THE NEW ENCOUNTER

THE NEW ENCOUNTER
Between Christians and Jews

John M. Oesterreicher

Foreword by Johannes Cardinal Willebrands
Introduction by Fr. David M. Bossman OFM

Philosophical Library
New York

NIHIL OBSTAT   Rev. Charles W. Gusmer
                          Censor Librorum

IMPRIMATUR   ✠ Peter L. Gerety, D.D.
                          Archbishop of Newark

Library of Congress Cataloging-in-Publication Data

Oesterreicher, John M., 1904-
   The new encounter

   1. Judaism—Relations—Catholic Church—Addresses,
essays, lectures.   2. Catholic Church—Relations—
Judaism—Addresses, essays, lectures.   3. Vatican
Council (2nd: 1962-1965).   Declaratio de Ecclesiae
habitudine ad Religiones non Christianas. Pt. 4—
Addresses, essays, lectures.   I. Title.
BM535.042   1985   261.2'6   85-36033
ISBN 0-8022-2496-2

In memoriam
Jacques Maritain
Anton Ramselaar
Leo von Rudloff
Karl Thieme

and
to all living pioneers
of the New Encounter

CONTENTS

THE VOICE OF VATICAN II

As this Sacred Synod plumbs the mystery of the Church, it remembers the bond that links the people of the New Covenant spiritually to Abraham's stock.

The Church of Christ thus acknowledges that, according to God's saving design, the beginnings of her faith and election go back as far as the Patriarchs, Moses, and the Prophets. She avows that all who believe in Christ are Abraham's children by faith (see Gal 3:7) and are thus included in the calling of that Patriarch. She also affirms that her salvation is mysteriously prefigured in the Exodus of the Chosen People from the land of slavery.

Wherefore the Church cannot forget that she received the revelation of the Old Testament through the people with whom God, in that enduring love words cannot express, deigned to conclude the Covenant of old. Nor can she forget that she draws sustenance from the root of that well-cultivated olive tree onto which the wild shoots of the Gentiles have been grafted (see Rom 11:17-24). For the Church believes that by His Cross Christ, our Peace, reconciled Jews and Gentiles, making the two one in Himself (see Eph 2:14-16).

Furthermore, the Church keeps ever before her eyes the words of the Apostle about his kinsfolk: "Theirs is the sonship and the glory and the covenant and the law and the worship and the promises: theirs are the Patriarchs, and from them is the Christ according to the flesh" (Rom 9:4-5), the Son of the Virgin Mary. No less does she recall that the Apostles, the Church's foundation-stones and pillars (see Ap 21:14; Gal 2:9), sprang from the Jewish people, as did most of the early disciples who proclaimed Christ's Gospel to the world.

As Holy Scripture testifies, Jerusalem did not recognize the time of her visitation (see Lk 19:44), nor did the Jews in large number accept the Gospel; indeed, not a few opposed its dissemination (see Rom 11:28). Nevertheless, now as before, God holds them most dear, for the sake of the Patriarchs; for irrevocable are His gifts and calling—such is the witness of the Apostle (see Rom 11:28-29).

In company with the Prophets and the same Apostle, the Church awaits that day, known to God alone, on which all peoples will address the Lord in a single voice and "serve Him with one accord" (Zeph 3:9; see Is 66:23; Ps 65:4; Rom 11:11-32).

Since the spiritual patrimony common to Christians and Jews is so rich, this Sacred Synod wishes to encourage and further their mutual knowledge and respect born principally of biblical and theological studies, but also of fraternal dialogues.

True, the Jewish authorities and those who sided with them pressed for the death of Christ (see Jn 19:6); still, what happened in His Passion cannot be attributed indiscriminately to all Jews then alive, nor can it be attributed to the Jews of today.

The Church's being the new people of God notwithstanding, the Jews may not be presented as rejected or accursed by God, as if this followed from Holy Scripture. May all, then, see to it that nothing be taught, either in catechetical work or in the preaching of the word of God, that does not conform to the truth of the Gospel and the spirit of Christ.

The Church, moreover, rejects all persecution against all human beings. For this reason and for the sake of her common patrimony with the Jews, she decries outbursts of hatred, persecutions, manifestations of contempt directed against Jews at whatever time in history and by whomsoever. She does so, impelled not by political reasons, but by the Gospel's pure love.

One thing remains: Christ underwent His Passion and Death freely and out of infinite love because of the sins of all humanity so that all may obtain salvation. This the Church has always held and holds now. Sent to preach, the Church is, therefore, bound to proclaim the Cross of Christ as the sign of God's all-embracing love and as the fountain from which every grace flows.

Nostra Aetate
Section Four

THE VOICE OF POPE JOHN PAUL II

I address a special word of greeting to the leaders of the Jewish community whose presence here honors me greatly. A few months ago, I met with an international group of Jewish representatives In Rome. On that occasion, recalling the initatives undertaken following the Second Vatican Council under my predecessor Paul VI, I stated that "our two communities are connected and closely related at the very level of their respective religious identities," and that on this basis "we recognize with utmost clarity that the path along which we should proceed is one of fraternal dialogue and fruitful collaboration." I am glad to ascertain that this same path has been followed here, in the United States, by large sections of both communities and their respective authorities and representative bodies. Several common programs of study, mutual knowledge, a common determination to reject all forms of Antisemitism and discrimination, and various forms of collaboration for the human advancement, inspired by our common biblical heritage, have created deep and permanent links between Jews and Catholics. As one who in my homeland shared the suffering of your brethren, I greet you with the word taken from the Hebrew language: Shalom! Peace be with you.

(New York City, 1979)

The bishops of the Federal Republic of Germany began their "Declaration on the Relationship of the Church to Judaism," published in April 1980, with the affirmation: "Who meets Jesus Christ, meets Judaism!" I want to make these words my own.

(Mainz, Germany, 1980)

If Christians are bound to see all human beings as their brethren and treat them accordingly, how much more are they bound by this sacred obligation when face to face with members of the Jewish people!

*   *   *

As sons and daughters of Abraham, Jews and Christians are called to be a blessing for the world (see Gn 12:2). They will be a blessing if jointly they stand up for peace and justice among all people and peoples. . . . The more this sacred duty puts its imprint on our encounter, the more does it redound to our own well-being.

In the light of this Abrahamitic promise and call, I look with you at the destiny and role of your people among the nations of the world. I gladly pray with you for the fullness of *shalom* for all your brethren of the flesh and faith, also for the land on which all Jews look with special reverence.

(Mainz, Germany, 1980)

I wish to confirm, with utmost conviction, that the teaching of the Church proclaimed during the Second Vatican Council in the Declaration *Nostra Aetate* . . . always remains for us, for the Catholic Church, for the Episcopate . . . and for the Pope, a teaching which must be followed—a teaching which it is necessary to accept not merely as something fitting, but much more as an expression of the faith, as an inspiration of the Holy Spirit, as a word of the Divine Wisdom.

(Caracas, Venezuela, 1985)

FOREWORD

I am very happy to introduce this collection of articles by
Monsignor John M. Oesterreicher, Director of the Institute of
Judaeo-Christian Studies in Seton Hall University, published
on the occasion of the 20th anniversary of the promulgation of
the Conciliar Declaration *Nostra Aetate*, the fourth section of
which deals with the relations between the Church and the
Jewish people.

In the first place this allows me to associate myself with a
publication which is a very special contribution to the celebration of that anniversary. The Declaration speaks indeed for
itself, and the time which has elapsed since its promulgation
has, if anything, made its message more clear and unequivo-
cal. However, those twenty years have seen not only its diffu-
sion around the world, but also a deeper understanding of its
contents and, to a certain extent, a wider practical application
of it.

In the Catholic Church magisterial documents have a certain life of their own. The work of those who try to interpret
them, of those who read them in the context of their daily lives
and help to put them into practice, contributes to it. Official
contributions to this work were made in the two documents
issued by the Holy See through its Commission for Religious
Relations with the Jews, namely the Guidelines of 1974 and the
Notes published 24th June this year.

However, official texts, necessary and important as they are, cannot cover all the ground nor can they deal with every objection and meet every particular situation that could arise in local Churches. This is where the work of theologians comes in, especially of those who may have contributed to the preparation of the official documents.

Msgr. Oesterreicher is perhaps the first one who ought to be mentioned in both of these categories. It is well known that he had an important role to play in the actual drafting of *Nostra Aetate*, and I dare say he remains the foremost witness of this exciting episode of modern history. His articles published here are proof enough, if that were needed.

But he is also known to us all as that untiring commentator, that authoritative interpreter, that precise exegete of the Council documents and those which have followed. The present collection gives proof of this for those who may have missed his texts when they were first published.

He was a forerunner of the developments which followed, a pioneer, or, if you will, a prophet. I believe no more need be said to invite the reader to delve into the pages which follow. It has been a privilege for me to have made such an invitation.

+ Johannes Cardinal Willebrands

INTRODUCTION

Christians and Jews lay claim to a heritage which in large measure has become the underpinning of western moral consciousness. The common ethos of this heritage is not, however, so singularly focused as to allow either Christian or Jew to differentiate which is exclusive and which is shared. Herein lies the challenge of dialogue—the need which both have to live harmoniously, acknowledging differences, owning similarities, and enacting separate but mutually compatible agenda for continuity.

Exclusivity has run its course, with a legacy of hatred and group self-righteous isolation. Mutual respect has grown in recent years, thanks in part to the efforts of such bridge-builders as John M. Oesterreicher and his colleagues in the Institute of Judaeo-Christian Studies at Seton Hall University. Bridge-building is not an enterprise which dissolves differences, but by acknowledging them constructively devises means whereby communication can take place. The enterprise of such bridge-building has succeeded in the form of "The Encounter" depicted in this present volume, the fruit of a lifetime of personal and group bridge-building.

One of the marvels of the new encounter between Christians and Jews is its ability to bring together the various parts which paved the way, for the endeavor of understanding is not a task for one person alone. Within each tradition there have been those of greater vision who did not shrink from expressing a desire for the harmony of diversity. Preparing the way is the task for prophets who dream of worlds not yet established.

Even the prophets won a hearing, and their legacy often was whispered to the next generation to produce a growth in perception—a new ability to see what before was obscure. The miracle of such growth is depicted in *Nostra Aetate*, an owning of Cardinal Bea's prophetic vision, in words not his own, by and for a new generation. It was an awakening of a new age. Twenty years later, John Oesterreicher carries on the work. Then he was Conciliar Consultor to the Secretariat for Unity. Today, he is a messenger of the prophetic vision.

Strange how diverse are the ways of God, especially when viewed from different perspectives. Yet, perspectives can be shared and diversity open new vistas for all to enjoy. Such is the enlightenment of the Second Vatican Council's confirmation that the experience of God is not the exclusive property of a few.

The love affair of life which privileged people enjoy can be shared in the common experience of forgiveness. Must we only count the sins of our neighbors and forget to remember our own? What joy is there in remembering only what destroys love? Living among people who choose to love rather than to hate is the joy which Jesus taught His disciples to cherish. But so often they forgot. We imagined that "they" killed God, while in fact we were only giving birth to a hatred in which God could not live.

The covenant is a sign of peace and beauty because it builds relationships. *Shalom* is not simply ceasing to fight. It is well-being which mutual acceptance and harmony produces. *Shalom* is not so much a promise as a challenge, a potential which we can create only by cutting a covenant into our hearts and sharing the blood of human compassion. In such an act, Christians and Jews discover one another in an old but ever new encounter.

The legacy of these pages can only serve to promote the continuation of the process they describe. Those who bear this message have trod the path before us. They invite a following to a land of new discovery.

David M. Bossman OFM

The link between Christians and Jews has been established by God, the Lord Himself. God has bound us together. Thus we are dealing not only with relations between men, but with God's own acting in history.

When we Christians and Jews try to understand one another better, we touch something of the Lord's presence in human history. Both of us have experience and knowledge of God in our lives and in our respective traditions. There are several fundamental differences in our faiths. And yet, we are linked together by the same Lord, who has chosen us in order to manifest His mysterious plan of salvation for all mankind. . . . Although in different ways, we try to be witnesses to this loving and saving action in the world. Thus we are "waiting for and hastening the coming of the Day of God" (2 Pt 3:12), when all the people will "call on the name of the Lord and serve Him with one accord" (Zeph 3:9).

+Johannes Cardinal Willebrands

PREFACE

Giving an Account

THIS BOOK CELEBRATES a train of wonders, events unexpected but welcome. The first of these wonders was the election of Pope John XXIII, a man old in years yet young in heart. While devoted to the Church's rich past, he wished to lead her into a bright future. He would have done no wrong had he limited himself to the care of the people entrusted to his pastoral office, but he wished to be a brother to all who dwell on earth. Wondrous, too, was his daring decision to convene an Ecumenical Council and place on its agenda the re-examination of the Church's bond to the people in whose midst she was born.

Another marvel was the Pope's happy choice of Augustin Bea, S.J., a priest advanced in age yet able to steer with youthful vigor, through ebb and flood tides to port, the Declaration of the Church's Relation to Non-Christian Religions, the Decree on Ecumenism, and the Declaration on Religious Liberty.

If I may strike a personal note, I consider it a wonder of grace to have been appointed a consultor to the Secretariat for Unity, and invited to help give life to Pope John's wish for a re-

19

ordering of the ties between the Church and the Jewish people. It was a bolt out of the blue when the letter from Vatican City arrived early in 1961, opening the door for me to contribute to a new Encounter of Christians and Jews.

No less surprising was it when a farsighted publisher asked me to gather and edit some of the papers I have delivered in the course of the years since the Council. The book salutes twenty years of the Conciliar Declaration *On the Church's Relationship to Non-Christian Religions*, the core of which treats her bond to the Jewish people. The Conciliar statement on this bond, in a new translation of mine, opens this book.

THE FIRST full-paper is about Augustin Cardinal Bea, the man and his work, a lecture given at the centennial of his birth commemorated by the Secretariat for Christian Unity in December 1981 in Rome. The second essay narrates the genesis of the Conciliar Declaration. It first appeared in German as part of the collection of Conciliar documents edited by Herbert Vorgrimler and published by Herder, Freiburg i.Br. The original translation was done in Great Britain and issued by Burns & Oates, London, as well as by Herder and Herder, New York. In this book, I use a revised translation.

"Humanity's Many Paths to God" was written for the March 1966 issue of *The Homiletic and Pastoral Review*. "The Rediscovery of Judaism" is the lecture that introduced a convocation of Catholic and Jewish scholars to honor the Fifth Anniversary of *Nostra Aetate* at Seton Hall University in October 1970. It was published as a pamphlet by the Institute of Judaeo-Christian Studies, SHU. "Teachers of Christians," never before published, was part of a convocation on the Tenth Anniversary, whose theme was "Learning One from the Other." Professor Michael Wyschogrod, Baruch College, CUNY, was the Jewish partner.

"Deicide Under the Microscope" appeared first under the title "Deicide as a Theological Problem" in *Brothers in Hope, The Bridge*, Volume 5. The three meditations on the Passion of Christ that follow are first, "Season of Love," a circular letter on preaching in Lent sent to the priests of the Archdiocese of Newark in 1979 on behalf of the Archdiocesan Commission for

Ecumenical and Interreligious Affairs; second, "Delivered Into Our Hands," part of a series of sermon aids for the Sundays of Lent of 1977 distributed among the same priests; and third, "It Was I," an introductory note that several times was used in the chapel of Seton Hall University prior to the reading of the Passion on Good Friday, and that could well be read in any Church.

While the first two studies seek to trace the development of the Conciliar Statement and several subsequent papers try to interpret the text, the last two look more toward the future. "The Covenant: Old, New and One," which appeared in October 1977 in the Jesuit weekly *America*, suggests a comprehensive covenant theology. The last of the papers, "The Challenge of Shalom," was delivered in April 1969 to the National Catholic Education Assocation at its convention in Detroit. Later published in pamphlet form it discusses the task of the Christian educator in establishing a creative relationship between Christians and Jews. A prayer for Jerusalem concludes the text.

The papers brought together in this book are not the sum total of my writings at the time and in the wake of the Council. Among those not included here I mention only two. First, a lecture I gave in 1964 to an assembly of Bishops and repeated in several German cities at the invitation of their respective *Gesellschaften für Christlich-Jüdische Zusammenarbeit* (Societies for Christian-Jewish Cooperation) on "Auschwitz, the Christian, and the Council," later published as a booklet. In it, I propounded the thesis that Hitler and his accomplice Himmler had millions of Jews murdered, mainly because Jesus was born of their stock—in other words, because the Jews were Christ-bearers not Christ-killers. I asked that in response to that horror the Council honor Jesus as a "son of David, son of Abraham" (Mt 1:1) and proclaim the Church's historical and existential bond to Abraham's stock.

Second, in the fall of 1972, Seton Hall's Institute of Judaeo-Christian Studies and the Theological School of the University of Lucerne held a symposium on "Judaism and the Church." I delivered the opening lecture on "Under the Vault of the One

Covenant." It was published in German as part of the Symposium's Proceedings. Though the thesis of that lecture has been
espoused by several scholars and received with interest by its
readers, the length of that paper prohibits its inclusion.

Since the present book is a mosaic of papers written on
different occasions, it is inevitable that certain important
themes have been treated more than once. I have not struck
such repetitions because I think their appearance and reap-
pearance may add both significance and strength to the
thoughts developed therein.

A brief remark explaining my spelling of Antisemitism, as it
appears in this book. Not only is the word a misnomer, it is also
deceptive. It was coined a little more than a hundred years ago,
to be exact, in 1879, by Wilhelm Marr, an anti-Jewish pam-
phleteer, with the purpose of avoiding the offensive word "Jew-
hatred." The latter might have made him suspect in certain
intellectual circles, while a pseudo-scientific term like "anti-
Semitism" might impress, indeed, fool many people. "Semitic"
denotes a family of languages. When the historian August
Ludwig von Schlözer, a few years before Marr, spoke of
"Semitic nations," he had in mind peoples that, without being
related, spoke one of the Semitic languages. Soon after, however, the linguistic term assumed ethnic significance, so that
Marr could use it to obscure the fiendishness of Jew-hatred.
Since I do not want to be a party to this cover-up, I avoid the
word Antisemitism as much as possible. When I quote another
author, I shun the hyphenated spelling, which misleads the
reader to think that "Semitism" is a reality.

WHAT JOHN DONNE said about every human being is dou-
bly true of an author, "No man is an island, entire of itself"
(*Meditation XVII*). An author's word would never reach the
printed page were it not for the help of other minds and hands.
Thus, I owe a great deal of gratitude to those who, in the name
of Pope John XXIII, called me to Rome. No less am I indebted to
many bishops and priests, to colleagues and coworkers at the
Council. I cannot list them all, but I would be remiss were I not
to honor Franz Kardinal König, Archbishop of Vienna, in
whose diocese I began my priestly ministry and whose gra-

cious friendship I have cherished through the years. With gratitude I remember the many fruitful conversations we had during the Council.

In the first two chapters of this book, I have tried to depict, as fully and fairly as possible, the initiative Pope John XXIII took to have Vatican II probe as well as articulate the relationship of the Church and the Jewish people. In the pages that follow, I have tried to delineate further Cardinal Bea's sure yet gentle guidance of a Conciliar Declaration from its first mention to its final vote. In having done so, I trust I have succeeded in erecting a monument both of them amply deserve.

It would be false modesty, I think, were I to disregard Pope Paul VI's graciousness to me. On the eve of the Promulgation of *Nostra Aetate*, the Pope received me at St. Peter's. I had gone there with the intention of thanking him for his fidelity toward Pope John's legacy. But he was quicker than I. Before I was able to say a word, he thanked me for my contribution to the fulfillment of Pope John's wish. "Tomorrow is a great day for you!" he said, "I will pray for you and your people, for its peace."

In his Foreword, Johannes Cardinal Willebrands, President of the Secretariat for Unity, warmly supports the interpretation of the history and theology of *Nostra Aetate* I develop in this book. I have known Cardinal Willebrands as a gracious fellow worker in the ministry of reconciliation. As Cardinal Bea's successor, he is ever the faithful servant of God and of His household. I deeply appreciate his magnanimity toward me. I also want the Secretariat's staff, past and present, to know that I value greatly their cooperation throughout the years. This is particularly true of Monsignor Jorge Mejìa, the Cardinal's right-hand man for Catholic-Jewish concerns.

Nor can I let go unmentioned the many kindnesses I have received from the late Archbishop of Newark, Thomas A. Boland, and the present Ordinary, Peter L. Gerety. Their generosity through more than the last three decades has permitted me to lead a richly rewarding life. Moreover, I consider it a particular favor to serve in a diocese whose Shepherd is, to my knowledge, the only Bishop to have issued two Pastoral Letters on the kinship of Christians and Jews.

Staying closer to home, I need and wish to thank Dolores Porrmann Cunningham, Assistant for Research and Publication at the Institute of Judaeo-Christian Studies, for her untiring help in assembling and making ready the various papers in this book. No mean task was performed by my assistant, SaraLee Pindar, who guided the manuscript through many stages and through what I consider the labyrinthine ways of the computer and word-processing world, for which she merits and has my thanks. For taking care of a hundred and one details necessary for completing my book, I express my heartfelt gratitude to my German secretary, Sister Sofie Müller.

Father James Sharp, University Librarian, demonstrated his usual kindness and concern for my research, as he has for that of others. Sister Anita Talar, R.S.M. of the library has been generous in her assistance by finding and checking titles as well as quotations. To both of them, I say, "Thank you." To the two pillars of the Graduate Department of Judaeo-Christian Studies, Rabbi Asher Finkel, and its present Chairman, Father Lawrence Frizzell, I am indebted for their friendship and frequent assistance. The University itself, its administrators and faculty members, has been kind in providing a congenial atmosphere for the ministry of reconciliation that is my life.

Of the long line of individual benefactors here at Seton Hall, I wish to single out Bishop John J. Dougherty, onetime Regent of the Institute of Judaeo-Christian Studies, and past President of the University, and the present Chancellor of Seton Hall, Monsignor John J. Petillo. I am particularly indebted to Father David M. Bossman, O.F.M., editor of *Biblical Theology Bulletin*, and Provost of this University, for his profound Introduction or, should I say, look into the future.

May I say again that I feel indebted to Rose Morse Runes, my publisher, for many kindnesses, but particularly for having encouraged me to save from oblivion articles, however modest, that might promote a fuller understanding of the gigantic step that the Church-in-Council took toward the New Encounter with the Jewish people.

Barukh ha-Shem! Praised be the Lord!

John M. Oesterreicher

PAVING THE WAY

"Paving the Way" recalls the pro-phetic announcement by the Second Isaiah of Israel's rescue from her cap-tivity in Babylon. Having been told to comfort God's people, speaking to it tenderly (40: 1-2), he is ordered to pro-claim: "In the wilderness clear a way for the Lord" (v.3). Can there be a better motto for Cardinal Bea's work in pre-paring the New Encounter of Chris-tians and Jews?

Cardinal Bea's Life and Work

AT NOON of every day the Second Vatican Council was in session, an unusual scene could be witnessed. After an active and sometimes tense morning, the Bishops and their assist-ants would rush to the nearest exit, while one man, bent by the burdens of a long life, walked with deliberate pace. From time to time, he would pause. It was not that he needed to draw fresh breath in order to continue; rather that someone—friend or stranger—sought the old man's wise counsel or wished to be strengthened by the warmth of his smile. No one was fooled by his apparent frailty; though the outer man had yielded to the weight of years, the inner man stood erect. You realize, of course, that I am speaking of Augustin Cardinal Bea.

I gladly admit that occasionally I myself stopped to watch

the unstaged meetings between him and other participants in the Council. The instance that I remember most vividly is his conversing with the two Brothers of the Community of Taizé who were among the official Observers at the Council, Frère Roger Schutz and Frère Max Thurian. In a simple way, these unplanned exchanges revealed the secret of his personality: strength in weakness, an epoch-making mission to all believers concealed by the modesty and inconspicuousness of an artless life.

The Cardinal was a rare person, indeed. A delightful tale from the early days of the pontificate of John XXIII underlines the Cardinal's singularity. At that time, while still a stranger to the day-to-day operations of the Vatican and not yet acquainted with all the members of the Roman Curia, Pope John paged—the story has it—through the *Annuario Pontificio*. Most names appeared but once in the roster of Roman Congregations, while one turned up time and again. A Father Bea was listed as "Consultor" of several bodies, the Biblical Commission, the Congregation for Seminaries and Pontifical Universities, the Congregation of Rites, and the Holy Office.

Perplexed, Pope John is said to have turned to one of his assistants: "Listen, the *Annuario* registers the name Bea several times. How many Fathers Bea are there?" "Just one, Holy Father," the assistant answered. "The four Consultors are one and the same person."[1] Pope John was impressed by Fr. Bea's gamut of concerns. A man of learning and of action, this Consultor was obviously one who trusted the gifts God had given him and who could, therefore, himself be trusted. Able to pay attention to a plurality of issues—not to one, at the expense of others, but to several, with fairness to each—he would, indeed, be suited to the mission the Pope was to give him. The various appointments he held spelled influence and power—power he wielded so humbly that he remained uncorrupted by it.

The breadth of Fr. Bea's interests was not only evidence of uncommon strength and keenness of mind but also proof of a great heart, ready to abandon particular causes in favor of universal concerns. Small wonder that Pope John told his friend Vittorino Veronese, a counselor-at-law and former Director General of UNESCO: "Do you realize how greatly the Lord has favored me when he permitted me to discover Cardinal Bea?"[2]

I have not the least desire to lessen Pope John's merit in having discovered Fr. Bea and having chosen him to lead Vatican II and thus the post-Conciliar Church on the road toward the unity of Christians. Much less do I wish to diminish his eminent role in the work of *rapprochement*, of reconciliation between the Church and the people of Israel. On the contrary, I happily acknowledge the debt the Church of today and of the future owes him for his choice of Fr. Bea. Still, he could not have discovered him, had not others done so before.

The Making of the Man

THE CARDINAL'S was a simple but solid origin, his father having been a farmer and carpenter, his mother the gentle mistress of the house. Like most of his ancestors of many generations, he was born in Riedböhringen, a small, little-known village situated on a plateau, called *die Baar*, to the east of the Black Forest. Because of its bleak climate, and biting cold winters, the plateau is often called "Baden's Siberia." Yet when summer comes, the meadows are transformed into a veritable garden of flowers, while the rich soil bears an abundance of rye and wheat.

It is not difficult to perceive that the earth underfoot and the sky overhead influence human beings; that the atmospheric conditions, the flora and fauna of a given region leave their marks on its inhabitants. It is thus possible, indeed probable, that the severe winters steeled the character of the young Bea, and that the bright and rich summers helped him to acquire the serenity of soul, the unruffled and friendly disposition that were his charm.

I owe the particulars of the Cardinal's development to Maria Buchmüller, the editor of what is, until now, the most comprehensive book about him. Her respect and affection, her research and gracious style are impressive; but I cannot accept the "environmental determinism" she seems to favor. She writes:

> To understand Cardinal Bea's spiritual make-up and his
> work, one must needs know the soil out of which he grew,
> the landscape, the region's history, the parental home
> along with the generations that preceded the present one,
> in short the milieu that fashioned him.[3]

It is an experiential fact that men and women the world over
are conditioned by their birth and upbringing. To acknowledge
this humbling dependence on external forces is a far cry from
even implying that human beings are what their descent and
environment have made them. The latter view springs, not
from experience, but from *ressentiment* against the uniqueness
of each man and woman. No one is ever the mere product of a
country and its climate, a people and its "blood," an age and its
events. I am impelled to reject even a mild form of environmental determinism, having been a witness to the horrible consequences of that ill-begotten ideology of *Blut und Boden*, the
worldview that sees in "blood and soil" the two great determi-
nants in the history of all humanity and that of each human
being.

Contrary to this notion, Cardinal Bea's life is distinguished
by his rise above what is commonly considered fate. He was an
only child who did not become the egocentric to which the
verdict of psychologists often condemns such children. Many
referred to him as *der deutsche Kurienkardinal*, "the German
Cardinal of the Roman Curia." This he was without doubt;
still, the title does not define him. His love and concern did not
remain within the borders of Germany or those of the Eternal
City; his sympathy and care were worldwide, all-embracing.
He was a Jesuit, in many ways an ideal one, at the same time he
was as atypical a Jesuit as there has ever been.

It is unlikely that in his younger years Cardinal Bea knew
any Jews, except those who walked through the pages of his
Bible History. Still, he was chosen to guide the work of reconciliation between Christians and Jews. To thwart this God-given
mission, enemies of the Council and the renewal it initiated
spread the rumor that he was of Jewish issue and—to make the
"indictment" complete—of being in the pay of "international
Jewry" or in the service of worldwide Freemasonry. Need I add

that these schemes to distort his dedication and purpose in the eyes of the Council's foes endeared him all the more to his friends and co-workers? All in all, by grace he transcended the measure nature seems to have prepared for him.

Early Steps. Augustin Cardinal Bea's earliest recollection went back to his third year. One Sunday, his father took him to the parish mass and, as was the habit of many men of country villages, walked up to the choir loft. This gave the little boy a vantage point from which he could easily follow the celebrant's action at the altar. He must have had an unusual affinity to the sacred; of all that he witnessed, it was the priest's blessing of the faithful that impressed him most. "In my childlike way," the Cardinal recalled, "I thought that it must be something really great to be a priest and be allowed to bless."[4] But, as far as we know, the experience remained his secret, not visibly affecting his childhood, though it may have been a decisive moment for his life and calling.

While the boy was in elementary school, the pastor of the village discovered his mental powers and began to instruct him in Latin, making possible his future ordination as priest. Before this could happen, he had to enter a *Gymnasium*, the preparatory school for university studies. It must have been a heartache for his parents to let their only child leave the bosom of the family when he was barely ten years old.

Young Bea did well in his studies. The last report card at the time of his graduation showed his knowledge and performance to have been outstanding in all disciplines, except music and gymnastics. While his marks in all the humanities were *A*, "excellent," that in religion was *A*-, "almost excellent." The slightly lower grade in religion resulted from a conflict between the young Bea and his professor who demanded learning by rote. "This did not suit me," the Cardinal said years later. "I wanted to think my faith through."[5] Far from being a rebel, he was adventurous enough to use his intellect to its limits so as to gain a personal understanding of the faith.

The customary course of studies would have been for the young man to spend a set number of semesters at a theological school of one of the German universities, and then transfer to a seminary in order to prepare for the priesthood. After a mere three semesters at the University of Freiburg, Germany, however, the young Bea decided to enter the Society of Jesus, which meant his having to move to Valkenburg, Holland.

In the latter part of the nineteenth century, the German Empire was governed by the "Iron Chancellor," Otto von Bismark (1815-1898). In a speech to the *Reichstag*, the German parliament, in 1888, he declared: "We Germans fear God but nothing else in the world." This provocative slogan is, to my mind, a partial explanation of the Chancellor's seeking to deprive the Catholic Church of her voice in matters of ecclesiastical appointments and the education of Catholic children. He wished to arrogate these prerogatives in the name of the State. This struggle—though but another instance of the age-old battle between Caesar and God, the secular and the spiritual orders—is euphemistically called *Kulturkampf*.

At the height of this conflict and in consequence of the law of July 4, 1874, the Jesuits were banned from German soil. It was this law that forced the young Bea to go to Valkenburg, Holland, for both his novitiate and further studies. After having completed the latter, he was ordained a priest, on August 25, 1912. He did post-graduate work in Near Eastern languages; yet, hardly had he begun them, when he was called back to Valkenburg as Dean of Philosophical and Theological Studies. In 1917, the law forbidding all activity of Jesuits was finally annulled. His superiors lost no time in naming him Provincial, that is, head of the Society's German province. As such he had to guard the life of the resurrected community. After having served seven years in that capacity, the superiors of the Society called him to Rome where great tasks awaited him.

A Move Forward.   Before departing, he saw his physician, who told him point-blank: "For you, Rome means death!"[6] The physician was no alarmist, rather did he know Fr. Bea's delicate constitution. In his youth, his lungs had been affected; and later on there seemed to have been warnings of a relapse. Even so, his body withstood Roman summers and winters for forty-four years.

In Rome, his superiors entrusted him with the direction of the Pontifical Biblical Institute. I cannot enumerate his various activities there, nor am I able to describe his many acts of devotion to the Popes from Pius XI to Paul VI. He was their inspirer, catalyst, and most conscientious assistant. There is no one term that aptly expresses the multi-faceted and selfless role that he performed during those decades—unless it be friend, "friend of Popes."

I just indicated that in this context I cannot list Fr. Bea's many achievements as co-worker of Popes. There are, however, two that I must discuss. The first is his translation of the psalms, the second his work on an encyclical of biblical studies, even though the encyclical antedated the translation. After having turned down as "too difficult" previous suggestions that the Psalter be rendered once more into Latin from the Hebrew original, Pius XII ordered, in 1941, that such a translation be undertaken. Immediately, a commission of six scholars under the direction of Fr. Bea went to work; in 1945, Fr. Bea was able to hand the Pope a copy of the commission's joint effort.

Pius XII received the fruit of their labor with satisfaction and praise, but many for whom the Psalter was the substance of their daily prayers, and whose ear was attuned to the diction and rhythm of the Vulgate found the new rendering into classical Latin strange, lacking the beauty and melodiousness of the older version. Though this translation was but short-lived, it was of historic importance. It was the first time that, following the direction of *Divino Afflante Spiritu*, the original text was shown to have the fullest authority and therefore should be preferred to any translation, old or new.[7]

Though Fr. Bea's Psalter was used only for a brief time, it nevertheless moved many in the Church to drink from the very fountainhead of Christian life and faith. For decades, it had been the fashion to seek the origin of all ideas and movements in Greece; now Catholics were reminded that the Church's cradle stood, not in Hellas, China, or India—outstanding though these nations and their cultures were—but rather in the midst of the Jews, the people despised by their overlords and neighbors but loved and inspired by God.

The Genius of Hebrew Speech

CHRISTIANS CANNOT ignore the fact that a great part of Scripture the Christian tradition calls the Old Testament, that is, a large portion of revelation by which they order their lives, was written in Hebrew.[8] Why in Hebrew? Because it was the language of those who were the first to hear God's revelation, its custodians and initial witnesses. To ask once more: Why Hebrew, the language of a small people that hardly commanded the attention of the rest of humanity? Why not one of the great languages of the world? Why not Greek, language of the Roman Empire and its Hellenic culture, the language in which the New Testament has come down to us?

If I dare read the Mind of God, the principal reason for His choice of Hebrew as the instrument of revelation seems to be His predilection for what appears insignificant to human eyes. For humanity to till the soil, to create works of art, to search for the "whatness" of things—in short—to follow its mission of cultivation and culture, it was placed in one of the smallest of the several celestial bodies of our solar system. The history of salvation, from the Covenant of God with Abraham to the Resurrection of Christ, took place, not in an Etruscan, Chinese, or pre-Columbian civilization, but in one of the least important and most despised corners of the Roman Empire. When God "looked" for a woman to give flesh to the Eternal Word, He did not select a princess from one of the palaces of the world, but a young maiden of no rank or reputation. Long before the axiom "small is beautiful," was coined,[9] it seems to have been the rule of God's dealings with humanity.

In addition to the mystery of election, God made Hebrew the vehicle of His grace because it lends itself to speaking of God and the world concretely in vivid images. When a simple Greek thought of the gods, he or she considered Olympus as a playground of immortals whose emotions were the lowest. The learned Greek saw God in sublime thought as the Prime Mover and First Cause. God's aseity, His being "of Himself, in Himself, and through Himself, grounded in no other,"[10] may be a feast for the intellect, but it is no comfort in the trials of human life. The God of Israel, however, in revealing Himself to Moses out of the bush burning but not burnt, called Himself *eheyeh asher eheyeh* (Ex 3:14). Generations of translators, influenced by Greek thought, have rendered this as "I Am Who I Am " but here God does not speak of His everlastingness, but of His lasting presence with His people: "I Will Be Who I Will Be," meaning: I will be present with you as the One who sustains, supports, and defends you.[11] The Hebrew mind moves in such dynamic speech and thus lives in the language God chose to speak to Israel and all humanity.

The Humanity of the Sacred Writers.   The Decalogue commands that no carved image may be made of God (see Ex 20:4), yet He is depicted most graphically as the Bearer of human traits. Though the book of Job emphatically disclaims that God has eyes of flesh to see as humans see (see 10:4), many biblical writers speak of God's eyes. They mean, of course, His watchful omniscience—a man's or woman's comfort or terror (see Prv 15:3, Am 9:4, Ps 11:4). Without being embarrassed, the sacred authors refer to God's arms, hands, fingers, and feet; to His face, mouth, lips and nostrils; even to His back. God's arms and hands obviously point to the power that created the world, directed Israel's history, and protected His people. What a difference between saying: "His power offers safety," and "Beneath His arms there is safety." The first informs, the second inspires. Once God's "holy arm" is bared, salvation comes to all the ends of the earth (see Is 52:10). Again, God's face means His presence—the people's guidance and support, their rescue by His love and pity (see Is 63:9). "To seek His face" is to seek Him, to long for His grace. "He hides His face" whenever Man falls into sin; in letting "His face shine," He is bestowing favor (see Pss 104:29; 31:17).

Untroubled by the simplicity—some will say the primitive character—of such anthropomorphisms, the sacred writers of the Torah kept, from ancient tales, images of God walking in the garden as the daily breeze cools the air (see Gn 3:8); shutting the door of the ark after Noah, his family, and his animals have entered (see Gn 7:16); coming down to see the city of Babel and the tower the *hubris* of its inhabitants built (see Gn 11:5).

The authors of these and similar passages even seem to have taken delight in depicting God as having the shape, manner, and feelings of a human. How is this possible, since the whole of Scripture proclaims God as the One who transcends time and space, the One not bound by the limits of tribe, people, province, and empire? How is it possible that the singer of one psalm passionately declares that Israel's Guardian neither slumbers nor sleeps (see 121:4), while the singer of another cries out:

> Awake! Why are you asleep, O Lord?
> Arise! Cast us not off forever!
>
> (44:24)

God is so rich, so incomparable, He cannot be grasped, except by opposites. He is at rest, ever at work; He is all stern, all gentle; He dwells in light inaccessible (see 1 Tim 6:16), and yet is near those who cleave to Him in prayer and right doing (see Dt 4:4f).

Again, the biblical doctrine about God is unmistakable: He is not a human being that He should change His mind, not a creature that He should repent His deeds (see Nm 23:19; 1 Sm 15:29). Yet, the teller of the flood story dares say: "When the Lord saw that the wickedness of Man on earth was great, and that Man's every thought and all the inclination of his heart were only evil, He regretted that He had made Man on the earth and was grieved to the heart" (Gn 6:5f). At first glance, this sentence seems to bring God down to our level; in reality, it exalts Him as much as human words can. For it attributes to Him none of the pettiness, the triviality many pagan myths ascribe to their gods—all caricatures of humanity—but the strong emotions of a lover. Nothing could be more truly human than to say, as does the inspired writer, that having had to watch the betrayal by His favorite creature, the Lord regretted having wasted His tenderness; that the heart of God was riven because His affection had been ignored and His gift scattered to the winds (see Gn 6:6). Nothing could be more human and, at the same time, more divine.

What the introductory sentence to the flood story wishes to

convey is that the Lord has not withdrawn from His creation. Present-day jargon notwithstanding, He is not an absent God. Rather does He love all things that are, and loathes nothing He has made; He, the Master, is the friend of life, and His "imperishable spirit is in all things" (Wis 11:24-26; 12:1). Man is especially dear to Him: without ceasing, He pursues the people He has made His own. Neither are the nations far from His care; to none does He deny His blessing. There will be a day when Isaiah's gospel will be fulfilled. The Lord of hosts proclaims:

> Blessed be Egypt, my people,
> Assyria, the work of my hands,
> And Israel, my inheritance.
>
> (19:25)

The reason, then, for anthropomorphisms is obvious. A human being—every man and woman of whatever century, land, and culture—cannot enter the realm of the spirit except through the door of the senses. To no other people of the ancient world was this approach as self-evident as it was to the Hebrews. Far from disdaining the world seen, heard, smelled, tasted, or touched, they valued it as the abode of the Word and, thus, a parable of things divine. In one of the great songs of Scripture, bearing Moses' name, the community of Israel is warned not to forget what it owes to the Lord. The singer knew no better way of describing God's work than the use of metaphors taken from nature. In rescuing the children of Israel from Egypt, He acted like an eagle: the mother bird incites her nestlings into flight, spreads her wings beneath them so that they will not be dashed to the ground, finally bears them up on her pinions (Dt 32:10f). These are the ways of God, our Deliverer.

The Rationality of Hebrew?   Hebrew folklore and legend, both being part of what the rabbis call *Aggadah*, attempt another answer to the question why Hebrew became the instrument of divine revelation. One legend has God use it in creating the world. Another has Adam speak it, when singing the first nuptial song: "Bone of my bone, flesh of my flesh," when calling his wife *ishah*, "woman" (Gn 2:23). But, when people rebelled against God by building a tower into high heaven, and setting up idols to replace the Lord, human beings became estranged from one another and their speech confused (see Gn 11:1-9). Up to then, Hebrew had been humanity's universal language; now it was assigned to the future people of Israel Gen. r. 18,4).[12] Charming though this look into the past is, it is mere fancy, it does not square with what we truly know about humanity's and Israel's early history.

The opposite of this mythical view is the rationalistic answer: The choice of Hebrew as the instrument of divine teaching was a mere accident of history. In Isaiah 19:18, Hebrew is called *sephat Kena 'an*, "the lip (speech) of Canaan." Far from its being the universal language, it was spoken only in a tiny corner of the earth, later called Palestine and today Israel. It is a dialect rather than the dominant member of a group of languages that together with Phoenician, Punic, Moabite, and Ugaritic make up Canaanite. Hebrew may have been a compromise between Aramaic and Canaanite speech, a composite that reflects the confluence of cultures in Israel's history. In Egypt, the "sons of Israel" (Ex 1:1) spoke, in all likelihood, an Arameo-Arabic dialect, discovering Hebrew only on their entry into Canaan after the Exodus. It then became their language and thus that of their sacred writings.

If one remains on the surface of things, it must appear that an "accident of history" made Hebrew the vehicle for conveying a unique religious experience. But was it merely a chance event that turned Hebrew into the medium of an extraordinary divine-human communication, the means of a revelation that demanded of its hearers the imitation of a God who is righteous, indeed, holy—something not at all common in the ancient world? Could it be that the rule responsible for God's choice of Israel as His very own also accounts for the rise of Hebrew from its low state to its noble dignity, from an unnoticed dialect to idiom of grace? Scripture speaks of the marvel of God's choice more than once, here is one, indeed, its most significant instance: "It was not because you are the largest of all nations that the Lord set His heart on you and chose you, for you are really the smallest of all nations. It was because the Lord loved you" (Dt 7:7f).

The Absurdity of Hebrew? In the eyes of many, the very thought that some obscure Hebrews should be the inspired bearers of God's Message is absurd. Even people who think of themselves as Christians take offense at the idea that the Bible, the Word of God, should have been spoken and written by Hebrew men. Are its authors, they ask, not members of the people described by their own Scriptures as sinful, stiff-necked, and rebellious, even worse? Yes, they are. Then, counter those skeptics, they are not worthy to play the role God is said to have assigned to them. True, they are not, but neither are the members of any other nation. Yet, to say that all peoples and people do not deserve to speak in the name of the living God does not touch the heart of our problem.

The heart of the problem is rather what the Apostle Paul calls the folly of the Cross, though it was expressed centuries before Christ's crucifixion. Speaking in the name of God, the Prophet Isaiah exclaims:

> I will destroy the wisdom of the wise,
>   and bring to nothing the cleverness of the clever.
>
> (29:14)

Though a stumbling block to Jews and an absurdity to Gentiles, Christ-nailed-to-the-cross is power and wisdom, God's power and wisdom, the Apostle proclaims (1 Cor 1:23, 24). He then tells the community of Corinth:

> My brothers, think what kind of people you are whom God has called. Few of you are wise by any human standard, few influential or well-born. Yet, to shame the wise, God has chosen what the world considers foolish, and to shame the strong, He has chosen what the world considers weak, so that no human being might boast in the presence of God.
>
> (see 1:26-29)

The same "revolutionary" move—God's sweeping away human illusions of grandeur—chose Hebrew, not Babylonian, Egyptian, or Greek writers as His "tongue."

The Dynamism of Hebrew.   Johann Gottfried Herder (1744-1803), poet, literary critic, and outstanding member of the Romantic movement in German literature—a movement that stressed the importance of imagination and emotion over and against reason, indeed, the strict canons of classicism—was the first to write on the distinctive character of Hebrew. In an essay, *Vom Geiste der Ebräischen Poesie*, he calls Hebrew a language of poets rather than of abstract thinkers. In it, action, description, passion, song, and rhythm prevail. For the Hebrew people, the verb dominates not only the sentence structure, but also the process of thinking. Indeed, in the forming of words, the verb is most important.[13]

The dominance of the verb accounts for the fact that in Hebrew speech and writing, the world is not at a standstill, it seems to move before one's eyes. Most of the time, the language is simple and direct, yet it is always vivid. Hebrew literature has a certain simplicity, but for all its simplicity, the mood is often expansive. Instead of saying that he will wait no longer, that now it is his turn to speak, Elihu, one of Job's friends, loses all restraint:

> I am bursting with words to utter,
>   the spirit within compels me.
> Like a new wineskin under pressure of new wine,
>   my bosom is ready to blow up.
> I must speak to find relief,
>   I must open my lips and answer.
>
> (Jb 32:18)

The expansive quality is but one side of the coin, here is the other. When an exaggerated report reaches David's ear that Absalom, avenging the shame of Tamar on his brother Ammon, had murdered *all* the royal princes, nothing at all is said of David's being sad, distressed, shocked, or angered, nothing of the agitation of his heart. It is even said that the

King bewailed their horrible end. Instead we are told: "The King stood up, rent his clothes, and then threw himself on the ground" (2 Sm 13:31). From these outer manifestations we are meant to infer the King's inmost thoughts and feelings. I can think of no presentation of the King's feelings that would be more concrete.

Biblical Keywords: Emet, Truth.   The genius of Hebrew speech is also manifest in the particular meaning of certain key words, such as *emet, shalom,* or *tzedakah.* When we, men and women of the West, speak of truth, we do so as heirs of a great philosophical tradition. We understand truth as *adaequatio rei et intellectus,* the equation of reality and mind, of thing and thought. This definition of truth, though intrinsically Greek, is generally attributed to the tenth-century Jewish philosopher Isaac Israeli.[14] In comparing truth in the Greek sense with the Hebrew *emet,* I do not wish to belittle the quality that determines so much of our daily lives. Our senses and minds would have to be dull were we no longer able to savor the import of statements like: one and one are two; protein is an essential component of our diet; no culture can be envisaged without works of art. Significant though these and similar truths are, they do not touch the core of our existence. Truth, in a philosophical sense, then, can be thought of, pondered over, meditated on, spoken of, even rejoiced in, but nothing more.

The Hebrew *emet,* truth, however, is something to live by, walk in, or do. *Emet* is formed from the root *'mn,* a root even one not familiar with Hebrew can easily detect in the word with which Jews and Christians end their liturgical prayers. Many people think that *Amen* always means "So be it," but this meaning is rare. Most of the time, it is best rendered "So it is!" Other expressions to convey the meaning of *Amen* are: "Indeed!" "It's true!" "It's certain!" "Yes" embodies its meaning well. *Emet* is thus something that is stable, firm, reliable, or enduring; it is sure or worthy of trust.

When Israel's Lord is called "God of Truth," the appellation means more than that He is truly God, in every respect unlike idols. It means that He is steadfast and faithful, true to His word and "keeping His gracious covenant with those who love

Him" (Dt 7:9). As He is "truth," so is His word, His law (2 Sm 7:28; Ps 19:10; 119:86, *passim*). True is everyone who obeys His will, keeps His Commandments. Scripture calls the obedient servant one who "does the truth," who "walks in truth, in faithfulness," *halakh be-emet* (2 Chr 31:20, 1 Kgs 2:4; Is 38:3). Thus, long before the word "existential" was coined and became fashionable, the ancient Israelite approached God, the people, and the world in a superbly existential manner, without ever philosophizing about it. Among the so-called Dead Sea Scrolls, discovered only in 1947, there is that amazing rule of the monks of Qumran. It demanded of the members of the community that they "do truth and justice" (1 QS I,5).

As he had done on other occasions, St. Paul (or one of his company) took the simple *aletheuo*, "to tell the truth," into Christ's service: he treated a plain word as if it were a precious cup that he could fill with strong wine. He then uttered the hitherto unheard-of sentence: *aletheuontes en agape*, "doing the truth in love" (Eph 4:15). It seems appropriate to deal here, however briefly, with what is often—and quite wrongly—called the Hellenization of the Church's Jewish heritage: no Greek perspective is superimposed on a Christian sub-structure, rather is Greek thought or speech received into the communion of the faithful by a "baptism." The Pauline phrase was unknown to Greeks, and in practice it is still little known among Christians. After all, it is not an easy thing that is demanded of a Christian. He or she ought to be driven, not by instinct, but by *dynamis*, by love's power that enables him or her to live for others, as Jesus, the *Ebed YHVH*, the Servant of the Lord, lived and died for His brothers and sisters.[15] An observant Jew will rightly say that he or she lives by the power of the Law, but that power is also Love's might.

In the *Tanakh*, the Jewish Bible,[16] *emet* means God's teaching or revelation in promise and precept (see Ps 86:11; Dan 8:12); in the New Testament, *aletheia* often refers to the Good News of Christ, to the gospel as preached by the Apostle (Gal 2:5, 14; 5:7; Rom 10:16; Eph 1:13; 2 Tim 3:8). In Rabbinic literature, *emet* is called one of the pillars that sustain the world (*Ab* 1,1) or "the seal of the Holy One, blessed be He" (*bYoma* 69b). In the Gospel according to John, Jesus says of Himself: "I am the Way, the Truth, and the Life" (14:6). In words less emphatic, less terse, He is the Road leading to the Father; the Revealer of the Father's saving will and plan, indeed, their fulfillment; the Giver offering us a share in the divine life.

Shalom, Well-being, Harmony. In certain pagan cultures, one had to know the secret names of their gods or goddesses to approach them. My discussion of certain biblical key words in no way implies that the knowledge of their meaning is necessary for loving God. That knowledge is, however, needed if our inner life and our self-understanding are to be what they should. *Shalom*, another word that dominates Scripture, is commonly rendered "Peace." Yet, its basic meaning is wholeness, perfection, integrity. It may mean well-being, prosperity as they touch daily existence; on a higher plane, it is life in harmony with oneself, with one's neighbor, with God.

The great vision of Messianic times, the vision of universal peace, exemplifies that meaning:

> Many peoples shall come and say,
>   let us climb the Lord's mountain
>   to the house of the God of Jacob,
> that He may instruct us in His ways....
>
> They shall beat their swords into plowshares
>   and their spears into pruning knives;
> Nation shall not lift sword against nation
>   nor ever again train for war.
>
> (Is 2:3-4; Mi 4:2-3)

Men and women become disoriented if they cease to dream; similarly, the faithful, be they Jews or Christians, will lose the passion of their calling if they no longer dream of, or rather hope for God's total reign; no longer reach for the seemingly impossible; no longer seek to shape the future in His name.

Jewish worship, throughout the ages, abounds with petitions for *shalom*. The high priestly blessing, dear to Christians as much as Jews, culminates in "The Lord look upon you kindly and give you [His] peace" (Nu 6:26). *Shalom* verges on blessing, glory, salvation, and life to such an extent that one can say that *shalom* is all these things. Peace is granted to the just, to those who lead the life of righteousness. It will accrue to those who live in accordance with God's will (see Is 32:16-18). It is the companion, as it were, of God's presence among His people (see Lv 26:1-13; Ez 37:23-27).

Similar tones are awakened by Jesus' saying: "I leave you peace, My peace I give unto you" (Jn 14:27). With these words He does not take leave of His disciples; on the contrary, He announces His abiding presence. All who seek to walk in the sight of God will see the words of one of the singers of Israel fulfilled in their lives:

> The Lord, He proclaims peace
>   to His people, to His faithful ones,
> and to those who put their hope in Him....
>   Kindness and truth shall meet;
> justice and peace shall kiss.
>
> (Ps 85:9, 11)

Tzedakah, Righteousness.   The difference between the Jewish tradition and our own world in the understanding of "truth" and "peace" is pronounced; but no other is as marked as that between "justice," in Israel on the one hand, and Western civilization on the other. As early as the twelfth century B.C., Deborah, the prophet, sang of *tzedakah* in an altogether unique manner. She delighted in the knowledge that, whenever people gathered at the wells, they extolled the *tzedakot YHVH*, "the just deeds of the Lord" (Jgs 5:11). These "just deeds" are really God's victories as Israel's Champion, the manifestations of His grace, His saving acts in history.[17] Other biblical books, too, use the word *tzedakah*, justice, righteousness, to proclaim God's saving power. (See 1 Sm 12:7; Mi 6:5.)

The one who sang best of God's justice as the well of salvation, and thus of the synonymity of the one with the other, was the Second Isaiah, the poet among the prophets. Some of his

hymnic utterances allow us a glimpse of the mysterious work-
ings of the God of Israel. He does not permit mathematical
equations to govern His actions. The Lord's disregard of what
men and women the world over consider equitable, the prophet
calls "just." What is thus a puzzle to the common sense of most
people, even confusion to their minds, is the strength and joy of
the faithful.

On several occasions, the prophet gloried in the identity of
justice and salvation. These are his words:

> Pour down, O heavens, from above!
>   Let the clouds gently rain [His] justice!
> Let the earth be opened and salvation bud forth.
>   Yes, let justice spring up.
> I, the Lord, created it all.
>
> (45:8)

> I bring my justice near,
>   it is not far off.
> My salvation shall not tarry,
>   I will grant salvation to Zion
> and my glory to Israel.
>
> (46:13)

> Lift your eyes to the heavens,
>   and look at the earth beneath;
> though the heavens vanish like smoke,
>   and the earth wear out like a garment,
>   and they who dwell on it die like gnats,
> my saving power shall last forever
>   and my justice shall never want.
>
> (51:6; see also 51:8)

The salvific character of God's justice is hailed also in other
parts of Israel's Scriptures. Jeremiah, for instance, warns the
wise, not to take pride in their wisdom; the strong, not to boast
of their strength; the wealthy, not to be blinded by their wealth.
Let them rather glory in being allowed to know God. They will
indeed delight in His presence:

> I, the Lord, bring to the earth
> *hesed, mishpat, tzedakah*,
> unfailing love, right, and saving justice.
>
> (9:23-24)

Pained by his or her sinfulness, a penitent turns to the God of the Covenant, hoping that His justice will save the sinner, and His goodness forgive the one who grieves over sin:

> Hear my prayer, O Lord,
> in your faithfulness give ear to my plea,
> in justice answer me,
> for none who lives is just in your sight.
>
> (Ps 143:1-2)

The first Epistle of John affirms that use of justice, towering as it does above any other meaning:

> If we acknowledge our sins,
> [God] is just and may be trusted
> to forgive our sins
> and cleanse us from every wrong.
>
> (9:1)

In his Epistle to the Romans, the Apostle Paul returns time and again to justice as the great attribute of God, designating His benevolence, His goodness, His devotion and fidelity to His partner in the Covenant. The gospel, he declares, is "the saving power of God for every one who believes." In explanation, he continues: "In it is revealed the justice of God, which begins and ends with faith" (1:16-17). God's saving presence is with the faithful at all times, working in them if they meet it in faith. (The translators of the New English Bible render the Greek *dikaiosynē* as God's "way of righting wrong".) Later in his Letter to the Christian Community of Rome, Paul writes: "The justice of God has been made manifest apart from Law, even though the Law and the Prophets bear witness to it. It is through faith in Christ that this justice becomes effective" (3:21-22).

I have spoken of God's justice as His countenance turned toward Israel and humankind or, to change the metaphor, God's arm ever reaching out to His favored creature. I have still to touch on human justice. At first sight, it may seem a totally different aspect of justice. In reality, it is a man's or woman's response to God's saving presence, to His commandments; it is the believer's conformity to the Lord's will.

Chapter eighteen of Ezekiel is devoted to a covenanter's responsibility before God, or conduct in His sight. In His name, the prophet calls "just" the one

> who does not feast on mountain-shrines,
> who does not lift his eyes to the idols of the house of
>   Israel,
> who does not dishonor another man's wife,
> who does not approach a woman during her period,
> who does not oppress anyone,
> who returns a debtor's pledge,
> who does not commit robbery,
> who gives bread to the hungry,
> who clothes the naked,
> who does not lend at interest,
> who judges fairly between a person and an opponent,
> who walks by my statutes,
> and faithfully observes my ordinances.
>
> (18:5-9)

The New Testament, too, hails "justice" as the human response to the divine law, as moral conduct in the light of Sinai. Zechariah and Elizabeth are said to have been "just before God, blamelessly walking in the way of all His commandments and ordinances" (Lk 1:6). After the wondrous birth of his and Elizabeth's son, Zechariah prayed with a prophet's ardor (see Lk 1:67) that the whole people,

> saved from the hands of [their] enemies,
> may serve God unafraid,
> in holiness and justice...
> all the days of [their] lives.
>
> (Lk 1:74-75)

Is not the meaning of "justice" best summed up in Jesus' demand: "Be perfect, as your heavenly Father is perfect!" (Mt 5:48)? The New English Bible says instead of "perfect" "all good"; thus, it reads: "Be all good, as your heavenly Father is all good!" Jesus' saying is a happy recast of the "Be holy as I am holy" (Lv 19:2; see 1 Pt 1:16).

Sublime though the rule of justice is, it does include the basic demand of evenhandedness (see Mt 23:23). True, the prophets' passionate castigations of the rich and mighty for exploiting the poor and downtrodden go unmentioned in the gospels, except in Mary's Song (see Lk 1:51-53); yet this does not mean that they have lost all validity. On the contrary, the prophets who were "the conscience of Israel"[18] continue to be the conscience of all those who worship the God of Israel. Social justice must be their concern.

Without in the least wishing to belittle the Christian's obligation of caring for the commonweal, I must repeat that Christ's message seems unconcerned with social, economic, or political relations among people. The justice Jesus proclaimed by His word and demonstrated on the Cross is not a good anyone can claim; it is gift, favor, grace. In His message, as in that of Israel's prophets and psalmists, justice and grace are synonymous, indeed, interchangeable concepts.

Once, a man, in a crowd that surrounded Jesus, called out to Him: "Master, tell my brother to give me my share in the family possessions!" It was a legitimate grievance that had him turn to one whom he recognized as a teacher in Israel. Still, Jesus answered: "Man, who made me judge or arbiter of your affairs?" (Lk 12:14). These seem hard, unfeeling words. Yet, what Jesus wished to bring home to the petitioner and the multitude was that He had been sent neither to adjudicate entitlements nor to guard property rights. No, His ministry was to dispense God's mercy, to proclaim divine, not human justice. The heart of His gospel is the proclamation of a justice that, outdistancing human measurement, invests believers with the ultimate gift, salvation.

Not the least of my reasons for dwelling on the significance of certain biblical keywords is the fact that a major barrier between Christians and Jews is one of language. To a large extent, we both use the same vocabulary—words like God, Man, Messiah, creation, redemption, sanctification, grace, law, sin, mercy, forgiveness, hope, and others—we do pronounce and accent those words differently. In order to encounter each other, not in hostility, but in truth and peace, Christians must learn the meaning these and other words had for the biblical authors; they must learn to read Scripture with a Hebrew, not a Greek or Western mind; they must learn patterns of thought and speech that are not native to them, but require them to be transformed. Likewise, Jews have to become aware of the Christian idiom to make the dialogue the two-way street, the interaction it ought to be.

Before continuing the consideration of Cardinal Bea's early work as the paving of the way the Council was to travel, it is appropriate to recall that my relatively long treatment of the meaning and importance of Hebrew was occasioned by Pius XII's directive to Fr. Bea that, with other scholars assisting, he translate the Psalms into Latin from the original text. Though he did not know what the future held in store, in carrying out his commission he strengthened the quest of alert Christians for a re-vision and re-ordering of the relationship between Christians and Jews. Another of Father Bea's involvements carried that unwitting preparation of the Conciliar encounter with the people of Israel still further.

Moved by the Breath of the Spirit

FATHER BEA'S colleague of long standing at the Biblical Institute, Fr. Max Zerwick, S.J., describes the former's work on *Divino Afflante Spiritu* in these words:

> Together with the Dominican exegete Père M. Vosté, at that time secretary of the Biblical Commission, Rome, Fr. Bea had a major, indeed, decisive part [in the writing of the Encyclical]. It seems safe to say that this is his greatest contribution to Biblical Science.... Yet, at no time, neither before nor after its publication, did he even hint how great his part in it had been. His work was like that of a mason,

the Pope, however, was the architect. Still, the spirit of the
Encyclical is that of Fr. Bea; its core, in particular, bears
his signature.[19]

For decades, the Roman authorities had seen the application
of modern critical methods to Holy Scripture as an alien
approach, even a hostile force invading sacred territory. When
eventually they realized that the treatment of the Bible as a
literary composition would not obscure but illumine its meaning, they took the methods developed by Protestant scholars
into the Church's service. A gift of the divine Spirit, the Encyclical was also an adventure of the human intellect. While "fundamentalists" see in the human authors of biblical books mere
tools of God, *Divino Afflante Spiritu* regards them as His living, loving co-workers.[20]

The Church, indeed, did away with an unsophisticated way
of ascertaining the meaning of a biblical passage in favor of
more intricate and demanding methods. In doing so, she
acknowledged the magnanimity of God who made His creatures partners in the business of revelation, thereby enhancing
the dignity of the sacred writers. It bears repetition that as the
bearers of His message to Israel and all humanity, God chose
not disembodied spirits, but men of flesh and blood, not beings
from a mythical realm, but creatures with a definite place of
birth, domicile, culture, and language. Further, to hear the
sacred writers really speak to us, we must learn thought and
speech patterns, emotional reactions that may not be our own;
we must take into account their inner make-up.

No human being, and thus no biblical author, can encom-
pass the infinite richness of God, or the whole marvel of Christ.
As it is with all men and women, so it is with the sacred writers
of Scripture: perceptions and utterances are bound to pass
through the prism of their differing personalities. Each of their
visions of reality is thus quite distinct, yet nonetheless true;
each portrays only a segment of the history of Israel, or of the
life of Christ; still, they are trustworthy. It makes me dizzy to
think that God reveals His will, shows His way, offers a share
in His life and righteousness through the individuality of the

Prophets and Evangelists. But such is the grandeur of our God, the God of Israel.

These thinking, rather than mechanical, instruments of the Holy Spirit were—with possibly one exception—"heirs of the covenant God made with [the] fathers when He said to Abraham, 'In your offspring, all the families of the earth shall be blessed' " (Ac 3:25). This happy truth seems to irritate some scholars: they prefer to speak of "writers of antiquity," of "Oriental" or "Semitic authors," to avoid calling them "Hebrews" or "Jews." Not that the former terms are incorrect, but they make no demands on us, while the challenge of the name "Hebrews" touches our very lives, elicits from us cheerful gratitude and love—or ought to.

The Encyclical and the Jews. In his Encyclical on Holy Scripture, Pius XII warmly acknowledges that the inquiry of modern exegetes "has also clearly shown the special preeminence of the people of Israel among all the other ancient nations of the East...." Today, we hear a statement like this without overtones, as something obvious, if not commonplace. In those days, however, with the Nazis in power, to praise the genius of the Jewish people was considered treason, an assault on the purity and grandeur of the Nordic race. Strange though it may seem to men and women of our generation, in the days of Hitler it was a courageous affirmation. He thus helped us become more and more aware of the authentic bond between the Church and the People of Israel.

I am sure that, without the much misunderstood, at times even maligned, Pius XII, John XXIII could not have convoked the Second Vatican Council. I am sure, too, that we must see in *Divino Afflante Spiritu* a first impetus to the realization of the genuine bond between the old and the new children of Israel, the firstborn and the secondborn.

Many will think it strange that I regard Pius XII as one who broke some ground for Vatican II, who helped prepare the climate for a re-vision and re-ordering of the relationship of the Church and the Jewish people. Let me take you back to 1950 when he invited all people to come to Rome for the celebration of the Holy Year, and included the Jews in his invitation:

> We open the Holy Door to all those who worship Christ and extend to them a fatherly welcome, not excluding those who sincerely but vainly await His coming and worship Him as one promised by the prophets and still to come.

Was this not an invitation altogether new? "Not so new," some will counter, "since it was but a disguised call to conversion." This may be. Even if it were, let us not forget the change in tone and heart the words of Pius XII make manifest. Time was when lack of psychological insights and certain misconceptions led Christians to see in Jewish aloofness from Christ nothing but stubbornness and ill will. Pius XII, however, calls the messianic expectation of Jews sincere.

Though I do not pretend to offer something other than a personal interpretation, I have little doubt that Cardinal Bea, too, saw in the words of Pius XII a first sign for a new vision of Jews and Judaism by Christians. Prior to the drafting of a conciliar statement on the Jews, I prepared a position paper, in which I offered a reading of the signs of the times, as I understood them, outlining the needs of the day as well as some actions the Church would have to take to quicken the kinship with the people of Israel. Among those signs I listed the welcome Pius XII extended to Jews in whom the messianic hope is alive. The Cardinal saw the position paper; to my knowledge, he never disagreed with my views.

All concerned with deepened Christian-Jewish relations remember with joy the spontaneity of Pope John's love. On Good Friday of 1959, when the Cardinal conducting the service was about to chant the intercessory prayer on behalf of the Jewish people, the Pope sent him word to delete the phrase *perfidia Judaica*. Pope John's loving gesture must not let us forget the preparatory work of several scholars who demonstrated that *perfidia* in the writings of Christian antiquity never meant faithlessness, infidelity, or perfidy.[21]

Nor ought we to forget the decree on the correct understanding of the prayer by the Congregation of Rites, bearing Pius

XII's signature. The decree clarifies the translation of *perfidia* by siding with those scholars who had proved that *perfidia* meant disbelief or refusal to believe [in Christ]. It was never meant as invective; it could well be taken as the term with which a Jew might describe his or her attitude toward Jesus as the Christ. Again, I feel conscience bound to hail Pius XII's initiative without lessening my gratitude to Pope John for the giant step he took in cleansing the Good Friday prayer for the Jews of phrases that may hurt. The final action came even later so that now the Jews are called "those to whom God spoke first" or "the first hearers of the word of God." This wholly positive phrase about "the other," in this instance, "the Jews," is a perfect example of ecumenical speech.[22]

There is still another aspect indicating the newness of Pius XII's approach to the Jews. I have only to mention the words "forced sermons" and "forced baptism," without giving some of the gruesome details. This use of force was denounced time and again by Popes as incompatible with the freedom which is essential to faith. Forcing Jews to believe in Christ was a sign of sickness, an aberration of Christian consciousness, worse, it was evil. Obviously, no one merits praise for not returning to those days, but in my role as historian of Cardinal Bea's paving the way to a new encounter of Christians and Jews, I have to record the change in tone and heart. In one and the same breath, Pius XII invited Jews and other Christians, seeing them as kin.

The Literal Sense. God's choice of Hebrew authors as the bearers of His revelation may well be called a paradox. Need I say that paradox in a theological context is poles apart from the "quaint paradox" of the *Pirates of Penzance*. The paradox I hail is not the incongruities and incompatibilities within a human being, its inner contradictions; it is rather the incomprehensible dwelling on earth, among men and women, of the God whose abode is "the inaccessible light" (1 Tim 6:16). The paradox with which I am concerned is the interaction between the sovereign Lord and the dependent creature, the meeting of the holy and the sinful.

Pius XII urges exegetes to pay attention to paradoxical modes of expression of the sacred writers. Other characteristics they ought to be aware of are their way of narration, their specific idioms, and their love of hyperbole. He adds that anyone familiar with the nature of biblical inspiration cannot be surprised at the fact that the sacred writers have ways all their own.[23] Tempting though it be to discuss these thought and speech patterns, I must refrain from doing so. A singular concern of the Encyclical is the demand that "the foremost and greatest endeavor of interpreters should be to discern and define clearly the literal sense of a given passage."[24]

The high regard in which Pius XII held the literal sense may seem perplexing. In everyday life, to be called "a literalist"is an insult; "literal" means "plain," "unimaginative," "superficial," and so on. Obviously, this is not the intention of Pius XII. To him, "literal" means "authentic"; his regard for it was but respect for, and fidelity to, the work of the human author.

Things Old and New.   During the two millenia preceding the Encyclical, there had grown, in the Jewish as well as the Christian tradition, a body of allegorical interpretations. The Rabbis thought that even every letter and number had a significance above and beyond itself. They attributed special dignity, indeed, sanctity to the letters of the alphabet. The letters, as written here on earth, are reflections of heavenly letters. The letters are indestructible, thus, when Moses broke the tablets of the Law, the letters flew upward, back to their Creator (*bPes.* 87b). R. Ḥanina b. Teradyon is said to have been wrapped in a Torah scroll and put to death by burning. Moments before drawing his last breath, his disciples, wishing to share in the vision granted him at the point of martyrdom, cried out: "Rabbi, what do you see?" He answered: "The parchments are burning, but the letters are soaring on high" (*Ab. Zar.* 18a).

Christian scholars hold that the search for the "deeper" meaning of biblical texts originated with the school of Alexandria, which maintained that the glory of God demands that we always unearth the spiritual sense underlying the text. Others trace the search back to the pagan Stoics. As appreciation of rabbinic thought increases among Christian scholars they, I am sure, will consider the influence of Midrashic literature more important than that of the school of Alexandria or of the Stoic philosophers.

I will go even further. The quest for other meanings as well as the love of metaphor are deeply rooted in human nature. An animal sees its surrounding as the senses present them. So does every human being, but the inner eye, or should I say the poet in every man and woman, sees more. It sees beauty, meaning, links between the material and the spiritual. Pope Pius XII had not the least intention of muzzling the poet in us. What he opposed was "bad poetry"—the misuse of figurative meaning, the clearest example being the allegorization of parables.

Would I could duly praise the five senses. A straight road leads from the at-homeness of the Hebrew Scriptures in the world of sound, color, and fragrance, to the parables and sacraments of Jesus. In the parables, a dutiful farmer, a daring merchant, a tired woman, and a quick shepherd—with the help of seed, pearl, coin, and sheep—act out the drama of God's dealings with humanity. In the sacraments, things of everyday life—water, oil, bread, and wine—are turned into instruments of grace; they are God's assistants in the work of sanctifying Man, and Man's helpers in the business of glorifying God. Sacraments are said to be foreign to Judaism. Whether they are or not, the Christian sacraments grew out of the Jewish world.

Christ's Parables: Their Intent. Joseph Klausner was the first Jewish scholar to discuss in Hebrew the uniqueness of Jesus; he did so in the light of the Jewish tradition and with the help of contemporary exegesis. Hence, he called Him "a master teller of parables."[25] More than that, Jesus is alive in His parables, His love moves through them.

Some parables begin without an introductory formula, just like any other story. The opening words of others relate the story to be told to the reign of God. For instance, "God's kingly reign is like a mustard seed," more precisely, "with God's rule, things are as they are with a mustard seed." An opening phrase like this one is not an oratorical device; through it, Jesus wishes to announce that the reign of God is at hand; that it is here, and yet still to come.

To repeat, in telling His parables, Jesus announces the advent of God's reign among His people, in the midst of humanity. Any interpretation of His parables must be done with this in mind. Their exegesis requires care and respect. The Fathers of the Church certainly held them in respect, but in their day the difference between parable and allegory had not yet been clearly established. As a rule, the parable has one salient point; in some instances, a principal and some minor points. All the details are without consequence. They are told for the sake of ornament; they dramatize the situation; they give the story life. In an allegory, the major, and at times even the minor, details are symbolic.

The Good Samaritan.   By turning the parable of the Good Samaritan into an allegory, certain Church Fathers gave it a direction that can scarcely be thought of as Jesus' intent. This is the way they understood the parable:

> A man—obviously, a Jew—travels from Jerusalem down to Jericho; he represents Adam who, having fallen into sin, had to go into exile. From the wonders of Paradise he journeys toward graceless Jericho. Adam, that is human-kind, now deprived of God's favor, and subject to the power of Satan, is wounded, all but dead. Thieves—evil spirits—tempt Adam and his spouse, mar their souls and the souls of their offspring with the lust of concupiscence. Is there no help for them, the Fathers wonder, no way of returning to their original friendship with God? Their answer is "no." The priest and the Levite, representing the Law and the Prophets, "the Ancient Dispensation," are unable to remedy the consequences of Adam's fall by bringing salvation to sinful humanity. Healing, the Fathers continue, comes only with the Samaritan, a scorned stranger. He stands for Christ, who came to His own, but His own received Him not. He was in the world, His world, but the world did not know Him (see Jn 1:10-11).
>
> The wine and oil with which the compassionate stranger

treats the victim is variously understood by the Fathers as His blood and His pity, or the blood of the Passion and the unction of the Holy Spirit, or the gnawings of conscience and the healing power of faith. [The diverse figurative meanings suggested by the Fathers show the arbitrariness of the allegorical explanation of parables.] The beast that carries the Samaritan stands for Christ's humanity, or His body bearing the cross, that is, the burden of our sins. The inn to which he brings the heavily beaten, almost dying man is the Church, refuge and home of all who are broken in mind or body. The two silver pieces given to the innkeeper, St. Peter, are the two commandments of love or the promise of life, this life and that of the world-to-come. Finally, the return of the Good Samaritan is Christ's Second Coming, when all things will be as they ought, when the full fruits of redemption will be ours.

This is a composite of the comments by Origen, Augustine, Ambrose, John Chrysostom, and others. I have taken the ensemble of their thoughts, as given by Cornelius a Lapide who concludes his rendering with these words: "this interpretation seems reasonable and true."[26] I regret to say, it is neither. If one is oblivious to the difference between parable and allegory, one may be enticed by the patristic interpretation, because it has everything fall neatly into place. Reading like a survey of salvation history, the patristic comments lack the challenge, the urgency that is the mark of Jesus' speech. His speech disturbs and comforts; accuses and offers pardon; warns and woos. He challenges His hearers to act, to make history, not to ponder it.

He came, not to offer overviews, however intriguing, but to summon me and you to a new life. Here as elsewhere, Christ's words are a call to renewal, to *teshuvah*, the turning to God with one's whole being. The allegorical interpretation, however, obligates the hearer to nothing; in fact, it never so much as touches the tasks that ought to be everyone's concern. It speaks only of others, of Adam and of the Jews, what they did, or did not do. It relates their failures, real or alleged, never those of the hearers, that is Christians. I have no desire to judge the Fathers—victims of an age teeming with allegorical interpretation—or imply that ill will permeated their sermons. Still, I must say their interpretation easily misleads the hearer into self-righteousness, into looking down on Israel as the people of failure, and looking upon the Christian community as faithful and obedient.

Homiletic Observations. The parable does no more and no less than answer the question, "Who is my neighbor?" It moves powerfully to the final imperative: "Go and do the same" (Lk 10:37). To spell out Jesus' terse words to the student of the Torah: Do *not ask* who is my neighbor! *Be* a neighbor to one in need, whoever he may be! This is the great theme of the parable, and nothing else. Cornelius a Lapide, however, holds that

> Christ here draws attention to the perversity of the priests of that day, who were zealous in carrying out all the outward observances of the law, but utterly wanting in true religion and in showing mercy and pity. For [the] priest [of the parable] left his fellow-countryman and neighbor in direst distress without even a word of consolation or comfort.[27]

This gratuitous charge clashes with Jesus' narration. He did not describe the priest and Levite nor did He tell what their motives were; they are there to flesh out the story. While preachers delight in analyzing the supposed motivation of priest and Levite, others see them as a portrayal of the alleged impotence of God's covenant with Israel. The parable's learner comes to Jesus with the query: "What must I do to inherit eternal life?" At Jesus' prodding, the searcher after the perfect life—an earnest student of the Torah—answers with Deuteronomy 6:5 and Leviticus 19:18: "Love the Lord your God...and your neighbor as yourself" (Lk 10:27).[28] Jesus confirms his answer by saying: "Right! Do so and you shall live" (10:28). Could Jesus have used a more powerful phrase to declare that the Old Testament or, might it not be better to say, the First Testament is life-giving? Were it not so, would one of the singers of Israel have prayed:

A lamp to my feet is your word
   a light to my path.

(Ps 119:105)

The Sin of Comparison.   A favorite topic of preachers on our
parable obviously is the question of everyone's neighbor. Many
a time, the sermon becomes a limited experiment in "comparative religion." In these attempts to compare Christianity with
Judaism, the latter is usually said to be inferior, while the
former is called superior, indeed perfect. Superiority and perfection are qualities best claimed by quiet deeds rather than by
noisy speech. A random example of the comparative approach
is that of Gunther Schiwy, a contemporary German Catholic
exegete:

> The law knew indeed "love of neighbor," even "love of
> enemy," but the common Jewish theology saw no one save
> a fellow national as neighbor or, at the most [*höchstens*], a
> stranger living in their midst: "When an alien settles with
> you in your land, do not oppress him. Treat him like a
> native-born. Love him as yourself, for you, too, were once
> aliens in the land of Egypt. I, the Lord, am your God" (Lv
> 19:33-34).[29]

I added to the quotation from Scripture the unique conclusion: "I, the Lord, am your God," because it marks the Law
proclaimed to Israel as God's gift—not pages of a code, but part
of her salvation. Further, there are other instances in which the
Pentateuch proclaims that justice is indivisible; it is either
all-encompassing or it is not. "The law shall equally apply to
the resident alien as to the native" (Ex 12:49). In contradistinc-
tion to the code of Hammurabi, which acknowledged class
privileges in its system of justice, the book of Leviticus emphatically declares: "Have but one rule, for alien and native alike. I,
the Lord, am your God" (24:22). It is puzzling that Schiwy
introduces his reference to Israel's exquisite law on the treatment of those born elsewhere or those of different stock and
culture, by the adverbial phrase "at the most," as if love of
foreigners and outsiders were held in high regard by all Christians, or as if it were practiced all over the globe.

I will return to Schiwy's opinion on what he calls "common Jewish theology," which I take to mean rabbinic thought, later. For the moment, I would like to examine briefly the penchant religious teachers or writers—be they Christians, Jews, Muslims, Hindus, or others—have for making comparisons. To compare one phenomenon with another can be most useful in obtaining deeper knowledge; it may even be a necessary means on the road to truth. Still, at times—indeed, many times—a comparison achieves the opposite; it may even be an occasion for sin. Were I to compare one of my special gifts or my faith with that of another—kin or stranger—I would, in all likelihood, fail to arrive at a balanced judgment. It is much more probable that were I to engage in such a comparison, I would be downcast because of my "inferiority" or overbearing because of my "superiority."

To top it all, can anyone believe, even for a second, that Jesus told this parable and others for the purpose of having His followers compare their Way to the Jewish Way and thus conclude that they are praiseworthy servants? Such self-praise would be at odds with Jesus' enjoinder to His disciples: "When you have done all you have been commanded to do, you should say, 'We are poor servants, deserving no praise; we have only done our duty' " (Lk 17:10).

The famous Billerbeck, an expert in the rabbinic tradition but lacking in sympathy for it, reasons:

> As the Old Testament...counts among those to whom Israel should show love only the alien dwelling in her midst, it is evident that, for her, love of neighbor is not universal, not love of humanity but merely love of another Israelite.[30]

Billerbeck seems unaware that neither the Jewish nor the Christian Way demands universal love, love of humanity; rather are Jews and Christians bidden to love individuals of flesh and blood, not "humankind."[31]

It is quite likely that when Israel was young the "neighbor to be loved" was understood as the one next door or every fellow-covenanter; after all, such was the frame of the people's experience. Later in Israel's life, when many non-Jews dwelled in the land and her life was touched by the lives of others, the frontiers of experience widened, and so did the understanding of the commandment, "Love your neighbor." Only then did the problem, "Who is my neighbor?" arise. Hence, to look down upon Israel for not having entered history with a mature understanding of moral requirements is inane. The preacher who speaks of the Jews in order to avoid reminding his congregation of their obligations and failures—not to mention his own—is untrue to his calling.

In treating the tale of the Good Samaritan, many Christian teachers succumb to the temptation of making Judaism the villain of the story, but our parable is not a drama with hero and anti-hero. It is not without reason that all the characters of the narrative, the Good Samaritan excepted, remain amorphous, that only the latter is fully alive, a creature of flesh and blood: a man of sensitivity and courage; a being of selfless heart and gracious hand. It is, therefore, hardly correct to say with Rudolf Bultmann: "The pith, the main issue of the parable is the juxtaposition of the loveless Jews and the love-filled Samaritan."[32] What really matters is the contrast between the Good Samaritan and me and, if I may be so bold, the Good Samaritan and you. Priest and Levite are but stand-ins.[33]

Love of Enemy in Judaism.   How sad that many ministers of the Word are not inspired by the Good Samaritan to meet Jews and Judaism with fairness and respect! By portraying Judaism negatively, they are unwittingly joining the highwaymen of the parable. What then is the true image of Judaism, its true voice? Shmuel Ha-Katan, Samuel the Small, a teacher of the first century A.D., warned:

> Do not rejoice when your enemy falls,
>   do not gloat when he stumbles;
> lest the Lord see it and be displeased with you,
>   and cease to be angry with [your enemy].
>
> (*Ab.* 4:24)

Without knowledge of the subtleties of the Jewish tradition, a reader may find the last line puzzling. In the opinion of the ancient Rabbis, God always sides with the wronged. Yet, when the wronged person looks on the ills of his enemy with glee, then the enemy, like all innocent sufferers, is granted God's favor.

The saying of Samuel the Small is remarkable for two reasons. First, it is taken, word for word, from Scripture. Samuel the Small quotes Proverbs 24:17-18, but without saying so. Why? He seems to identify himself so strongly with the inspired word that it flows from his lips as if it were his own. Second, his personality is enigmatic. He is the same man whom Patriarch Gamaliel, around the turn of the first century A.D., asked to draw up an imprecatory petition against the *minim* and make it part of the Morning Service.

Who Are the Minim?   The meaning of the term varies from one period to another. Their identity in that malediction has been the object of lively discussions among scholars. Many take them to have been Jewish Christians, suspected of making common cause with the Roman rulers. As alleged collaborators, they were considered traitors and thus would have to perish. Others think *minim* to have been antinomian gnostics, whose teaching and life were a peril to the Jewish Way.[34] In either case, the prayer sought the exclusion, if not the death, of Israel's imputed enemies.

The suspicion that Jewish Christians informed on their fellow Jews was ill-founded. Moveover the Romans despised Christians even more than Jews. Judaism was, a faith community, a *religio licita*, enjoying certain privileges: Jews were permitted, above all, to worship the One God in accordance with their own laws and dispensed from the cult of the emperor and other idolatrous practices. Christianity, on the contrary, was considered a *superstitio*, that is, an unrecognized religion whose god was not allowed to have his image in the *Pantheon* where all the gods of the Empire were given homage.

Now, is Samuel the Small a split personality, preaching, at one and the same time, love and hatred of enemies? How can one reconcile the two seemingly irreconcilable attitudes? Could the answer be that in quoting Scripture, he referred to personal enemies, while the "violence" of the petition was directed against the supposed enemies of God?

Another sage who based his teaching on the Scriptures is Rabbi Hama ben Hanina, of the third century, A.D. On one occasion, he followed the lead of the book of Proverbs:

> If your enemy be hungry, give him bread to eat,
>   if he be thirsty, give him water to drink;
> You will heap live coals on his head,
>   and the Lord will reward you.
>
> (25:21)

He did not quote the biblical saying verbatim; what he said was:

> Even if your enemy has risen early
>   to kill you
> and comes to your house hungry and thirsty,
>   give him food and drink.

The Rabbi then continued: "Read not *yeshallem*, 'He will reward you,' but *yashlimenu*, 'He will make peace between you and your enemy' " (*Midr. Prov.* 25:21). Is not this Rabbi's guidance bewildering? Does it not go too far? Is it, one wonders, only the Rabbi's personal persuasion? Or is it a companion saying to Jesus' counsel of offering "the other cheek" (Mt 5:39)?

There are other powerful sayings, handed down, not as one man's opinion, but as the consensus among the Rabbis. This is one of them:

> Our masters have taught:
> "Scripture says: 'You shall not hate your brother
>   in your heart'
> Lest anyone [be tempted to] think, ' I must not strike him,
>   beat him or curse him
>   [but I may hate him].'
> Therefore Scripture states: 'in your heart'."
>
> <div align="right">(<i>bArak.</i> 16b)</div>

Another counsel representing the mind of the sages is this:

> Our masters have taught:
> Those who are insulted and do not insult,
>   those who hear themselves reviled and do not reply,
> Those who act from love, and rejoice in their suffering,
>   of them Scripture says:
> "Your friends are as the sun rising in its might."
>
> (Jgs 5:31; *bShab.* 8b)

Contrary to what many Christians think of rabbinic teachings, the Rabbis say again and again that it is better to be among the oppressed than among the oppressors. Rabbi Abbahu, of the early fourth century A.D., held that "a man should always strive to be of the persecuted rather than of the persecutors" (*bB.K.* 93a).

These are but a few examples of rabbinic attitudes toward others, particularly enemies; another setting would be necessary for a complete and systematic exposition of the Rabbis' views on love and hate, concern for, and neglect of, others. What I would like to accomplish is to alert particularly teachers and preachers to the prejudices they may have inherited from the misrepresentations of pamphleteers who portrayed the Talmud as the seedbed of all anti-Christian thinking.

I would like to close this sketch with a brief rabbinic tale that, in a way resembles the parable of the Good Samaritan. Of several variations, here is one:

> A man walking along the road sees that his enemy's ass has fallen down under the burden it had to carry. He goes over to his enemy, lending a hand to help him reload the burden. The task completed, the two enter an inn where they talk with one another like friends. The man whose ass had collapsed says to himself: "I always thought of him as an enemy but he has proved himself to be a true friend." They talk some more, and peace envelopes them.
>
> (*Midr. Pss.* on 99:3)

Genres and Forms. "How inscrutable are God's judgments, how incomprehensible [His] ways" (Rom 11:33). With such wonderment does the Apostle conclude his vision of God's sovereign design for humanity's salvation, and Israel's role in it. I recall his exultation as I realize that *Divino Afflante Spiritu* contributed to a new encounter of Christians and Jews, though the authors of the Encyclical do not seem to have been aware of it. They give no evidence of having discerned the signs of the times; nonetheless, they were able to offer the tools with which to remove some of the obstacles to the meeting of Jews and Christians, indeed, to remove major sources of their age-old conflict.

The Encyclical urges all biblical commentators not to lose sight of "the manner of expression or the literary mode adopted by the sacred writer [of any biblical book]."[35] A knowledge of genres and forms, as modern scholars call these modes, is indispensable for a valid interpretation of any given unit. Let us take, for instance, the words of Paul to Timothy:

> Wondrous, indeed, is the mystery of our faith:
> He was manifested in the flesh,
>   vindicated in the Spirit,
>   seen by angels,
> proclaimed among the Gentiles,
>   believed in throughout the world,
>   taken up in glory.
>
> (1 Tim 3:16)

Obviously, this is not a cold statement of fact or a set of propositions speaking only to the mind, not to the heart. Were we to take it as such, and not as an exultant profession of faith, we would miss its moment, its true significance.

Quite different in form is Genesis One. It is a hymn praising the goodness of the Creator, and that of His work: it is the Gospel of Creation. If it is read, not as a hymn, but as a series of scientific data, as a chapter from a cosmological handbook, such reading distorts the true message and becomes a well of mis-knowledge rather than of light and gladness.

Hebrew Polemic

AMONG THE MANY forms that give the Hebrew Scriptures
their literary character, their texture, their sometimes terrifying beauty is one—polemic—whose special quality has not
always been appreciated. Christians have often taken its
severe language as evidence of God's utter disgust with, and
final condemnation of, the people He had once made His own.
Biblical polemic, however, does not spring from contempt,
from the desire to vanquish the other. It is love become righteous anger; it is fruit of an impassioned concern for the integrity of the people covenanted with God.

The Thunder of Prophets.   Polemic is part of prophetic speech.
As such, it calls for repentance, renewal, and the seeking of
God's presence. It is related to what German exegetes call
Mahnrede, "exhortation" or "warning"; *Scheltwort*, "rebuke";
Strafpredigt, "threat of punishment." Moreover, it is woven
through Israel's entire tradition, the Scriptures (Jewish and
Christian), the writings of Qumran, the body of rabbinic
thought. Strangely enough, its identity was determined and its
make-up analyzed only a little more than two and one-half
decades after the publication of the Encyclical.[36]
   To turn to Scripture, the Book of Isaiah begins with what has
been called "The Great Arraignment," God's putting His people on public trial. Its proceedings are extraordinary: God is
both plaintiff and judge; He calls heaven and earth—the whole
of creation—to witness that He has been true to the Covenant
He had concluded with Abraham and his descendants, but that
they have turned their backs on Him and forsaken the bond of
love. The prophet reminds them of how severely they have been
punished: their land laid waste and their abodes destroyed by
flames of judgment, and yet the avenging Lord is full of pity
and pardon. Were it not for God's grace and mercy, Israel's life
would be ended:

> Were it not for the survivors
>   the Lord of Hosts has left us,
> we would become as Sodom,
>   no better than Gomorrah.

(1:9)

Two great motifs—punishment and pardon—vibrate in this "covenant trial" (1:2-9) as in the next one (1:11-20); in fact, they move throughout Scripture:

> Blessed be the ever-living God,
>   [blessed] His everlasting Kingdom,
> He afflicts and He shows mercy.

(Tb 13:1)

In the second "lawsuit," the Lord tells His people with the most graphic of words, that their worship, feasts, offerings, prayers, and vows are futile, indeed, loathsome. None of them reaches Him because Israel's ranks are full of evildoers, their hands stained with crime. No sooner has the Lord said that the deepest abyss separates them, than He invites them to seek His pardon:

> Though your sins be like scarlet,
>   they may become white as snow:
> Though they may be crimson red,
>   they may become white as wool.

(Is 1:18)

This scene with its dark terror and bright promise is introduced by piercing words. The prophet calls those to whom he is sent, "Princes of Sodom!...people of Gomorrah!" (1:10). There can be no more stinging address. To be identified with (not just compared to) the cities of perversion and doom, seems to be the worst form of rejection. Here, as with all polemic remarks, the great rule of the Encyclical that the literal meaning be neither forgotten nor side-stepped does not hold. Censures are not to be taken literally; they are not to "finish off" a person. They hurt;

in fact, they are meant to hurt, but only in order to awaken the one chastised and push the sinner toward a new life.

The Monks of Righteousness.   Polemic, the distinctive mark of prophets, is also at work in post-biblical literature. Its presence demonstrates quite clearly that polemic utterances are integral to the Jewish tradition. The monks of Qumran did not hesitate to think of themselves as "children of righteousness..., walking in the ways of light," while they saw in those outside their community "children of falsehood..., walking in the way of darkness" (1QS III:21) or "men of falsehood who walk in the way of wickedness" (1QS V:10-11).

The opponent of the Teacher of Righteousness, their leader, is called "Wicked Priest" or "Spouter of Lies" (1QpHab IX:9; X:9). The Pharisees are disposed of as "seekers after smooth things" (1QpNah I:2; II:2), "leading many astray through their false teaching, their lying tongue, and their deceitful lips" (1QpNah II:8). These indictments parallel the Hebrew Scriptures, yet lack the full biblical spirit. Their judgments seem distressingly final. The wicked cannot escape their wickedness. There is no pardon in sight for them; no love ought to be lost on them.

A Rabbinical Duel.   The Rabbis of old pored over scrolls, searched Torah, and issued legal decisions—in the minds of some, a not very exciting occupation. Hence some see the Rabbis as men not to be moved. Yet, the opposite is true. They are impassioned human beings whose passion is rarely their ego, rather God's cause.

In 538 B.C., Cyrus, the king of Persia, seeking to end the captivity of Israel in Babylon, gave the exiles the opportunity to return to the Promised Land. Though the Persian treasury financed the move, by no means all Babylonian Jews availed themselves of it. The Talmud (*bYoma* 9a) tells that Resh Lakish, a Palestinian teacher of the third century A.D., was swimming in the Jordan, one day. As he was about to step out of the water, Rabbi b. Bar Hana, who had but come back from Babylon, held out his hand to help the swimmer ashore. Not at all happy at the offer, Resh Laḳish exploded: "By God! I hate you. For it is written: 'If she be a wall, we will build upon her a turret of silver; if she be a door, we will enclose her with boards of cedar' " (Ct 8:9).

Here "wall" is the symbol of a firm character, "door" that of a vacillating one. Had many exiles not lingered, but come home to the land of their fathers at once, the Chosen People, in and through its wholeness, would have been able to support weak members and withstand assaults from without, such is the view of Resh Lakish. To understand his outburst better, one must appreciate the meaning of the Land for the Jewish people. God's gift, the pledge of His love, the sign of His fidelity, it is the very earth on which Israel is called to walk in the sight of the Lord. Resh Laḳish's anger at his fellow Rabbi was no act of personal animosity but one of concern for God's glory and the well-being of His people.

Still, the Rabbis' polemic often appears pitiless; the God they preach seems to be one of utter severity. Yet, when one contemplates the whole gamut of their teaching, God's tender mercy radiates. Rabbi Helbo taught that prayer is like a *mikveh* (the place for taking ritual baths) while repentance resembles a sea. For a bath is at times open, at others shut; in like manner, the gates of prayer are sometimes shut, sometimes open. The sea, however, is wide open at all times; similarly, the gates of repentance are ever open. A sinner may always walk through them. Rabbi Anan, however, contradicting his fellow teacher, proclaimed: The gates of prayer are never locked (Lam.r-3:4,6). No avenue to God is ever closed.

The Chastisement of Erring Jews. In their polemic against fellow Jews who had strayed or were considered to have strayed from the path of Judaism, the Rabbis used a variety of names. The most common designation of a "heretic" was *min*, one who rejects the unity of God or seems to do so, denies bodily resurrection or Israel's election by God, or makes of evil something godlike. The most colorful name the Rabbis gave to their opponents in the war for the triumph of righteousness was, and still is, *apikoros*, an adaptation of the Greek *apikoureios*. An *apikoros* is one who with Epicurus, the Greek philosopher (ca. 340-270 B.C.), holds pleasure to be the only good, the very goal of all morality. The Talmud makes the appellation derive from the Aramaic root *p-k-r*, "to be free of restraint." Hence, an *apikoros* is a worldly minded person, given to the gratification of the senses or one who, denying divine providence and retribution, feels not bound by the precepts of Torah.

Another polemical title is *kofer*, "freethinker," one who asks irritating questions, playing one Scripture passage against another. *Kofer ba-ikkar* is one who disavows essential truths or fundamental dogmas of Judaism. *Mumar*, from the Hebrew *hemir*, "to change," is a convert to a faith other than Judaism, "an apostate." *Meshummed* conveys the same meaning. All these designations are at times uttered with great bitterness that turns the original polemic device into an invective. Still, one must bear in mind that the Rabbis, even when uttering their most bitter invectives, were animated by concern for the unity of Israel, the integrity of her service. They were pained by a real or an alleged violation of the bond that encompasses all the members of God's covenant with Israel.[37]

Scholars Battling Scholars.   At the beginning of the rabbinic tradition, two schools, *Bet Hillel* and *Bet Shammai*, the House (i.e., disciples) of Hillel and that of Shammai, frequently confronted one another. The Hillelites were broadminded, lofty and courageous in their interpretation of the Law; the Shammaites narrow, indeed, petty of spirit. The school of Shammai taught, for instance, that in the evening a man should recite the *Shema Yisrael*, "Hear, O Israel, the Lord is our God, the Lord alone" (Dt 6:4) while reclining, whereas in the morning he should do so standing.[38] The Shammaites took the time references, "when you lie down and when you get up" (6:7) in the most literal way, as the mode of fulfilling the commandment of professing the Uniqueness or Oneness of God. The Hillelites, however, held that a Jew may recite the *Shema* while sitting or reclining, while walking on a road or staying at home.

Strangers to the rabbinic tradition may find it difficult to take the question of a worshiper's posture quite so seriously. Yet, disagreements like this one often led to heated polemic, harsh disputes, even violence between members of the two schools. Rabbi Naḥman Bar Isaac (fourth century A.D.) held that "one who follows the rule of *Bet Shammai* makes his life forfeit." Legend has it that once, away from home, Rabbi Tarfon (late first century A.D.) recited the *Shema* in the manner prescribed by *Bet Shammai*. The punishment was instantaneous: R. Tarfon fell among robbers. The bandits must have been gentle people, they did not touch him. They only sent him away with the warning: "You deserved to come to harm because you acted against the opinion of *Bet Hillel*." (*bBer.* 11a).

One first day of the Days of Awe, the Temple's courtyard was empty, because the people followed one of Shammai's rulings. When Bava ben Buta—himself a Shammaite, though in this matter living by the opinion of the School of Hillel—saw this he uttered this curse against his own: "May their houses be desolate for they have made desolate the house of our God" (*jBetsah* 2:4). Again, when the School of Shammai enacted eighteen preventive measures that made contacts and exchanges between Jews and Gentiles difficult—arguments arose between the Hillelites who opposed those enactments and the Shammaites who favored them. The arguments must have stirred their emotions to such a pitch that several Hillelites were killed (*jShab.* 1:4).

Initially, the Talmud maintains, there were but few disputes in Israel; with the lapse of time, contentions increased, the Torah split, as it were, into two: the two schools held conflicting opinions and issued contrary rulings (*bSanh.* 88b). It has been said that during the first hundred years of their existence— from 30 B.C. to 70 A.D.—the two clashed with each other on points touching "the very heart of Judaism" three hundred and fifty times.[39]

The Enigma of the Am ha-aretz. Fierce though the "war" between the two rabbinic schools was, the animosity they felt, one against the other, pales before the Rabbis' contempt for the *amme ha-aretz* and the latters' contempt for the "Disciples of the Wise," as the students of the Torah were called. It is even said that the loathing of an *am ha-aretz* for scholars was worse than that of the heathens for the people of Israel (see *bPes.* 49b).

One Rabbi went so far in his rancor as to allow the stabbing of an *am ha-aretz* on the Day of Atonement that falls on a Sabbath, that is, the holiest day possible (*ibid.*). Such "bloodthirst" is obviously hyperbole; savage though the words sound, they were no imperative to kill.

Even so, the language compels us to ask, "Who were the *amme ha-aretz* that they evoked so violent a rejection?" The Rabbis have given various answers. One replies: Whoever does not properly tithe his fruits; another, whoever does not recite the *Shema* in the evening and morning; still another, whoever does not wear fringes on his garment; yet another, whoever has no *mezzuzah* on his doorpost (see *bBer.* 47b). But these replies are not definitions, rather are they outward signs of the *amme ha-aretz*.

Claude G. Montefiore has deliberated at length on what precisely made them so abhorrent to the Rabbis.[40] He insists that the *amme ha-aretz* must neither be equated with the "poor in spirit" of the Sermon on the Mount, nor with the insignificant and despised members of society. Rather were they the opposite of the "humble of heart." Praise of humility is, after all, a frequent note in the teachings of the Rabbis. As the greatest of virtues, it leads to the life to come (*bSanh.* 88b). Indeed, "the Holy One blessed be He says of the arrogant, 'I and he cannot dwell in the same world' " (*bSot* 5a).

Montefiore likens the *am ha-aretz* to a boor (see *Ab.* 2:6) or a cad. The *am ha-aretz* is an ignoramus, though being ignorant of the Law does not mean being unlettered; rather is he defiantly ignorant of decency, refusing to amend. "Decency" here means, not modesty, but moral integrity. This may be the reason for the Rabbis having engaged in tirades like the one in *Pesaḥim* 49b: "A man should not give his daughter in marriage to an *am ha-aretz* because they are detestable and their wives vermin, and of their daughters it is said, 'Cursed be he who lies with any beast' " (Dt 27:21).

How are we to take this almost unpardonable language? It is no doubt the speech of a man passionately devoted to the Law and the holiness it demands. But this does not justify its use. It is an abberation of traditional polemic whose purpose is no less than to make ready, in the moral wasteland of this world, "a highway for our God" (Is 40:3).

Jesus, the "Beguiler." Since the Rabbis shot their arrows at all Jews who, in their eyes, had chosen a route different from the main road of Judaism, it is not surprising that they did not spare the infant Church living in Judaism's bosom, and the young Church after their parting of the ways. The name Jesus gave to His teaching was *besorah tovah*, "good tidings," an expression that as part of Hebrew speech antedated His coming. As such, it is good news in its common meaning. Only with the advent of Jesus did it receive a new, that is, a salvific accent. The Rabbis, however, saw in His proclamation, not the "joyous news of salvation," but utterances that brought in their wake enmity, jealousy and strife to Israel. Understandably, the Rabbis did not take kindly to the expression "good news." So strong was their irritation that some mocked it. Rabbi Meir (130-160 A.D.) turned the Greek word *evangelion* into the Hebrew *aven gilayon*, the "sheet of sin," while Rabbi Yohanan, his contemporary, twisted it into *avon gilayon*, "sheet of falsehood" (*bShab.* 116a).

It is but natural for the Christian world to have resented these and other derogatory passages, and to have sought their removal. Still, the actual censorship, not to speak of the burning of the Talmud, was hardly a mature reaction. Christians would have done well to realize that even a stinging epithet may be a cryptic acknowledgment. The Rabbis obviously disbelieved the Christ event; their polemic, however, is evidence that they took it seriously.

Contrary to the opinion of many, allusions to Jesus in the Talmud are not numerous; in fact, the entire Second Temple period is largely ignored. In the few instances where the Talmud, according to the opinion of major scholars, refers to Jesus, the loving witness of the disciples is turned into its opposite. On the lips of Jewish and pagan opponents of Christianity, "all the noble qualities of Jesus which the disciples had found in him, were twisted into defects, and all the miracles attributed to him, into horrible and unseemly marvels."[41]The

Rabbis taking this stance did not do so because they were too far removed from the days of Jesus to be able to see Him ministering to the people. Rather did they continue the charge reported in the Gospels. There, scribes from Jerusalem maintain: "He is possessed by Beelzebul," "He casts out demons by the prince of demons" (Mk 3:22; see Mt 12:24-28).

A "sinner," "sorcerer," "beguiler," "idolater," or more fully a "sinner in Israel," a "scoffer against the words of the wise," are misrepresentations Rabbis of old used to gainsay Jesus' ministry of mercy. Joseph Klausner calls them titles "of little historical value," instances "of vituperation and polemic against the founder of a hated party."[42] Christians cannot hear these titles dispassionately. Still, they must not forget that the Apostle felt bound to acknowledge the sincerity of his kinsmen disbelieving in Christ: "I bear them witness, they are zealous for God" (Rom 10:2). Christians may be inclined to agree with Paul that the zeal having animated the ancient Rabbis was ill-informed or misguided. Nevertheless, it was zeal, that is, a fervent love of God, an ardent desire to hallow His name.

In a similar spirit, Christians ought to listen to the Talmud's testimony on the reality of Jesus' death. I think it most remarkable that the Rabbis—quite unlike the author of the Koran and some modern writers—never seemed to have been tempted to deny the fact of Jesus' death, even though they could not accept the affirmation of faith that Jesus died to save men and women everywhere. This, then, is the talmudic reconstruction of the events that led to Jesus' execution:

> On the eve of Passover Yeshu was hanged. For forty days prior to the execution, a herald went forth and cried "[Yeshu of Nazareth] is going forth to be stoned because he has practiced sorcery and beguiled Israel, leading her astray. Let everyone who knows something in his favor come forward in his defense." He was therefore hanged on the eve of Passover.
>
> (bSanh. 43a)

This talmudic description of Jesus' trial and execution is rather vague and confused, it is definitely at variance with the

Passion narratives of the Gospels. Jesus is said to have been "hung," not "crucified"; the protracted judicial inquiry of which the talmudic story speaks is unknown to the Evangelists. Still, it is worthy of special notice that the Rabbis did not suppress the fact of Jesus' violent death, even though they rejected the Christian claim that He gave up His body and shed His blood for the sins of the world. Remarkably, though it was Pontius Pilate who sentenced Jesus to death, the talmudic story does not even mention the Roman governor. They had to assume some responsibility, since their charge against Jesus was that "he had practiced sorcery, deceived Israel, and led her astray."

This polemic stance, once the dominant view of Jews, has given way, at least in part, to admiration and love. However deep the wonder and affection of modern Jewish scholars and poets may be, it is still far removed from the profession of Ignatius of Antioch: "Him I seek who died for us; Him I love who rose for our sake" (*Ign.Rom* 6:1). Yet, these differences and disagreements, even the old dissensions and conflicts notwithstanding, Christians and Jews are members of faith communities oriented toward redemption. They are brothers and sisters in hope.

A midrashic exegesis of Psalm 40:1, "I hoped in the Lord and He heard my cry" offers this solace:

> Nothing is left for Israel but to hope in the Holy One blessed be He, that He may reward them for saying, "I hoped in the Lord".... It is written: "The Lord is good to those who wait for Him" (Lam 3:25) and "Return to the Stronghold, prisoners of hope" (Zach 9:12). "Wait for the Lord with courage; be stouthearted, be strong, wait for the Lord" (Zach 27:14). "Wait for the Lord," "Hope in the Lord," keep on hoping and hoping. So, even if you hope and still are not saved,...hope and hope again.... For God desires neither burnt offerings, nor peace-offerings, nor sacrifices—only hope.
>
> (*Midr. Pss.* 40:1-2)

The Apostle's thought resounds with the same motif: "We have been saved, though only in hope" (Roman 8:24). "And may the God of hope fill you will all joy and peace—by your faith in Him—until, by the power of the Holy Spirit, you overflow with hope" (Rom 15:13).

Polemic in the New Testament

IN THE PRECEDING pages, I have glanced quickly but, I trust, adequately at the role polemic plays in Israel's sacred writings of biblical and post-biblical times. With the help of this brief examination, I have tried to demonstrate that polemic as well as related literary forms are integral, authentic parts of the Hebrew tradition. Once this is accepted as reality, it follows that polemic in the New Testament cannot be seen as "anti-Jewish," "anti-Judaistic," or "anti-Semitic." On the contrary, Jesus' controversies, even His rebukes, warnings, and "Woes!" hurled at Pharisees, spring from Jewish ardor, from His Jewish soul. Other New Testament utterances—those of John the Baptist and those of the Seer of Patmos, "brother in tribulation and endurance" (Ap 1:9), show the profound concern for God's revelation, the righteous life, and the hallowing of the Name which marks all that is best in Israel, and gives those literary efforts their special Jewish imprint.

The "Seven Letters to the Churches of Asia" that make up the beginning of "Revelation" contain a message to the Christian community of Smyrna. In this message, the community is praised for its steadfastness in the face of slander and persecution, both the work of the Jews of that city (see Ap 2:9-10). Yet, those Jews were far from being authentic Jews. Even though they pretended to be, they had ceased to be true Jews, indeed, lost their claim to the dignity of Israel. They had become the opposite of what they were called to be, for one of two reasons: either because they prayed to the God of Israel and Zeus[43]—a syncretistic worship that a Jew worthy of his name considers utter abomination—or because they proved themselves hostile to the spreading of the Gospel and the salvation of Gentiles which, in the eyes of Christians, made them servants of the Adversary.

All this is said, not of *the* Jews, but of the Jews of *Smyrna*.

The text of this indirect polemic is clear. Two renderings of the Greek original, varying in details, but alike in substance, speak for themselves. The first reads: "I perceive the blasphemy of those who call themselves Jews, and are not, but are of the assembly of Satan" (Ford);[44] the other: "I know how you are slandered by those who claim to be Jews, but are not—they are Satan's synagogue" (NEB). The two translations leave no room for misunderstanding. Yet, Christians and Jews, some Christians and some Jews, have read the sentence as if it condemned all Jews, indeed, Judaism itself.

True, the words of the Apocalypse are as strong an indictment as one would find anywhere, but why would anyone wish them to say something different from what they do? Why would anyone wish to turn a specific judgment into a general one? I can think of no other cause than some emotional disorder. Could it be that here the old enmity between Jews and Gentiles that Christ meant to tear out by its roots (see Eph 2:13-16) raises its ugly head again? Could it be that lingering memories of their estrangment color the reading of Scripture? Or, is it a morbid assumption of a tragic structure of the universe, a neurotic preference for a warped interpretation of reality?

Early in the Gospel according to Matthew, the Baptist called the people to total renewal: "Turn, for the Reign of Heaven is at hand" (3:2). Multitudes from Jerusalem, from all over Judea and the land around the Jordan responded; they went out to John to be "baptized in the Jordan River while they confessed their sins" (3:5). Among them, Matthew reports, were a goodly number of Pharisees and Sadducees. John "welcomed" them with a salutation that sounds like a rejection: "Brood of vipers! Who told you that you would escape the coming wrath? Give evidence that you mean to change your lives" (3:8). Jesus uses the same address in 12:34 and 23:33. The harsh metaphor may have had its origins in the writings of Qumran. In one of their Hymns of Thanksgiving, the speech of dissidents within the Brotherhood is likened to "venom of adders" (1QH 5, 27; see Dt 32:33). Why this fierce accusation? The Baptist certainly did not wish to abuse the men standing before him, nor did he wish to characterize all Pharisees as a "slippery band of knaves."

But then, why? To jar the complacent out of their self-complacency and to warn them against mistaking baptism for magic.

John wished to call his hearers to a complete turning to God, to a new vision of values. No easy task, to be sure. Not because they were Pharisees, not because they were Jews, but because they were human beings, weighed down by a second law of gravity, one affecting the soul. In other words, they were afflicted by that inertia or that resistance to the touch of grace which tempts every man and woman. To help them surmount the difficulty of such turning, John (and Jesus, too) had to use hard and bitter words. Yet, we must not forget that in polemic speech, the words which seem to condemn are meant to help restore those so addressed to true righteousness.

The Devil's Children.   Another crux, not to say pitfall, for scholars and preachers alike, is what Bultmann calls: *Die Teufelskindschaft der Juden*, "The Jews, the Devil's children."[45] To single out Bultmann may be unfair, for few are the exegetes who read without bias the dramatic composition in which the Fourth Evangelist pits Jesus and a group of Jews against one another. The bias I have in mind is the ease with which interpreters apply the expression "the Jews" of a given narrative, not only to that specific audience, but to the Jewish people as a whole. The same bias reads "the Pharisees" of a certain passage, not as the handful of Pharisees present, but as the several thousands of Pharisees throughout the land.

Jesus is not a philosopher who enunciates general principles, but a lover of people who speaks to one or more persons, in a setting always unique. Yet, the particular and the universal need not be opposites. What Jesus said to one or a few may well be extended to His kin, the Jews, indeed to all His kin, human beings of every time and place. But this ought to be done, only if the meaning of an utterance or event demands it. So as to clarify the use of the collective "the Jews," I will treat the scene in John 8:31-59 as a real encounter, and not a literary composition, as many exegetes assume it to have been.

There is no compelling reason for seeing in the crowd of pilgrims at the Temple, who had come to Jerusalem to celebrate

Sukkot, the Feast of Booths, and with whom Jesus is said to have crossed verbal swords, the representatives of all Israel. There is no compelling reason for identifying "the Jews" of this scene (or many another) with all the Jews alive then and now.

When Jesus began His discourse in John 8:12 with: "I am the Light of the world," the pilgrim crowd is portrayed as not convinced of His mission. Yet, as He went on to say: "The One who sent me is with me....I always do what pleases Him" (8:29), we are told that "many believed in Him" (8:30). But when He continued, offering them freedom—an existence chained to neither self nor sin—they were incensed. They were in no need for further freedom, they maintained; being Abraham's children, freedom was already theirs.

Were these demurrers—creations of the Evangelist—the same people whose trust in Jesus the Evangelist had especially noted? Not likely. For Jesus accuses His antagonists of wishing to see Him dead. But could it not be that the same people who a moment ago took Him to their hearts now wished to banish Him from their presence so utterly that they contemplate murder? Yes, human fickleness could have made them switch from love to hate. There is no way to determine definitively whether those charged with seeking Jesus' death were the ones who, for a moment, had embraced Him, or whether they were other pilgrims—those who had remained cold to Him.

It was particular men in His audience, not the whole nation, He is related to have charged with plotting His death: "You look for a chance to kill me.... The devil is your father,...a murderer from the beginning" (8:37,44). If one reads these words, indeed, the whole scene without preconceived ideas about the theology of the Evangelist, one concludes that Jesus addressed people within His hearing, the same who later are said to have "picked up stones to throw at Jesus" (8:59). The attempt to stone Him was an unpremeditated act of rejecting the assumed blasphemy in Jesus' proclamation: "Before Abraham came into existence, I am" (8:58). It must have been unreflected, for had the stoning been planned, Jesus could not have escaped, that is, "slipped out of the Temple precincts" (8:59).

Though large as life, the interplay of charge and counter-charge does not seem to be the record of an actual confrontation between Jesus and some antagonists. (My assumption that Jn 8:31-59 is not the account of a real clashing between Jesus and some of His kinsmen does not imply that they never came into conflict with one another; moreover, it may well carry some features of a true incident.) The various scenes of the Fourth Gospel are vibrant; still, the Gospel was not composed during the two generations following His death and rising. The majority of scholars holds that the time in which it received its present form is about 100 A.D., the time after the "parting of the ways," the painful separation of the young Church and Israel. The author of the scene may have been an *aposynagōgos*, one banned from the faith-community of Israel and kept from joining in its worship and life (see Jn 9:22; 12:24).[46]

If this is so, then our scene may well express the grief of "John's" wounded soul and his anger at the forced isolation from his people. His personal sorrow, however, is not all that is reflected in John 8:31-59. The evangelist is stirred by a wider concern: he is afflicted by the tension between Church and Israel—tensions created by the similarities and dissimilarities of the two bodies. This hurting experience may have made him shape that artful polemic I have been discussing. It is important to remember that this literary form dictates the use of hyperbolic language; the accusation, "the devil is your father," must not be taken literally. Thus, we must not hear in the incident an invective or, what would be worse, a dogmatic statement.

My understanding of John 8 and its polemic is, alas, diametrically opposed to that of quite a few exegetes. One of the most offensive examples of their understanding is that of Hermann Strathmann. In connection with Jesus' exclamation: "The Truth will set you free" (8:31), the Truth being the revelation of God in Jesus, Strathmann writes:

> The Jewry of those days [*Die damalige Judenschaft*] took its stand against the Truth. Such is the Evangelist's total verdict on Judaism. Jesus appeared [on earth] as the Truth

incarnate. [The Jews], however, opted for the lie. He came as the Savior of the world. They sided with the one who is the murderer from the beginning. They shut themselves off from grace and turned themselves over to hate. How was this possible? In the same way as Judas' betrayal. [The Jews] are Satan's instruments.[47]

Strathmann calls our gospel narrative the "merciless unmasking of Judaism in its depravity."[48] I find it hard to understand that, while the Nazi mass murder of Jews and the apostasy of the "German Christians" is still a vivid memory, a German exegete suffers no qualms of conscience in calling the Jews "Satan's instruments," a people who "opted for the lie." Earlier in his commentary, he went so far as to declare:

The stance of the Jews [toward Jesus] is based on their lack of comprehension (v.37 tells that His word found no place in them). Their lack of perception is not accidental; no, they were objectively incapable of hearing His word. Their descent from the devil—whose wish determines their will— makes it impossible for them even to listen to His words. Jesus came to destroy the devil's works (see Jn 3:6); hence the devil's children and servants have neither the faculty nor the inclination to give Him a hearing, much less their love. They are compelled to seek His death; in fact, it corresponds to the very nature of the devil that the divine truth Jesus proclaimed is exactly the reason for the desire to kill Him. Murderous lust and lying determine the devil's mode of existence. Hence, the fact that Jesus speaks the truth is paradoxically the grounds for [the Jews], the devil's children, not to trust Him, not to believe in Him. And yet, in view of Jesus' indisputable sinlessness, their unbelief is unnatural, explainable only by the fact that they are not of God, that God is not their Father.... Here the antagonism between Jesus and the Jews is stripped to its essence, expressed in the sharpest formula.[49]

Incredible! Here the imagination of a noted scholar has run amuck. The Book of Job as well as the Gospels portray the devil as the great tempter. Strathmann, however, invests him with Godlike power. Allowing the devil to determine the way and goal of human beings is theology gone insane. Some of the names given the devil in the New Testament: "Prince of this world" (Jn 12:31; 14:30; 16:11), "the Evil One" (Mt 13:19; Eph 6:16), "the Enemy" (Mt 13:39) may strike terror in our hearts, but they do not imply that he is God's equal, directing or shaping human lives.

Another gospel narrative—Matthew 16:21-23—may shed light on the role the devil plays in Jesus' controversy with some Jewish antagonists, as described by John. The Gospels of Matthew and John differ in time and temperament, in their vision and portrayal of Jesus. Still, Matthew's story may help us understand better Jesus' reproach in John's narrative. In the former, Jesus foretells that He will have to suffer greatly and die, but will be raised from the dead. To this prediction, blundering Peter replies: "Heaven forbid that such a thing should ever happen to you!" (v.22).

Unable to understand why our salvation should need Jesus' sacrifice on the Cross, Peter speaks his heart. Jesus responds: "Get behind me, Satan!" (v.23). The violence of these words shocks us. Translators have tried their best with them, but phrases like "Get out of my sight!" or the softer, "Get out of my way!" obscure the love hidden in Jesus' rebuke. "Get behind me" does not mean "Get away!" or "Leave me!" It reflects rather the order in which, according to Jewish custom, master and disciples walk through streets or countryside. The master leads; the disciples follow. What sounded like a rebuff was in reality a call to Peter (and us), not to walk the easy, self-chosen road, but to obey Jesus' voice.

In the context of this Gospel, Satan means simply "the Adversary." The New English Bible renders Jesus' reproach: "You are a stumbling block to me! You think as men think, not as God thinks." The Jerome Biblical Commentary reads: "You are a scandal to me!" while the New American Bible has Jesus say: "Get out of my sight, you Satan! You are trying to make me trip or fall!" In pointing to these translations, I wish to make the meaning of Jesus' answer clearer, without draining it of its enigmatic character, its power, its *tour de force*. It is the singularity of Jesus' polemic that severity of speech hides gentleness of meaning; that rebuke serves as invitation; that Israel chastened is really Israel embraced.

In his essay on polemic to which I referred before, Otto Michel calls it one of the most "dangerous weapons in the life of the Church and that of Israel." We will not walk the road of righteousness, he continues, simply by rejecting polemic, but rather by keeping it free of malice and repeatedly testing it against the truth of Scripture. A Christian, in particular, while giving witness to his faith, must be aware of a Jew's lofty calling. Whenever a Christian reaches boundaries that separate one faith from the other, the separation signaled by these boundaries must be illumined by God's all-encompassing love.[50]

The Pontifical Biblical Institute

IT MUST HAVE cheered Cardinal Bea to see his co-workers of yesteryear, fellow scholars of the Biblical Institute, stand out among those who, in answer to an official request, submitted themes for deliberation and decision by the Council. Whereas many other proposals had to do with matters of narrower perspective, that of the scholars of the *Istituto Biblico* was concerned with an issue that at one and the same time touched the heart of the Church and the well-being of men and women outside it. Their petition was titled *De antisemitismo vitando*, "On shunning antagonism to Jews."[51] I think it of great significance that men who teach, indeed, live with the Scriptures asked that the Council clarify and, when needed, correct those theological affirmations and biblical sayings that were made to serve as basis for the teaching of contempt. Their call for a Christian life and theology without rancor against the Chosen People implies, without doubt, the conviction that Scripture is free of aversion to Jews; it implies no less the firm wish that its interpretation be so, too.

The members and associates of the Biblical Institute requested that, when considering ecumenical matters, the Council turn its attention, not only to other Christians, but also to the Jew-ish people. In asking that it reflect on the destiny of Israel within an ecumenical framework, they affirmed that, the cleavage of faith notwithstanding, a genuine kinship envelops Jews and Christians. They are both children of Abraham, the first by birth, the other by adoption. Christians are, the schol-ars of the Biblical Institute recalled, true heirs of the faith of Abraham "our Patriarch," as the First Eucharistic Prayer calls him. At the major stations of his life, the biblical Abra-ham is tested by God and proven true because he believed. He believed contrary to experience, instinct, and the opinion of the "world." The Christian's faith, too, goes contrary to what our senses and drives expect, to what the "mainstream," the "world" seeks.

No one has expressed this dichotomy more strikingly than Tertullian (ca. 155-220 A.D.). In the lines that follow, the first sentence is always a profession of faith, the second the objec-tion of the "world," while the third is the love-born defiance of the Christian:

> The Son of God was born. How shameful!
> Yet this is exactly the reason for not feeling shame.
> The Son of God died. How senseless!
> Yet this is precisely the grounds for believing.
> He was buried and rose from the dead. Impossible!
> Yet this is what makes it certain.
> (*De Carne Christi*, V; *PL* 2,761)

It is a pity that this forceful argument is always misquoted by this poor abbreviation: *Credo, quia absurdum*, "I believe because it is absurd." If one wishes to shorten Tertullian's saying, one might render it as: "I believe [in Christ's saving deeds], even though, nay, because Philistines of faith think them absurd."

The learned men of the Biblical Institute asked the forthcom-ing Council to declare that Christians are truly included in the blessing Jacob bestowed on Joseph's sons:

The God in whose ways my fathers Abraham and Isaac
    walked,
  the God who has shepherded me from birth to this day,
The Angel who redeemed us from all evil,
    bless these lads.
Through them may my name be remembered,
    and the names of my fathers Abraham and Isaac.
May theÿ grow in number upon the earth.

(Gn 48:15-16)

At the same time these scholars insisted that such inclusion
did not rob Israel of its dignity. The Chosen People is not
"rejected," not "accursed;" nor is it "collectively guilty" of
Christ's death on the cross. The petitioners pleaded with the
Fathers of the Council that they admonish the faithful to shun
all offensive speech and that they warn all preachers not to
succumb to false exegesis that upholds—sad to say—the thesis
that God did cast off the people of His predilection.

Some writers on Jewish-Christian relations seem eager to
adjust New Testament pronouncements or dogmatic statements by the Church to whatever they assume the spirit of
reconciliation demands. Vital though the concern of the theologians who make up the Biblical Institute was, their frame of
reference was quite different. They, too, wanted change—not
one that seeks accommodation to the real or imagined wishes
of Jews, but one that strives for greater conformity to the
substance of faith. In a true dialogue, one partner does not suit
his or her beliefs to the views of the other, real or alleged.
Rather do they share, one with the other, the fullness of his or
her faith-given vision.

Obedience to biblical teaching, regard for the integrity of the
faith, and not Jewish pressure—as enemies of the Council at
times suggested—moved the scholars of the Biblical Institute
to present their hopes for the renewal of the Church. They went
so far as to point to specific narratives that by faulty exegesis
have become forces for engendering and sustaining the "myth"
of Israel's lasting fall from grace. These are, among others,
Matthew 27:25 and 1 Thessalonians 2:14-16.[52] I do not think

that the men of the *Biblicum*—the Institute's popular name—
expected the Fathers of the Council to offer a detailed interpretation of these passages. After all, such an exegesis would not
have been within the compass of this or any other Council. But
is it not incumbent on me to undertake what neither the petitioners as well as the bishops by their respective responsibilities were kept from doing?

Israel's Self-Malediction?　I do not know how Cardinal Bea
and his confreres would have solved the problems the passages
quoted pose, but I hope that my interpretation of at least one of
them will be close to what they would have offered, had they
spoken. At present, I can deal only with the outcry of the crowd
gathered before the Governor's residence, after he had interro-
gated Jesus as to whether He was a dangerous rebel or a
religious enthusiast that need not be feared: *His blood be on us
and on our children* (Mt 27:25). These words are part of a scene
so frightening that many think it unhistorical—a peg on which
the Evangelist wanted to hang his reflections on Israel's guilt
and punishment. I wonder whether to declare the event but a
figment of the Evangelist's imagination, a creature of his ill
will toward Jews, is not too easy a solution of a torturing riddle.

The setting is the Praetorium, the Roman Governor's palace.
Jesus stands before the Governor, accused of sedition, of seeking to overthrow the Emperor's rule over Israel, and making
himself its King. Pilate asks: "Are you the King of the Jews?"
Jesus gives a noncommittal answer: "You have said it" (27:11).
Were He to say "Yes," He would nourish the misunderstanding
of His kingship; were He to say "No," He would deny His
mission.

The moment Pilate realizes that his direct examination will
not bring to light Jesus' political stance, he tries another tack.
He offers to release either Barabbas, a notorious leader of
freedom fighters, or Jesus whom many call the "Messiah"
(27:17,22). The crowd opts for the "bandit," the guerilla chief;
as to Jesus' fate, their answer is a determined "Let Him be
crucified" (27:22). In mock obedience to the biblical ordinance,
Pilate washes his hands:

If a corpse of a slain man is found lying in the open, in the land which the Lord your God is giving you to possess, the identity of the slayer not being known..., the elders of the town nearest the corpse shall wash their hands in the ravine over the heifer whose neck has been broken. Solemnly they shall declare: "Our hands did not shed this blood, nor did our eyes see it done. Absolve, O Lord, your people Israel whom you redeemed, and let not the guilt of the innocent rest on your people Israel."

(Dt 21:1, 6-8)

By washing his hands, Pilate dodges his responsibility as man and governor: "I am innocent of this man's blood; see to it yourselves" (27:24).

To this, the crowd [the Evangelist writes: "the whole people"] exclaims: "His blood be on us and on our children!" (27:25). What are we to think of this unsettling outcry? Several commentators pass over it in silence. A few, it seems, approach the event with heart neither shaken nor sorrowing. Paul Gaechter, for instance, argues like this: "Only a Jewish apostate of the worst kind, only a hater of Israel," he reasons, "could have invented the outcry. But neither the Evangelist nor his fellow disciples were men of that ilk." Still, according to Gaechter, the Jewish stamp of the narrative, especially of the cry, proves its historicity beyond the shadow of a doubt.[53] Gaechter goes on:

The monstrous cry is tantamount to a self-malediction. It is the final point in a long development of the people's view. In fact, there was only this alternative: either they acknowledged Jesus as the Messiah sent by God or they demanded his destruction, at any price. The people's stance means that it has broken the covenant for the last time, has renounced the blessings of the messianic age, in short, has pronounced its own rejection. This is what makes the scene so shattering. I admit that, theologically, the extent to which God took note of Israel's self-cursing, and the extent to which He did not is a question still unanswered.[54]

Gaechter did not seem to notice that he embroiled himself in some difficulties. Both the story and the editorial gloss "the whole people" cannot be factual. Nor can it be maintained that the crowd acted in the name of "the whole people"; no one had appointed it Israel's representative.

To fathom the meaning of the incomprehensible outcry, to understand what prompted the crowd to shout it, we must, I think, inquire after the composition of the group. Among them, there must surely have been pilgrims from far away who were in Jerusalem for the celebration of Passover, most likely unaware of Jesus' ministry and the problems it caused. Righteous Jews of Jerusalem, too, may have come to the Praetorium, heartbroken because they sensed that the arrest of Jesus was not an incident of every day but an event of infinite dimension. News of Jesus' trial, spreading like wildfire, easily brought people out of their houses. Although they may have been there in considerable number, they had little influence, because they were not committed to one side or the other. The most involved and most vocal body was made up, I have no doubt, of freedom fighters. They had looked up to Jesus as the one who, when the time was ripe, would lead them in battle to gain Israel's freedom from the pagan occupier.

The Zealots and Jesus. It is said that when Jesus fed five thousand pilgrims en route to Jerusalem, many wanted to proclaim Him king throughout the land (see Jn 6:15). They saw in Him a man of heavenly power who could, as easily as He fed His kinsmen, drive the hated oppressor out of the land. There were other instances of Jesus' power that impressed them, and nourished their dream of a realm in which pagans would not be able to hinder them in serving God.

Their and Jesus' political theories—if I may use this expression—were diametrically opposed. The freedom fighters held firmly that God's kingdom—rather, His reign—could not come as long as the Roman idolaters and their idols polluted the land. Thus, the freedom fighters saw it as imperative that the Romans be expelled by force, if necessary in blood-drenched combat.[55] Jesus' vision may be summed up as follows: Even if the political circumstances are sad, even if pagan idolaters rule the land, the reign of God can be inaugurated here and now.

Whenever He is loved with everything a man or woman is and has, and whenever other human beings are loved as God loves them, His rule is confirmed, His kingdom is here.

How is it possible for Zealots not to have seen that there was an irreconcilable difference between the two positions, theirs and that of Jesus? Their desperation so blinded and their wishful thinking so dominated them that they sought to have Jesus fit in with their dream world. This is not meant in a derogatory way. The incitement was strong. Just remember, Jesus rode into Jerusalem, mounted on an ass; He allowed the multitude to wave palms in His honor and spread garments in His path to pay Him tribute. He let them shout "Hosannah! Praise God! Blessed be the King of Israel!" (Jn 12:13). The freedom fighters took the whole event as a sign that Jesus, the Son of David, was now ready to assume command of their forces.

Yet, when these Zealots saw Jesus stand before the Emperor's representative, unable or unwilling to fight, a picture of misery, the embodiment of weakness, they were thrown into despair. They felt betrayed. Here was the one who could have led them and all Israel to victory; yet, He refused to act. He could have brought freedom from the idolaters who ruled the Land, and new life in the sight of the Lord, true Ruler of Israel and of the universe; yet He did not take the needed step. Like Samson He could have laid the Palace in ruins; He could even have made the Empire collapse; yet, suddenly He had lost His nerve.

The freedom fighters were offended; Jesus had become a scandal to them. They were furious, nay, fury took possession of them. No wonder they demanded that He be crucified. In a way, they relished the irony: crucifixion, Rome's punishment for rebels and seditionists, was to become the penalty of Him who refused to lead the revolt.

In shouting "His blood be on us and on our children!" they cursed neither themselves nor their offspring. On the contrary, they protested their innocence. Their line of thinking may have been like this: Jesus bolted us and our cause, no, the cause of God. He thus deserves to be punished as a deserter. It was within His power to become Israel's King-Messiah, but at the decisive hour He failed miserably. So the partisans may have thought. In calling for His death, in delivering Him to the disgrace and pain of the cross, they were sure of being allies of truth. Though they had sought vengeance, they thought themselves to be the voice of justice.

I have little doubt that my departure from the conventional interpretation will startle most readers. As far as I can see, my thesis cannot be found in the major commentaries on Matthew, but I am equally sure that they do not offer an interpretation that sensibly explains the action of the crowd. As further argument for my thesis, let me change the scene and take you to Golgotha. There you see Jesus crucified between two "robbers," or "bandits," as most translations read. The comment attached most likely says that "to mock Him, Jesus was nailed to the cross between two criminals." The Greek text calls them *lestai*, literally, "robbers," or "bandits;" here, however, the word means "insurrectionists," fighters for the sovereignty of their land and God's supreme reign, not shared with any emperor or king.

The two "robbers" differed totally in their understanding of Jesus (see Lk 23:39-43). One was not only convinced that the Romans had to be driven out, violently at that, but also that Jesus was the man—perhaps the only one—to lead an armed campaign. He could have marched at their head, but He spurned the offer. He had chosen—perversely, one of the partisans crucified with Him thought—to accept suffering and death with perfect resignation. There could be only one reason for this nonviolence, for this "aid to the enemy": ill will. So the "bad thief" (to use for a moment the popular nomenclature) thought, and raged against Him.

The "good thief" looked at the same Jesus, but in a completely different light. Penetrating the surface, he saw in Jesus' self-imposed weakness the movement of divine grandeur. Jesus could have had a host of angels to help Him but paradoxically He sought to defeat violence, not with violence, but with non-violence. In all His wretchedness, He proved Himself truly a king. Hence, the "good thief" could beg: "Remember me when you enter upon your reign" (Lk 23:42). Both scenes, the one at the Praetorium and the other at Golgotha, make us witnesses to Jesus as He accepted the role of the Suffering Servant of YHVH.

In the light of all this, what does the editorial gloss, "all the people," imply? Would it suffice to point out that the use of "whole," "every," and "all" is one of the peculiarities of Matthew's literary style? In chapter four, verse twenty-three, for instance, he writes that "[Jesus] went about all Galilee"; "He taught in their, [that is, all the] synagogues," healed every disease and every infirmity. I do not think it would answer adequately the question I just asked. Nor can I side with Schiwy who maintains, with the help of verses 24 and 25, that Matthew wished "to make it impossible for Jews to lay the blame for Jesus' death on Pontius Pilate."[56] The opinion of another well-known exegete, Josef Schmid, is even less convincing:

> The Jews (the Evangelist deliberately chose the expression "all the people" i.e. "the whole nation," represented here by the members of the High Council and the crowds present) declare solemnly to take upon themselves and their descendants the responsibility for the blood, the death of Jesus. Thus the Jewish people cursed itself.[57]

I wish I knew by what authority an exegete of Schmid's caliber asserts that the crowd at the front of the Governor's residence acted in the name of all Israel.

A somewhat different perspective is that of Walter Grundmann, a Protestant exegete. He writes:

> Matthew concluded the trial before Pilate...with the release of Barabbas and the abandonment of Jesus.... This decision was of special significance for the Jewish-Christian community from 30 to 70 A.D. In that decision, the contest with the ideology of the Zealots reached its climax, sealing the fate of a major part of the Jewish people. In having rebuffed Jesus and His community, the Zealots came to grief in [fighting] the catastrophic Jewish war.[58]

Here Grundmann seems to be on the right track, but a few lines earlier he writes: In having "all the people" cry for Jesus' blood, "Matthew wishes, I suppose, to say that the people, as the People of the Covenant, bears the blame for Jesus' death."[59]

An Unbiased Interpretation.   For a Catholic to continue the formerly dominant interpretation and to insinuate that the Evangelist preaches the theological monstrosity of collective guilt is to be at variance with Vatican II. It is for this reason that I am so adamant in my disagreement with the many exegetes who hear "His blood be on us and on our children" as the unrestrained outcry of the whole people, cursing itself for all times; worse, bringing down on itself God's ban, His malediction forever. However frequent it may be, this kind of exegesis is like the behavior of a bull in a china shop. But to ask again, how does one interpret this frightful sentence? As I see the problem, Matthew somehow telescopes this scene of the Passion narrative with the hardship of his own time. "The whole people," then reflects the tensions between the Jewish-Christian community and its maternal body, the Jewish people. The entire scene mirrors their mutual animosities.

It is a pity that their differences of faith, weighty though they were, turned into enmities. My heart deplores the fact that their beliefs not only kept them apart, but also set them against each other. My heart weeps that mother and daughter were not only estranged but turned hostile to one another. Perhaps their youth—I mean that of Pharisaic Judaism and that of the infant Church—compelled them to be at strife, indeed, to war against each other. I do not think it helpful to inquire which of the two is more to blame.

To change my metaphor of the Jewish-Christian relationship: I do not wish to explore who began the fratricidal strife, who sinned more against truth, justice, and love. Nor do I want to dwell on which of the two was more tenacious, which inflicted the greater pain on the other. The answer to that question is obvious: the Christian world. I do not mean that we should ignore the past; rather, that we advance toward the future, that we are moved, stirred by the future, by its opportunities. If I am right in thinking that their youth caused the "storm and stress" of their coexistence, may I then say that the maturity we acquired in so painful a way has brought us to the threshold of a new vision of one another.

Whether we read the narrative as an actual event or as a theological perspective, we must be certain that the cry does not imply the global accusation of collective guilt, but rather the delicate relationship that we may call communal responsibility or, better, covenantal solidarity. The Rabbis teach that the Covenant rests on the axiom: *Yisrael 'arevin zeh lezeh* (*bSheb.* 39a), all "Israel are sureties one for another" or all "Israelites are responsible for one another." The grandeur and beauty of this principle is beyond telling. Let me then quote Rabbi Simeon b. Yohai in explanation of it: A group of Jews were together in a boat when one of them began to drill a hole under his seat. His companions took him to task: "Why are you doing this?" He replied, "What does it matter to you? I am only drilling under my own seat." They countered, "You will flood the boat for all of us." According to Ephraim E. Urbach, the concept of mutual responsibility is inherent in Israel's election but this reciprocal surety also makes possible atonement and the preservation of a "special relationship between Israel and his God."[60]

Let me sum up: It is my conviction that the common understanding of the scene before the Governor's palace has to be turned upside down. Daring though it seems, what sounds like a curse is another praise of God's love for Israel. I gladly confess that I am committed to happy endings, for I believe with the writers of Holy Scripture and with Dante that the history of all humanity is a *Divina Comedia*, the triumph of Love.

IN THE PRECEDING PAGES I have tried to elaborate on Cardinal Bea's achievements as Rector of the Biblical Institute and on some of the teachings of Pius XII's Encyclical on Biblical Studies. In my opinion, they were building stones of the new structure of Christian-Jewish relations. Such retrospect is necessary for a proper understanding of the genesis of the Conciliar Statement on the Church and the Jewish People, a fair picture of Pope Pius XII's historic significance, and Cardinal Bea's role as a man for our times. His finely tuned mind and resonant heart fitted him well for his work at the Council.

Firmly anchored in his faith in Christ, Cardinal Bea was lovingly open to the faith of others. Intent upon elucidating the relationship of Catholics to other Christians, to the sons and daughters of Abraham and Sarah, and to the members of the world's various religions, he loyally served his Church and, at the same time, humanity.

When the Cardinal presided over the plenary sessions of the Secretariat, he often closed his eyes while the members discussed a text before them. I confess that the first time I witnessed his seeming inattention, I thought to myself: "If anyone has a right to rest, surely it is this hard-working man." But as soon as the last participant had spoken, the Cardinal, with eyes opened, recapitulated the substance of the discussion in flawless Latin, even though the participants had used several languages. His apparent slumber had hidden but not suppressed his alertness. The encounter of Christians and Jews needs men and women as awake to truth and love as the Cardinal was.

NOTES

[1] Variations of this anecdote have been told. To my mind, they do not gainsay but rather confirm the authenticity of the charming vignette.

[2] Maria Buchmüller, ed., *Augustin Kardinal Bea, Wegbereiter der Einheit* (Augsburg: Winifred Werk, 1971), p. 20. Most of the particulars that follow are taken from this book even when not expressly mentioned.

[3] *Ibid.*, p. 24.

[4] *Ibid.*, p. 54.

[5] *Ibid.*, p. 52.

[6] *Ibid.*, p. 70.

[7] *Ibid.*, p. 78. The official English translation of *Divino Afflante Spiritu* was published by the National Catholic Welfare Conference, Washington, D.C.

[8] The Catholic Church has in its Bible books that are not part of the Hebrew or Palestinian Canon. They were part of the Septuagint, the Greek version of the Bible compiled by Jews of Alexandria around 250 B.C. Among these are I and II Maccabees, Judith, parts of Daniel and Ezra, also stories like that of Susannah.

[9] E.F. Schumacher, *Small is Beautiful: Economics As If People Mattered* (New York: Harper and Row, 1973).

[10] Karl Rahner and Herbert Vorgrimler, *Theological Dictionary*, ed. C. Ernst, O.P., transl. R. Strachan (New York: Herder, 1965), p. 39.

[11] For a fuller explanation of the rendering of the Divine Name that I have used, see the study by Martin Buber and Franz Rosenzweig, *Die Schrift und ihre Verdeutschung* (Berlin: Schocken, 1936), pp. 185-210. The English text of the study is called "The Burning Bush," and appeared in *On the Bible: Eighteen Studies by Buber*, ed. Nahum Glatzer (New York: Schocken, 1968), pp. 44-62. For an overview of several exegetical interpretations, see Myles M. Bourke, "Yahweh, the Divine Name," *The Bridge*, ed. J.M. Oesterreicher (New York: Pantheon, 1958), 3, 271-287.

[12] For the role of Hebrew in the life of Israel and humankind, see Louis Ginzberg, *The Legends of the Jews*, transl. Henrietta Szold (Philadelphia: Jewish Publication Society, 1940), 1,181; 5,204ff., n. 91.

[13] J. Herder, *The Spirit of Hebrew Poetry* was published in English in Vermont, 1833. Since the book is out of print and found in few libraries, the entry in the *Encyclopedia Judaica* (Jerusalem: Keter, 1971), 16, 1395, may serve as a substitute. For a more comprehensive explanation of Hebrew words, see one of the biblical dictionaries, such

as: *Encyclopedia of Biblical Theology*, ed. Johannes B. Bauer, transl.
J. Blenkinsopp, D.J. Bourke, N.D. Smith, W.P. van Stigt (New York:
Crossroad, 1981); *Dictionary of Biblical Theology*, ed. Xavier Léon-
Dufour, transl. P.J. Cahill, S.J., and E.M. Stewart (New York: Sea-
bury, 1973); John M. McKenzie, S.J. *Dictionary of the Bible* (Milwau-
kee: Bruce, 1965); see also *Bible Key Words*, based on Gerhard Kittel's
Theologisches Wörterbuch zum Neuen Testament, transl. and ed.
D.M. Barton, P.R. Ackroyd, and A.E. Harvey (New York: Harper,
1960).

   [14]   In his Introduction to Thomas Aquinas' *De Veritate*, Robert W.
Mulligan writes: "It is worthy of note that the famous definition of
truth, *adaequatio rei et intellectus*, used at the beginning of these
Questions is not from any known text of Isaac Israeli's *Book of Definitions*, in spite of the fact that many editions of St. Thomas imply that
its source is there." Mulligan refers to J.T. Muckle's edition of *De
diffinicionibus*, where the often cited definition of truth does not
appear. See Mulligan, transl. and ed., *Truth* (Chicago: Regnery, 1952),
p. xxiii.

   [15]   See the Servant Songs, Is 42:1-4; 49:1-6; 50:4-11; 52:13-53:13. The
common Jewish interpretation of these songs is a collective one, seeing in them a portrayal of Israel, as God's Chosen People. The traditional Christian reading of them is that of prophetic oracles, fore-
telling Jesus' Messianic ministry in life and death. The most likely
exposition is one that combines the collective and the individual
views. As the ancestor stands for his descendants, so the people fore-
shadow in their existence the One-to-come who, in this case, is Jesus,
the Sum, the Perfection, of all that Israel is meant to be. For the link
between forebear and descendants, see H. Wheeler Robinson, *Corporate Personality in Ancient Israel*, Facet Books (Philadelphia: Fortress, 1964).

   [16]   *Tanakh* is an acronym formed from the initial letters of the three
divisions of the Hebrew Bible, *Torah*, ("Guidance," "Law"), *Neviim*
("Prophets"), and *Ketuvim* ("Writings," "Hagiographa").

   [17]   On God's saving acts on behalf of His people, see Gerhard von
Rad, *Old Testament Theology* (New York: Harper, 1962), 1,372.

   [18]   The designation of Israel's prophets as "the Conscience of
Israel" is drawn from the book by Fr. Bruce Vawter, C.M., bearing
that very title (New York: Sheed and Ward, 1961).

   [19]   Max Zerwick, S.J., in his article, "Am Päpstlichen Bibel-institut
In Rom," quoted in Buchmüller, *ibid.*, p. 75.

   [20]   See *Divino Afflante Spiritu*, p. 18.

   [21]   See Kathryn Sullivan, R.S.C.J., "Pro Perfidis Judaeis," in *The*

Bridge, 2, 212-223; see also my study "Pro perfidis Judaeis," *Theological Studies*, 8, 80-96.

[22] The four progressive stages of change of the Good Friday prayer for the Jewish people are discussed on pp. 108-110 of this book.

[23] See *Divino Afflante Spiritu*, p. 18.

[24] *Ibid.*, p. 14.

[25] See Joseph Klausner, *Jesus of Nazareth*, trans. H. Denby (New York: Macmillan), p. 414. Klausner concludes his book with the statement that for the Jewish people, Jesus is neither the Son of God, nor one of the prophets, nor a Pharasaic rabbi, but "a great teacher of morality and an artist in parable."

[26] Cornelius a Lapide, *The Great Commentary*, transl. G. Gould Ross: St. Luke's Gospel (London: John Hodges, 1887), p. 258.

[27] *Ibid.*, p. 261.

[28] I think it of some moment that Martin Buber translated Lv 19:18 as: *Liebe deinen Genossen dir gleich*, or *Liebe deinen Genossen, er ist wie du*, "Love your fellow; he (she) is like you" (*Das Buch ER Rief, Die Schrift*, 3 [Berlin: Lambert Schneider, n.d.]). Buber's and Rosenzweig's translation began to appear in 1925. In 1924, the Catholic exegete Paul Riessler rendered the verse as: *Liebe deinen Nächsten wie einen deinesgleichen*, "Love your neighbor as one like you"; the NEB has "Love your neighbor as [one] like yourself." A recent Latin American version reads: . . . *que es como tu mismo*.

[29] Schiwy, *Weg ins Neue Testament* (Würzburg: Echter, 1965), p. 335.

[30] Herman L. Strack and Paul Billerbeck, *Kommentar zum Neuen Testament* (Munich: Beck, 1922), 1,353.

[31] To the best of my knowledge, the first thinker to unmask "love of humanity" as sham is Max Scheler. I cannot embrace humanity, nor can I exchange gifts with it. Humanity dwells in Plato's realm of ideas, not on earth like my neighbor, whom I can touch and by whom I can be touched; whom I irritate at times, and who at other times irritates me; against whom I, alas, sin, and who sins against me. Scheler sees in "humanitarianism" a rebellion against the twofold commandment of love of God and of neighbor. See Scheler, "Christian Love and the Twentieth Century," *On the Eternal in Man*, transl. Bernard Noble (New York: Harper, 1960), p. 367.

[32] See Bultmann, *The History of the Synoptic Tradition*, transl. John Marsh (New York: Harper & Row, 1963), p. 178.

[33] To acknowledge a debt to a mentor of my youth, it is in Søren Kierkegaard's *For Self-examination* that I first found the counsel to read the Word of God as we ought. To read it with profit, we must say

again and again: "It is I who am addressed," "It is I for whom the message is meant." Kierkegaard takes the parable of the Good Samaritan as an illustration. He warns the reader not to seek a subterfuge or try to be witty by saying, "O! the parable speaks of a priest, and I am not a priest. But how wonderful that, for once, the Gospel gives it to the priests, for the priests are the worst of all." No, rather you must say, he tells his reader: "This is I. How could I have been so heartless; I, who call myself a Christian, and therefore am in a certain sense a priest." Kierkegaard continues in this vein until he comes to the Samaritan. Here he admonishes his reader to change his speech: "This is not I: no, alas, this is not the way I am." Yet, when Christ summons, "Go and do likewise," then say, "Yes, this concerns me. I will start right now." (In formulating this précis, which lacks some of the power of the hardhitting original, I used the German edition, *Zur Selbstprüfung der Gegenwart Empfohlen* (Jena: Diederichs, 1922; pp. 33-35). English editions of Kierkegaard's works, translated by Walter Lowrie, have been published by Oxford and Princeton University Presses.

   34   Among the recent literature on *birkat ha-minim*, the imprecatory petition that the Lord put an end to the *minim* and their hostility to Israel, are two essays discussing their identity. Jacob J. Petuchowski, "Der Ketzersegen" in Brocke-Petuchowski, *Das Vaterunser* (Freiburg: Herder, 1974), pp. 90-101, sees in the *minim* Jewish Christians. Asher Finkel, "Yavneh's Liturgy and Early Christianity" in the *Journal of Ecumenical Studies* (Spring 1981), 18, 231-250, offers weighty arguments in favor of the view that the *minim* in *birkat ha-minim* are gnostics who had naught but contempt for the Law.

   35   *Divino Afflante Spiritu*, pp. 19, 5, 16.

   36   Otto Michel, "Polemik und Scheidung" in *Judaica* (Zürich: Zwingli, Dec. 1, 1959), 15, 193ff.

   37   For a comprehensive treatment of the various appellations given to dissidents by the Rabbis, see the *Encyclopedia Judaica*, 8, 358-362.

   38   The controversies between the Houses of Hillel and Shammai are treated extensively in the entry "Bet Hillel and Bet Shammai," *ibid.*, 4, 737-741.

   39   See *ibid.*, p. 738, where the pertinent sources in the Mishnah are listed.

   40   Montefiore, *Rabbinic Literature and Gospel Teachings* (London: Macmillan, 1930), pp. 3-15.

   41   Klausner, *ibid.*, p. 19.

   42   *Ibid.*, pp. 18-19.

   43   In her commentary, J. Massyngberde Ford speaks of the Jews of

Smyrna as given to syncretistic worship. Together with other Jewish communities, they seem to have prayed to Zeus, whose altar is at times called "Satan's seat." See Ford, *Revelation*, in *The Anchor Bible* (Garden City: Doubleday, 1975), 38, 393.

⁴⁴ *Ibid.*, p. xxiv or p. 392.

⁴⁵ Bultmann, *Das Evangelium des Johannes* (Göttingen: Vandenhoeck & Ruprecht, 1964), p. 238.

⁴⁶ On excommunication from the Synagogue, see Raymond E. Brown, *The Gospel According to John* in *The Anchor Bible*, 29, 374, no. 22.

⁴⁷ Strathmann, *Das Evangelium nach Johannes* in *Das Neue Testament Deutsch* (Göttingen, 1963), 4, 147.

⁴⁸ *Ibid.*

⁴⁹ *Ibid.*, p. 146.

⁵⁰ See Michel, *ibid.*, p. 212.

⁵¹ For a more extensive analysis of the petition of the *Biblicum*, see "Waking the Dawn," this book, pp. 114-116.

⁵² Like all other suggestions, those by Bishops or Pontifical Universities, the *Votum* of the Biblical Institute was sent to the Council's Preparatory Commission. They were all collected in volumes to be sent to Bishops, Abbots, in short, all prospective members of the Council. The Institute's petition was sent on April 24, 1960.

⁵³ Gaechter, *Das Matthäus Evangelium* (Innsbruck: Tyrolia, 1963), p. 914.

⁵⁴ *Ibid.*

⁵⁵ The Zealots are discussed in the popular work by J. Pikl, *The Messias*, transl. A. Green O.S.B. (St. Louis: B. Herder, 1946), and in M. Hengel's *Die Zeloten, Untersuchungen zur judischen Freiheitsbewegung in der Zeit von Herodes I. bis 70 n. Christus* (Leiden: DLC, 1976).

⁵⁶ Schiwy, *ibid.*, p. 174-176.

⁵⁷ Schmid, *Das Evangelium nach Matthäus* in *Regensburger Neues Testament* (Regensburg: Friedrich Pustet, 1959), 1,371.

⁵⁸ Grundmann, *Das Evangelium nach Matthäus* (Berlin: Evangelische, 1968), p. 555.

⁵⁹ *Ibid.*

⁶⁰ Urbach, *The Sages: Their Concepts and Beliefs*, transl. Israel Abrahams (Jerusalem: Magnes, 1975), pp. 539-540.

WAKING THE DAWN

"Awake, harp and lyre! I will wake the dawn." These words are part of Psalm 57, a psalm that begins as a lament and ends as a song of thanksgiving. Its singer prays for the morning light to conquer night's darkness and anxiety. "Waking the Dawn," then, seems a fitting title for the Conciliar struggle to bring about the end of alienation and hostility between Christians and Jews through the melody that sings of their kinship.

The Genesis of Nostra Aetate

THE COUNCIL'S MESSAGE on the Church's bond to the Jewish people, the core of the Declaration, On the Relationship of the Church to Non-Christian Religions, holds a special place among all the documents of Vatican II. It, and no other, owes its existence to an express mandate of John XXIII. The total Declaration is unique in that, for the first time in history, a Council has acknowledged the groping of individuals, tribes, and peoples for the Absolute. For the first time, a Council has bowed in awe before the truth and holiness in other religions, acknowledging even halting steps toward the living God.

In Section 4 of the Declaration, the Church has, again for the first time, publicly proclaimed the Pauline vision of the mystery of Israel. Thus in the Declaration, the Church has professed her faith in the omnipresence of grace, active in the many religions of humankind. Beyond that, the Church's message gives glory to God for His everlasting fidelity to the Jews, His Chosen People. In presenting the genesis of this Declaration, I wish to strengthen the proper understanding of its vital message.

The Origins

ON SEPTEMBER 18, 1960, Pope John commissioned Cardinal Bea as President of the Secretariat for Promoting Christian Unity to prepare a draft declaration on the inner relations between the Church and the people of Israel. At the first session of the Secretariat, the Cardinal reported that various inquiries had reached the Pope from the Jewish community. He had been asked if there would be a possibility of Jews being kept informed about the Council and if memoranda could be submitted. Some had even asked for the establishment of a separate commission.

Pope John had decided, however, to entrust these concerns to the Secretariat for Unity. The Cardinal said that there had been various reasons for this, but did not give them. One may well suppose that the risk of setting up an excessive number of commissions counted, in the Pope's mind, against the establishment of a separate Commission *De rebus iudaicis*, "On Matters Jewish," or *De Ecclesiae affinitate cum populo Iudaico*, "On the Kinship of the Church with the Jewish People." One may safely assume that the Pope was moved to entrust the treatment of Jewish-Christian relations to the Secretariat for Unity by virtue of the role the Jewish people play in the history of salvation and, no less, by the personality of the Cardinal, a man of wide experience in whom he had great confidence.

The Visit of Jules Isaac. Cardinal Bea's reference to Jewish inquiries doubtless included that of the French historian Jules Isaac, the most important advocate of Jewish concerns prior to the Council. Early in the summer of 1960, he went to Rome with the support of the French branch of B'nai B'rith[1] and equipped with a letter of introduction from Archbishop de Provenchères, of Aix-en-Provence, his home town, to make known his requests to Pope John. After initial difficulties, he succeeded in obtaining an audience on June 13 of that year.

The Pope began the conversation with his characteristic ease of manner by confirming his great reverence for the Old Testament, especially for the Prophets, the Psalms, and the Book of Wisdom. Isaac, however, a man who feared he did not have much longer to live, came straight to the point. He referred to the great hope that the measures taken by the Pope concerning the Jews had awakened in the hearts of his people. "If we expect still more," he added, "what is responsible for that, if not the great goodness of the Pope?"

During the audience, he gave the Pope a three-part dossier: [1] A brief for the correction of false and, indeed , unjust statements about the people of Israel in Christian instruction. [2] An example of such statements: the theological myth that the scattering of Israel was a punishment inflicted by God on the people for the crucifixion of Jesus. [3] An extract from the so-called "Catechism of Trent" which, in its treatment of the Passion, emphasized the guilt of all sinners as the fundamental cause of Christ's death upon the cross, and thus, in Isaac's view, proved that the accusation of deicide raised against the Jews did not belong to the true tradition of the Church.

The Tridentine Catechism was published in 1566, not by the Council of Trent but as one of its fruits, under Pius V, its proper name being *Catechismus Romanus*, its special significance resting on its pastoral character. Unlike other catechisms, it was designed to assist preachers and catechists and to lay down guidelines for authentic instruction in Catholic faith and life. It was drawn up at the express resolution of the Council and advocated by many Popes; it comes close to being a pronouncement of *magisterium*, the Church's teaching office, despite the little use which has been made of it. From Chapter V, which deals with the fourth article of the Creed, Isaac cited pertinent paragraphs:

> The first part of the [fourth] article [of faith] sets forth the truth of faith that Christ the Lord was crucified, at the time when Pontius Pilate was administering the Province of Judea in the name of the Emperor Tiberius. It was then

that Christ was arrested, ridiculed, loaded with every kind of insult and torment, and finally lifted up on the Cross.

The pastor of souls should not omit to speak frequently of the history of the Passion, so carefully recorded by the Evangelists, in order that the faithful may be well informed, at least, about the major points of this mystery which seem necessary for the securing of our faith. For on this article, as their foundation, rest the religion and belief of the Christian; and if this has been laid, then the rest of the edifice will hold firmly together. If there is anything which creates difficulties for the human mind and heart, then certainly it is the Cross, the most difficult of all mysteries. We are scarcely willing to comprehend that our salvation should come from the Cross, and from One who was nailed to the Cross for us. But it is precisely here, as the Apostle says, that we may wonder at the infinitely wise Providence of God.

Anyone seeking . . . the principal reason [for the sufferings of Christ] will come upon sin, the original sin passed down from our first parents, and then all the sins possible which humans have committed from the very beginning right up to the present and which they will commit up to the end of the world. That, indeed, was the intention of the Son of God, our Savior, in His suffering and death: to take upon Himself the sins of all ages, to wipe them out and to offer the Father superabundant satisfaction for them. The sublime magnitude of this expiatory suffering is made all the greater by the fact not only that Christ suffered for sinners, but also that these same sinners were themselves the authors and instruments of all His sufferings. The Apostle reminded us of this when writing to the Hebrews: "Consider Him who endured from sinners such hostility against Himself, so that you may not grow weary or faint-hearted" (12:3). This is preeminently the guilt of those who repeatedly fall back into sin. It was our sin which drove Christ the Lord to His death on the Cross: those, therefore, who wallow in sins and vices are in fact crucifying the Son of God anew, in so far as it depends on them, and holding Him up to contempt (Heb 6:6). And this is a crime which would seem graver in our case than it was in that of the Jews; for the Jews, as the same Apostle says, "would never

have crucified the Lord of glory if they had known Him"
(1 Cor 2:8). We ourselves maintain that we do know Him,
and yet we lay, as it were, violent hands on Him by disown-
ing Him in our actions.

Nonetheless, according to the words of holy Scripture, . . .
Christ delivered Himself up for our sake. In Isaiah, God
says: "I struck Him for the transgression of the people"
(53:8). And shortly before this, the prophet says, on seeing
in spirit the Lord full of wounds and stripes: "All we like
sheep have gone astray; we have turned every one to his
own way; and the Lord has laid on Him the iniquity of us
all" (53:6). Of the Son Himself it is said: "When He has
given Himself up for sin, He shall see everlasting offspring" (53:10). The Apostle has uttered this truth even
more emphatically, though for another purpose, which is
to show how much we are permitted to expect of God's
immeasurable goodness and mercy: "He did not," says
Paul, "spare His own Son but gave Him up for us all—how
should He not also give us all things with Him?"
(Rom 8:32). . . .

Men of every estate and rank "took counsel against the
Lord and against His Christ" (Ps 2:2). Gentiles and Jews
were the instigators, authors and executors of His sufferings. Judas betrayed Him, Peter denied Him, and all
abandoned Him.

The reasons all these great and supernatural benefits
accrued to us from the sufferings of the Lord are these:
First, His suffering was the complete and, in all respects,
perfect satisfaction which Jesus Christ made to God the
Father in a unique manner for our sins. Indeed, the price
which He paid for us was not only equal to our guilt, but
even exceeded it by far. And then, His suffering was an
offering infinitely pleasing to God. The Son Himself
brought it to the altar of the Cross, and thus it could not fail
to reconcile the Father's anger and disfavor completely.
This is the opinion of the Apostle, when he says: "Christ
loved us and gave Himself up for us, a fragrant offering
and sacrifice to God" (Eph 5:2). Finally, His suffering was
our ransom. Of this the Prince of Apostles says: "You know
that you were ransomed from the futile ways inherited
from your fathers, not with perishable things such as
silver or gold, but with the precious blood of Christ, like
that of a lamb without blemish or spot" (1 Pt 1:18). . . .

There is still one other thing in addition to all the immeasurable graces mentioned, and it is perhaps one of the greatest. In this suffering alone we have the most resplendent example of every virtue: patience, humility, unequalled love, meekness, obedience, and supreme fortitude not only in His endurance of pain for the sake of righteousness, but also in His submission to death. All this shows Christ's suffering in such perfection that we can truly say that the commandments which our Redeemer gave us in words during the whole time of His teaching activity He put into action during the one day of His suffering.

Towards the end of the audience, which lasted almost half an hour, Isaac expressed his deep gratitude, then asked anxiously whether he might take away with him a little hope. John XXIII reassured him: "You have reason for more than a little hope." But he went on to say with a smile that, though he was indeed the head here, a matter such as this needed consideration and study in the appropriate quarters: "What you see here is not an absolute monarchy."[2]

The Initiatives of John XXIII. That Jules Isaac's visit had a lasting effect on John XXIII cannot, in my opinion, be doubted. Yet, it is questionable whether his was the decisive influence in moving the Pope to act, as is sometimes asserted. What he did, however, was to cause the Pope's sentiments, until then not fully expressed, to come to the fore. It was, after all, the measures taken by John XXIII prior to the audience to remove hurtful phrases from liturgical texts that had encouraged Isaac, as he himself acknowledged, to put his requests before the Pope.

In 1959, John XXIII had given a new face to the Good Friday Prayer for the Jews. He had deleted from the text the adjective *perfidus* in the exhortation *Oremus et pro perfidis Iudaeis*, "let us pray for the unbelieving Jews [that is, unbelieving in Christ]" and also the expression *perfidia Iudaica*, "Jewish disbelief." Ignorant of the Latin of Christian antiquity, translators misunderstood both expressions and rendered them in various modern languages by false cognates like "perfidious" and "perfidy." At first the suppression of these wounding phrases on March 21, 1959 seemed to extend only to the churches of Rome itself. But, on July 5 of the same year, the Sacred Congregation of Rites issued an instruction that expressly extended the papal decision, as had been its intention, to the liturgy of the whole Church.

The edict had been passed on to all the Bishops through the Nuncios and Apostolic Delegates. Since then, the intercession has been revised more than once. The first revision read:

Let us pray also for the Jews,
that our God and Lord will be pleased
to look graciously upon them,
so that they, too,
may acknowledge our Lord Jesus Christ
as the Redeemer of all....

Almighty and eternal God,
You gave Your promises to Abraham and his posterity.
Heed the prayers of Your Church
that the people chosen by You of old
may attain the fullness of salvation:
through our Lord Jesus Christ, Your Son,
who lives and reigns with You
in the unity of the Holy Spirit,
God, world without end. Amen.

To appreciate the nature of this first revision, it is necessary to recall the Good Friday intercession prior to 1966. Previously, the faithful prayed for the "unbelieving" Jews, i.e. the Jews who withheld their faith from Christ. The revised prayer simply asked: "Let us pray for the Jews."

The simplicity of this petition is the fruit of a newly acquired *discretio*, an awareness that it is not for us to pass judgment on others. Earlier, Catholics prayed "that our God and Lord will remove the veil from their hearts," a negative expression which has been replaced by the more positive "that our God and Lord will be pleased to look graciously upon them." Formerly, the worshipers spoke of Jesus Christ simply as "our Lord," which could easily lead to proprietary arrogance, as though the Lord were their own property. Now, He is called "Redeemer of all humankind." Before 1966, the prayer spoke of the Jewish people as being blinded and living in darkness, while now it recognizes that the Jews are still God's "special possession" and voices the hope that they may attain "the fullness of redemption." The wishes and even the faith of the worshipers must stand humbly aside. It is for God to decide when and how His plan of salvation will be brought to completion.

The present version calls Jews the people "to whom God spoke first." The whole prayer now reads:

Let us pray also for the Jews,
to whom God spoke first.
May He grant that they advance
in the understanding of His word and love.

Almighty and everlasting God
You made Abraham and his descendants
bearers of Your promise.

In Your loving kindness
hear the prayers of Your Church
so that the people You made Your own in olden days
attain the fullness of salvation.
Through Christ our Lord.

A further measure, taken in the same year, was the deletion of a part of the prayer dedicating humanity to the heart of Jesus.[3] In this prayer, originally from the hand of Leo XIII, various sentences were inserted during the pontificate of Pius XI, including the following: "Look finally with great pity on the children of the people who were once your Chosen People. May the blood that once was called down upon them flow over them now as a fount of salvation and life." The "once" of the first sentence is obviously a mistranslation. The word used in the original Latin text, *tamdiu*, means "for so long." But even this almost tender "for so long Your Chosen People" is not in harmony with the Pauline assurance: "For the gracious gifts of God and His calling [of Israel] are irrevocable" (Rom 11:29).

"The blood that once was called down upon them" is doubt-less an allusion to the words shouted by the crowd gathered before the governor's palace: "His blood be on us, and on our children" (Mt 27:25). The historicity of this cry is doubted by several exegetes. Nonetheless, it is not unthinkable on the lips of a group composed largely of disappointed resistance-fighters. If this assumption is correct, we must go one step further and declare that the zealots, blinded by their guerilla ideology which sought, above all, freedom from the Roman yoke, per-ceived neither the mystery of the person of Jesus nor the depth of His message. His refusal to put Himself at their head might have so enraged them that, at the decisive moment, they aban-doned Him and, sure of themselves, accepted the responsibility for His fate.

If the outcry was indeed an impulsive acceptance of respon-sibility by a small group, it cannot be considered a self-malediction by the whole people, though the author of the prayer of dedication and many others took it as a self-imprecation. Even if one assumed that the Evangelist wanted the outcry of the crowd to be understood as the expression of that anger which led, not only to the rejection of Jesus, but also to the involvement of the Jewish people in a suicidal war with Rome, the words of the crowd can in no wise be interpreted as a self-curse that God made His own. In any case, the exclusion of these two exegetically doubtful sentences from the prayer of dedication prepared the way, not by design, but in deed, for the Council's understanding of the faith, in harmony with the New Testament view of Israel's destiny.

The climax of the more or less spontaneous actions of John XXIII that in a way prepared for the Conciliar Declaration on the Jews was a meeting between the Pope and a group of American Jews in October, 1960. This party of well over a hundred, making a United Jewish Appeal study-trip through Europe and the State of Israel, stopped in Rome in order to thank the Pope for his many efforts to save Jews during the time of Hitler's persecution. As Apostolic Delegate in Turkey, the Pope had succeeded in rescuing thousands from the clutches of those who sought to exterminate them. Deeply moved by the visit, he sought to hold fast to the passing moment and make it bear fruit in the future. He greeted his visitors with the words, *Son io, Guiseppe, il fratello vostro!*, "I am Joseph, your brother!" Alluding to the way Joseph, then Egypt's governor, revealed his identity to his brothers (Gen 45:4), this greeting gave the Pope the opportunity to use his baptismal name Joseph, instead of the official John. It showed clearly that Pope John wanted to overcome the barriers that had kept Christians and Jews apart for centuries.

Pope John knew, of course, that there was an inevitable tension between the beliefs of Christians and those of Jews; at the same time, he was convinced that this division ought not degenerate into hostility. Hence, he added to his greeting this reflection:

> There is a great difference between the one who accepts only the Old Testament[4] and the one who joins to the Old the New as the highest law and teaching. These differences, however, do not extinguish the brotherhood that springs from a common origin [of Christians and Jews]. We are indeed all children of the same heavenly Father and the light and work of love must always shine among us all. *Signatum est super nos lumen vultus tui, Domine!* "The light of Your countenance, O Lord, is signed upon us!" (Ps 4:7)[5]

The Pope ended his address with a reference to the solidarity extending to all people, thus pointing out that the brotherhood for which he had called was the debt everyone owes the other as his or her fellow creature.

The fact that on a few occasions John XXIII spoke of himself as "Joseph, your brother," shows that in his view the relationship of Christians and Jews, though in a way unique, is part of the oneness of all humankind. His first encyclical, for example, was devoted to the themes of truth, unity, and peace. In the course of this document, he turned toward all Christians separated from Rome, expressed his longing for their presence, and recommended urgently that they pray for the unity of the Church and the spreading of Christ's kingdom. Having also asked their leave to call them sons and brothers, he went on to say: "To all our sons and brothers ... who are separated from the See of Peter, we address these words: 'I am Joseph, your brother!' "[6]

It may not be inappropriate to cite a statement by Cardinal Suenens on the occasion of the tenth anniversary of the Jewish weekly, *Belgisch Israelitisch Weekblad*, as a proof of how Pope John's idea of the kinship of Christians and Jews has penetrated Catholic consciousness. In his article of congratulations, he said that fundamentally Christians have received everything through the Jews, both what they hold in common with them, and what obviously separates them from each other. Everything that Christians have received obliges them to deep gratitude toward God for His purposes with the people of Israel. Moreover, all these gifts ought to produce close ties, strong in love and authentic in character. In the eyes of God, Christians and Jews are kin.[7]

When John XXIII was Apostolic Delegate in Bulgaria and Turkey, he had experienced at close hand the many sufferings of Jews and also of Eastern Christians separated from Rome. In Turkey he was kept informed, to an extent not generally realized, of the horrors of the National Socialist extermination camps and the anguish of Jews threatened with deportation "to the East." He struggled to ward off these dangers wherever and however he could.

Eyewitnesses testify to the Delegate's constant alertness and never-failing activity. One of them speaks of the goodness of his intervention, his warmth, his dynamism and his sympathy.[8] Another stresses that his participation in the tragedy of the Jews in those days was no mere formality. "Deeply and sincerely moved by the suffering of the Jews, he showed a strong desire to help in every way possible." When reports of atrocities were brought to him, he received them "with hands folded in prayer and tears in his eyes."[9] He asked to be made aware of the details concerning deportation orders, and noted them carefully. He never handed these matters over to a member of his staff. It was he who personally saw to it that they were dealt with, the same eyewitness reports. In this way, he succeeded in preventing many deportations from Slovakia, Hungary, and Bulgaria, thus saving the lives of thousands.

Once one realizes how much John XXIII as Apostolic Delegate regarded these rescue activities as matters of heart and conscience, one cannot help seeing his papal measures as a continuation of the earlier work. When he purged liturgical texts of wounding or merely misleading expressions, when he commissioned Cardinal Bea to prepare a Conciliar statement on the relationship between the Church and the Jewish people, he extended his previous labors. The work initiated by Pope John is seen by some, Cardinal König and Abbé Laurentin among them, as the Church's response to Auschwitz, the epitome of Hitlerian atrocities. Cardinal König writes:

> As Apostolic Delegate in the Near East, John XXIII had come to know the distress and the mortal anguish of the Jews fleeing from their persecutors . . . . He felt an urgent desire to set against the immeasurable and bottomless hate of those days a lasting word of love.[10]

Abbé Laurentin interprets John XXIII's wish for a special Conciliar declaration on the Jews as follows:

> This intention had deep roots in his heart: his memory of the persecuted Jews and the powerlessness of an Apostolic Delegate in Istanbul, who could render no more than limited assistance.[11]

The actual source of the decision to propose that the Council issue a declaration on the relationship of the Church to the Jewish people lay, therefore, in the heart of John XXIII, in particular in his understanding of the suffering of the Jews. Compared with this, the action of Jules Isaac and other earlier or later interventions were of secondary importance. Nevertheless, they deserve to be recorded here since they disclose the situation concerning the problems of Catholic-Jewish relations as they were before the Council opened.

The Petition of the Biblical Institute. The proposal of Rome's Biblical Institute to the Council's Central Preparatory Commission must be mentioned first. Dated April 24, 1960, it is signed by the then Rector, Ernst Vogt, S.J., also in the name of eighteen teachers at the Institute, all Jesuits hailing from several countries. The last paragraph of the dogmatic section contains a proposal to the Council Fathers entitled *De antisemitismo vitando*, "On shunning Jew-hatred."[12] Its line of thought and manner of expression suggest that it was written by Fr. Stanislas Lyonnet, S.J.

The petition asked that the Council include the existence of the Jewish people and their relation to the Christian Church while considering ecumenical questions. It went on to say that Christians are without doubt true descendants of spiritual Israel, the authentic heirs of the faith of Abraham "our Father in faith," as the first Eucharistic prayer calls him, and of the blessing of Jacob. The Christian profession of faith can thus fittingly and rightly be called "the dignity of Israel," as does the liturgy of the Easter Vigil. Never should it be alleged that the Jewish people is rejected. Already in the past, a part of the Jewish people turned to Christ (Rom 11:1-2). We know, the authors of the petition continued, that the part disbelieving in Christ will not remain forever fixed in this position. In several passages, whose value as evidence cannot be doubted, the Apostle explains that this part of the Jewish people, too, will eventually turn to Him (Rom 11:15, 26). This teaching which, in the opinion of the petitioners, belongs definitely to the deposit of faith, has, it is true, never been proclaimed by the teaching office of the Church. It does, however, seem capable of effectively countering many of the prejudices that promote antagonism toward Jews.

I deeply value this move of the *Institutum Biblicum*, the Church's most prestigious body of biblical scholarship. My esteem for some of its members notwithstanding, I cannot agree with all the points they make in their presentation. "The dignity of Israel," for instance, is not another term for the Christian creed. In the prayer recited at the Easter Vigil, the expression means exactly what it says: the dignity of the Israel of the Patriarchs and Prophets. The prayer avows that those who are one with Christ are the Patriarchs' kin, the Prophets' companions, the people's fellow wayfarers. They are incorporated in the first Israel, sharing in its dignity, that is the Covenant, its summons to follow God's way and bear witness to Him.

To return to the Institute's petition, it then stressed that Christians must be warned to avoid ways of speaking that could cause offense. To underline this point, the instructions for expurgating the texts of various prayers mentioned before were explained. The urgency of the petition arose from sermons and teachings which, on account of defective exegesis, maintained the "accursedness," "rejection," and also the "collective guilt" of the Jewish people.

For the true proclamation of the mystery of the Passion, the Biblical Institute rightly pointed to the catechism of the Council of Trent with its emphasis that all sinners, that is, all human beings, are to be reckoned as Jesus' crucifiers. A special reason brought forward for the petition was the "error of the ultimate rejection of the 'Chosen People' " which rested on a false interpretation of such passages of the New Testament as Mt 27:25; 24:2; 1 Thess 2:16; Rom 9:22. Finally, the signatories of the petition saw in the Pauline teaching, that a time would come when "the full number of the Gentiles will enter in" and "all Israel will be saved" (Rom 11:25, 26), the best weapon with which to put a stop to any theologically embellished Antisemitism, or make its revival impossible.

The Request of the Institute of Judaeo-Christian Studies, Seton Hall University. At about the same time the Biblical Institute's petition was drawn up, another written request was being considered in the United States. As it was to express the common desire of a loose working group scattered throughout the country, it took some time to draft, although the requests it contained were kept to a minimum. It was signed by John J. Dougherty, then Professor of Exegesis at the Seminary in Darlington, New Jersey, today a Bishop and past-President of Seton Hall University, and by me as Director of the Institute of Judaeo-Christian Studies attached to the same University, together with ten fellow priests: Monsignori Myles M. Bourke, Edward G. Murray and William Ryan; Fathers Gregory Baum, O.S.A., Joseph P. Brennan, J. Edgar Bruns, Edward H. Flannery, Isaac Jacob, O.S.B., Ambrose Schaeffer, O.S.B., and Quentin L. Schaut, O.S.B. On June 8, 1960, shortly after it became known that Cardinal Bea had been named President of the Secretariat for Promoting Christian Unity, I was able to submit the petition, written in English, to him and ask him that he take the necessary steps for the realization of the desires expressed in it. A Latin version was sent to the Cardinal on June 24, 1960.

The signatories saw the petition as continuing the work of reconciliation begun by Pius XI as well as Pius XII, and greatly strengthened by John XXIII. It referred to the measures of Pope John discussed previously, as well as to the words with which Pius XI rejected Antisemitism at the time the persecution of the Jews by Hitler was mounting day by day. He branded hatred of the Jews not, as one might have expected, an injustice, a violation of the moral law—that was self-evident. He saw the hater of Jews much more as a rebel against the reality of salvation history, which makes the Christian a supernatural descendant of Abraham, the common Father of Jews and Christians. In the words of the Pope: "Through Christ and in Christ, we are of Abraham's spiritual stock. Spiritually we are Semites."[13] Social psychologists see in the aversion to Jews, not without reason, a variant of xenophobia. There is no doubt that for Pius XI, hatred of the Jews was the rancor of apostates against God's singling out of the Jews as bearers of His revelation. Thus Pius XI was convinced that Jew-hatred was not only a danger to the life and limb of Jews, but also a threat to the Christian existence.

The petition added to the oft-quoted maxim of Pius XI a little known saying by Pius XII. On the occasion of the Holy Year, 1950, more precisely at its opening on Christmas Eve, 1949, Pius XII invited all people to Rome. In particular, he bid welcome to Christians separated from the See of Peter and, together with them, to the Jews: "We open the holy door to all who worship Christ, not excluding those who await His coming in good faith though in vain, and honor Him as the One whom the Prophets proclaimed who has not yet come. We offer them a fatherly greeting and welcome."[14] There was a new spirit at work, even though the "old language" remained. Today we give a more positive value than this to the Jewish expectation; we no longer speak of a vain, senseless, and fruitless waiting. However much the two differ, the Jewish and

Christian hopes are deeply related to each other. The Pope's invitation was a great advance. It was the first ecclesiastical text that placed Christian-Jewish relations in an ecumenical framework. The Jews were mentioned here in the same breath as non-Catholic Christians—the subtitle of the printed text speaks of "dissident Christians." As I understand this phrase, it does not view Jews as "crypto-Christians" but, rather, as the kin of Christians.

The signatories of the petition, supported by the teaching of the last three Popes, in particular, by the loving concern of Pope John, formulated the following requests:

> 1.   That, were the Council to inquire into the nature of the Church in the course of its deliberations, it proclaim the call of Abraham and the deliverance of Israel out of Egypt to be part of the genesis of the Church, so that she can fittingly and rightly be called "the Israel of God" (Gal 6:16), the Israel renewed and exalted by Christ's word and blood. Such a proclamation would correspond entirely to the way the Church sees herself when, for example, she looks upon the wonderful acts that accompanied Israel's Exodus as present in her life in a new manner. Thus she acknowledges at the Easter Vigil that God, who saved Israel from Egyptian persecution, now accomplishes for all nations, through the waters of regeneration, what He did then for the One People. Impelled by this spirit, the prayer uttered at the Easter Vigil ends with a request that is characteristic of the Church's understanding of herself: "Grant that the whole world may become Abraham's children and share in the dignity of Israel."[15]

> 2.   That the Council give further liturgical expression to the unity of salvation history, which comes to life especially in the prayers surrounding the administration of the sacraments. This could be achieved if the Masses now peculiar to the Patriarchate of Jerusalem became votive Masses of the whole Church, or a universal feast of the Just of the Old Testament was introduced. Feasts celebrated by the Patriarchate of Jerusalem include—among others— those of St. Abraham, Patriarch and Confessor, St. David, King, Prophet, and Confessor, and St. Jeremias, Prophet

and Martyr. The signatories are confident that much would be gained by extending these feasts to the whole Church. In this way, the marvel of the unbroken history of our salvation would be actively experienced, not mechanically learned, by the faithful. Thus, the consciousness of God's unceasing guidance of humanity through grace, and of the relationship between Christians and Jews would be made a part of their lives. A liturgical renewal along these lines would surely lead to a growth in love and gratitude among the faithful.

3. That, "for the love which Christ had for His kinsmen," misleading phrases be changed, particularly in the lessons of the Divine Office, distorting as they do the true teaching of the Church and her real attitude towards the Jews. Were the Council to turn its attention to the problems of our own time, the Church ought to denounce, as she has in the past, hatred of the people whose "is the human stock from which Christ came; Christ, who is God over all, blessed forever, Amen" (Rom 9:5).

As has been mentioned before, these were minimum requests. This appeal was, after all, the first advance into an area that had lain neglected for so long, and indeed seemed to be unknown territory to most people; it was, therefore, advisable that the appeal be limited to certain essential points. Furthermore, at the time it was drafted, the scope and procedure of the Council were unknown—one was simply unaware of what to expect.

The Memorandum of the Apeldoorn Working Group. Much more comprehensive and profound than the petition described above is a study carried out by a group of priests and lay people that met at Apeldoorn, Holland. Its last meeting, prior to the Council, was from August 28-31, 1960. The international group consisted of men and women who regarded it as their special task in life to serve the cause of reconciliation between Jews and Christians. Some represented a periodical or center that was trying to reassess the problems concerning the Church and the Jewish people: Anton Ramselaar, the *Katholieke Raad voor Israel*, Holland; Karl Thieme, together with Gertrud

Luckner, the *Freiburger Rundbrief*, Germany; Paul Démann, the *Cahiers Sioniens*, France; Jean Roger, the *Oeuvre de St. Jacques*, Israel; and I, the Institute of Judaeo-Christian Studies of Seton Hall University, and its Yearbook of those days, *The Bridge*.

In retrospect, one may well say that together they formed the prophetic element that over the years had prepared a place in the Church, intellectually, spiritually, emotionally, and theologically, for the Conciliar Declaration. The meeting in the summer of 1960, however, was prompted by the prospect of the Council, of which they, as yet, knew little. Still, the Memorandum drawn up by Paul Démann, after thorough discussion by the whole group, was not addressed to some organ of the Council but to "those who in any way, direct or indirect, have a part in the teaching office of the Church or informing the mind-set of the faithful, whether their field of work be the training of priests, catechesis, preaching, journalism, or writing in general."

The men and women to whom the Memorandum was addressed were mentioned in the preamble; it recognizes, among other things, that the Church has never lost her interest in that part of Israel which did not follow Christ but has been preserved in continued existence by the hand of Divine Providence. The Church knows, the preamble goes on, that she is deeply rooted in the people of the Old Dispensation. No less is she conscious of the fact that Jesus, the Christ, who stands as a sign of contradiction between her and the Jewish people of today, is at the same time the deepest bond between the two. The Church is fully aware of the heritage she has in common with the people of Israel in the writings of the Old Testament, and feels in her depths the solidarity which today still links her destiny to that of the Jews.

The Church lives, faithful to the Apostle's teaching, in unceasing hope of a reconciliation, a restoration of separated Israel to the unity of the one people of God. The Church well knows that Israel's continuance in history, with its richness in human loyalty and abundance of suffering, lays upon the former great tasks and responsibilities. Not in the least can she pass over the torments that Jews have suffered in the midst of Christian peoples. She laments the ignorance, the deformities in thought and attitude on the Christian side which have been, all too often, the cause of those sufferings. She knows, finally, that the prejudices that gave rise to contempt and hatred have not yet disappeared.

On this basis, the Apeldoorn meeting proposed the following guidelines for reshaped preaching and catechesis. As the group owed its existence to private initiative and, therefore, held no official commission, it could put forward only suggestions. This, however, it did freely:

1.   In the eyes of the Church, the Old Testament has the same claim to be accepted as God's revealed word as has the New. The revelation given in the Old Testament and the saving history recorded in it must keep their traditional place in Christian education and witness. Any attempt to reduce the value of the Hebrew Scriptures, any attempt to present its imperfections or the unfaithfulness of the Jewish people in a way that engenders contempt or even mere dislike, is contrary to the spirit of the Church.

2.   As the Word made flesh, Jesus transcends the Old Dispensation. In His humanity, however, He is a part of His people and land, steeped in their traditions. The spirit of the Patriarchs and the Prophets continues to live in Him. He did not "come to abolish the Law and the Prophets, but to fulfill them" (Mt 5:17). Neither He nor the Church can be understood outside this framework.

3.   That framework had many facets, and our knowledge of it is incomplete. Nevertheless, we can say with confidence that at the time of Jesus, Jewry presented a picture of exuberant life, not of degeneration. We have to give the faithful a true picture of Judaism of those days, as far as the state of historical studies allows. It would be unjust to draw a caricature of Judaism in order that the greatness of Jesus and His teaching stand out by contrast.

4.   It would be contrary to the spirit of the Church to pit Old and New Testaments against each other, the "God of wrath," against the "God of love," the "law of fear," against the "law of love." The same divine grace is pro-

gressively revealed throughout both Testaments and the same command of love is present in them.

5.   When seen historically, the dramatic conflict between Jesus and the leaders of His people, which led to His condemnation and crucifixion, is an intricate problem. Certain facts have, in any case, to be borne in mind. In Jesus' time, most Jews were already dispersed throughout the Mediterranean countries; of those settled in Palestine, only a fraction could have known Him. Those who met Him were not only His enemies and opponents, but also the enthusiastic crowds and the disciples. According to the Gospels, the actual opposition came only from a group of spiritual and political leaders, and the condemnation of Jesus was their work also. Yet even they—whatever their personal responsibilities may have been—acted, so Jesus declared, and following Him, Peter and Paul, "in ignorance" (see Lk 23:34; Ac 3:17; 1 Cor 2:8). If the events of this vital period are presented in a historically inaccurate way, Christian instruction is itself led into error.

6.   Even more important is a theologically accurate understanding and explanation of the drama of Golgotha. Jesus suffered and died on account of the sins of all of us and for our salvation. No one stands outside the solidarity of sin, no one. is excluded from the grace of salvation. (Mary, free of any sin, received an extraordinary favor in that she, in anticipation of the saving sacrifice, was preserved from all guilt.) All the participants in the drama of Golgotha, Jews and Gentiles alike, believers and unbelievers, represented humankind as a whole: they stood there, in place of all of us. What makes us accomplices of Christ's enemies and executioners is not nationality or religion, but simply and solely sin, the rejection of grace.

7.   It is, therefore, of extreme importance to avoid the fatal error that holds responsible for the death of Christ all Jews of that time, indeed, the Jews of all time, and them alone. This gives rise to the absurd conception of a "deicidal people" and works upon the feelings of the faithful in regard to the Passion, instilling in them revulsion against those immediately responsible, and not only against them

but against the whole Jewish people. Such errors not only falsify the meaning of the Passion, they also deform the spirit of the faithful. The Cross, this unique source of love, humility, and expiation becomes a source of aversion and hatred, and a reason for shifting the blame for one's own sins on to others. In the past, such errors helped feed hostile feelings toward Jews among Christian people, and roused them to scorn and persecution. These false ideas led to situations in which Jews were crushed to the ground under the weight of the Cross, and the appalling consequences of those ideas have helped hide the true meaning of the Passion from Jews.

8. The central place of the Passion in the life of the Christian, the gravity of the errors already mentioned, the extent of the persecutions of the Jewish people in the midst of the Christian world, and the abysmal depths of the roots of Jew-hatred, all these ought to prompt the Church to warn her priests, catechists, indeed, all believers against these distorted notions. The Church ought to call upon them to avoid not only the errors themselves, but also all forms of expression that reflect and nourish those errors, for example, generalizations such as "*the* Jews rejected Christ," "*the* Jews crucified Christ." In expounding St. John's Gospel, one must be certain to take into account the fact that, in a great many places, the Evangelist uses the expression "the Jews," to mean simply and solely the "Jewish leaders hostile to Jesus." The Church is the true "remnant of Israel," increased by the entry of those Gentiles who became children of Abraham by faith: as such, she must unite within herself both Jews and Gentiles. Thus, one should not say that the Jewish people are rejected or that, within the Church, the Gentiles have taken Israel's place. Nor should one depict the reality of salvation as if the Church had supplanted Israel, as one people might another. Certainly, the transition from the Old to the New Dispensation was accompanied by radical changes—institutions were superseded, a new all-embracing structure appeared—but what had happened was that the *same* people of God had been thus transformed in moving forward the fullness of their vocation.

9. That portion of Israel which kept apart from this

transformation has survived in present-day Judaism. Its preservation and presence in the world are a basic element of God's plan of salvation, and, therefore, cannot be without significance for the Church. Christians may not disregard this present reality, nor may they consider it from a purely human and political point of view, as do those who lack faith. They should rather draw near the Jewish world with the insight and awe due its past, its faith, and its trials. The Church expects of her children that they leave nothing undone to tear down the wall of separation between themselves and the Jews, a wall which the misunderstandings of centuries have rendered almost impenetrable; and, further, that they leave nothing undone to establish amicable relations with the Jews.

10.   To interpret the destiny of the Jewish people over the centuries as a result of their rejection by God is misleading; the teaching of the New Testament, especially that of St. Paul, leaves no doubt that this perspective is wrong: "God has not rejected His people whom He foreknew" (Rom 11:1-2). Despite resistance to the Gospel, "their election stands, they are [God's] beloved" (11:28), and "the gifts and the call of God are irrevocable" (11:29). And does not the Apostle teach that "all Israel will be saved" (11:26)? Day by day, the providential preservation of the Jewish people gives evidence to the faithfulness with which God stands by His plan for the salvation of the world. It would, therefore, be contrary to Scripture and to the true spirit of the Church were one to assume, as often happens, that there lies upon the Jewish people a sentence of rejection, indeed, a curse. It would be absurd to give such a meaning to, for example, Matthew 27:25, "His blood be on us and on our children." As if God could ratify the outcry of a group of demonstrators, worked up by their ringleaders, and have it descend as a curse upon millions of innocent people! To interpret the destruction of the Temple, the Diaspora (which predated the Crucifixion) and Jewish sufferings and humiliations over the centuries as the result of their rejection by God would be contrary to the Church's teaching on the meaning of suffering. One would do well to warn priests and the faithful, in all earnestness, never to adopt

these inaccurate and hardly Christian ideas about the destiny of the Jewish people.

11. The divinely guaranteed hope of the reunion of Church and Israel is an integral part of Christian hope. At the same time, it is the key to the mysterious destiny of the Jewish people, so that without it there can be no real Christian understanding of that destiny. When and wherever this hope is obscured or forgotten, the Christian vision is distorted. If, according to the teaching of the Apostle, the failure of many in Israel furthered the spread of the gospel and with it the salvation of the Gentiles, how much more will Israel's reunification reveal God's mercy and faithfulness? This revelation will be so glorious that the Apostle could portray it as *vita ex mortuis*, "life from the dead" (Rom 11:15). This eschatological hope has always been present in the Church. It urges believers to be fired with this expectation in thought and prayer, and, not least, in their attitude toward the children of the people "of whom is Christ, according to His humanity, who is God over all, blessed for ever, Amen" (Rom 9:5).

A few weeks after its completion, the Apeldoorn text was sent to the Secretariat for Promoting Christian Unity in the hope that the former would have a favorable influence on the latter's work. From the start, there prevailed in leading Conciliar circles a desire to keep the Statement on the Jews short, thus the Memorandum could not exercise the influence it deserved. For years, it lay in the files of the Secretariat and of those who had taken part in the conference. Though unknown to the Church as a whole, even to most members of the Council, the Memorandum was influential. Its words did not find their way into the Conciliar text, but its spirit did.

Only two of the Memorandum's assertions need be altered in the light of the Declaration. In the future, expressions of hope for union at the end of time will have to be reshaped more humbly. Similarly, the Memorandum, together with other documents examined in this book, takes the expression "Israel of God" in the greeting that concludes the Letter to the Galatians: "Peace and mercy upon all who walk by this rule and upon the Israel of God" (6:16) to refer to the Church as the "true, new

Israel," terms, incidentally, that do not appear in the New Testament. This is the way exegetes of the past used to interpret the phrase, while a few contemporary scholars hold that, in the Letter to the Galatians, the designation "Israel of God" has the same significance as "Israel" in the liturgical formulae of Ps 125:5, Ps 128:6, and of the Eighteen Benedictions. It is the historical people Israel upon which the Apostle, with Israel's singers, invokes the grace and mercy of God.[16]

Other Endeavors. I cannot consider in detail other attempts to gain a hearing for the cause of reconciliation between the Church and the Jewish people. There was a lively interest in quarters other than those mentioned. One example is the inquiry by the editors of *Wort und Wahrheit*, a Catholic journal of opinion and concern, into the question: "What do you expect from the Council?" This inquiry among German-speaking Catholics was, no doubt, encouraging, but the fact that of eighty-one answers, only three were concerned with questions regarding the Church and the Jewish people was regrettable. The three who hoped and asked that the Council concern itself with this theme were the Dominican Friars of Walberberg, Karl Thieme, and I.[17]

Démarches of Jewish organizations and individuals also deserve mention, even though they were made at a later stage, and had no influence to speak of on the discussion of the Conciliar Declaration or the shaping of its text. I am thinking here of the Memoranda of the American Jewish Committee, one on the image of the Jew in Catholic instruction (June 1961), another on anti-Jewish elements in the Catholic liturgy (November 1961), and still another by Rabbi Abraham Joshua Heschel, of the Jewish Theological Seminary, New York (May 1962).

The first Memorandum gave a list of "slanderous statements in text books encouraging hostility toward the Jews." It requested the "serious support of the Vatican" in defeating blind fanaticism and creating a prejudice-free climate of opinion, especially in the United States. The second quoted from a series of liturgical texts in which, according to the authors, the Jews were represented as a worthless and morally contemptible people who were motivated only by vengeance and hatred.

The signatories went on to ask "respectfully that the Church, in accordance with the precedents laid out, take all available steps to correct those passages which . . . provoke and encourage the slanderous idea of Jews as a cursed and despised people responsible for the death of God."

In his Memorandum, R. Heschel rightly declared that Antisemitism is an ancient evil, so complex that it is impossible to attribute it to any one cause, or to make any one institution responsible for its persistence. Yet, Jews, in response to the Prophets' call for justice and out of reverence for six million martyrs, were bound to request *all* institutions to investigate and block every possible source of Antisemitism. R. Heschel demanded the extirpation of the religious roots of Antisemitism, making four proposals for the improvement of relations between Catholics and Jews.

> First: That the Council brand Antisemitism as a sin and condemn all false teachings, such as that which holds the Jews as a people responsible for the crucifixion of Christ and sees in every Jew a murderer of Christ.
>
> Second: That without wishing to impugn the rights of any religious group to win supporters by honest means, Jews feel it a spiritual torment that their sanctity as Jews, in their faithfulness to the Torah, is not accorded recognition. Genuine love, however, requires that Jews be accepted as Jews, and it is their sincere hope that the Council recognize the integrity and the continuing value of Jews and Judaism.
>
> Third: That in order to eliminate mutual ignorance every possible means be used to make Christians truly familiar with Judaism and Jews with Christianity, e.g. through public discussions in which Christian and Jewish scholars exchange opinions and tackle controversial and decisive issues. Plans should also be made for joint research projects and publications.

The fourth proposal asked that a high-level commission be set up at the Vatican, with the task of erasing prejudice and keeping a watch on Christian-Jewish relations everywhere. It is also desirable to have similar commissions at the diocesan level to ensure that attention be paid to the demands of justice and love.

A further Memorandum of the World Conference of Jewish Organizations (February 1962) contented itself with one major plea. I quote a passage which, to my mind, states the essence of the whole document:

> Encouraged by the historical initiative [John XXIII's removal from the liturgy of certain expressions susceptible of misinterpretation] and by many sympathetic actions of His Holiness, we turn to the Church with a respectful appeal that she may adopt such measures as appear appropriate to her to put all men, both inside and outside her ranks, who listen to her voice, on their guard against the great—religious and social—dangers inherent in racial fanaticism and in all teachings which stir up hatred and bring suffering upon defenseless people.

The major reason for the ineffectiveness of the Memoranda just sketched may well have been that they were drawn up without knowledge of the possibilities open to a Council. Their proposals went into too much detail, and the fulfillment of some of their requirements presupposed a mentality which the Conciliar Declaration had yet to create. Some have claimed an influence for these Memoranda on the Council they did not exercise. They remained largely unknown. Still, they have value as signs of an incipient dialogue.

The History of the Text

AS HAS BEEN mentioned, Cardinal Bea announced at the first meeting of the members and advisers of the Secretariat for Unity on November 14 and 15, 1960, that Pope John had entrusted to the Secretariat responsibility for dealing with the theological problems posed for the Church in her relationship with the Jewish people. The Cardinal asked for volunteers to accept responsibility to work for the Pope's mandate. As an appointed advisor, Fr. Gregory Baum offered to collaborate in the task. Cardinal Bea accepted this offer, and commissioned

Baum to produce a short exposition of the problem: that exposition was presented to the second plenary meeting of the Secretariat in Ariccia in the Alban hills from February 6 to 9, 1961.

Baum's thesis was that the teachings and actions of recent Popes made it clear by word and deed that the Christian bond to the Jewish people was a theological one, but that certain patristic and medieval conceptions about Jews could no longer be held. In order to make the "mystery of Israel" known (see Rom 11:25) to the faithful so that hostility toward Jews would be uprooted, and to give Jews a correct picture of the Church, it was of greatest importance that the Ecumenical Council issue authoritative statements on three points:

> 1. In speaking of the origin and nature of Christ's Church, her close affinity with the Israel of old should be made unmistakably clear. Thus, it should be shown that the New Covenant confirmed, renewed, and transcended the Old, and that the New Testament fulfilled the Old, without, however, invalidating it.
> 2. In order to correct the widespread notion that *the* Jews had rejected Jesus as the Christ, it should be stated firmly that a holy remnant of the Jewish people acclaimed and accepted Him as Savior of all. In any case, it is unjust to call the Jews an accursed race or a people rejected by God.
> 3. The Church's unceasing hope of Israel's final reconciliation with herself should be solemnly proclaimed. Till that day comes, the Church must declare again and again that the attitude of Christians toward their Jewish neighbors must be one of love and respect. Contempt for and hatred of Jews is to be condemned.

The Subcommittee on the Jewish Question. At the beginning of February, 1961, the late Abbot Leo Rudloff (Jerusalem and Weston, Vermont) was appointed a member of the Secretariat while I was named consultor. Together with Gregory Baum, we formed the core of the "Subcommittee to Deal with the Problems of the Church's Relationship to the Jewish People." On occasion, the Subcommittee co-opted other members. On its behalf, I was asked to prepare a study of the whole matter for the forthcoming meeting of the Secretariat.

The Secretariat had scarcely taken its first steps toward carrying out the papal commission when it ran into opposition. It seems that a confidential conversation with Cardinal Bea, understood by a journalist to be an ordinary interview, alerted the world, and with it the Arab governments, to the Secretariat's intentions. The anxiety and annoyance of Arab leaders bore no relation to the facts. In their minds, they transformed a pronouncement intended as a pastoral and theological one into a political document.

The line of thought of the Arab representatives may well have been as follows: Were the Council to proclaim the kinship of Christians and Jews, such a proclamation might well help the two to live together in peace in the countries of the West, but above all it would redound to the advantage of the State of Israel. Once Catholics began to take a friendly interest in Jews and Jewish matters, it would not be long before they extended their interest to the State of Israel. Thus, the Council document would undeniably intrude into the sphere of politics and become a preparatory step toward the diplomatic recognition of the State of Israel. It is not surprising that Arab leaders, unable to forget for a single second the political tensions in the Near East, were determined to prevent a Conciliar statement "favoring the Jews." Before and during the Council, they tried every conceivable avenue to suppress such a Conciliar declaration.

The attempt to undermine the endeavor of the Secretariat started with representations by diplomats accredited to the Holy See. Great pains were taken to make it clear to the representatives of the Arab countries that the Holy See was not playing a kind of chess game, or engaging in intrigues. Yet, I suspect they were never given to understand unambiguously that the proposed Declaration was a measure necessary for the inner life of the Church, and that she could not renounce it; nor were they ever told that the Council had to be kept free of any improper influence, and that, accordingly, no intervention by political bodies would be tolerated. The slanders that appeared from time to time in a section of the Arab press, and likewise the occasional threats, could have been met with the assurance that, rather than give in, an appeal would be made to world opinion. Historical accuracy, however, requires the admission that what was perfectly possible after the Council was unthinkable before.

In the period before Vatican II, Roman officials still expected to achieve much by diplomatic efforts. When they were unable to convince the Arab leaders, they became uneasy and began to waver. Accordingly, a certain insecurity often hampered the Secretariat's work during the preparatory period and during the Council itself. From minute to minute, one could not be sure whether the Central Commission, as the highest organ of the Council, would permit a separate decree or whether the pronouncements on the Jews would be incorporated into other documents. There were even hours when it was doubtful whether there would be a Conciliar pronouncement at all, in which the Church could make known her in-depth vision of the mystery of Israel. One must be aware of this situation in order to understand the ups and downs in the history of the text.

At the third meeting, which again took place in Ariccia, from April 6 to April 21, 1961, Abbot Rudloff, as chairman of the Subcommittee, pointed to the seriousness and importance of the theme. He wanted only to bring out certain points, by way of introduction, and define the extent of the problems. He shared the wishes expressed in the Memoranda described before, and added to them certain other suggestions, for example, that the Holy Week liturgy of the Byzantine rite be subjected to a fundamental reform, and that the proper authorities remove from Church buildings all pictures and sculptures of the ritual murder charge, together with other representations insulting to Jews and untenable in the light of historical investigations.

Abbot Rudloff's main emphasis was that, at the end of time, the two Israels would be reunited as, in his view, stated in Romans 11:26-29. The Church had to live in the expectation of this event, which will be brought about by God's grace. There was, however, no doubt that the majority of her members were not inspired by this great hope. He believed that a Conciliar pronouncement on the relation of the Church to the Jews would give promise of a renewed Advent spirit.

After this, I developed the thesis that the time of the Council was the God-given moment to speak in an ecumenical spirit of the people from whom Christ in His humanity had descended. I offered the following reasons for the Church's having been called at precisely this time to give expression to the role of the Jews in salvation history and thus put in its true light the bond between the Church and the Jewish people:

1.   The biblical revival of our time and the accompanying rediscovery of Hebrew thought and speech patterns made possible, as never before, a sensitive perception of Jews living both before *and* after Christ. Certain exegetes have aroused from its long slumber the Apostle's teaching concerning Israel's way of salvation in Chapters 9 to 11 of the Epistle to the Romans. In addition, modern Popes have broached the idea that, despite their aloofness from Christ, Jews are our "separated brethren." They are our brothers and sisters in Abraham, the "Father of our faith." It was therefore appropriate, indeed urgent, that the Council continue the Popes' work of reconciliation.

2.   The Council would doubtless be dealing with the relationship of Catholics to Christians separated from Rome and with the Church's concern for non-believers. Yet, if the Council were to show no regard for Israel's place in God's plan of salvation, it might appear that the role of the Jews was the same as that of the pagans. Thus, to ignore them, or fail to single them out, would be contrary to the spirit of Scripture and the tradition of the Church.

3.   Were the Council Fathers to remain silent, they would be accused of having capitulated to opponents of the Declaration. One ought to recall the meeting of the World Council of Churches at Evanston, Illinois, in 1954, when even a brief reference to Christian hope concerning the people of Israel, an eschatological one at that, was voted down by a coalition of Near Eastern (or Arab-sympathizing) and American liberal delegates, the former intimidated by

the Arab governments and the latter afraid of hurting their Jewish neighbors and friends. Instead of creating an amicable atmosphere, the suppressed reference to hope caused more dissension. Thus, the forthcoming Council must not allow itself to be guided by similar fears.

4. Since it was uncertain whether the resistance to a special decree on the Jews could be broken, and since the Subcommittee never took the position of "all or nothing," its members would not under any circumstance insist upon a special pronouncement. Still, I earnestly pleaded with the Council Fathers to advocate certain essential truths concerning the Jewish people. If necessary, these could be incorporated into other decrees. Were the Council to proclaim that the Christian faith was rooted in that of the people of the Old Covenant and that we await a final reconciliation between the Church and the Jewish people, and were the Council solemnly to condemn hatred of Jews, such declarations would, without doubt, contribute to an atmosphere of friendship between Christians and Jews. The memory of persecutions and oppressions of the past is most deeply imprinted on the consciousness of many Jews. All too often, these sufferings were, alas, inflicted "in the name of Christ." Conciliar statements expressing the love of Christ and the fondness of the Church for the people of Israel would help take away the burning sting of injustice and insult as well as bring peace.

Finally. A profound knowledge of Christ and the Church is impossible without a knowledge of God's deeds at the time of the Patriarchs and Prophets, without a loving awareness of the *magnalia Dei*, "God's mighty acts" (Ex 14:13) at the time of Israel's departure from Egypt. Again, there could be no good news of salvation without the good news of creation. The latter is no empty phrase. Against the background of those pagan myths which represent the birth of the world as the outcome of a pitiless quarrel among the gods, the first chapter of Genesis, which sings the praises of the Creator who is good and by whose work there has come forth a world that is fundamentally good, is truly a hymn, a gospel. Jesus would not be God's Anointed and the Savior of all humankind without the promises and prefigurations of the First Covenant, without those figures who in their lives in some measure foreshadowed His work and suffering. In conclusion, Christian hope cannot be complete without the healing of the breach between the Church and the Jewish people. The restoration of their unity will be the "happy ending" of the drama of salvation. In the words of St. Thomas Aquinas: *Ignorantia huius mysterii nobis esset damnosa*, "Ignorance of this mystery would harm us spiritually." (Commentary on Letter to the Romans 11:25).

Basing my appeal to the members of the Secretariat on St. Thomas' saying, I concluded:

For this reason, not only for the well-being of Jews, but also, indeed much more, for the spiritual progress of the faithful and for a testimony to the perfect unity of the Church which was, is, and always will be the Church of Jews and Gentiles, we seek your agreement to the requests we will now present.

Gregory Baum read aloud a study of the affirmations on which the Declaration was to be based, a study I had written, which the Subcommittee, after thorough discussion, had made its own. The study had been drafted in English and was available to the Secretariat in Latin and French translations. I am happy to recall that at the study's first reading in Ariccia it was greeted with applause—contrary to all customs of the Secretariat. At that stage, Fr. George Tavard, A.A., joined the Subcommittee. Later, it was submitted to the fourth general meeting in August, 1961, at Bühl, Germany.

Cardinal Bea was, beyond doubt, the ideal chairman. He steered the Secretariat's meetings firmly but gently. All discussions followed parliamentary procedure, but without rigid formality. During the preparatory period, the Secretariat's members met, for the most part, away from Rome. They lived in the same house, they prayed and ate together, they also met informally so that the Secretariat took on the character of a community. Still, outbursts of applause were not a daily occurrence. On the contrary, if my memory does not deceive me, the spontaneous clapping that greeted the preliminary study on April 20, 1961, was the only time that such a reception was given to a preparatory document. It must have expressed clearly matters that most members had hitherto only vaguely sensed. What formerly had lain dormant in their hearts was now brought out into the full light of day.

Underlying Affirmations

The study, that prepared the way for the carrying out of Pope John's mandate, was divided into three parts.

Dogmatic Principles. No one can truly understand the Church as Bride and Body of Christ, as the people of God and the community of believers, unless he or she is lovingly aware of the fact that the Church is rooted in the life and faith of ancient Israel. In the *City of God*, St. Augustine sees God's call and Abraham's response as *articulus temporis*, "a hinge of time," that is, a pivotal moment in history (*PL* 41,492). So much were this call and response a turning point—the end of idolatry in Abraham's life, the birth in his heart of belief in the living God, and his total surrender to Him—that at the consecration of an altar, a bishop speaks of the Patriarch's life as the *seminarium fidei nostrae*, "the seedbed of our faith" (see *Pontificale Romanum*). Similarly, according to St. Augustine, Israel was blessed not merely with prophetic figures, the existence of the entire people was prophetic. For him, the people as such was the divinely inspired herald of the Messiah and His Kingdom (*PL* 42,283).

On many occasions the Liturgy celebrates the *Ḥasidey YHVH*, "the favors of the Lord to the people of Israel" (Ps 89:2) as true elements of the Church's history. Thus, the *Exsultet* of the Easter Vigil proclaims: "This is the night when, long ago, You led *our forefathers*, the children of Israel, out of Egypt and made them pass dryshod through the Sea," in all likelihood imitating the statement at the Seder about Passover night. Thus, the Christian theologian sees the Israel of the Patriarchs and Prophets as the Church in the making, while the Church herself is Israel fulfilled, renewed in the blood of Christ and spread over the whole earth. Just as the Israel of the time of expectation served as matrix of the Church, so the Church glories in her transformation by Christ's word and her hallowing by the fire of the Holy Spirit. None of this is to be understood as if Israel's role had been nothing but a preparatory one. A woman's dignity and work have not ended by having given birth to a child. Moreover, Judaism, too, is a development of the Israel before the Babylonian exile or its return from there under Ezra.

Despite their differences, the two Covenants do not contradict each other, rather are they two stages in God's dealings with humankind. Doubtless the New, in several respects, transcends the Old. But it would render little honor to Christ were we to slight the stock from which He came and the order of grace into which He was born. St. Peter proclaimed that the God who had "glorified His Servant Jesus" was none other than the "God of Abraham and of Isaac and of Jacob, the God of our fathers" (Ac 3:13). One and undivided is God's counsel, one and indivisible the history of salvation: therefore, the Church prays at the Easter Vigil: "Grant that the world in its fullness—all men and women—may become children of Abraham and share in the dignity of Israel."

A second section of the first part spoke of the Jews as forever loved by God. The enmities that in our day tear humanity apart make it necessary to recall time and again the universality of the Church. For Christians, at least, this could be done in an impressive manner, were the Council to proclaim that in Christ the Church embraces Jews and Gentiles with a single love[18] and that she is, therefore, the Church of Jews and Gentiles. The separation and reconciliation of the two is of fundamental significance in Pauline theology. So long as the division lasts, God's sovereignty is not fully acknowledged. In Christ, however, the breach is healed, and thus Scripture rejoices: "He is our peace. He made the two [Jews and Gentiles] one, breaking down the enmity that stood like a dividing wall between them" (Eph 2:14). As willed by God, the healing of this breach between Jews and Gentiles is a sign of His all-embracing love; indeed, it is evidence that salvation has come in Christ, evidence that must be made known and accessible to all.

It is misleading to say that "the Jews" had rejected Christ. First, one must not forget that, long before Jesus' coming, millions of Jews were living in the Diaspora. Second, the attitude of the People of Israel toward the gospel of salvation had been divided. While those in power opposed Jesus, even aimed for His death, multitudes listened to Him eagerly and heard Him with delight (see Mk 12:37), and a remnant chosen by grace accepted Him (see Rom 11:5). Many were led by the forces of society; under the influence of the emotional climate of those days they acquiesced in their leaders' decision. The first communities of the early Church consisted almost entirely of men and women of Jewish origin, and of proselytes. The proselytes were Gentiles who had taken refuge under the wings of the God of Israel (Ru 2:12). Though of alien descent, they became Jews by belief and often by observance of the whole Law. From the Jews of Jerusalem who had become Christians there came—to use a phrase of the late Cardinal Journet—"the first heartbeats of the Church, which determined the whole future rhythm of Christian life."[19]

Still more pernicious than the misconception that "the Jews" had rejected Christ is the notion that God has rejected them, that they are an "accursed" people. Quite apart from the indefensible assumption that the outcry of a raging mob: "His blood be on us and on our children" (Mt 27:25) had bound God's hands, so that this cry became His decree, the shouts of the crowd were not the voice of the whole people.[20] In the same Jerusalem in which the shouts of the liberation fighters gathered before the Governor's palace resounded, there were also "a great multitude of the people, and of women" who followed Jesus on His way to the place called The Skull, "bewailing and lamenting Him" (Lk 23:27).

If we separate the Gospels from their historical context, and take no account of the fact that they originated under the influence of Hebrew forms of speech, certain passages of the Gospels can easily give rise to the impression that God repudiated the Jews, as if He were "finished with" the people He had chosen and had made the original guardians of His revelation. If, however, we keep in mind Hebrew speech patterns and adopt the Pauline interpretation of Israel's destiny, we know that they do not involve the inescapable finality which they seem to express.

The Apostle often spoke boldly and impulsively; yet, he chose with extreme care the words with which he characterized those in Israel who did not know the time of their visitation (see Lk 19:44). He did not hesitate to say that their strivings were without insight, that they were not enlightened but, at the same time, he felt bound to testify that "they have a zeal for God" (Rom 10:2). Had Paul so wished, he could have found in the prophetic tradition a whole series of violent expressions with which to castigate the leaders and the masses. He contented himself, however, with speaking of their "unreceptiveness" towards the truth of God's grace, a word which most translators, alas, render as "hardening" (Rom 11:7, 25).[21] With tender restraint he termed their failure to recognize Jesus as a "misstep" and a "blunder" (Rom 11:11).

Paul did not, it is true, explicitly record the ignorance of Jesus's adversaries, as Peter had, but it would not be wrong to characterize their attitudes the way he did his own while persecuting the Church: "I did not know what I was doing in my unbelief" (1 Tim 1:13). The Apostle also speaks of the powers that rule this world, fallen angels, who did not understand God's hidden wisdom, else "they would not have crucified the Lord of glory" (1 Cor 2:7-8). Those of his kinsmen who resisted God's plan of salvation, seeking to thwart it, still remained God's favorites. "For the sake of their forefathers, they are forever dear to Him" (Rom 11:28). Even when they are unaware of it, they testify to God's loving kindness and gracious rule among human beings, as revealed in Christ Jesus.

It was in this spirit that the Bishop of Lille, Cardinal Liénart, had written his famous Lenten pastoral of February 21, 1960. In it, he rejected as un-Christian the notion that the Jews are an accursed people, a race of deicides deserving our contempt, as if they, and not all humans, bore the main responsibility for the Lord's death. "It is simply untrue," the Cardinal asserted, "that Israel, the Chosen People of the Old Covenant, has become an accursed people under the New. In reality, the religious destiny of Israel is a mystery of grace, which Christians need ponder with respectful sympathy."[22]

In its third part, the study of affirmations dealt with the final reconciliation of the Church and the people of Israel. A view of the Church that did not include this imperishable hope seemed to the Subcommittee's members incomplete. In the words of the Apostle, Israel according to the flesh[23] had been divided: the smaller part, "the elect" (Rom 11:7), was the means of the Church's growth and extension over the whole world, while the larger part, despite what the Apostle calls its disobedience, has been preserved as witness to God's mercy and reminder of His faithfulness (Rom 11:30-32). God's steadfastness and pity went far beyond Israel's mere physical preservation, for "the gifts and the call of God are irrevocable" (Rom 11:29). Israel according to the flesh, at present aloof from Christ, would be united with Him on the day foreordained by God, so the Committee held.

Admittedly, some few exegetes had been thrown off balance by the Apostle's unexpected but compelling statements in his Letter to the Romans. They believed that his assurance "all Israel will be saved" (11:26) must be understood as the Apostle's reference to all who, throughout history, had believed and would believe in Christ. But the majority of exegetes, past and present, agreed that the Apostle was speaking of the salvation of the Israel according to the flesh.[24]

Among the Fathers of the Church, and also later, there were two ways of understanding the future "conversion" of Israel. One approach was that with Israel's final turning to Christ, history would reach its completion; therefore Paul's phrase "life from the dead" (Rom 11:15) could mean none other than the resurrection of all flesh. The other approach, however, gave the words "life from the dead"—a phrase not found elsewhere in Scripture and, therefore, peculiar to Rom 11:15—a spiritual meaning. The adherents of this interpretation saw in Israel's future turning the signal for a new outpouring of grace, a reawakening of love over the whole earth. It cannot be the task of a Council to choose between these two exegeses.

Similarly, one can only speculate on the ways and means of

that "turning" and its immediate results. Theodore of Mop-
suestia assumed that the Jews of those days, like the Apostles,
would be teachers of the Gentiles.[25] Gregory the Great saw
them as imitating the Passion of Christ, as martyrs insulted
and tortured, giving witness by their blood.[26] Photius' view was
that the readmission of Israel would bring with it the great
kingdom of the future, "perfect and universal joy," as if the
dead had risen.[27] But according to Origen, it would actually
transform this perishable world into an imperishable one.[28]

We know little of the circumstances and consequences of
Israel's final "ingathering," thus it could not be the subject of a
Conciliar decision; still, the essence of this hope is certain (see
Rom 11:12, 15, 25-26). As a divine promise and apostolic legacy,
it is an integral part of the Church's never-failing expectation.
A solemn declaration giving expression to this truth would
certainly be a blessing.

Moral and Liturgical Considerations. The first section of this
part pointed out that a Christian aware of the continuity of the
old and the new order of grace, conscious of the bond between
the two, must meet his Jewish neighbors with respect and love.
God chose His people not because of their merit; in His unfath-
omable predilection, He gave His word to their ancestors, binding Himself to their descendants forever. A Christian who
bears in mind God's constant fidelity to His people will experience his or her own kinship to them, even though faith in
Christ separates one from the other. This awareness of being
related to one another is part of the rejection of Jew-hatred by
Pius XI, discussed earlier, and no less of the address by John
XXIII to a group of Jewish visitors.

The Church abhors all racial fanaticism. But hatred of Jews
has a special quality of evil. It violates truth, justice, and love;
over and above that, it deals a blow to faith. Considered from
without, Jew-hatred, like any other form of hatred, contradicts
the article of faith that every human is created in the image of
God. At its core, however, Jew-hatred wishes to deny, even do
away with the fact, that at the Incarnation the eternal Son of
God became a Jew, son of David and son of Abraham (Mt 1:1).

For most of the faithful, the liturgy has become in fact their teacher in the spiritual life. An old axiom, *Legem credendi lex statuat supplicandi*, may be understood in a wide sense, namely that the way one prays shapes not only one's convictions of faith but also one's inner life. At the time of the document's writing, there was only one commemoration of Old Testament figures in the calendar of the Latin Church, that of the Maccabees, on August 1. But the spiritual significance of the Maccabees is not nearly as great as that of many other men and women of Israel. Would it not be of help to many believers, the study asked, if those feasts of the Just of the Old Covenant that are celebrated by the Latin Patriarchate of Jerusalem were in some way extended to the whole Church? This could be done, for example, in the form of a new feast of Patriarchs and Prophets. Yet, as it is the wish of the Church today to have the celebrations of feasts of Saints yield to the celebration of the events of our Redemption, the preliminary study suggested that the feasts of the Jerusalem Patriarchate be incorporated, where possible, in the Roman Missal as votive masses.

Liturgical prayers, especially those bound up with the admission of the sacraments, quite often show that the figures and events of the Old Covenant not only live on in the New, but also acquire a new significance. For many people, special Masses in honor of the various Patriarchs and Prophets would anchor even more deeply in their hearts and minds the knowledge of the unity of saving history. If these Masses were celebrated only occasionally, their introduction into the Roman Missal would contribute, on the one hand, to a fruitful atmosphere in Jewish-Christian relations, on the other, the life of grace among the faithful would undoubtedly be enriched. To give but one example, one of the prayers from the Proper of the Jerusalem Patriarchate reads:

> Almighty, everlasting God, in Your fatherly goodness, through the intercession of blessed Jeremiah, the prophet, release from the bondage of sin Your servants who plead guilty in Your sight. Let the pain of remorse which is their punishment be outweighed by Your gracious mercy which brings them pardon. Through Jesus Christ our Lord. Amen.

Concrete Proposals. A number of books of religious instruction for various age groups have not yet [that is, at the time this study was written] absorbed the spirit that animates it. Thus, it would be of great value were the Council to induce those responsible for the formation of priests and lay instructors in religion to treat the role of the Jewish people in the history of salvation in such a way that their instruction stands in full harmony with God's marvelous saving design.

The signatories also requested that Pope John's desire of creating a climate of respect and affection, begun by him, not be forgotten. At the time this study was written, the third nocturn for Good Friday contained a number of misleading and wounding expressions. They have now, however, been eliminated from the Breviary. The second Response of the second nocturn of Maundy Thursday contained the following sentence: "For a handful of coins, he delivered Christ *to the Jews.*" Similarly, the second Response of the second nocturn for Good Friday said: "Darkness fell [upon the earth] when *the Jews* crucified Jesus." These were but a few examples.

It is a commonplace among exegetes that the expression "the Jews" in St. John's Gospel rarely means the Jewish people as such, but rather stands for Jesus' opponents, in particular, for the officialdom that rejected Him. I think it wrong to see in the Johannine use of the expression "the Jews" a hostile attitude toward the whole Jewish people. This view ignores altogether the manifestly Jewish character of the Fourth Gospel. Various attempts have been made to give historical reasons for this usage, for instance, that of Hans Kosmala, who thinks it may be part of the Qumran tradition. "Israel," he says, is one of the cover-names of the community of Qumran, while "Judah," "land of Judah," or "house of Judah" denote the enemies of the community. Those "ready to repent" "the chosen of Israel," are said to "have gone out of the land of Judah" (*CD* II, 5; IV, 2f, 3f).[29]

The Scandinavian exegete N.A. Dahl thinks the Johannine usage can be traced to the biblical and the rabbinic traditions concerning the representative role of Israel. "The Jews," he suggests, is not merely a synonym for the high priests and elders of the people, but stands for the hostility of the "world" toward Christ. In the Jewish tradition, Jerusalem, especially Mount Zion, is the center of the world. According to the rabbinic view, Jerusalem will be the "mother city" of the human race in the days of the Messiah. For the prophets before them, Jerusalem was the place to which the nations would flow and from which the Torah would go forth (Is 2:2-3). The Holy City, accordingly, is the center of salvation, the focal point of grace, and the home of faith. The Evangelist saw Christ's mission to Israel as a mission to the whole world: it was there that He carried out His service to humanity. Yet, the Evangelist added to it a negative aspect. He saw the resistance of the world, too, centered or crystallized in Jerusalem. The resistance of the officialdom in Jerusalem against the Redeemer mirrors the resistance of human beings everywhere. Thus, the authorities of the biblical city, "the Jews," are made to stand for the permanent and ubiquitous resistance to the divine offer of renewal. To sum up, the Johannine use of the expression "the Jews" may be a literary device that is to bring out a profound theological idea.[30] This is yet another example of the way in which the uninformed will take as anti-Jewish something which, in reality, forms part of Israel's so frequently ignored heritage.

Some modern translations of the New Testament contain footnotes that give the reader this essential information. It would greatly help a correct understanding of the mystery of the Passion if such footnotes were also introduced into the peoples' Mass books. No texts, liturgical or otherwise, should be tolerated that are not worded in such a way as to serve truth and love.

Finally, Church buildings in various countries have memorialized the ritual murder libel in stone or painting. Although several Popes have declared that the various accusations against Jews of having killed Christian children for the purpose of offering sacrifice on Passover, or drinking their blood have no other source than the wickedness and greed of the accusers, reminders of these evil tales remain untouched. The authorities of the Anglican cathedral at Lincoln were the first to remove all memorials in honor of the alleged martyrdom of Little Hugh of Lincoln.[31] In several places, Catholic Bishops have tried to obtain the removal of similar memorials by the local population. Resistance to such action comes, at times, not from antipathy against Jews, but rather from an ingrained attachment to old village customs that have become part of the peoples' identity.

I find it imperative, therefore, to quote one of several ecclesiastical documents denouncing the "blood libel." On July 5, 1247, Pope Innocent IV issued a Letter to the Archbishops and Bishops of Germany and France:

> We have received a tearful complaint from Jews of [your country] telling how some princes, both ecclesiastical and lay, together with other nobles and powerful persons in your cities and dioceses, plot evil schemes against them and invent various pretexts in order to rob [Jews] of their goods by appropriating them. This they do without prudently considering that it is from the archives of the Jews, so to speak, that the testimonies of the Christian faith came forth. Among other commandments of the Law, Holy Scripture proclaims *"Thou shalt not kill,"* forbidding them even to touch a dead body at the time of their Passover. Nevertheless, Jews are falsely accused of having communion with the heart of a slain child at that feast. This is alleged to be enjoined by their Law, though it is in fact manifestly contrary to it. Moreover, when the body of a dead man happens to be found anywhere, [their enemies] maliciously ascribe the cause of death to the Jews.
>
> On this, and many other fictitious pretexts, [these same princes] rage against the Jews and despoil them of their possessions, in opposition to the special laws, that is, the privileges graciously granted them by the Holy See, in opposition further to God and to justice, even though they have never been indicted, never have confessed, never have been convicted [of these alleged crimes]. The selfsame rulers oppress [Jews] by depriving them of food, by imprisoning, and by persecuting them. They afflict Jews with punishments of diverse sorts, and condemn a great many of them to the most shameful kind of death. Hence these Jews, living under the domination of the aforesaid princes, nobles, and lords, are in worse condition than that of their fathers in Egypt, and are forced to go miserably into exile

from places where they and their ancestors have dwelt from time beyond memory.

Fearing their own destruction, [the Jews] have had recourse to the discretion of the Apostolic See. We, there-fore,... command that you show yourselves favorable and benign toward them. Duly redress all that has been wrought against these Jews by the aforesaid prelates, nobles, and lords. In the future do not allow them to be harassed unjustly in these or in comparable ways by anyone.[32]

Several requests were attached to the preliminary study. Directed to the Fathers of the Council, these proposals pleaded for earnest consideration. First, that, should the Fathers come to define the nature of the Church, they teach: according to God's plan of salvation, the Church has her roots in the Israel of the Patriarchs and Prophets. May they further proclaim that the calling of Abraham and the deliverance of the Jewish people out of Egypt form part of the genesis of the Church.

Second, that they teach: the Church is the Church of Jews and Gentiles. The reconciliation of both in Christ prefigures and announces the reconciliation of all human beings in the Church, which, therefore, makes her the core of humankind. The Jewish people, however, even if far from Christ, does not in any way stand under God's curse. On the contrary, it remains forever dear to Him because of the Patriarchs and the promises made to them.

Third, that they teach: the reconciliation of the two Israels is an integral part of Christian hope and the Church awaits this hour of grace with longing and unshaken faith. It is true that she knows neither the day nor the hour, but with Paul, she is convinced that it will be an event full of grace, indeed, "life from the dead" (Rom 11:15).

Fourth, that they proclaim the dignity of every human being as an image of the Creator, and condemn racism in all its forms. May they especially brand hostility to Jews, not only as a sin against justice, love and the common bond of human kinship, but also as an onslaught on Christ, who, in His humanity, is of the House of David.

Fifth, that the feasts of the Just of the Old Covenant, as they are, at present, celebrated in the Latin Patriarchate of Jerusalem, be extended to the whole Church, either as votive Masses or as a feast of the Patriarchs and Prophets.

Sixth, that guidelines or directives be issued on the best ways of teaching, in seminaries as well as in adult religious instruction Israel's role in salvation history, and, no less, the post-biblical history of the Jewish people.

Seventh, that the work of love begun by Pope John be perfected by banning statues or pictures that preserve the slanders accusing the Jews of ritual murder. Prayers, paintings, and sculptures which injure and inflict injustice on the people from which Christ came in His humanity must be removed.

The Discussion. In discussing the seven requests during the general meetings of April and August, 1961, attempts were made to deepen certain affirmations, or clear up misunderstandings. At the April plenary meeting, for instance, it was suggested that with regard to the first request, greater emphasis be placed on the unity of the two Covenants, and the impossibility of understanding the New Testament without the Old. Another member wanted the terms "Old" and "New" Israel to be dropped, as they only preserved the idea of opposition between the two. To speak comprehensively of the "Israel of God" would be far better.

In its original form, the second request held that the Jewish people were in no way rejected by God, although the majority of them have stood apart from Christ. A prominent member of the Secretariat protested against the word "majority" as going beyond the words of Scripture. In this connection, another speaker recalled that the dispersion of the Jews was a reality already at the time of Christ. Two-thirds of them lived in the Diaspora, and had therefore never heard Jesus' preaching, and scarcely that of the Apostles. So, they could not have rejected Him in their hundreds of thousands, much less in millions.

Another member found the expression "the Church of Jews and Gentiles" unsatisfactory. It does, indeed, describe the character of the Church in the time of the Apostles, but not that of the Church today. As most Christians in Western countries sprang from a centuries-old tradition, one could not properly call them "Gentile Christians." The answer to this objection, a member countered, was the fact that the phrase "Church of Jews and Gentiles" is not divisive, but is intended to proclaim the unity of all, that it describes an event in salvation history, not a personal or temporary situation. "Church of Jews and Gentiles" means, among other things, that "God has surrendered all to [their] disobedience, that He may have mercy upon all" (Rom 11:32). Henri de Lubac, as the discussant quoted, avows that the Church, as regards the majority of its members, is descended from the Gentiles, but that the idea of the Church is descended preeminently from the Jews.[33]

Someone else pointed out that "the Church of Jews and Gentiles" was not coined in modern times, but was already known in Patristic literature, and furthermore, the art of Christian antiquity gave testimony to what it denoted. One such instance is that of the mosaic in San Lorenzo at Rome depicting Christ as Pantocrator, "Ruler of the Universe." Christ is seated on a globe, with Peter and Paul to His right and left, and with the holy cities at their feet : at Peter's feet Jerusalem, the temple of which had long been the place of God's special presence; at Paul's feet Bethlehem, the scene of His manifestation to the nations and their representatives, the Wise Men from the East. These two holy cities, the one of the Jews and the other of the Gentiles, constantly reappear in early Christian works of art; out of them goes forth the flock of Christ, made up of twelve sheep, symbolic of the twelve apostles and the twelve tribes. Twelve was considered the number of universality, *sacramentum est cuiusdam universitatis* (Augustine, *In Psalm.*; *PL*, 37,1104).

Another instance is the mosaic in the apse of S. Pudentiana. It shows Christ as Ruler and Teacher, enthroned in Jerusalem: the One to whom all authority in heaven and on earth has been given (Mt 28:18) and who bade His Apostles to preach the gospel to the whole creation (Mk 16:15). At His right is the Apostle who, on the day of Pentecost, urged his kindred to acknowledge Christ (see Ac 2:36), at His left the one who brought the Gospel to the Gentiles (see Ac 15:7). Behind Peter stands the *Ecclesia ex circumcisione*, behind Paul the *Ecclesia ex gentibus.* The two women, who symbolize the twofold yet single Church, are about to crown the messengers of Christ with a garland.

With regard to the reconciliation of "the two Israels," one of the Bishops complained that the teaching had largely fallen into oblivion. Another questioned whether the Jewish people still had a role in saving history. The questioner thought the answer was "No," while others replied "Yes."

The fourth request stressed Christ's descent from the House of David. One Bishop proposed that the envisaged Declaration should also give prominence to the Jewishness of the Blessed Virgin and the Apostles.

The fifth request was originally addressed to the Sacred Congregation of Rites. Again, one of the Bishops declared that, on the one hand, the Congregation of Rites did not favor additional feasts, and on the other, that the Patriarchs and Prophets were already invoked in the Litany of the Saints, while Abraham occupied an important place in the Canon of the Mass.

There was no discussion on instructions for seminaries because all seemed to agree that it was of the greatest importance. Regarding the seventh request, I think it was the consensus of opinions that the new Good Friday intercession on behalf of the Jewish people was highly beneficial.

The Discussion Resumed. At the plenary session of August, 1961, the seven requests were taken up again. The first comment concerned the origin of the Church. She was not simply rooted in Israel, one discussant maintained, for Christ was not only the son of Abraham, but also the only-begotten Son of the Father. Thus, the deepest roots of the Church lay in the Triune God. This observation was undoubtedly correct in itself, but it was not a relevant objection, since the theme of the first request was the origin of the Church in time.

One speaker found the words "a people of deicides" slanderous. True, he said, the accusation was refuted, but even the expression itself must be totally rejected. The second request, too, sparked a far-reaching discussion, though no decisive solution of the problem of Israel's rejection of Christ was reached. One speaker held the extreme position that the New Testament taught, in several places, that Christ was rejected by the *whole* people, but was firmly contradicted. Another maintained that "His blood be on us, and on our children" (Mt 27:25) was not correctly interpreted in the discussion preceding the request. This passage, he said, was prophetic: in it the blood of Christ was called down *non in damnationem, sed etiam in salutem*, "not to condemn but to save [the people]." Another speaker answered that it was highly unlikely that the crowd shouting before the praetorium thought of either salvation or damnation.

As the discussion continued, someone reminded the Fathers that Pope John had deleted from the prayer of dedication of humanity to the Heart of Jesus an expression along these lines. Also, the crowd which had gathered in front of the Governor's palace could not possibly represent the whole people. If the Evangelist speaks of the "whole people," *pās ho laos*, in this scene, then it was certainly not to report a fact, but to express a *theologoumenon*, his own evaluation of what had happened. The nation as a whole was bound to feel the temporal consequences of preferring Barabbas to Jesus, that is, the loss of sovereignty. This preference should be allowed to stand as a presentiment of the self-destructive course upon which Jerusalem was later to embark. In this, all the nations, of today and tomorrow, should see a warning ever to take the road toward peace. One should always distinguish between the Jews as a corporate entity, a collective, and the Jews as a sum total of individuals. It is to be deplored that preachers speaking of "the Jews" give the impression that they have in mind every individual.

To avoid this pitfall, the global expression "the Jews" ought to be shunned. The discussion then took up the objection against calling the Church the new Israel because it seemed to involve a rejection of the old. It was much more a matter of a new beginning, indeed, a "schism" within the people of Israel. Again, an outstanding member of the Council held that one should distinguish between Israel, being part of the economy of salvation under the Old Covenant, and Israel as an ethnic body. The economy had not been rejected but brought to perfection in the New Covenant. The Jewish people, however, no longer were part of the order of the Old Dispensation. As far as salvation is concerned, they are in the same position as all other nations. This view was strongly contradicted. It could hardly be said that the Jews are in the same spiritual situation as other people. The special promises given them had made them a special people in God's eyes, not because of their own merits, but solely through God's predilection and faithfulness. Their singularity, therefore, remains.

One speaker returned to the third request, objecting to calling the reconciliation of the two Israels an integral part of Christian hope. He said "integral" meant that "our salvation depended on this hope." This objection, someone replied, was perfectly well-founded if the words "our salvation" were to be understood as the salvation of individual Christians. It was, however, invalid if one took them to mean the salvation of the world, that is, the fullness of redemption, its ultimate unfolding and the final ripening of the fruits of that love which was at work upon the Cross and in the tomb.

An English member raised the question of whether one was really bound to say that hope for the salvation of all peoples formed part of the Christian expectation. Whereupon another Englishman replied that Scripture said nothing about the conversion of the English, but most definitely spoke of the final embrace of Christ by the Jews. Someone else pointed out that the requests were speaking of the Jews because they were the subject of the Declaration. That others were not mentioned in no way implied an absence of interest in their welfare. Yet, it must be said that a Christian's faith was incomplete if he or she considered Chapters 9 to 11 of the Epistle to the Romans unimportant. No one wishes the Council to explain in detail what every verse of these three chapters teaches. It was then agreed that the request must be so formulated as to be above and beyond the various theological opinions. It was not admissible to turn theses still under discussion among theologians into the subject of a Conciliar statement.

Only one alteration was suggested for the fourth request. One could not simply say, as in the original text, that the Antisemite "sinned against faith." One should attach to this

categorical statement a "maybe," "perhaps," or "possibly,"so
that the request would read something like this: "Hatred
against Jews is not only a sin against justice, love, and the
bond of brotherhood, but may well be a sin against faith." This
suggestion was not accepted, but the final sentence of the
request was redrafted in a more concrete form, so that it no
longer spoke of the Antisemite sinning "against faith" but
against "the humanity of Jesus Christ, who was of the house of
David" (see Mt 1:1, 21:9; Lk 1:32, Rom 1:3).

Curiously, the fifth request unleashed a very lively debate. It
was pointed out that the Carmelites celebrate a Mass in honor
of the holy Prophet Elijah, and that the Office for Advent
remembered the Patriarchs and Prophets again and again. We
must not forget that in so meaningful an hour as that of death
itself, the Church commends the dying Christian to God, that
He have mercy on him or her as He did on the Just of the Old
Covenant. God is implored, in a whole series of liturgical invocations, to set free the soul of His servant from the agony of
death, as He had freed—to mention only the most important
invocations—Enoch and Elias from death, Abraham from the
superstition of Ur, Job from his sufferings, Lot from Sodom
and the flames of its destruction, Moses from the power of the
Pharaoh, Susanna from false accusations, and Daniel out of
the lions' den. Another comment referred to the holy women,
who must not be overlooked.

A Bishop noted for his frankness, held that introducing a
special feast of the Just of the Old Covenant was unnecessary
since, as he pointedly declared, "the feasts of Our Lord, the
Blessed Virgin, and the Apostles are all 'Jewish feasts'."
Another objection raised was that the feasts of the Jerusalem
Patriarchate were largely of a local nature, and that it was not
the prevailing custom to extend to the whole Church feasts
linked only to a particular locality. Besides, the present time,
with its liturgical renewal, was not a favorable one for the
introduction of new feasts.

Concerning the sixth request, the question was raised whether
it would not be advisable to prepare a document concerning the
Jews for the Commission on Seminaries and Studies. Another
participant suggested that the sixth request be phrased as

follows: "Everything not in agreement with the Church's teaching set out here is to be removed from text books." One member believed that it would be difficult to introduce the post-biblical history of the Jewish people into the already over-loaded teaching syllabus. Another inquired: "Is the study of the entire history of the Jews really necessary and required for an understanding of the plan of salvation?" He was answered that there are current among Christians many false notions and popular beliefs concerning Jews that give Christians a distorted image and must, therefore, be rooted out. The conclusion then was, as was so often, that the request could not be detailed but must be kept in general terms such as: "In the theological formation of seminarians, one ought to be attentive to all that is part of [post-biblical] Jewish history."

In connection with the seventh request, one speaker asked for the insertion of Mary's name. He was told that the request cited a text by the Apostle Paul in which Mary was not mentioned. The further discussion of the request led to the conclusion that, there were, indeed, many paintings and sculptures that had to be removed but the Council's Fathers could not list the individual sites.

As the discussion was winding up, one Bishop admitted that, pleased though he was with the general teaching presented in the study of the underlying affirmations, he found the presentation too long, and hardly serviceable. The petition should refer only to the teaching of the Church, while the practical applications should be reserved for directives to be worked out after the Council.

At the end of November, 1961, a new plenary session took place in Ariccia, at which the proposed declaration was again on the agenda. The discussion revolved around two points. First, the difference between Israel "according to the flesh" and Israel "according to the Spirit." One speaker maintained that the promises given to Israel were of a spiritual nature, and their fulfillment was to be sought in the spiritual realm of the Church. There was not only a continuity, but also a disconti-nuity between the Old and New Covenants: the Church was a new creation. Another participant wondered whether it was correct to speak of Jews as our "separated brethren," since the expression related to people baptized in the name of Christ but not united with Rome. Peter Canisius, the first to use it, was referring to Protestants, while Leo XIII applied it to Evangelical and Orthodox Christians.

A theological adviser of the Secretariat hoped to speed up the phrasing of the Declaration a little. In dealing with the entire problem two courses of action had to be taken: [1] A Conciliar denunciation of Antisemitism. Here, the theological substantiation was simple and the need obvious. [2] A Conciliar proclamation on human dignity: It ought to bear witness that the world is the creation of God and that the dignity of human beings consists in their likeness to Him. Within this framework, a special reference to the Jews could be made, at which the Arabs could not take offense.

The speaker continued his exposition of the theological standing of the Jews, and concluded with the following questions: [1] What meaning has the Old Testament for the Church? [2] What is the status of the Jewish people up to the end of the world? [3] What is the significance of the promises given to the Jews? All in all, a Conciliar Declaration may much more readily condemn Jew-hatred than argue controversial questions of theology, let alone solve them.

The discussion then turned to the ways and means of putting into effect the Pope's commission. One member pointed out that Jew-hatred was such a complex historical problem that the Council could hardly go into it. It would be far better to affirm before the whole world the rights of the Jewish people. This suggestion met with agreement: a document prepared by the Secretariat could not possibly deal with the history of Antisemitism. Its task was rather to delineate the duties of Christians and their correct relationship with Jews.

A leading Bishop said that he had no objection to the proposed approach, but wanted to make clear that many questions concerning the Jews still remained open. The Jewish people perdures through the ages, and our salvation springs from them. But what place do they hold in God's plan today, and what is the true attitude of the Church toward them? The Bishop wondered whether that attitude could best be joined with that of tolerance. (The theme of "tolerance" was later

154 THE NEW ENCOUNTER

dropped, since "toleration" of other beliefs represented a phase of ecclesiastical attitude the Council had abandoned because it easily leads to condescension. Tolerance does not accord with religious freedom as proclaimed by the Council.)

Another discussant suggested that the Secretariat prepare a text that could be built into the draft On the Church while another thought it better to phrase the draft in such a way that it could be incorporated into the draft On Religious Liberty. Several members replied that both ideas were acceptable, but that the mandate given to the Secretariat for Unity was to present to the Council a text bearing its imprint.

After continued discussion, in which a wide range of members took part, two questions were put to the plenary meeting:

1. Whether a theoretical and practical decree concerning the Jews should be worked out. The question was answered affirmatively by some three-fifths of the members.

2. Whether additional proposals ought to be forwarded to the Theological Commission and the Secretariat's Subcommission, On Tolerance and Religious Freedom. This was agreed to unanimously.

I have dealt extensively, without, however, exhausting the discussion through three plenary sessions, in order to demonstrate to as great a degree as possible the tenor of the Secretariat. Some critics asserted, in a fit of bad temper and a rare kind of illogic, that the length of the Council proceedings and the ebb and flow of debate proved that the Declaration on the Jews did not come from the heart. There were also people like Moses Sachs, Minneapolis, who valued the Council Fathers' efforts, and declared that it required courage on the Church's side to probe into her position, tackle the problem amid full publicity, and show concern for the feelings of non-Catholics.[34]

Fraud and Other Problems

At the risk of tedium, I have reported the deliberations at length, because an attempt to veil the Council's history in silence would be doomed to failure. Concealment encourages rumormongers. While the Council was meeting, it was a necessity of life to keep the preparatory work confidential, but now it would look like secretiveness. If one does not present the stages of the Council soberly, one is only helping those who know how to transform the tiniest fact into a sensation, or give a false emphasis to every word and event.

The most alarming examples of "disclosures" which, for want of better information, are accepted by many as authentic reports, are *The Pilgrim* by M. Serafian, and an article on the history of the Declaration on the Jews, entitled "Vatican II and the Jews" (*Commentary*, January, 1965) by the same author. He is an ex-Jesuit, Malachi Martin, this time using another pseudonym, F.E. Cartus. The article contains a prayer ascribed to Pope John that has had wide currency, though everyone who knew the Pope's mind and style is convinced that it was fabricated. Moreover, Mr. Martin has in all these years refused to offer any proof of the prayer's authenticity, a photocopy of the original, for instance. Nor did he ever reveal how he came into the possession of the alleged prayer of Pope John.

This is the prayer that Mr. Martin maintains was found after the Pope's death, without telling us by whom:

> We are conscious today that many, many centuries of blindness have cloaked our eyes so that we can no longer see the beauty of Your Chosen People nor recognize in their faces the features of our privileged brethren.
>
> We realize that the mark of Cain stands upon our foreheads. Across the centuries our brother Abel has lain in the blood which we drew, or shed tears we caused by forgetting Your love.
>
> Forgive us for the curse we falsely attached to their name as Jews. Forgive us for crucifying You a second time in their flesh. For we knew not what we did.

The prayer reads as a careful composition. The Pope's style, however, was unassuming, conversational rather than literary. No one I know had ever heard Pope John speak in a similar vein. I, myself, had had a long audience in which he told me how he viewed his role in the history of Catholic-Jewish relations. I was also present when he addressed all the members of the Secretariat for Unity, and had seen a communication to Cardinal Bea about the contemplated Declaration on the Church and the Jewish People. In not a single instance did he utter words that bore the slightest resemblance to the alleged prayer.

Why am I so adamant in rejecting the prayer? First, I would not want to base the new Christian-Jewish encounter, indeed, any relationship, on a lie. Second, I consider the prayer harmful to Jews. In my opinion, phrases like "the beauty of Your Chosen People" and of "the features of our privileged brethren" are intended to beguile, not to honor Jews. They bespeak flattery rather than love. It treats Jews as immature, needing assurance and approval, when they should be given the justice and esteem that are their due. It is not mean-spirited to distrust a former Jesuit and priest, at odds with his Church, when he publishes an alleged Vatican secret in an influential Jewish journal!

By having the Pope say: "We bear the mark of Cain on our brows" (incidentally, the mark of Cain is not a brand of guilt, but a sign of protection), "our brother Abel has lain in the blood we have shed," and "Forgive us for crucifying You a second time," the prayer locks Christian-Jewish relations into a paternalistic frame rather than reshaping them in a new spirit. By using such language, the tendency of the prayer seems to be the opposite of the Conciliar Declaration. While the Declaration rejects the collective guilt of the Jews, the prayer lays a universal guilt on Christians, even those of today, for the wrongs and sufferings inflicted on Jews by one or another Christian generation of the past. Here, truth and fairness have given way to sensationalism.

There are other unanswered questions. If Pope John really considered the prayer a kind of testament, a message to the whole Church, why did he not see to its publication during his lifetime? Further, if Mr. Martin held the prayer to be of vital importance, as he says he did, why did he wait a year and a half to publish it? One need not wait for an answer; the questions themselves divulge that "we have been had."

In a treatment intended to be of more than ephemeral interest but to serve serious and scholarly research into the history

of the Declaration on the Jews, it would be out of place to treat
as secrets facts that have long since been known. Pope John
would have given the lie to any kind of "secretiveness" declaring as he did to a series of journalists accredited to the Council's press office that the Church had nothing to hide and called
on them to testify to this.[35]

The invitation to openness given to the men and women of
the press applies with still greater force to an historian. In the
long run, frankness can only be of advantage to the Church in
general and the purposes of the Council in particular. In the
spirit of that candor, may I say that the Secretariat took great
care to protect freedom of expression. While this was much to
the Church's credit, there was another factor arising out of the
reports of the discussions which was not at all beneficial. The
public and press were inclined to see the démarches of the Arab
governments as the main obstacle to the Declaration on the
Jews. It would be wrong to underestimate the constant and,
indeed, growing pressure from the Near East powers. But there
was another factor that worked against the Declaration to the
same, if not to a greater, extent: the theologians were not prepared for it.

From the time of Christian antiquity up to that of Vatican II,
there had been hardly any development of the Church's teaching on the mystery of Jewish existence. Many other mysteries
had been subjects of meditation in prayer and intense intellectual activity, for example, those of the Triune God, of the person and office of Jesus, and of the Eucharist. There was a
constant clarification of concepts and continual refinement of
language in order to render supernatural realities as exactly as
possible in human speech. But nothing of this kind had
occurred with regard to the relationship of the Church to the
Jewish people. The problem was really the Cinderella of
theology.

From the point of view of post-Holocaust Jews—their inner
needs scarcely understood by the surrounding non-Jewish
world, including some ecclesiastical circles—the Declaration
came somewhat late; some say with resentment, too late. But
from the point of view of theologians and their quite different
needs, the Declaration came rather soon, one is tempted to say,

too soon. I think it well to reconcile the two extremes and to say that the Declaration came just at the right time. It is still possible to comfort the present generation of Jews, hoping that they will not become victims of despair. Equally, the Declaration could rouse theologians from a centuries-long sleep. To a small extent, it has already done so. From the point of view of scholarship, the theological situation is today better than it has ever been. Advances in philosophy, especially the unexpected penetration into the spirit of the languages of the Near East, an exegesis enriched by the researches of form criticism, a growing appreciation of rabbinic literature and, not least, the insights conveyed by modern psychology—these all enable theology to come to a proper understanding of the post-biblical role of Israel and to express it in a valid manner.

The First Draft: Decretum de Iudaeis. In accordance with the expressed wish of the plenary meeting, that is, the vote taken then, the first draft, *Decretum de Iudaeis*, was worked out in Ariccia from November 27 to December 2. For this special task, the following members, had been added to the Subcommittee: Bishop Émile de Smedt, Bruges; Msgr., now Cardinal, Jan Willebrands, General Secretary, now President of the Secretariat; and Msgr. Francis Davis, Birmingham.

Before the end of the session, the Subcommittee was able to present the following text:

> The Church, the Bride of Christ, acknowledges with a heart full of gratitude that, according to God's mysterious saving design, the beginnings of her faith and election go as far back as to the Israel of the Patriarchs and Prophets. Thus she acknowledges that all Christian believers, children of Abraham by faith (see Gal 3:7), are included in his call. Similarly, her salvation is prefigured in the deliverance of the Chosen People out of Egypt, as in a sacramental sign (*Liturgy of the Easter Vigil*). And the Church, a new creation in Christ (see Eph 2:15), can never forget that she is the spiritual continuation of the people with whom,

in His mercy and gracious condescension, God made the Old Covenant.

The Church in fact believes that Christ, who "is our peace," embraces Jews and Gentiles with one and the same love and that He made the two one (see Eph 2:14). She rejoices that the union of these two "in one body" (Eph 2:16) proclaims the whole world's reconciliation in Christ. Even though the greater part of the Jewish people has remained separated from Christ, it would be an injustice to call this people accursed, since they are greatly beloved for the sake of the Fathers and the promises made to them (see Rom 11:28). The Church loves this people. From them sprang Christ the Lord, who reigns in glory in heaven; from them sprang the Virgin Mary, mother of all Christians; from them came the Apostles,the pillars and bulwark of the Church (1 Tim 3:15).

Furthermore, the Church believes in the union of the Jewish people with herself as an integral part of Christian hope. With unshaken faith and deep longing the Church awaits union with this people. At the time of Christ's coming, "a remnant chosen by grace" (Rom 11:5), the very first fruits of the Church, accepted the Eternal Word. The Church believes, however, with the Apostle that at the appointed time, the fullness of the children of Abraham according to the flesh will embrace Him who is salvation (see Rom 11:12, 26). Their acceptance will be life from the dead (see Rom 11:15).

As the Church, like a mother, condemns most severely injustices committed against innocent people everywhere, so she raises her voice in loud protest against all wrongs done to Jews, whether in the past or in our time. Whoever despises or persecutes this people does injury to the Catholic Church.

With the completion of the draft on the Jews, the preliminary work was concluded. There seemed to be no obstacle to the Council Father's discussing this draft during the Second Session. Accordingly, at the appropriate time, the Secretariat submitted the draft to the Central Preparatory Commission, whose task it was to oversee all documents destined for the Council Fathers. In the summer of 1962, however, a "bombshell" exploded that seemed to destroy all these plans.

The First Setback, On June 12, Dr. Nahum Goldmann, President of the World Jewish Congress, announced that it intended to dispatch as representative of the Congress in Rome Dr. Chaim Wardi, a senior official of the Ministry of Religious Affairs in the State of Israel. Dr. Wardi worked in the Ministry as an expert in Christian matters. Moreover, he had attended as official observer the World Council of Churches' Third Assembly at New Delhi in the late autumn of 1961, and similarly the pan-Orthodox Conference at Rhodes during September of the same year. In the eyes of the leaders of the World Jewish Congress, these duties seemed to equip him particularly well for his new task, while, for others, they made his appointment suspicious.

As the World Jewish Congress later explained, the appointment was just an attempt to put into practice the principle of having representatives in the world's most important capitals. Dr. Wardi was to serve the Congress as adviser on those Christian affairs that concerned Jews, without intending any special role for him in relation to the Vatican or the Vatican Council.[36] A section of the world's press, however, depicted the matter as if the World Jewish Congress had attempted on its own account to send a diplomatic representative to the Vatican or a semi-official observer to the Council. It is difficult to decide whether the misunderstanding was caused by the journalists' quest for sensation, or by the (perhaps not unintentional) lack of clarity on the part of the leaders of the Congress, or by both.

The announcement aroused general disquiet. Jewish organizations expressed consternation at the proceedings of the Congress. Quite a few Roman officials were offended, as diplomatic representatives are never nominated without previous consultation; no religious communion sent observers to the Council without having been invited. As it appeared from press reports, the imprudence of the Jewish Congress in appointing a government official as its representative made it seem as if they were trying to interfere. The Arab governments saw their worst fears confirmed and let loose a storm of protest against the allegedly preferential treatment of the Jews. It seems that at a given moment Arab leaders assumed that the Jewish Congress' decision had Vatican approval. Yet, they certainly believed that the State of Israel stood behind the plan and was trying to force its way, under false pretenses, into the Council, or at least into its "antechambers."

The result of this unhappy affair was that the Central Preparatory Commission decided, at their last session in June 1962, to remove the draft decree on the Jews from the Council's agenda, not, as some then speculated, on account of the teaching it contained, but simply and solely because of the unfavorable political circumstances then prevailing.[37]

The decision of the Central Preparatory Commission to remove the *Decretum de Iudaeis* from the agenda could easily have led to the question's never being taken up again, so that the first draft would instead have awaited rediscovery by a historian in the Council's archives. Yet, once the question had been brought up, the draft could no longer be ignored. Often it seemed that it was of such weight and force that it created a hearing for itself. In any event, the first draft found persistent advocates.

Though not referring to any definite text, the Chief Rabbi of Rome addressed this message to the Fathers:

> Jews are fully conscious of the great significance of this Council and of the effects that it will have on the spiritual and political life of many nations. May we express the wish that this assembly of the Church will take decisions which may establish peace, mutual understanding, cooperation and tolerance among people. Judaism and Christianity are today conducting a common and difficult struggle for religious freedom, one of the fundamental means of expression in civilization.
>
> Jews hope that the Council, in accordance with the shining example given by Pope John, . . . will understand the need to eliminate all expressions still in use in the Liturgy and in religious instruction which continue even today to evoke mistrust and ill will towards Jews. Jews hope further that the Council Fathers will solemnly and without ambiguity condemn all forms of Antisemitism and also those people who make use of Christian teaching to justify their hostile feelings and actions against the Jewish people and the Jewish religion.[38]

Another advocate of concern for the Jewish people was Bishop Arceo Méndez of Cuernavaca, Mexico, who broached the problem of Jewish-Christian relations in the Council chamber at the beginning of December, 1962. He wanted to know "whether pastors of souls, and the faithful, are following the example of the Pope and showing real love toward the children of our common father Abraham, or whether they are not displaying an unconscious Antisemitism."[39]

By far the most powerful advocate of a Declaration was Cardinal Bea. So convincing was his intervention that he might well be called the father of the Declaration on the Jews. He spoke with sympathy of the anxiety of Christians in the Near East who feared that their religious life would be repressed. He held that, to judge from all appearances, this alarm was deliberately sounded by certain quarters. It would be bad policy to give way to the pressure of the opponents. If one stood firm against this pressure, it would probably crumble into nothing.

Appeal to Pope John. In the wake of the "Wardi Affair," the Cardinal appealed directly to Pope John, requesting that he decide what was to be done. In a memorandum he reminded the Pope that the Secretariat had striven, on the basis of a special mandate, to throw light upon the bond between the Church and the Jewish people. It had drafted a decree which declared, among other things, that the Jewish people, although separated from Christ, was not to be regarded as accursed by God, but was, on the contrary, exceedingly loved by Him and must therefore also be loved by the Church.

Cardinal Bea recalled that the draft had been put before the last session of the Central Preparatory Commission by special papal instruction, but had then been removed from the agenda because of the action of the World Jewish Congress and the excitement caused by the often exaggerated press reports. One had to consider whether reasons, understandable at the time of the initial agitation, still remained valid and were sufficient to remove the problem altogether from the Council's program. He judiciously stated that there were important reasons in favor of taking up the theme again:

[To put the draft *De Iudaeis* before the Council] is demanded by the bond of kinship between Christians and Jews, which is far deeper than the bond which unites all humans. Equally, the incredible and appalling crimes of National Socialism against six million Jews—atrocities for which the ground had been prepared by an extensive propaganda machine—require a purification of spirit and conscience.

One has also to acknowledge that even Catholic preachers have not always been inspired by the spirit of Jesus in their presentation of the Lord's Passion. All too often the Jewish people as such, that is, all generations since Christ, had been accused of deicide and depicted as accursed by God. There is a real need for inner renewal here.

Finally, we ought to be spurred on by the decisive attitude of the World Council of Churches, which adopted a resolution on Antisemitism on December 3, 1961, at its third general assembly in New Delhi. The resolution began by repeating the stand taken by the first Assembly of the World Council in the year 1948 in Amsterdam.

> We call upon all the Churches we represent to denounce Antisemitism, no matter what its origin, as absolutely irreconcilable with the profession and practice of the Christian faith. Antisemitism is a sin against God and humanity. Only as we give convincing evidence to our Jewish neighbors that we seek for them the rights and dignity which God wills for His children, can we come to such a meeting with them as would make it possible to share with them the best which God has given us in Christ.

The resolution of the World Council of Churches continued:

> The [Third] Assembly renews this plea in view of the fact that situations continue to exist in which Jews are subject to discrimination and even persecution. The Assembly urges its member Churches to do all in their power to resist every form of Antisemitism. In Christian teaching, the historic events which led to the Crucifixion should not be presented so as to place upon the Jewish people of today the blame

which belongs to our corporate humanity, not to one
race or community. Jews were the first to accept
Jesus, and Jews are not the only ones who do not yet
recognize Him.[40]

The question of whether the Council Fathers could assume
the reponsibility of bringing new suffering down upon the
Catholics of the Near East was countered by Cardinal Bea with
another question: Was it permissible to endanger the renewal
of the whole Church by discounting the Jewish question for
reasons significant in themselves but still conditioned and
limited by factors of the day? The Cardinal made concrete
proposals and summed up by saying that the Council should
take its stand with apostolic frankness, and overcome obstacles fearlessly, though with deliberation. It was necessary,
indeed absolutely urgent, that the Council discuss the matter.[41]
    On December 13, 1962, Pope John replied with a short per-
sonal note: "We have read Cardinal Bea's memorandum with
care and entirely share his opinion that a profound responsibility requires our intervention." The Pope went on to say that the
words: "His blood be on us and on our children" (Mt 27:25) did
not relieve believers of the duty laid upon them to work for the
salvation of all the children of Abraham and, similarly, that of
every other human being on earth. He ended with the prayer
from the Te Deum: "Help us, then, we entreat You; help Your
servants whom You have ransomed with Your precious blood."
    The second part of the Pope's note seems at first disconcert-
ing. It can be understood only if one realizes that Pope John
knew very well that certain circles wanted to use the difficulties
in the Near East, and also the obscurity of some passages in
Scripture, to persuade the Council to evade its responsibility
for treating the Church's bond to the Jewish people. Moreover,
the prayer with which the Pope sealed his agreement with
Cardinal Bea's memorandum shows that for him, the most
human of Popes, the Declaration on the Jews was not only a
matter of the heart but also an act of faith and a work of piety.
    The public mind, formed and in many ways guided by the
press, became an unexpected helper to the Declaration. It can

be asserted without exaggeration that the efforts made on behalf of the Declaration, as in other Council matters, would have come to nothing, had not the press repeatedly directed the eyes of the world toward them. The regular reports by the great daily newspapers of Arab intrigues and attempted obstruction not only pilloried these activities, but also torpedoed them. One can even go further and say: Had the Arabs not attempted, in various ways, to sabotage the Declaration—and had the press not repeatedly unmasked these intrigues, and, indeed, repudiated them with indignation—the effect of the Declaration would have been significantly less than it was. Had the Declaration been accepted without ado at its first presentation, it might long since have been forgotten. The objections and attempts at intimidation by the Near East Governments and the subsequent reverberations in the press made apparent the extraordinary importance of the Declaration, and carried its proclamation to the furthest corners of the world.

It must also be said, unfortunately, that the communications media did perceptible damage to the Declaration and to other plans of the Council as well. Certain misinterpretations have to be attributed to journalists. Harried editors, nourishing their readers' eagerness for "sensation," composed headlines such as "Acquittal of the Jews by the Council," or "Church Absolves Jews from Guilt of Crucifixion." Here the emphasis of the Declaration is completely distorted. The Council's intention— to restore the Pauline view of the Jewish people and to put an end to certain interpretations of Scripture that contradicted its true meaning—is misunderstood in such a way that the humble revision of a centuries-old stereotype is transformed into a condescending gesture. If some Christians in earlier times were arrogant enough to think that they were chosen by God to punish the Jewish people for its refusal to believe in Christ, now there is attributed to the Council the perhaps even more offensive arrogance to claim for itself God's prerogative of forgiveness. Thus, the press makes the Church appear the epitome of presumption and contradiction: she teaches that a presumed guilt of the Jews does not exist and then is reported to have forgiven that same guilt.

Another Obstacle. Despite John XXIII's call for "tact and discretion," "understanding and accuracy,"[42] correspondents of major newspapers treated rumors as proven facts and their own guesses and constructions as if they were the firmly based results of careful investigation. Journalists would doubtless reply that they were often forced to make guesses because full information was withheld from them. The latter is true. Nevertheless, it must be said that some—to quote John XXIII again—"were more concerned about the speed than the accuracy of reporting," and that they were more interested in "a scoop" than in truth.

To this category belongs the "Weigel incident." At the end of June, 1963, the distinguished ecumenist Fr. Gustave Weigel, S.J., spoke at a meeting of a Jewish umbrella organization, the "National Community Relations Advisory Council," at Atlantic City, New Jersey, on a subject not directly connected with the Declaration. During the discussion that followed, he was caught off guard by a *New York Times* reporter, who asked what the situation was concerning the condemnation of Antisemitism by the Council. As Weigel himself later explained, he replied without sufficient reflection that such a denunciation had indeed been prepared, but that it had not been discussed during the First Session, and probably would not be during the Second, because of the opposition of Arab governments, who had interpreted a purely moral pronouncement as declaration of political support for the State of Israel.

In some points, Fr. Weigel's answer did not fully correspond to the facts: It was never planned to issue merely a condemnation of hatred of Jews. Again, Fr. Weigel was not aware of the most recent state of affairs, as he had not been present at the latest session of the Secretariat. His forecast was, however, trumpeted to the world. It was feared that his answer would make the situation even more difficult. This, thank God, did not happen. In fact, the sensational report may even have aroused consciences. Fr. Weigel frequently indicated that he deeply regretted his overhasty and ill-considered reply. All the same, he could not help seeing the favorable consequences of his "indiscretion."[43] At a meeting of the Secretariat during the Second Session, we happened to sit next to each other. When he saw how well things were going, he took pleasure in the thought that some small credit was due him, and whispered to me that his imprudence had been "a blessing in disguise."

With this recollection, I have somewhat anticipated the course of events in the Council. Cardinal Bea, after Pope John had assured him of his full support, took the necessary steps to bring the Declaration once more before the Coordinating Commission, and thus before the Council. In his judgment, the one great chance of achieving this lay in incorporating the Declaration into the draft on Ecumenism. At his suggestion, this diffident reference to other religions was to precede the Statement on the Jews:

> Having dealt with the basic principle of Catholic Ecumenism, we do not wish to pass over in silence the fact that these principles are also to be applied, with due regard to the given situation, to dialogues and acts of cooperation with people who are not Christians, but adore God or, at least, impelled by God's will, try to keep the moral law implanted in human nature according to their conscience. This is particularly true of the Jews who, after all, are linked to the Church to an extraordinary degree.[44]

The Second Draft: Chapter IV of the Schema on Ecumenism. In addition to this modest introduction, certain other changes were made in the text. Some were purely stylistic. The most important was certainly an additional passage rebutting the charge of deicide and warning catechists and preachers not to fall into a hostile exposition of the Passion story. Another part was inserted into the second draft between the statement establishing that the Jews were not a people accursed by God but ever dear to Him, and the one declaring that the Church has kept in mind that her risen Lord was of Jewish descent, as were His Mother and His Apostles:

> The Chosen People cannot without injustice be termed a deicidal one, as the Lord has expiated through His suffering and death the sins of all, the [actual] cause of [His] Passion and [His] dying (see Lk 23:24; Ac 3:17; 1 Cor 2:8). His death was certainly not brought about by all Jews

living at that time, much less by those of today. Priests must be careful not to say anything in their teaching or sermons that could create hatred of Jews or contempt for them in the hearts of their hearers.

In place of the last two paragraphs in the first draft, the conclusion now read:

As the Church shares with the Jewish people so great a heritage, this holy Synod wishes expressly to encourage and recommend the mutual understanding and respect that is attained by theological studies and brotherly conversations. Further, as the Church repudiates injustices committed against human beings everywhere, similarly, indeed even more, does she deplore and condemn, in the spirit of a mother, the outbreaks of, hatred and the persecutions of which Jews have been the victims, in the past and in our own time.[45]

Although the new draft, as Chapter IV of the Decree on Ecumenism, was approved at the Secretariat's session from February 25 to March 2, 1963, and was later handed over to the Coordinating Commission, it was not sent to the Council Fathers, together with the first three chapters of the schema, before the Council opened. It was issued only on November 8, 1963, that is, two months after the Second Session had opened. The no less embattled Declaration on Religious Freedom, now Chapter V of the draft on Ecumenism, was delivered to the Fathers only on November 16 of the same year. This delay, a consequence of the attitude prevailing in leading Council circles, was very regrettable, as it cut down the time available for study and discussion; still, it was not able to stop progress of these two drafts.

The impossibility of silencing the desire for clarification of the relation of the Church and the Jewish people was due to the fact that, within the first week of the Second Session, Bishops had stood up in the *aula* to urge that this theme be dealt with.[46] On October 2, 1963, Bishop Johannes van Dodewaard, Haarlem, recommended, in the name of the Dutch hierarchy, that the Church give renewed expression to the close bond between the Church and the Jewish people. In anticipation of the text, he called the children of Abraham a people who belonged in their God-given nature to the true olive tree (Rom 11:24) and who for the sake of their Fathers were especially dear to God. Whereas in the language that prevailed before the Council, the Jews were termed *perfidi*, "unbelievers," and reckoned among the *infideles*, Bishop van Dodewaard called them *populus ille fidelis*, "that faithful people." As he himself later declared, he saw beyond the people's unbelief in Christ, and the abandonment of the traditions of their Fathers by many of them today, to their vocation as the people of faith. Above all, he saw in them the people to whom God had pledged His unchanging troth. Whatever Israel's shortcomings or failures might be, God is its faithful Shepherd.

On October 3, 1963, Archbishop (later, Cardinal) Franz Sheper, Zagreb, asked that in the treatment of the mystery of the Church, the place occupied by the Chosen People in God's plan of salvation be described as precisely as possible. He stressed that the people of Israel was not rejected by God, that it rather shared with the Church a common heritage. "The Jews have far more in common with the Church than have all other peoples." The Archbishop himself later explained that, in order not to overrun the prescribed time limit for speeches, he left unspoken the final sentence of his prepared text: *Nemo est qui non viderit populi Israelitici relationem erga Ecclesiam omnino specialem esse, cum nullo populo communem*, "No one can remain unaware that the relationship of the people of Israel to the Church is a quite special one, unlike that of any other people."

Like a bolt out of the blue, on November 18, the leaders of the Eastern Churches struck out against Chapter IV. Since no discussion was planned, those who favored Chapter IV were not prepared to speak; they were waiting for the day reserved for statements on this matter. Those opposed, however, made use of the general debate on the draft on Ecumenism to proclaim their rejection of the Chapter on the Jews. They fell into two groups: those who wished to give way to the pressure of the Arab governments, and others who in fact supported the

statement as such, but thought it a mistake to include it in the
schema on Ecumenism.

Cardinal Tappouni, Patriarch of the Syriac Rite at Antioch,
objected to treating statements about the Jews and about religious freedom together with that of Christian unity. He
acknowledged that those who had worked for the text were
guided by spiritual motives, but the current political situation
was such that it could too easily be misunderstood. In countries
hostile to the Jews, Chapter IV would do the Christian Church
serious harm.

Coptic Rite Patriarch Stefanos I of Alexandria spoke in the
same vein as Cardinal Tappouni. In a discussion of Christian
unity it was completely out of place to devote a whole chapter to
the Jews, he said. Furthermore, when the Nazis persecuted the
Jews, the Church had given clear proof of her attitude. On
other occasions, measures that might have made the Church's
position in various countries more difficult had been avoided.
Why not in this instance? The difficulties under which the
Church was living in the Near East were already great enough
without adding a gratuitous provocation.

The Melchite Patriarch of Antioch, Maximos IV, was of
exactly the same opinion as the previous speakers: "Ecumenism is the striving for reunion of the entire Christian family,
that is, the reconciliation of all who are baptized in Christ." It
was impossible to understand how the Jews got into a draft on
Christian Ecumenism. If one really wished to speak of the Jews
at the Council, that could be done either in the document on the
Church or in that of the Church in the Modern World. In his
account of the Second Session, Antoine Wenger, A.A., entitles
the corresponding chapter: "When Politics Held Theology in
Chains." He writes: "The unity of the three Patriarchs living in
Arab countries was all the more remarkable as Patriarch Maximos usually disagreed with the other two in theological
matters."[47]

On November 19, 1963, these three were joined by the Latin
Patriarch of Jerusalem, Alberto Gori, and the Armenian Patriarch of Cilicia, Peter XVI. The former approved of the Council's
taking an interest in non-Christians, but maintained that it
should treat either all non-Christian religions or none. Favor-

ing the Jews would endanger Christian minorities in many countries. The Armenian Patriarch also held that the chapter on the Jews fell outside this framework. To quote Fr. Wenger again: "On hearing these interventions, we felt uneasy. It seemed to us that, from a theological point of view, the draft on Ecumenism provided the natural setting for discussion of the Jewish question."[48]

There were other speakers, such as Cardinal Léger of Montreal, Canada, who welcomed the statement on the Jews and religious freedom, but wanted these themes to be discussed in a different context. A special position was taken up by Cardinal Ruffini of Palermo, who declared as early as the first day that if one really wished to speak of the Jews, one should also deal with other religions whose adherents were less hostile to the Church than the Jews.[49]

An Ecumenical Concern. The objection of those who reacted against the inclusion of the Jewish question and that of religious freedom in a decree on Ecumenism seemed plausible. It is, however, noteworthy that theologically trained commentators, like Fr. Wenger, and the experts whose special field was the relation of the Church and the Jewish people, approved the inclusion of the draft concerning the proper attitude towards the Jewish people in that on Ecumenism. The supporters of that inclusion knew that the original reason for it was not theological, but arose purely out of practical considerations of Conciliar politics.

When asked by some journalists whether the Declaration on the Jews would not be better attached to the Declaration on the Church in the Modern World rather than to the Decree on Ecumenism, I stated:

> Human relations exist on various levels. . . . The relation of Christians and Jews is no exception. Its most obvious element is the social one. In the society of today, Christians and Jews live side by side. They are neighbors. . . . Their social proximity and equality as citizens—both characteristics of a pluralistic world—are without doubt of the greatest importance. Yet, in my opinion, it is not the task of an Ecumenical Council to discuss the constitutional privi-

leges of Jews and Christians and their respective place in the political sphere.

A much more basic and fundamental element in social and political relations between Jews and Christians is their life as persons. Every Christian, every Jew, is a person, and that means more than merely a member of a group . . . he or she is a special thought of God in the flesh, unique and unrepeatable. Few things have to be so much emphasized today as the respect due to each single human being. . . . Humans possess a dignity that has no equivalent among the other living things on this earth. For this reason the Council, at the beginning of its First Session, proclaimed the exalted status of each human being in a solemn "Message to Humanity."

The relation of Christians and Jews has, however, another, deeper dimension that is peculiar to it: a dimension rooted, not in common human nature or citizenship, but in sacred events in which both have a part, that is, in the history of salvation.

Abraham, the Father of the Jewish people, is at the same time the Father of all who believe in the living God, in the "goodness and loving Kindness of God our Savior, revealed to us in Jesus Christ" (Ti 3:4). "Peerless Abraham, Father of faith," the Roman Liturgy calls him. All the Patriarchs, Prophets, and Psalmists, all the Just of the Old Covenant, but also its sinners, are the spiritual forebears of Christians. Thus, it comes about that the world's salvation is most intimately linked to the glory of Israel, but also to its failure; to its election, but also to its "misstep" (Rom 11:1, 11).[50]

This dimension suggests the ecumenical vision of the mystery of Israel; it would thus justify the inclusion of the statement on the Jews in the decree On Ecumenism, though it does not make it mandatory.

In the daily conference at the American Press Office, Gregory Baum, too, defended the placement of the statement on the Jews in the decree On Ecumenism:

1. We believe that the roots of the Church are in the Israel of old. To understand her mystery one must turn to the

people of Israel. The Church is grafted onto the well-cultivated olive tree.

2. The division of the Jewish people into those who accepted Jesus as Messiah and those who did not accept Him prefigures all the subsequent schisms within Christianity.

3. Christians believe that Israel is part of the eschatological dimension of the Church, in accordance with the saying of St. Paul, who teaches that the Church and Israel will be a single people.[51]

Those who approved the new framework for the Declaration included René Laurentin, theologically one of the best-schooled commentators, who wrote:

It is said "Ecumenism is the union of Christians. Jews are not Christians. Therefore they are not included in Ecumenism."

Now it is certainly true that Israel's position is not that of Orthodox Christians and Protestants who explicitly profess their faith in Christ. Israel's position is unique. . . . It is important to recall certain fundamental facts:

1. We have common roots or, to put it more exactly, the same roots as Israel:

Common writings, the whole Old Testament which speaks of Christ. "He wrote of me," said Jesus of Moses (Jn 5:46; see 5:39; 8:58; 12:41; etc.).

A common history, the whole history before Christ, but not that alone. Jesus lived within Judaism and its laws. He sought out "the lost sheep of the house of Israel" (Mt 15:24). The Virgin Mary, the Twelve, and the principal witnesses to the faith of the first Christian generation were part of the Jewish people. At her beginnings, the Church lived within the framework of Judaism. The problem of baptizing Gentiles seems to have arisen only some years later (Ac 11:19). For hundreds of years Jews (including proselytes) had a special position in this respect, corresponding to the practice recorded in Ac 8:36-38 and 9:18. They were regarded as fit for immediate baptism the moment they acknowledged Jesus Christ. Adherence to Judaism was equivalent to the catechumenate.

One can, accordingly, speak of common roots in a quite special sense: "It is not you that support the root, but the root that supports you," says St. Paul to the community of Rome with its many Gentile members (Rom 11:18). Indeed, it is not enough to speak of a root, it is much more a question of a common stem. According to St. Paul, Israel is still "the well cultivated olive tree" onto which [the Gentiles] were grafted "contrary to nature." The "natural branches" are summoned to return to life (Rom 11:17-25).

2. There is a unity of goal and destiny. Israel is still the Chosen People, and "all Israel will be saved" (Rom 11:26, 32, etc.).

3. The rift between Israel and the Church—which is, in any case, only partial—is nothing but a parenthesis, an unnatural situation which at the deepest level forms part of the mystery of salvation and contributes to its realization (see Rom 11:14, 18-22, 30-31).

4. There is a deep solidarity and even a certain unity between Israel and the Church in their expectation of oneness at the end of time. Christ has made Jews and Gentiles one "and has broken down the dividing wall of hostility . . . that He might create in Himself one new man in place of the two" (Eph 2:14-15).

If it is the intention of Ecumenism to create a universal community based on the fullness of Christian values, it cannot discount the vocation of Israel—a vocation included unambiguously within that of the Church. Thus, St. Paul cannot imagine the Church's eschatological fulfillment without Israel.[52]

So far as I know, the ecumenical theologian[53] who first dealt in detail with "Israel as an ecumenical problem" was Bernard Lambert, O.P. He wrote:

Judaism remains outside the Church: yet it never ceases to act on and in the Church. It acts in the Church through the Jewish origins of Christianity. It acts on the Church in virtue of a kind of destined solidarity that brings Jews and Christians together at all the great crossroads of history. The Jew cannot lose sight of the Christian, the Christian cannot ignore the Jew. Something unique brings us together and yet separates us, as if neither of us can quite

pass the other. The relations between us are governed by
an odd alternation of rejection and acceptance....

The problem of Israel is not extra-ecumenical. It concerns the reconciliation of the two parts of the *Oikoumenē*:
the Jews and the Gentiles. For measured by God's plan for
human salvation, this is the fundamental division of
humanity: on the one hand, the Jewish people, the People
of the Covenant; and on the other, the pagans, the Gentiles. Neither the Old Testament nor the New knows
another division of human society in the economy of salvation: on the one hand, so very few, from whom, however,
came salvation; on the other, the mass of humanity. The
question is not one of numbers, but of election and new
birth. Abraham was chosen to be the Father of all believers, the starting-point of a new humanity moving forward
in faith to the promised land, gathering in as many Gentile
peoples as it pleased God to lead that way. . . .

An ecumenism that limited itself simply to the relations
among Christians would, in principle, be condemned never
to succeed, because it would be established on too narrow a
foundation.[54]

I have described in some detail the views of those who regard
the relation of the Church and the Jewish people as an ecumenical, indeed, *the* ecumenical problem because in those days this
question stirred the minds of many. Despite the help of theologians and journalists, and the support of Bishops and Bishops'
Conferences for the thesis it contained, Chapter IV of the draft
on Ecumenism was denied success. On the second day of the
general debate, November 20, 1963, Cardinal Meyer of Chicago
applauded the draft. He found especially praiseworthy the
inclusion of Chapters IV and V. It was true, he said, there are
differences of opinion as to whether these two chapters are
correctly placed, but it is the wish of many of the Fathers,
particularly of those from North America, that the draft
remain as it stands.

Bishop Jelmini of Lugano, in the name of all the Swiss
Bishops expressed his joy that the Church could be seen in this
draft, not as a closed community, but as one open to the world.
He thought it desirable to speak here not only about the Jews,
but also about the adherents of Islam, and even about unbe-

176 THE NEW ENCOUNTER

lievers. A succession of Bishops greeted the draft as "an event, truly a gift of God's grace." This latter description comes from the Mexican Bishop Méndez, who laid particular stress on the bond between the Jews and the Church in salvation history, and declared, no doubt in deliberate reference to the opposite opinion of the Near Eastern Bishops: "It is extremely opportune to condemn the hatred of Jews."[55]

All these interventions seemed to be of no avail. Although on November 21, 1963, the Council's Secretary General, Archbishop Felici, offered the prospect of an early discussion ("in the immediate future"), none took place. To overcome the deadlock that seemed to have been reached, Bishop Helmsing of Kansas City concluded his speech of November 29 concerning Chapters II and III of the draft with an urgent demand that in the few remaining days at their disposal, the Council Fathers proceed to a decisive vote on Chapters IV and V.

"The Bishop gave expression to the concern and indeed the anger of many Council Fathers lest [the total silence concerning any discussion] might prove to be a well-planned attempt to delay a decision on these chapters and to bring the Session to an end without their coming to the promised vote."[56] This fear was only too justified. The Council closed on December 4 without having taken the procedural vote on whether to accept or reject a given draft as a basis for discussion. Only such a vote would have made the two chapters into an unalterable part of the Council proceedings and have thus withdrawn them from the competence of the Coordinating Commission.

Ups and Downs. There was no discussion, but when the possibility of such a defeat had to be taken into account, Cardinal Bea was, curiously, given the opportunity to expound Chapter IV of the draft on Ecumenism to the Fathers. In his presentation, the Cardinal began by pointing out that this chapter dealt with a question that was not political but religious. He said:

> The aim of this very brief decree is to call to the attention
> of Christ's faithful these truths concerning the Jews that
> are affirmed by the Apostle and contained in the deposit of

faith, and to do this so clearly that in dealing with the children of that people the faithful will act in no other way than did Christ the Lord and His Apostles Peter and Paul.[57]

Of much more importance, in fact simply decisive, is the example of burning charity of the Lord Himself on the Cross, praying: "Father, forgive them, for they know not what they do." This is the example to be imitated by the Church, the Bride of Christ. That is the road to be followed by her. This is what the draft proposed by us intends to foster and promote.[58]

Felicitous as is the reference to the two Apostles, that to our Lord's prayer on the Cross (Lk 23:34) is questionable.[59] It was hardly the Jewish people for whom our Lord asked forgiveness here, but only those immediately concerned with the Crucifixion: that is, the high priestly clique, the Governor, the soldiers, and those who mocked. If the Lord's prayer for forgiveness of His tormentors is mentioned in connection with this issue in the Council discussion, the impression could easily arise that Christians are called upon to display mercy toward Jews, whereas what the Christian world truly owes to Jewry and Judaism is, in the first place, justice.

My great respect for the Cardinal and his wisdom and goodness notwithstanding, I must say that this urgent request to the Council to imitate our Lord in its conduct toward the Jewish people, and to teach others to do likewise, was mistaken for the notion that the Council had, so to say, absolved the Jewish people from the guilt of the Crucifixion. A distinguished observer from the Dutch Reformed Church, in a public discussion with me, misinterpreted this passage of the Cardinal's speech to mean that the Church was presuming to forgive the Jews. This, of course, is to misjudge the Cardinal's intention. His plea meant no more and no less than that the cause of Chapter IV represented not only the legacy of Pope John XXIII but also, and above all, the will of Christ.

The question of why it was necessary to drive home yet again the truths set out in the draft was answered by the Cardinal in these words:

> Some decades ago Antisemitism, as it is called, was preva-
> lent in various regions and in an exceptionally violent and
> criminal form in Germany under the rule of National
> Socialism, which through hatred for the Jews committed
> frightful crimes, extirpating several millions of Jewish
> people—we need not at the moment seek the exact number.
> Moreover, accompanying and assisting this whole
> activity was a most powerful and effective propaganda
> against the Jews.[60]

The Cardinal went on to say that this propaganda might well
have had a pernicious effect upon Catholic Christians, too,
especially as it often pretended to draw its arguments from the
New Testament and from Church history. He pointed out that
the Declaration was principally concerned with the proper
understanding of Scripture and a true interpretation of the
intentions of the Apostles and Evangelists, and thus with the
rebirth of the Church.

His next sentence was truly one of the most impressive and
illuminating of the whole speech:[61]

> Since the Church in this Council is striving to renew itself
> by "seeking again the features of its most fervent youth,"
> as John XXIII of venerable memory said, it seems impera-
> tive to take up this question.[61]

The quotation from Pope John comes from his address of
November 14, 1960. In the original it reads: *ricercare le tracce
della giovinezza più fervorosa.*[62] Following the will of John
XXIII, the Church sought, in the Declaration on the Jews, as in
the Council itself, to rediscover the imprint of her Pentecostal
zeal so that her countenance might again become as fresh and
pure as in the days of her "first love" (see Ap 2:4).

The Pilgrimage to the Holy Land. From all evidence available,
it seems that discussion of Chapter IV was postponed to facilitate Pope Paul VI's pilgrimage to the Holy Land. In fact, Paul
VI hoped this journey of prayer would help expedite the issu-
ance of the Declaration. The idea of such a pilgrimage, a return

to the "cradle of Christianity,"[63] was a stroke of genius that seemed to justify the postponement of the debate. If inspiration were equivalent to success in this world, then the journey of January 4 to 6, 1964, would surely have cleared the way for the Declaration on the Jews. On January 6, the Pope declared, in Bethlehem, that the "mission of Christianity was one of friendship among peoples, of understanding, of encouragement, of furthering, of lifting up and, to say it again, one of salvation."[64]

Thus Paul VI, as *Le Monde* acknowledged with respect on January 7, 1964, "was the first to dare speak of peace on either side of the Israel-Arab border." In the same spirit, he quoted to King Hussein of Jordan, on January 4, the words of the Psalm which St. Peter had already made his own (1 Pt 3:10-11):

> He that would love life and see good days,
> let him keep his tongue from evil
>   and his lips from speaking guile;
> let him turn away from evil and do right;
> let him seek peace and pursue it.

(See Ps 34:12-16.)

When the Pope entered the Holy city, he turned to the officials and the inhabitants of Old Jerusalem and called out:

> Jerusalem! At this moment in which we stand within your walls, the joyful song of the inspired author comes to our lips: "May they prosper who love you. Peace be within your walls, and security within your towers . . . peace be within you . . . I will seek your good" (Ps 122: 6-9).

On taking leave of the people and the King in Amman, the Pope saluted them with the words *Salam aleikum!* and warned with apostolic earnestness: "Put away all bitterness, wrath, anger, clamor, slander, indeed, all malice. Be kind to one another, tender-hearted, forgiving one another, as God in Christ forgave you" (Eph 4:31-32).

On entering Israeli territory on January 5, the Pope was greeted by the President of the State of Israel, Zalman Shazar.

Paul IV closed his speech of thanks with a renewed call for peace:

> As a pilgrim of peace, we beg above all for the blessing of a humanity reconciled with God and of deep and genuine concord among people and nations. May God hear our prayer, God who, as the prophet proclaims, has plans for our "welfare and not for evil" (Jer 29:11). May He in His goodness pour forth upon the tormented world of today that incomparable gift, whose echo resounds on every page of the Bible. With it we are glad to sum up our greeting, our prayer, and our desire: "Shalom, shalom."[65]

During the penitential devotions led by him in the Church of the Holy Sepulcher in Jerusalem, on January 4, 1964, the Pope took up another theme: the inadequacy of Christian witness in the world, the manifold failures of Christianity in the course of history. In his own name and that of all Christians, he uttered this confession:

> Lord Jesus,
> We have come here as guilty people
>   to the place of our crime.
> We have come like the one who followed You
>   and yet betrayed You.
> We have so often been both true and false.
> We have come to proclaim the mysterious link
>   between our sins and Your suffering,
>   between our deeds and Your redeeming work.
> We have come to beat our breast,
>   to ask for Your forgiveness,
>   to implore Your mercy.
> We have come because we know that You have
>   the power and the will to forgive us,
>   because You have atoned for us,
> You, our salvation, You, our hope.[66]

No less significant were several signs of the Pope's respect for the Jewish people. His first words in Israel witnessed to the emotion he experienced on seeing and walking on the land where in days past lived the Patriarchs, our Fathers in the faith, where the voices of the Prophets resounded through the centuries in the name of the God of Abraham, Isaac and Jacob; the land that, finally and above all, the presence of Jesus Christ has blessed and made holy forever for Christians and, one can truly say, for all humankind. From this land, unique in the grandeur of the events it has witnessed, our humble entreaty goes up to God, on behalf of all people, believers and unbelievers. We gladly include therein the children of the People of the Covenant, whose part in the religious history of humanity we can never forget.[67]

It was, no doubt, the sign of a new vision of Jewish existence and of the new relationship of Christians and Jews that Cardinal Tisserant, who accompanied the Pope on the journey, as well as a dignitary of the Eastern Orthodox Church lit candles at Israel's Memorial of the Martyrs, to honor the memory of the Jewish victims of Nazism. Jews, however, were disappointed that in all his communications Pope Paul avoided calling the Holy Land by the name Israel. Had the Pope been confronted with this criticism, he probably would have remarked that, indeed, he avoided "Israel" out of delicacy, that is, so as not to worsen the tensions between Arabs and Jews.

The highlight of the pilgrimage was, however, neither the encounter with representatives of the Islamic and Arab world, nor that with representatives of the State of Israel, but the brotherly meeting of the Church of the West with that of the East. Late in the evening of January 5, 1964, the Ecumenical Patriarch of Constantinople, Athenegoras I, on the occasion of his visit to the Pope at the Apostolic Delegation in Jerusalem, said to Paul VI:

Venerable brother in Christ . . . for centuries the Christian world has been living in the darkness of separation. Her eyes are tired of straining into this darkness. May this meeting become the dawn of a bright and blessed day in which coming generations will partake of the same chalice of the Lord's holy body and precious blood, in which they

will praise and glorify the one Lord and Savior of the world
in love, peace and unity.[68]

After an exchange of gifts and joint recitation of the Our
Father in Greek and Latin, the Pope took the Patriarch's arm
and led him to the door, at which the Patriarch exclaimed: *Oui,
la main dans la main pour toujours*, "Yes, hand in hand
forever."[69]

The Pope's pilgrimage left a powerful impression. "This
Pope is a man of spirit, of courage. He is making history.
Christianity presses . . . toward a new vitality." Thus wrote a
German newspaper,[70] while an American paper summed up the
event: "A lodestar is risen, a goal has been set."[71] Despite such
manifestations of joyful approval, the pilgrimage did not fulfill
the expectations of those who had hoped for a relaxation of the
political situation in the Near East and, with it, an end to Arab
opposition to the Declaration on the Jews. Although the Pope
had come, not simply as a pilgrim, but almost as a beggar for
peace, the Jordanian radio repeatedly punctuated its reports in
Arabic with this hateful remark: "Two thousand years ago, the
Jews crucified Christ, and fifteen years ago, they attacked the
people of Palestine." Again: "Truly of all the world religions it
is the Jews who are the enemies of God. Truly, the crimes of the
Jews shall never be forgiven them."[72]

The Jordanian radio seemed to let no opportunity pass to stir
up hatred against the Jews. On leaving the State of Israel, Paul
VI took up the defense of Pius XII against the crude and malicious attacks made by the German dramatist Hochhuth. Some
were alienated by this farewell speech. In my opinion, the
Pope's intention was to ask Jews not to pay attention to those
who were spreading slanders and trying to sow seeds of dis-
cord. To many people, however, it seemed as if the Pope were
holding the Jews, not the dramatist, responsible for the play
"The Deputy." A Jordanian newspaper, in its coarse way,
wrote that Pope Paul's defense of his predecessor against the
charge of not having stood by the Jews in the face of the Nazis'
attempt to exterminate them, was a refutation of the accusations of the "Jewish propaganda apparatus." An Israeli paper,
the *Jerusalem Post*, countered that "whatever our opinions are

in this matter, one could not be but deeply moved by the courage and frankness of the Pope's plea."[73]

It is appropriate to remark here that from the very outset there have been Jewish voices expressing dissociation from the play and its thesis, though quite a number of Jews, still under the traumatic influence of the Hitler years, did welcome Hochhuth's attempt to shift the guilt from "the many" in the West and lay it on the shoulders of one man. It was not long, however, before they realized that the playwright was by no means a friend of the Jews. All Jews who appear in the play are caricatures and freaks; not one of them is an upright man. One of them speaks in accents which seem to have been taken from an Antisemitic handbook. When Jacobson, who has "been in hiding" as Gerstein's librarian, hears that his parents have passed through the Nazi death factory, he bursts out: "I wish to go only in order to return as an avenger .... I will come back—a murderer myself . . . as a bomber pilot. Murder for murder. Incendiary for gas, fire for fire!" In a stage direction, Hochhuth describes this downtrodden man as speaking with "almost Old Testament-like harshness" (Act 1, Scene 3).

It could be deduced from the statements of the Jordanian radio and press that the Arabs were not going to allow the Pope's pilgrimage to have any effect upon their propaganda machine, not to mention their further pressure on the Vatican. This pressure must have been greater than was publicly apparent. If it seemed to some that the Secretariat for Unity had slackened its grip on the reins and was letting itself drift rudderless, this was a false impression. Such a judgment of the situation discounts the pressure to which the leaders of the Secretariat were subjected, and betrays the irresponsibility of the armchair strategist, or of criticism based on hindsight. At any rate, at a plenary session of the Secretariat in Ariccia, from February 24 to March 6, 1964, to which, however, not all non-episcopal members and advisers were invited, a new text was produced. This revealed only too clearly the wounds inflicted by the Declaration's opponents. An attempt had been made, by omissions and by watering down many expressions, to appease its enemies. In order to take into account the formal objections to Chapter IV, the Declaration was now banished to the

184 THE NEW ENCOUNTER

appendix of the draft on Ecumenism. The one on religious liberty was similarly treated. The two drafts were now called the "First" and "Second"' Declaration, corresponding to the time of their completion and delivery to the Fathers.

The Third Draft: Appendix to the Declaration on Ecumenism. In the "Second Declaration," that is, the third draft of the Declaration on the Jews, the Church gladly acknowledged that the beginnings of her faith and her election were to be found in the Israel of the Patriarchs and Prophets. Nor could she forget that she, although a new creation in Christ, continued God's covenant with Israel. She further believed that her Lord had suffered and died freely for the sins of all people. She remained conscious that Mary, Mother of Christ, and the Apostles, the pillars of the Church, sprang from the Jewish people. For the sake of her common heritage with Judaism, the Council encouraged and promoted studies and discussion that would further mutual knowledge and respect. The Church rejected and deplored outbreaks of hatred and persecution against Jews, whether in the past or in our own times. She warned [all to whom this applied] not to represent the Jewish People—in religious instruction, preaching, or ordinary conversation—as accursed or deicidal. Furthermore, nothing should be said that could produce hatred or contempt for Jews in the hearts of those who heard it. To do so would be contrary to the will of Christ, who loves Jews and Gentiles with one and the same love.

In my opinion, a solid frame had been left here, but only a frame. It lacked any links with Pauline theology. What the advocates of this version expected from its meagerness of expression is not clear to me. The hatred of the State of Israel by Arab governments and their fear of Judaism's dignity being restored were so deeply rooted that no impression could be made on them by minor concessions. Despite all whittling down, the Coordinating Commission was not satisfied with the new text and summarily recast it—an extraordinary and unprecedented proceeding. It was now entitled On the Jews and Non-Christians.

The Evangelical pastor Johann Christoph Hampe, an always

astute and usually well-informed commentator, though occasionally erring in detail, was on firm ground in what he wrote
about the period between the Second and Third Sessions.

> There must have been, during the summer of 1964, a new
> and still more ominous phase in the destiny of the state-
> ment on the Jews, which called into question its whole
> future. The Coordinating Commission did not approve the
> latest text, and the State Secretariat was again clearly
> impressed by the Arab opposition within the Unity Secre-
> tariat, under its leading spokesman, Bishop Mansourati. It
> was at this time that a plan appeared to separate the
> chapter on the Jews completely from the draft on Ecumen-
> ism and to hand over the task of producing it to the newly-
> formed Secretariat for Non-Christian Religions. But since
> this Secretariat had nothing to do with the Council and
> was, therefore, not entitled to submit drafts to it for discus-
> sion, and a draft on all religions did not exist, the proposal
> amounted to an attempt to abandon any statement on the
> Jewish question. Exposed by the world's press, this
> attempt was defeated. It looked as if the statement as given
> above, in the form and place already indicated, would come
> before the Council at the beginning of the third session.
> Experts in this field hoped for a short debate and a positive
> vote.[74]

Through an indiscretion, the revised form of the "Second
Declaration" reached first the American and then the world
press. The immediate reactions were anger, sorrow, and
lament. In many circles, this unconsidered response, based
upon inadequate translation, was all there was. The Declaration was divided into three sections, of which the first spoke of
the "heritage which Christians have in common with Jews."
This was its wording:

> The Church of Christ gladly acknowledges that in
> accordance with God's mysterious saving design, the
> beginning of her faith and her election go as far back as to
> the Israel of the Patriarchs and Prophets. Thus she pro-
> fesses that all Christian believers, children of Abraham by
> faith (see Gal 3:7), are included in his call. Similarly, their

salvation is prefigured, as in a sacramental sign, in the deliverance of the Chosen People out of the land of bondage.

For this reason, the Church, "new creation" in Christ (see Eph 2:15) and People of the New Covenant, cannot forget that she is [at the same time] the spiritual continuation of that people with whom God in earlier times, through His inexpressible mercy and gracious condescension, made the Old Covenant, and to whom He entrusted according to His will the Revelation contained in the books of the Old Testament.

Nor does the Church forget that Christ springs, according to the flesh, from the Jewish people; from them descends the Virgin Mary, mother of Christ; from them come the Apostles, the foundations and pillars of the Church.

The Church also keeps, and will always keep, in mind the words of the Apostle concerning the Jews, that "to them belong the sonship, the glory, the covenant, the giving of the Law, the worship, and the promises" (Rom 9:4).

Since Christians have in this way received so great an inheritance from the Jews, this holy Synod wishes emphatically to promote and recommend the mutual knowledge and respect that is achieved by theological studies and brotherly discussion. In addition, she strongly deplores and condemns outbreaks of hatred and acts of violence against Jews, just as she strongly disapproves of injustices committed against human beings everywhere.

In addition, it is worthy of remembrance that the union of the Jewish people with the Church is a part of Christian hope. With unshaken faith and deep longing, the Church awaits, in accordance with the Apostle's teaching, the entry of this people into the fullness of the People of God which Christ has founded (Rom 11:25-26).

May all, therefore, take care, that in catechetical instruction, in preaching the Word of God, and in daily conversation, the Jewish people is not represented as rejected, and equally that nothing is said or done that could alienate minds from the Jews. They should also guard against attributing what was done during Christ's Passion to the Jews of our time.[75]

In passing, it may be of some profit to quote here a rendering by the German Evangelical minister, Jörgen Zink, of Romans 9:4, which one could well call a modern targum:

> God gives them the prerogative to be His sons. Splendor and light, His loving-kindness and His holy nearness rest on them. God has bound and obligated Himself to them. They know how to worship God worthily by their celebrations and feasts. They have promises for their future and know He will be the succor of His people.

The next two sections of the "Second Declaration" were entitled "The Fatherhood of God Over All People" and "The Abomination of Demeaning and Wronging Others." In the first of them, it is said that the Lord Jesus wondrously confirmed the teaching of the Old Testament and the light of human intuition that God is the Father of all. Christians cannot invoke and adore Him as Father of the human race as long as they refuse to meet all people as brothers and sisters created in His image. Every "No" to brotherly and sisterly love among people is ultimately a "No" to God.

In obedience to the love for our brothers and sisters [urged upon us by Christ], we ought to give real attention to the opinions and teachings [of non-Christians] which, though they differ from our own in many ways, contain nevertheless many rays of that truth which enlightens everyone on earth. This applies above all to Muslims, who worship the one God, just Judge that He is, and stand close to us not only in religion but also in many cultural achievements.

As far as the wrongness of discriminating against others is concerned, the draft said that the sense of kinship makes it impossible to differentiate between one person and another, or one people and another, in relation to their human dignity and their rights. All people of good will, therefore, especially Christians, should avoid every kind of degradation and persecution of others, whether on account of their origin, color, religion, or status. Furthermore, with burning love the Council summoned all Christians to "maintain good conduct among the Gentiles" (1 Pt 2:12) and, so far as lay in their power, to live peaceably with all (see Rom 12:18). The Council also enjoined Christians to love not only their neighbors, but also their supposed enemies, that they might be true children of their Father in heaven who made His sun to shine upon all (see Mt 5:44-45).[76]

A New Draft. On September 25, 1964, Cardinal Bea solemnly introduced another draft of the Declaration. He began by saying that no other draft had so held the public mind in suspense, and had been discussed so widely in papers and journals. The interest was so deep that one might well say: Many people will judge the Council by the stand it takes on this question. This interest, however, was not the foremost reason why it was impossible to delete the "Jewish question" from the list of subjects to be considered by the Council. Its necessity arose much more out of the Church's faithfulness "in following the example of Christ and His disciples in love for [their people]."[77]

The Cardinal went on to say that the further work done on the draft submitted during the Second Session was to be explained by the fact that the Secretariat had thoroughly examined the suggestions made by the Council Fathers and had made careful use of them. At the same time, he gently reminded the Bishops that the text now before them did not originate with the Secretariat, when he said: "The members of the Coordinating Commission of the Council know, too, that this short document took a great deal of their time."[78]

The principal part of the Declaration that spoke of the Jews was that of deicide. Its treatment had been considerably altered. The question was whether and in what manner the Jewish people as such was guilty of condemning and crucifying Jesus. Many of today's Jews are of the opinion that this prejudice of Jewish culpability is the principle root of hatred of Jews and thus the source of the many evils and persecutions

Jews suffered over the centuries. The Cardinal emphasized that this opinion could not be sustained; it was nevertheless indisputable that, in the course of the history of various peoples, the notion of a universal Jewish guilt misled many Christians "to consider and name Jews a deicidal people, rejected and cursed by God; this [those Christians] held to be a warrant for despising, even persecuting them."[79] For this reason Jews today expect the Council to condemn solemnly such an attitude.

The point to be discussed now, the Cardinal continued, is whether the Council should declare that Jesus' death must not be charged to the Jewish people as a whole, and if this is the Council's wish, in what way it should be done. There can be no question of impugning the findings of Scripture or denying any point of doctrine contained in the Gospel. The question is rather this: the leaders of the Sanhedrin in Jerusalem, though not elected by the people, were doubtless to be regarded as the legitimate authority according to the ideas of that time and of Scripture itself.

The Cardinal's statement needs, I think, some qualification. Undoubtedly, "the authorities" were in possession of their office; it would scarcely have occurred to the majority of Judaeans to question such problems of principle. But we must not forget that the men of Qumran, however insignificant they may have been in number, denied the legitimacy of the high priests of their day. The high priests, descended from the Hasmoneans, received their positions by the "largesse" of the Romans, not the grace of God. The procurators, who were by no means averse to bribes, appointed and dismissed the high priests quite arbitrarily. Since these frequent dismissals were illegal—the office of high priest was for life—it is hardly possible to consider the subsequent appointments fully valid. Now and again, one or another of the "aristocratic" families sought to snatch the high-priestly office with the assistance of armed bands. We must keep in mind that the people, to all appearances, had no confidence that members of aristocratic families, especially that of Annas, were exercising their office properly.

At any rate, the people hated the incumbents of this high office. The Talmud has preserved this lament:

Woe is me because of the house of Boethius,
  woe is me because of their clubs!
Woe is me because of the house of Ḥanin,
  woe is me because of their whisperings!
Woe is me because of the house of Ḳathros,
  woe is me because of their pens!

Woe is me because of the house of Ishmael ben Phabi,
  woe is me because of their fists!
For they are high priests
  and their sons [Temple] treasurers,
  their sons-in-law trustees,
  while their servants beat the people with their clubs.

(*b Pes.* 57a)[80]

The fact that the high priests were considered legitimate authority, the Cardinal continued, is what makes their decisions and actions, leading as they did to the condemnation and death of Christ, grave and tragic. And yet, one must ask, how grave? "Did those 'rulers' of the people in Jerusalem fully understand the divinity of Christ and so become formally guilty of deicide?"[81] The answer to this question can only be "No," since the Lord prayed for His crucifiers: "Father, forgive them; for they know not what they do" (Lk 23:34). If one does not wish to devalue this prayer so that it becomes an empty formula, then it meant, without doubt, that "the Jews"were by no means fully aware of what they were doing. Peter and Paul also excused the authorities on grounds of ignorance (see Ac 3:17; 13:27). Yet, whatever their knowledge may have been, the Cardinal proceeded, can one accuse the *people* of that time of having killed Christ? Even in those days, the Jewish dispersion within the Roman Empire consisted of some four and a half million people. Moreover, if one could indict the people of those times for the crimes of their leaders—which cannot really be upheld—what right would we have to blame these actions on the Jewish people of today?

If I may reflect on the words of the Cardinal once more, can one really ask whether the Jerusalem authorities *fully* grasped the divinity of Christ? Is it not more likely that they had no inkling whatever of the mystery of God-made-man? After all, the Apostles themselves had to wait until the grace of Pentecost before the wonder of Jesus dawned on them. And even Mary and Joseph are said not to have understood the question asked them by the twelve-year-old Jesus in the Temple: "Did you not know that I must be in my Father's house?" (Lk 2:49). Moreover, the assumption (so often recurring in old polemics against the Jews) that belief in Christ as the incarnate Son of God was so "self-evident" that the failure to accept it was undoubtedly evil, minimizes the world-shaking mystery of the Incarnation. This view equates the mystery with nothing more than an observation like: "What nice weather we're having!"

Nothing that the Cardinal said hit the mark more exactly than this simple question: Is there any other case in which we reproach a people for the actions of their ancestors of nineteen hundred years ago? Cardinal Bea went on to say: "Because of the difficulty of the subject, it is understandable that many different formulas were tried, one after the other, in order to deal with the wishes and the criticisms of the Fathers."[82] On various occasions, the

> Council Fathers and others, including non-Catholics and non-Christians, petitioned that the question of "deicide" receive some treatment. It would be tiresome to describe all the deliberations in detail . . . they took a long time. Consequently, we were unable to submit this part of the Declaration for examination by members of the Secretariat. Since the Secretariat had dealt with all other business at its March meeting, it was decided not to recall the members to Rome for discussion of this one section. All that now remains, Venerable Fathers, is to examine and discuss this draft.[83]

It can be said in advance that the Fathers made liberal use of this invitation.

Despite the Cardinal's efforts to win understanding for the new draft, it had a bad press. In many instances, it was described as completely unsuitable—one of the many exaggerations of those days. Looking at the matter soberly, one has to say that the revisions had significantly weakened the Declaration and thus made it more palatable to its opponents. Despite that fact, it was not a bad document. It was only if one compared it with its predecessors, and if one followed the principle that the good is the enemy of the better, that it became disappointing. The most noteworthy alterations that the Coordinating Commission had made in the Secretariat's third draft were:

1. The ill-conceived word "deicidal" was dropped from the summons directed to all Christians not to call the Jewish people accursed or deicidal. There were various reasons for this, which will be discussed later. Yet, it must be said at once that the condemnation of this most deeply harmful expression had, indeed, certain tireless champions, but not many friends. Most Bishops declared that they had never heard the accusation: "You are a Jew, therefore you are a deicide!" They were accordingly convinced that the proponents of a denunciation of this expression—whether they were Christians or Jews—were attaching much more importance to the problem than it actually possessed. They also felt an unspoken discomfort in using the very word "deicide," even when used negatively.

While the debate on the use of "deicide" was going on, the late Cardinal (then Bishop) Wright came up to me and said: "Look here, John, this won't do. We cannot tell the world: 'Trust us, the Jews are not deicides'." I answered, "Why not?" Upon which the Bishop explained his objection like this: "Why not? Simply because it is insulting to utter the word even to deny it. What would you say if someone suddenly announced, in public, Oesterreicher is not a thief? How would you like that?" "My dear·Bishop, that depends on the situation. If this 'defense' came like lightning out of a clear sky, I should of course be bewildered. But if, for years, I had been the victim of slander, then I should feel that I had been set free by such a public vindication. I should in fact be pleased about it." The Bishop was evidently impressed by this argument, as he asked me to prepare a memorandum for him on the matter. But I am not sure that I convinced him in the depths of his heart. This little incident shows how greatly we are tied to our emotions, and how much our judgment depends upon our experiences. The uneasiness of many friends of the entire Declaration I have just described enabled its opponents to win a victory on the deicide issue.

2. A further, much-commented-on statement was the acknowledgement of the Church's eschatological hope for the union of Israel with herself. This passage was much warmer in tone than the rest of the Declaration, and this could give the impression to a hasty reader, particularly a Jewish one, that what was intended here was nothing but proselytizing. An unprejudiced reader, however, who examines the statement carefully is bound to conclude that it does not recommend a "mission to the Jews," but expresses simply and solely the belief that at the end of time God will gather into union with Himself all who profess His name.

The statement was so greatly misunderstood that the late Rabbi Abraham Joshua Heschel—a man of deep insight, whose blood, however, boiled easily—felt himself obliged to protest against it. He declared that faced with the choice of conversion or death in the gas chambers of Auschwitz, he would choose the latter.[84] This reference to Auschwitz equates the Church's profession of faith in the union of all who worship the God of Israel with the ghastly excesses of the Middle Ages, when Jews were more than once faced with the choice of baptism or exile. It is too fantastic to be refuted. The late Cardinal (then Archbishop) Heenan of Westminster, however, took it up at a press conference on September 26, 1964, and called Rabbi Heschel's declaration, that he was ready to go to Auschwitz if he were forced to choose between conversion and death, "pure rhetoric." True conversion means the free acceptance of faith. It was, moreover, far from the intention of the Secretariat to use the Declaration for an attack upon the "convictions of our Jewish brethren."[85]

Three days later, Archbishop Heenan addressed the Bishops in Council. He said that the wording of the document they had before them was not entirely the work of the Secretariat, and that he had no idea which theologians were entrusted with drafting this latest version of the Declaration. He went on to say that he in no way questioned the good will of these men, but it was probable that they had little experience with ecumenical matters. Such questions, however, required a special tact and sensitivity, particularly when they concern the Jews, whom frequent persecution had made understandably sensitive. He stressed that the Jews were mistaken if they regarded the text [of this profession of faith] as a demand that they give up their religion. But the fact that the Jews had taken this statement amiss was, he continued, sufficient reason for him to have the relevant passage removed.[86]

One of the most curious misunderstandings in the history of the Declaration concerned the warning addressed to all the faithful not to say or do anything *quod animos a Judaeis alienare potest*, "which could alienate [Christian] souls *from* the Jews." Someone who had forgotten the rudiments of Latin or had read the text with great carelessness, read *animos Judaeorum*, "the souls *of* the Jews," and understood it as follows: nothing should be said that could alienate the souls of the Jews [from the Church]. As was to be expected, this mistranslation was regarded as a new proof of the Declaration's proselytizing character.

It was remarkable how the critics saw only the inadequacies of this draft, and not its merits. If I am right, this failure is a symptom of the way many of us have lost all theological sense. Were that not so, Christians and Jews alike would surely have pricked up their ears and rejoiced when they saw this insertion:

> The Church also keeps and will always keep in mind the words of the Apostle concerning the Jews, that "to them belong the sonship, the glory, the covenants, the giving of the Law, the worship, and the promises" (Rom 9:4).

In my opinion, these are powerful points of departure for a theology of post-biblical Israel. In the future, anyone who attempts to reflect on the role of Judaism in salvation history, or to express the relationship of the Church and the Jewish people in theological terms, will have to draw support from the assurance given by the Apostle and now recalled to Christian consciousness by the Council. It seems to me an encouraging feature of this addition that it did not originate among the members of the Secretariat. Though I have no secret information or other proof, I cannot escape the feeling that the reference to Romans 9:4 was added by Pope Paul.

As so often in the history of the Declaration, real or imagined setbacks proved a spur to new efforts and helped make truth and justice prevail. The defects in the draft originating from the Coordinating Commission gave the Bishops the opportunity for a far-ranging discussion not only of the wording of the Declaration, but also of its deeper meaning. The interventions were so much to the point and so well coordinated, one could assume with great probability that the skillful hand of a stage manager was engineering the event. The fact is that there was no plan, but only the highmindedness of the speakers, their feeling for the signs of the times, their keen ear for God's message uttered through these signs, and their earnest devotion to a renewal of the Church.

Many of the speeches on September 28 and 29, 1964, are so important that I reproduce large extracts from them, since they represent a climax in the history of the Declaration. Of course, they do not have the status of the Conciliar Declaration itself, giving as they do only the opinion of an individual, but in this precisely lies their charm and value. It would be a real benefit were they always printed with the Declaration itself, as they support, explain, and sometimes also develop it.

The Great Debate. At its beginning, the members of the Bishop's Conference of Fulda, assembled in Rome, issued the following statement:

> We German Bishops welcome the Conciliar Decree on the Jews. If the Church in Council makes a statement concerning her own nature, she must not fail to mention her bond with God's people of the Old Covenant. We are convinced that this Conciliar Declaration provides an opportunity for renewed contact and a better relationship between the Church and the Jewish people.
>
> We German Bishops welcome the Decree especially because we acknowledge the grave injustice done to the Jews in the name of our people.[87]

The Swedish journalist G. Vallquist wrote in her report of
September 28, 1964:

> Today was the greatest day of the present Council Ses-
> sion. The Declaration on the Jews was sped on its way with
> drums beating and trumpets blowing in a succession of
> speeches, each more positive than the one before.[88]

Every speaker was candid and to the point; the speeches themselves were a happy combination of serenity and warmth.
There were moments when an atmosphere of awe lay upon the
Council. It could be perceived that what was being dealt with
here was not an abstract principle, but the most concrete concern: the encounter of Man and Man and of God and Man.

The speech of Cardinal Ritter of St. Louis was a fine example
of decisiveness.[89] He said:

> With all my heart I make this Declaration my own. Quite
> clearly, it responds to a need of our age. I speak of a need,
> not of some political or national pressure to be evaded or
> appeased, nor of some human approval to be sought for,
> but quite simply of a centuries-old injustice that cries aloud
> for reparation. For many centuries we Christians have
> been guilty of error and injustice toward the Jews. In many
> ways we have assumed that God . . . had abandoned this
> people. Christians, even ecclesiastical documents, have
> charged the Jewish people with the suffering and death of
> Christ. . . . We who are gathered here in this Ecumenical
> Council have been given an opportunity to root out such
> errors, as well as injustices, and make reparation.
>   The draft before us is . . . a good start in this direction. It
> could, however, be much better constructed. It seems to me
> to require certain corrections. . . . The Declaration should
> speak more fully and explicitly of the religious heritage
> which in our own day still binds Jews and Christians
> closely together. The promises which God, who can neither
> deceive nor be deceived, made to Abraham and his de-
> scendants are still theirs. Both Jews and Christians are, in
> a special way, vessels of Divine Love, and a powerful unity
> of love and respect should therefore prevail between them.
> This spirit of love, which was alive in the original draft,

should radiate more strongly from this Declaration, too. We must joyfully proclaim our debt and loving attitude toward the Jews, which this draft acknowledges only with hesitation.

Venerable Fathers, we must eradicate that error which considers a [whole] people guilty of the crime committed by individuals, that error which fills even the hearts of children with hatred of the people God so greatly loves. The last part [of the Declaration] should be removed and replaced by the following paragraph, or something similar:

> For this reason, all must take care that they in no way present the Jewish people as rejected or deicidal, or throw the blame for all the crimes committed during the Passion of Christ upon the whole people then living and, *a fortiori*, upon the Jews of our own time. All these [evil deeds] are really the responsibility of all sinful people and especially of Christians who have fallen into sin. The catechism of the Council of Trent recalls this truth in all bluntness: the guilt of the Crucifixion rests above all upon those who repeatedly relapse into sin. For as our sins brought Christ the Lord to death upon the Cross, so those who wallow in sin and vice in fact crucify the Son of God anew in so far as depends on them, and hold Him up to contempt (see Heb 6:6).

Another American Bishop, Cardinal Cushing of Boston, spoke even more frankly and firmly:

> The Church must proclaim through this Ecumenical Council her unfeigned concern, universal respect and true love for the whole world and for all human beings. In a word, she must show forth Christ. . . . With regard to the Jews, I propose three amendments:
> 1. We must cast the Declaration on the Jews in a much more positive form, one not so timid, but much more loving. . . . For the sake of our common heritage we, the children of Abraham according to the spirit, must foster a special reverence and love for the children of Abraham according to the flesh. As children of Adam they are our kin, as children of Abraham they are Christ's blood relatives.
> 2. So far as the guilt of Jews in the death of our Savior is

concerned, the rejection of the Messiah by His own is, according to Scripture, a mystery—a mystery given us for our instruction, not for our self-exaltation.... We cannot sit in judgment on the onetime leaders of Israel—God alone is their judge. Much less can we burden later generations of Jews with any guilt for the Crucifixion of the Lord Jesus, for the death of the Savior of the world, except that universal guilt in which we all have a part. . . . In clear and unmistakable language, we must deny, therefore, that the Jews are guilty of Our Savior's death.... We must condemn especially those who seek to justify, as Christian deeds, discrimination, hatred and even persecution of Jews. . . .
3.   I ask myself, Venerable Brothers, whether we should not humbly acknowledge before the whole world that, toward their Jewish brethren, Christians have all too often not shown themselves as true Christians, as faithful followers of Christ. How many [Jews] have suffered in our own time? How many died because Christians were indifferent and kept silent? . . . If, in recent years, not many Christian voices were raised against those injustices, at least let ours now be heard in humility. . . .

Most of the Fathers called for a return to the earlier text, in which the charge of deicide was explicitly rejected. The following Cardinals spoke in this vein: Liénart (Lille), König (Vienna), Léger (Montreal), Meyer (Chicago), Shehan (Baltimore). The Auxiliary Bishop of San Antonio, Texas, Stephen Leven, spoke with particular force:

In Chapter IV of the draft on Ecumenism, presented to us last year, it was said that the Jews were not guilty of deicide. Now, in the present text, this statement is missing. Some say that it has been suppressed because the word "deicidal" is philosophically and theologically absurd, self-contradictory and therefore unworthy of a Conciliar document.... Fathers of the Council, we have to deal here not with a philosophical entity, but with an infamous abuse that was invented by Christians for the sole purpose of bringing shame and disgrace upon Jews. For hundreds of years, and even in our own century, Christians have flung the word "deicide" into the faces of Jews in order to justify all kinds of excesses, even murder. . . . We must remove this word from the vocabulary of Christians, so that it can never again be turned against Jews.

Altogether, twenty-one Bishops demanded the restoration of the text used at the Second Session.[90] As has already been mentioned, Cardinal Meyer, too, regretted that in the Coordinating Commission's text the rejection of the pseudo-theological imprecation "deicide" was inadequate.

> Is it not much more our duty in this connection to present the fullness of truth concerning the Jews, in the spirit of St. Thomas (*S.Th.* q. 47, a.5 ad c.)? . . . Following the teaching of Scripture, St. Thomas makes two points: [1] No single individual Jew of Christ's time was subjectively guilty of deicide, since all acted in ignorance of Christ's divinity. This must be said explicitly in our text. [2] The bulk of Jews should be acquitted of any formal guilt because they followed their leaders out of ignorance. As a proof of this, St. Thomas refers to St. Peter: "I know that you acted in ignorance" (Ac 3:17). Finally, it must also be said where the real guilt for the torments of Christ lies: "He died for us and for our salvation!" (Nicene Creed)

Archbishop (later Cardinal) O'Boyle of Washington, D.C., expressly associated himself with Cardinal Meyer's view. He found the statement limited as it was, to saying that the ill-treatment of Christ was not to be attributed to the Jews of our own day, too spare. Only a full vindication of the Jewish people would free them "from the insult laid upon them for centuries. The love of Christ impels us to make such a Declaration." Archbishop O'Boyle also addressed himself to other problems touched upon in the text. He said:

> It is true that this Declaration is conceived as one by Catholic Bishops, directed above all to Catholics. Nevertheless, it must be ecumenical in spirit. The statements concerning the Jews will be carefully studied by them. The spirit, the style, and the words of the Declaration must, therefore, be directed to this ecumenical goal. The love of Christ impels us to formulate our thoughts in such a way that they do not give needless offense; equally, that they be

expressed in a manner clear to Jews, and that they be in harmony with the hopes and aspirations of the Jewish soul.

The first example of disregard for ecumenical style that struck him was the use of the expressions "union of the Jewish people with the Church" and "entry of this people into the fullness of the people of God." In Jewish understanding, both would seem to indicate a passionate desire on the part of Catholics for the "conversion" of the Jews:

> The word "conversion" awakens in the hearts of Jews memories of persecutions, sufferings, and the forced denials of all truths that a Jew loves with sincerity and good faith. So a Jew, when he hears that Catholics are seeking to further his "conversion," thinks of the re-introduction of that type of proselytism that for centuries assaulted his rights and personal dignity. . . . The [spiritual] destiny of the Jewish people depends totally on the ways of Divine Providence and the grace of God. If we express our hope [for the eschatological union] in words [that give the impression] we are guided by the definite and conscious intention of working for their conversion, we set up a new and high wall of division, which makes any fruitful dialogue impossible. What is said in the Declaration on this point . . . goes beyond the precise limits of doctrine. A text is, in fact, cited in the Declaration, from St. Paul's Letter to the Romans (11:25), in which he uses words which are so uncertain and mysterious that the exegetes suggest quite diverse interpretations. It would therefore be better for us to remain within the limits of our knowledge and respect the hidden ways of Divine Providence. It would be better were we to express our hope for the turning of the Jews [to Christ] in such a way that they, too can perceive with respect its honesty and our humble recognition that the mystery of salvation does not depend upon us, but upon God's transcendent act.

I therefore suggest that we replace the section under discussion with the following words:
Furthermore, it is worthy of remembrance that the

union of the Jewish and Christian people is part of
Christian hope. With unshaken faith and deep longing the Church awaits that union which God will
bring about in His own time and in a way still hidden
in His wisdom. . . .

Finally, I should like to suggest that the Declaration
include an act of humility and repentance, which alone
moves human hearts. Our Lord taught the Church to pray
daily "forgive us our trespasses." A truly Christian Declaration concerning the Jews cannot ignore the fact that for
centuries Jews have been the victims of the injustice and
cruelty of Christians. The best way of witnessing to our
love for the people chosen by God in ancient times . . . would
be for us explicitly to ask their forgiveness for the pain and
injustice with which certain Christians have dishonored
history.

The late Cardinal (then Archbishop) Pocock of Toronto
began his speech by joining with appreciation in the praise of
the other speakers, and by making his own their demands
concerning the deicide problem as well as the condemnation of
the persecutions that had occurred. He continued:

May I be permitted to add a few words in defense of the
Declaration against those who object that in it the Jews
are presented in a much better light than in Scripture itself.
It is indeed true that the prophets of Israel not infrequently
accused the people of being stiff-necked and hard-hearted.
These accusations resound again and again, right into the
New Testament. Christ Himself sternly rebuked the high
priests and Pharisees, and sometimes the people also. The
same way of speaking is to be found in the preaching of St.
Stephen (Ac 7) and in St. Paul's First Letter to the Thessalonians (2:15-16). In these passages, the people of Israel are
accused of repeated unfaithfulness.
One should, however, not forget that these accusations
against the Jews come from men who were themselves
Jews. Christ, Stephen, and Paul are indeed sons of the
Jewish people. Their stern language is therefore nothing
else than an admonition for an inner turning of the people

whom they love, to whom they belong, and with whom they know themselves in a way to be one. Their statements should, therefore not be understood as a literal description of the people. They were much rather a form of emphatic and impassioned preaching intended to stir the hearts of their hearers.

Some of the Fathers who took part in the Great Debate did not content themselves, in their criticism of the text, with pointing out its defects, but went further than the original draft. Cardinal König of Vienna, for example, demanded that, in connection with the warning to avoid any unjust judgment concerning the Jews in preaching and catechesis, one should not merely return to the original draft. He went on to say that it was not the task of Christian preaching to assess the exact degree of guilt of Caiaphas, Pilate, and others, as in fact all of us were the cause [of Christ's Death on the Cross]. The foremost task of Christian preaching was to show that in the Cross lies salvation. The Cross should be presented as the source of all graces, as the sign of love and salvation for all.

Cardinal Liénart of Lille, whose pastoral letter[91] of 1960 in many ways anticipated the Conciliar Declaration, suggested the following wording for the warning discussed above:

> All possible care should therefore be taken to exclude from catechesis and preaching of the word of God everything that could instill contempt and hatred for the Jews. In particular, this Holy Synod commands that words which brand the Jews as rejected, even a deicidal people are to be most strictly avoided, because they in no way agree with the pronouncements of holy Scripture. Priests and catechists must instead take pains to show that the vocation of the Jewish people still continues. . . .

Of the need to issue this Declaration, the Cardinal bluntly stated: "Truth, not only love, impels it."

Two German speakers, Cardinal Frings of Cologne and Bishop Hengsbach of Essen, found it regrettable that in the text now laid before them, "that most beautiful and magnificent theology" of the Epistle to the Ephesians was completely absent. "According to it . . . Christ established peace between those who were far and those who were near, that is, between the Gentiles and the Chosen People when He, the Crucified, broke down the wall of hostility between them and created a single new humanity in His body" (Eph 2:15). Here, the Cardinal continued, was the classic scriptural passage concerning the relation between the peoples of the Old and the New Covenant.

Bishop Hengsbach expressed his gratitude to Pope John for the mandate given to the Secretariat to prepare a Declaration on the Jews. He was convinced that it represented a precondition for genuine contact and better relations between the Church and the Jewish people. He also mentioned the special satisfaction of the German episcopate, as already expressed in their statement at the beginning of the debate.

Among the outstanding speakers of the two-day debate were undoubtedly Cardinal Lercaro of Bologna and Archbishop Elchinger of Strasbourg. The Cardinal began with a notable affirmation:

Other speakers have discussed the immediate grounds, the importance, and the effective significance of this Declaration. Confining myself to one point, I should like to throw some light on the ultimate reason, the deepest motive which, it seems to me, is leading the Church of Christ in this historic hour inescapably to such a decision. This reason has nothing to do with political affairs and anxieties, nor with relations between states. It is not even the events during the last great war—by which all people have indeed been deeply shaken—nor feelings of moral obligation and humility, binding though they are, which are leading the Church to make this Declaration precisely at this time. It is much more due to inner impulses which have come to maturity at the deepest, supernatural core of the life and consciousness of Christ's Church, quite apart from any external event and stimulus.

That the Church is only now taking into account these considerations is due to the fact that she has only now attained a deeper insight into certain aspects of the mystery of her existence and the fullness of her life. One should say, therefore, that the Declaration on the Jews is a fruit of that self-examination which found its rich expression in the Constitution on the Church and, especially, in that on the holy Liturgy. . . . When the Declaration speaks of the "great spiritual heritage common to Christians and Jews," it seems to look back, in the words of the Declaration itself, to the "beginnings of her own election and faith," that is, to everything that the Church has inherited from the Jewish people, back to the days of the Virgin Mary, Christ Jesus, and the Apostles.

In the eyes of the Church, the Jewish people has a dignity that has supernatural roots and a corresponding value, not only in the past, at the time of the Church's beginnings, but also in the present day. This is particularly true about the basic and divine elements of her daily life. It is precisely this feature upon which the Constitution on the Liturgy is to shed light, and make effective in the Church today. Here is the culminating point of her action and the source of her strength. These are the gifts on which the Church is daily fed and lives, the Holy Scripture, as proclaimed in the Service of the word, and the Lamb of God offered in sacrifice. But these two blessings, this precious inheritance of the Church, come from the heritage of Israel, not only Scripture, as is obvious, but also the Eucharist, which is prefigured in the paschal meal and in manna, the bread from heaven in the desert (see Ex 16:4, 13-35), and was instituted by Christ according to the pattern of the Paschal Haggadah of the Jews. In addition, the Word of God and the Eucharist ["Behold, the Lamb of God . . ."] effect even now a certain union between the liturgical assembly, the Church, at the moment of her supreme action on earth, and the holy *Kahal*, the assembly of the children of Israel. Likewise, they keep alive, at the deepest level, the exchange of word and life, so that at the most exalted moment of the divine liturgy, we can rightly call Abraham our Patriarch, that is, the Father of our people: "Deign to regard [the gifts You have given us] with a favorable and gracious countenance, and accept them as it pleased You to accept . . . the sacrifice of our Father Abraham. . . ."

Even if this exchange is not at present fully unveiled to the Jews, it is still a powerful and ever-present bond of a

quite special nature and strength. It therefore seems to me
necessary that biblical exchanges should be explicitly
mentioned and that the role here and now entrusted to the
Jews should be honored. Even in the present order of salvation, they are able to give a certain biblical, a paschal
witness, so long as they are humbly faithful to the ways of
their Fathers. . . . This witness, though still covered by a
veil (see 2 Cor 3:15), can be of great use to us Christians, in
that it supports the spirituality of the Church, which must,
more and more, become paschal and biblical. . . .

The reverence and respect which the Church owes and
wishes to show to all humans, all peoples, and every sincere religious belief, suffers no injury if our Council
expresses a special veneration for the Jews, whom we, in
this context, regard solely as a religious community. . . .

The "union of the Jewish people with the Church," of
which our Declaration speaks, could easily appear suspect,
if understood in a crude and superficial sense. Our desire,
however, is simply to profess the faith and hope of Paul,
namely that God "has not rejected His people whom He
foreknew" (Rom 11:29), that [the Jews] are "beloved" of
God (Rom 11:28), and that "their full inclusion" is not yet
revealed (Rom 11:12). But in what ways will their fullness
be revealed? Certainly, in ways that are religious and mysterious, whose mysteriousness we must respect. Those
ways are hidden in the wisdom and knowledge of God.
Therefore, they should not be confused with human ways,
that is, with methods of propaganda and external arts of
persuasion. Only an eschatological turn of events will
bring [Jews and Christians] to the common messianic
meal of the eternal Pasch.

Coadjutor-Archbishop (later Cardinal) Elchinger of Strasbourg declared:

Our Vatican Council is striving for a sincere dialogue
with all people of this age. It is necessary and desirable,
indeed, demanded by our times that the Council promote
especially the dialogue with the Jews. I should like to speak
briefly about the meaning and conditions of this dialogue.
After the last war, which was for the Jews a time of
immense horror, a great Synagogue was built in the city of

Strasbourg, where I shepherd the faithful of the Church.
The synagogue is called "Synagogue of Peace." There, I
often had the opportunity to talk with Jews. I, therefore,
make so bold as to offer a modest testimony concerning
two questions.

[First], what is the significance of present day Jews for
the Christians of our time? Not only the Jews of the Old
Testament, but also the Jews of today deserve special
regard, in as much as they remain living witnesses to the
biblical tradition. This they are through their knowledge
and understanding of the sacred books of the First Covenant. In many regions, Jewish children spend at least an
hour every day studying Holy Scripture—a very fine
example for Christians. For those Jews, the Bible is not a
dead document, not past but living history. I acknowledge
that I have often been stimulated to a better understanding
and more vital love for the Fathers of the First Covenant
by some of these Jews.

Quite certainly, joint research into the Law, the Prophets
and the Writings—common study, that is, by Jews and
Christians learned and devout—brings with it the greatest
spiritual benefit. Many Jews of today testify to the biblical
tradition by practicing in their life certain religious virtues
which are praised by the Law and the Prophets. Thus, to
give only one example, they have an extraordinary sense
of God's transcendence, so that they are often called in
French *les pèlerins de l'Absolu*, "pilgrims of the Absolute."
They render obedience to the injunctions of the Divine Law
and, in particular, the Ten Commandments—an obedience
that is not only moral but also most deeply religious. They
trust in the liberation of God's people from bondage.
Divine worship and prayer, for which the liturgical setting
is not only the synagogue but also the home, strengthens
and sanctifies the religious ties of the family.

We believe with steadfast faith that God through all
eternity does not recall His decrees. When He concluded
the First Covenant, in His love He foresaw the Second.
Hence, the Second does not annul the First. Did not the
Lord Himself say of the Law and the Prophets: "I have
come not to abolish but to fulfill them" (Mt 5:17)? We Christians are therefore not permitted to look upon the Jews as
the rejected members of God's people. On the contrary, we
are bound, so far as possible, to search out the treasures we

hold in common, and together put them to use at present. Anyone can see how effective this would be precisely now, when atheism has spread and flourishes everywhere. Since Christians and Jews are witnesses to the Word of God and to the history of salvation, they can no longer, as worshipers of the one God, present to the champions of unbelief that saddest of all testimonies, a grievous lack of mutual knowledge and love.

[Second], what does our Declaration mean for the Jews of our time? Our late Pope of blessed memory, whom the Jews called "John the Good," awakened an immense hope among them by his truly evangelical attitude. Today we must let the same evangelical spirit govern our Declaration, which pre-supposes sober humility and proper respect for Jews. Without doubt, the Declaration is of the greatest significance for the much-needed dialogue between the Jews and the Catholic Church. Our text, awaited by Jews around the world, not without anxious questioning, will be a source either of peace and joy or of deep bitterness and grave harm. What then is required?

Jews expect from our Ecumenical Council a solemn word of justice. We cannot deny that, in this century as in previous centuries, crimes have been committed against Jews by members of the Church and, not infrequently, quite improperly in the name of the Church. We cannot overlook the fact that in the course of our history the Jews have been subjected to harsh measures, have been slandered, have had their consciences violated, have even been forced to convert. Nor can we deny that up to the most recent times there crept, all too often, into sermons and catechetical books, errors contrary to the spirit of the New Testament. Why can we not draw from the Gospel the magnanimity to beg for forgiveness, in the name of many Christians, for many and great injustices?

No doubt, Jews have their faults, they too have committed errors and made mistakes. Nobody denies that. But regardless of this, the Gospel of Christ demands that we acknowledge our guilt, without expecting the Jews to do the same. Besides, it is the office and bounden duty of our Ecumenical Council to purge our catechetical instruction of false teachings concerning the Jews, as our Declaration very justly demands. We must reject unconditionally the expression that turns the Jews into a deicidal people.

208 THE NEW ENCOUNTER

> Our Declaration must, however, avoid any kind of invitation to the Jewish people to convert. At the present time, it is simply impossible for the Jews to conceive that their passing over to the Gospel of Christ would be no defection, but true fulfillment. We do not, and cannot yet, know that hour appointed by God of which St. Paul speaks in his letter to the Romans, that is, the hour of the ultimate union of the Chosen People in its entirety.

In a similar spirit, Archbishop (now Cardinal) Sheper of Zagreb regretted that the Declaration considered the Jews too much in the context of the Old Testament, and applied itself far too little to the Jews of today. He suggested a complete rearrangement of the text so that it might not be overly didactic, but truly pastoral. In his opinion, it should begin with a description of the "vis-à-vis" of the Church and the Jews of today, that is, their situation and mutual relationship. Then all their common patrimony should be discussed: the sacred books of Israel; their common hope of salvation—the idea of a Messiah is unique to Judaism and Christianity—the history of salvation, in part identical, in part intimately linked together. After all this, there should be a call for dialogue and sincere cooperation in archeological digs, in the study of Jewish history, and in scriptural exegesis. Here would be the place to repudiate hatred of Jews. "The Church's children are called upon to avoid carefully everything that could insult the Jewish people." This new structure for the text was, however, not accepted. The Archbishop, with his emphasis on the present situation, seems to have been ahead of his time. In conclusion, he spoke of the necessity of drawing up a detailed directive to regulate the dialogue with the Jews. In addition there should be established, within the framework of the Secretariat for Unity, a well-organized permanent department for relations with the Jews.

Bishop Daem of Antwerp offered a timely contribution:

> Let us condemn the injustices done to Jews, the outbreaks of hatred, of tortures, of murder, and pogroms. Let us hope for a speedy end to every kind of racial and religious hatred. Let us honor those Christians who, filled

with love, are trying to establish and maintain better relations between Catholics and Jews. . . . The Declaration on the Jews could take on greater pastoral value if historical and theological considerations were accompanied by a concrete account of the relationship of Christians to Jews in our countries. The Declaration puts great emphasis on love. This would come to us more easily if we kept constantly before our eyes the positive value of the Jewish soul of our time. Is not the fact that today believing Jews are still mindful of the Covenant between their people and YHVH a visible proof of this value? It is of great significance that believing Jews wish to be loyal to God's commands, even when they are difficult, as for example observance of the Sabbath. In their liturgical assemblies they read the Sacred Books which are also our own. They sing the same Psalms that we sing. They see and deplore the dangers of a growing materialism and combat it, so far as they are able. They implore God's mercy and forgiveness for their sins, especially when they observe the Day of Atonement. They strive from the heart to give example of loyalty to their traditions; they press onwards, filled with a great hope for the good things to come. Impelled by their vocation to make a better world, they strive passionately [for this goal].

These various human and religious values, so much prized in our times, are important because they determine the boundaries of the dialogue, which is, however, fundamentally conditioned for us by Sacred Scripture. The Christian has to explain a certain antinomy in Sacred Scripture. The New Testament teaches that Jesus prophesied: "I tell you, many will come from east and west and sit at table with Abraham, Isaac, and Jacob in the kingdom of heaven, while the children of the kingdom will be thrown into the outer darkness . . . " (Mt 8:11-12). This warning cannot be the final revelatory word concerning the fate of Israel. St. Paul says: "As regards the gospel they are enemies, for your sake; but as regards election, they are beloved for the sake of their forefathers. For the gifts and the call of God are irrevocable" (Rom 11:28-29).

Jesus' stern warning and the Apostle's loving assurance must be related to the historical realization of the divine decree. From the context of the former, it is clear that Jesus is speaking of the immediate consequences that its failure to recognize Him would have for Israel. St. Paul, on the other hand, has in mind the ultimate destiny of Israel, its completion in God. . . . This shows plainly that the two statements do not contradict each other. Christ did not exclude the Jews from eternal salvation. . . . Loudly though the Apostle laments that "they have stumbled over the stumbling stone" (Rom 9:32), he still rejoices over God's mercy which will save Israel. "For God has consigned all men to disobedience, that He may have mercy upon all" (Rom 11:32).

It will be very useful for the dialogue of Christians with Jews if the Christians follow the norms that the Apostle has laid down for their attitude.

1. The Christian must avoid any kind of pride. Coming from the Gentiles, a Christian must acknowledge that, being a wild shoot, he or she does not support the root, but the root him or her. . . . "You stand fast only through faith. So do not become proud but stand in awe. For if God did not spare the natural branches, neither will He spare you" (Rom 11:20-21).

2. The Christian must be conscious of the divine decree revealed through the Apostle. If Israel has not so far grasped [it], even so, the day will come when God's mercy takes its full effect. "For if you [the Christian coming from among the Gentiles] have been cut from what is by nature a wild olive tree, and grafted, contrary to nature, into a cultivated olive tree, how much more will these natural branches be grafted back into their own olive tree" (Rom 11:24).

3. The Christian must bear in mind that, in accordance with the divine decree, Jews and Christians are moving toward the same fulfillment—the revelation of God's mercy in a common bond. We must follow this divine decree, not by means of unseemly proselytism, but in plain dealing and complete humility.

In order to bring to a meaningful conclusion this survey of the Council's mood, or, more precisely, the attitude of its leading personalities to the Declaration on the Jews, I should like to cite a few more short and impressive statements. Bishop Leven repudiated the general indictment of the Jewish people:

At the time of Christ, a great many Jews, especially in the Diaspora, were completely unaware of Him, and therefore could not have consented to His death in any way. It is as senseless to blame all Jews of Christ's time for [having brought about] His death as it would be to accuse all the Romans of that time of being guilty of Jesus' death, because the Roman Pilate handed Him over [to his soldiers], and Roman soldiers crucified Him.

Archbishop Heenan, rejecting the use of the Declaration for attempts at conversion, declared:

The text contains these words: "[The Catholic Church] has a sincere respect for those ways of acting and living, those moral and doctrinal teachings which differ in many respects from what she holds and teaches, but which nonetheless are often rays of that Truth which is the light of all men." If those [other religions] are rays of Truth, how much more luminous is the Jewish religion which is, at the same time, the root of our faith? As Pius XI said many years ago, "[Spiritually] we are Semites!"

On the question of collective guilt, he said:

In this century, the Jews have endured grievous, indeed, inhuman sufferings. In the name of our Lord Jesus Christ, who on the Cross forgave [His actual] persecutors, I humbly ask that our Declaration publicly acknowledge that the Jewish people, as such, is not guilty of the Lord's death. It would doubtless be unjust, were one to blame all the Christians of Europe for the murder of six million Jews in Germany and Poland in our own day. In the same way, I maintain that it is unjust to condemn the whole Jewish people for the death of Christ.

As was only to be expected, there were in the course of the Great Debate one or two negative voices. The most striking was the warning delivered by Cardinal Ruffini. He demanded that as Christians are to be enjoined to love Jews, "this glorious stock, from which came Jesus Christ, the Virgin Mary, and the

Apostles," so Jews should be urged to love Christians or, at least, not do them injury.

As a basis for this last expression he referred to the Talmud which, he said, teaches Jews to despise all other people, as if they were wild animals; he mentioned further the harmful influence exercised by the Freemasons. "Is not this pernicious sect . . . , this continual conspiracy against the Church, sustained and promoted by the Jews?"

Cardinal Ruffini's view of Freemasonry is, I am happy to say, unreal. Whatever influence individual Jews may have exercised on it, Freemasonry is not a stronghold of Jewry. The Cardinal seems to see the Jews through the diseased eyes of the forgers of the Protocols of the Elders of Zion. Of course, there have been, and always will be, conspiracies. But the attempt to represent conspiracies as a major historical factor is something which comes out of the vagueness of the subconscious and not from the lucid sphere of knowledge. Ayone who is himself caught up in a web of inward conflicts may be inclined to presume the existence of a web of conspiracies threatening both Church and culture.

The source adduced by the Cardinal (*bB.M.* 104b) contains no vilification of non-Jews as "wild animals." There are instances in rabbinic literature when Gentiles are compared with raging beasts, as in the comparison of the Gentiles with wolves and Israel with a lamb (*Pes.R.* 9). But the Gentiles here are not all Gentiles, but those oppressing Jews. To understand the attitude of the Rabbis toward non-Jews, one must try to understand a given hostile pronouncement in its context, that is, in the light of the historical circumstances and, so far as can be ascertained, the state of the writer's mind. Again, isolated statements should not be generalized. The renowned Rabbi Akiba used to say:

> Man is loved, for he was created in God's likeness; by a
> very special love, however, it was made known to him that
> he was created in God's likeness. As it is written: "God
> made Man in His own image" (Gn 9:6). The people of Israel
> are loved, for they are called children of the all-present
> God; it was a special love which made known to them that

they are children of the all-present One, as is written: "You
are the sons of the Lord your God" [Dt 14:1] (*Ab.* 3:18).

These words most successfully combine God's preeminent attachment to Israel with the favor with which He embraces all
creatures. The Rabbis' views on the Gentiles are often no more
than the expression of personal experiences. To list them here
would take too much space.[92]

The October Crisis. The panorama unfolding on these pages,
and before that, in the *aula* of St. Peter's, confirms the new
awakening to the mystery of Israel in the hearts of many
Bishops. The question that occupied them was no longer that of
better or worse relations between the Church and the Jewish
people, but rather of a deep mutual bond. The initiative had
now passed, in part, from the Secretariat for Unity to the
Bishops. In the revised draft put before the Fathers toward the
end of the Third Session, their influence was quite plain. The
introductory sentence recapitulated an argument of Cardinal
Lercaro, the final sentence was an echo of the plea made by
Cardinal König. The images of the olive tree, the return to the
Pauline profession of Christ as Peacemaker between Jews and
Gentiles, indeed, of Himself being that Peace, the recasting of
the Church's eschatological hope, the strengthened warning
against a biased, one-sided interpretation of Scripture, the
clear rejection of collective guilt—all these changes, which
gave the draft that followed the Great Debate its special
character—derive from suggestions made by Bishops.
   This new awakening thus proves that the Declaration on the
Jews was not simply the work of a minority or, as has been
intimated, the product of an energetic and well-organized
"lobby." There was, indeed, a Jewish lobby at the Council,
which at times drew considerable attention to itself. Whether it
should be described as "energetic and well-organized," as has
been done, is another question. All rumors to the contrary, it
must be said that the influence of that lobby, or of individual
rabbis, on shaping the text was minimal. Only the hypersensi-
tive who are afraid to look the facts of life straight in the eye,
could be scandalized that such lobbyists tried to make their

wishes and opinions known. There was a lobby of pacifists, another of vegetarians, another for equal rights for women in the Church, and other lobbies. It is only natural that particular interest groups should want to get a hearing at so unusual an event as an Ecumenical Council.

After the Great Debate, one would have to be quite blind to attribute the Declaration to the powerful influence of lobbyists. In a communiqué published after the Third Session, Patriarch Maximos attributed the progress of the Declaration to the skill of the Jews in the art of propaganda, and even went so far as to assert (which he later regretted) that the mighty intervention of the American Bishops in favor of a strongly-worded Declaration was the result of the commercial interests of many Americans who had close business relations with Jews.[93]

The Patriarch apparently did not content himself with this attempt to depict a section of the Declaration's advocates as having been "bought." In the same communiqué, he disassociated himself from the Declaration by explaining, in opposition to the great majority of the Council, that "so long as the Jewish people stands apart from Christ the Savior, there rests upon the brow of that people a mark of shame, as the Prophets of the Old Testament foretold. This mark of shame is not, however, equivalent to a personal crime." The Patriarch, who was otherwise an excellent theologian, neglected to give a scriptural reference. He would have found it impossible to produce evidence from any of the Prophets.

However much I regret the slanderous remarks of the Patriarch, fairness requires that I insert a different statement of his. After Maximos IV's return from Rome, he confronted some Muslims who were worked up over the Declaration with an excellent argument:

> It is a contradiction if someone speaks of deicide who does not believe in the divinity of Christ; the fact that the Council has repudiated the accusation of deicide should present no difficulties for a Muslim, for the Koran itself states that the Jews believed they had killed Jesus, whereas in reality they had crucified not Him, but a double [see Fourth Sura].[94]

As early as October, 1964, it was reported that the Arab Supreme Committee for Palestine had sent a deputation to the Vatican in order to counter the efforts being made at the Council "to declare the Jews innocent." A communiqué issued by this Committee saw behind the Council's efforts "imperialist-Zionist maneuvers to lead the Church to take up a position in the Palestine conflict favorable to international Jewry."[95]

From these desperate attempts to bring the Declaration on the Jews into disrepute, with the help of pseudo-theological and pseudo-historical arguments, one can imagine how strong were the repeated remonstrations of the Arab governments with the Secretariat of State. It is no wonder that the elderly Secretary of State, Cardinal Cicognani, felt himself driven into a corner. To do him justice, it must be borne in mind that he was coming under pressure not only from Arab governments, but also from other quarters. In this tense situation, the idea may have come to him, not to untie the knot, but to cut it.

Late in the afternoon of October 9, 1964, a Friday, the Secretariat for Unity held a plenary meeting. At the fixed time, Cardinal Bea came in, took two letters out of his pocket, and read them aloud, without comment or explanation. They came from Archbishop Felici, the Secretary-General of the Council, who stated that he was writing "on higher authority." This gave the impression that he was communicating the wishes of the Pope. But, it seems, he was acting in the name of Cardinal Cicognani who, to all appearances, had neglected to ask the other members of the Coordinating Commission for their opinions.

One letter contained the information that the Declaration on Religious Freedom must be examined again by a mixed commission. What this "examination" would be like one could see from the fact that the majority of the proposed members were outspoken opponents of that Declaration. The second letter concerned the Declaration on the Jews. It required that this, too, be submitted to a renewed examination by a Commission of Six (three members were to be nominated by Cardinal Bea, and three others by Cardinal Ottaviani, the Chairman of the Theological Commission). It was said that the object of this examination and recasting was to shorten the Declaration so that it could be incorporated into the draft of *On the Church*.

These two letters had the effect of a bomb; their aftermath was felt all over Rome. There was general consternation. The instruction was seen as a clever maneuver to defy the authority of the Bishops, circumvent the rules of the Council,[96] and, not least, cripple the Secretariat for Unity, that is, to rob it of its Conciliar status by withdrawing from it further responsibility for the Conciliar documents that had originated within its province.[97]

It is said that Cardinal Bea spoke with Archbishop Felici, and demanded to know whether he had acted on papal authority. The Secretary-General answered this question in the negative, but at the same time gave to understand that he had acted according to the mind of the Pope. To this Cardinal Bea is supposed to have replied: "I cannot accept this as the last word." It is said that he then went directly to Pope Paul, who informed him that a mixed commission had in fact been discussed, but that no definite decision on its establishment had been reached.[98]

Shortly before this crisis, the four Patriarchs of the Near East had called on the Pope, doubtless to implore him urgently for support. Even during the Great Debate, the Patriarch of Antioch, Cardinal Tappouni, had entreated the Council in the name of all the Near Eastern Patriarchs:

> I most earnestly request that this totally inopportune Declaration be completely abandoned. It is not that we are hostile to the Jewish religion or in favor of discrimination against a particular nation. Nearly all of us are ourselves Semites. If we do not want this Declaration, it is because we desire to avoid the great difficulties which it would, without any doubt, put in the way of our pastoral activity. It will be said that the Declaration is pro-Jewish and this would be seriously prejudicial to our work. After giving the matter due consideration, in all conscience, we submit once more that this Declaration is not opportune and request that it be struck off the agenda of the Council.

To make only one comment, the Jewish religion does not exist, indeed, has never existed, apart from the Jewish people.

Jews are a people unique in that their peoplehood and their bondedness to God are inseparable. No matter how the individual Jew thinks, believes, or behaves, Jews are a covenanted people. Hence, were someone to argue: "I am not against Judaism as a faith, I am only against Jews as a people or nation," such argument would be untenable.

In his intervention during the Great Debate, Bishop Tawil, Melchite Patriarchal Vicar for Syria, went even further:

> Although it is necessary to condemn Antisemitism, there are other persecutions. It is forgotten that millions of refugees were driven out of Palestine. The Jews have already forfeited the friendship of the Arab world; the Declaration will shut all doors for ever. For this reason, it is extremely inopportune: it will have grave consequences and make whole nations enemies of the Church.

I have never been able to understand why Arab apologists like to maintain that, at the time of the War of Independence, millions of Arabs were driven out of Israel. First, there were not millions of Arabs in the Land. Second, the relatively small Jewish defense force, engaged in a war with the armies of all neighboring Arab countries, could not have taken on millions of Arabs living within the newborn State. Third, if it were true that millions, I repeat millions, of Arabs fled before the untested Israeli army, it would be so cowardly and shameful that I do not understand why it is part of Arab propaganda, and was even taken to the *aula* of St. Peter's.

The Patriarchs probably came before the Pope and the Secretary of State with the same "heavy artillery" that Bishop Tawil used. I speak of "heavy artillery" because such emotionally charged arguments make those who offer counterstatements appear as people lacking in feeling, and so disarm them. If I see things rightly, it was mainly the regrettable, if understandable, failure to resist this pressure which brought on the October crisis.

To return to that crisis, Cardinal Bea's intervention was not the only one. On the evening of Sunday, October 11, at the invitation of Cardinal Frings of Cologne, a group of leaders of the Council, assembled at his residence, among them the Cardinals Alfrink of Utrecht, Döpfner of Munich, König of Vienna, Léger of Montreal, Joseph Lefèbvre of Bourges, Liénart of Lille, Meyer of Chicago, Richaud of Bordeaux, and Ritter of St. Louis. The fourteen Cardinals present drew up a letter to the Pope, beginning with the now famous words *magno cum dolore*:

Holy Father,

With great sorrow have we learned that the Declaration on Religious Freedom, although it stands in harmony with the wish of the majority of the Fathers, is to be entrusted to a mixed Commission. Three of its members seem to be hostile to the sense of the Council in this respect.[99]

The letter, which dealt only with the Declaration on Religious Liberty, spoke of the extreme concern and great disquiet of the signatories, in whose opinion even the "appearance of a violation of the Council's rule and its freedom" would compromise the Church before most of the world. They asked the Pope "with the utmost urgency" for a return to the normal procedures of the Council and for all questions to be dealt with in accordance with the existing rules, in order to avoid great harm to the whole people of God. The letter was subsequently signed by several Cardinals who were unable to take part in the meeting. In all, it bore seventeen signatures.

According to R. Laurentin,[100] this letter was delivered to the Pope on Monday, October 12. J. Schmitz van Vorst, [101] however, reports that Cardinal Frings handed it to the Pope personally in his one-hour audience on Tuesday, October 13. It is probable that the Cardinal chose the more polite way, giving the Pope time to examine the matter as well as to consider further steps. The Pope was pained, not to say deeply disquieted. It is difficult to know how far he was offended by the concealed abuse of his authority. In any case, he quickly restored both his own and the Council's threatened role, by assuring Cardinal Frings that the Secretariat for Unity would remain responsible for both Declarations.

The changes in the Declaration on the Jews forecast in the second letter would hardly have been rejected, had they not been combined with the proposal to cut it to one paragraph. Many Fathers and theologians had held that the Constitution on the Church was the right place for a Statement on the bond of the Church to the Jewish people. But an abridgment which reduced the document to a fraction of its original would have been unacceptable. In the early stages of the crisis, Paul VI is supposed to have assured Cardinal Bea that the Declaration on the Jews would be "neither amputated nor diminished."[102] It is also difficult to see how a smooth incorporation of the Declaration on the Jews could have been possible at such a late stage when the Constitution on the Church was already complete. In any case, the Theological Commission, which was responsible for the Constitution on the Church, refused to consider the proposal of Archbishop Felici's letter; thus in the end, the Declaration was not made, as had also been proposed, an appendix to *Lumen Gentium*, the Constitution On the Church, but became the heart of a separate declaration on the relation of the Church to other religions.

The Expansion of the Declaration. During the Great Debate, and even before it, several Fathers had expressed the wish that the Declaration on the Jews be made comprehensive, so that the new spirit of encounter would extend not only to the Jews, but to all non-Christians. During the Second Session in 1963, this was suggested by Cardinals Bueno y Monreal of Spain and Doi of Japan, but most emphatically by Bishop da Veiga Coutinho of India. In the Third Session in 1964, the idea of a structured, yet all-inclusive declaration was represented mainly by Bishops Plumey of the Cameroons, Sfair of Lebanon, Descuffi of Turkey, Nagae of Japan, and Nguyen Van Hien of Vietnam. A number of African Bishops desired that Animism be expressly mentioned.

Thus, many Fathers avowed the dignity of genuine spiritual experience; still, the leading men of the Secretariat refused for a long time to express this view in greater detail, rather than in a general way. Not, indeed, because they believed that God did not address those outside the sphere of the biblical revelation, in any way, but because they felt that the Secretariat for Unity was not authorized to produce such a declaration; it had neither the competence nor the experts needed for drafting a declaration on the all-embracing salvific will of God and His saving work among the nations. After the Great Debate, however, the Secretariat for Unity began to appoint a number of special temporary committees to which belonged, among others, Georges Anawati, O.P. (Egypt), Yves Congar, O.P. (France), Canon Charles Möller (Belgium), and Josef Neuner, S.J. (India).

In February 1964, the Institute of Judaeo-Christian Studies had submitted a Memorandum to the Secretariat for Unity and several Bishops; it had been drawn up by Dr. Barry Ulanov of Columbia University, New York. According to him, it was not only extremely suitable but, indeed, necessary that the Council celebrate the variety as well as the essential unity of the inner experiences of human beings. In Dr. Ulanov's view, the Church has been entrusted with the task of joyfully praising every just deed and every just person, every loving deed and every loving person, every opening of a soul to God, every movement of the heart, however weak, that announces the goodness of God and the goodness of people toward each other. The recognition of religious experiences outside her own sphere does not mean that the Church fails to realize the great differences between herself and those who do not believe in Christ. Dr. Ulanov continued:

> By affirming the work of the Spirit who blows where It will, she deepens her own asceticism and piety, her own sympathy and incessant prayer. At the same time, she shows herself as the faithful companion and intercessor for all those who seek permanent peace.

From the very beginning of his pontificate, Paul VI had supported this wider outlook of the Church, and thus encouraged an expanded declaration in part consciously, in part without realizing it. He had first sounded this theme in his opening speech for the Second Session:

The Catholic Church looks beyond the frontiers of Christianity. How could she limit her love, as she is to imitate the love of God the Father, who gives His good gifts to all people (see Mt 5:48) and so loves the world, that He gave His only Son for its salvation? (see Jn 3:16). Thus, she looks beyond her own sphere to the other religions which have preserved the sense of the Divine and the idea of the one supreme and transcendent Creator and Sustainer. These religions venerate God by sincere acts of piety, a piety which, like their convictions, forms the foundations of their moral and societal life. The Catholic Church sees, not without regret, in these religions gaps and errors. It cannot but turn also to them in order to tell them that the Catholic religion gives due respect to everything true, good, and humane she finds in them. She also assures them that she is in the forefront of those who, among our contemporaries, protect the sense of religion and worship, both conditions of and obligations for the earthly commonweal, in order effectively to defend, as it were, the rights of God over humanity.[103]

After this, Paul VI returned to this theme more than once. In his Easter Message of March 29, 1964, the Pope proclaimed:

Every religion contains a ray of the light which we must neither discount nor extinguish, even when it is not sufficient to give people the clarity they need, or to realize the miracle of the Christian light in which truth and life are wedded. But every religion raises us toward the transcendent Being, the sole Ground of all existence and all thought, of all responsible action and all authentic hope. In every religion faith dawns, but we expect that when the evening comes, we will see the unfolding of each in the radiant light of Christian wisdom.[104]

Paul VI's first encyclical, *Ecclesiam Suam* of August 6, 1964, was devoted to the task of the Church to enter into a dialogue with "the others." He said there:

Then we see another circle around us. This, too, is vast in its extent. . . . It is made up above all of men and women

who worship the one, supreme God whom we, too, worship.
We note briefly: first, the children of the Jewish people,
worthy of our affection and respect, faithful to the religion
which we call the Old Covenant; then, the worshipers of
the One God, the Muslims, deserving our admiration for all
that is true and good in their worship of God; and finally,
the followers of the great Afro-Asiatic religions.

The Pope said further that evidently the members of the
Church cannot share in these various forms of religion, nor
could they pretend that all are of equal value, and that these
religions absolve their followers from the duty to seek God in
the perfect and definitive form in which He has revealed Himself and in which He demands to be known, loved, and served.
The Pope continued:

We will not deny to these religious affirmations the respect
that their spiritual and moral values demand, and we wish
to join them in promoting and defending common ideals of
religious liberty, human solidarity, culture, societal welfare and order. For our part, we are ready to enter into
dialogue on these common ideals, and will not fail to take
the initiative where our offer of dialogue in genuine, mutual respect, is well received.

The idea of giving the Declaration on the Jews a catholic
framework, encompassing the earth, was tremendously advanced by the Pope's plan to attend the Eucharistic Congress
at Bombay after the Third Session. The new Declaration was
passed "in the first reading," even before the end of the Session. On December 3, 1964, the Pope delivered a speech to the
representatives of non-Christian communities in Bombay. It
was a programmatic statement applying the Conciliar Declaration to a concrete situation. He said:

Your country is a country of an old civilization, the cradle of great religions, the home of a nation which has
sought God in constant desire, in deep meditation, in
silence and in ardent hymns. Only rarely has this longing
for God been expressed in words so full of the Advent spirit

as those in your holy books written many centuries before Christ:

> From unreality lead me to reality,
>   from darkness to light,
>   from death to immortality!
>   (*Upanishads, Brihadaranayaka* 1)

This prayer is relevant in our time. Today, more than ever before, it should ascend from every human heart. Humankind passes through profound changes; it is groping for guidance and new forces that will lead it into the world of the future.

Going on to the special problems of India, the Pope continued:

> You, too, are struggling with the evils that darken the lives of innumerable people throughout the world, such as poverty, hunger, and disease. You fight an inexorable battle for more food, clothing, and houses, for education, for a just distribution of the riches of this world. Are we not all united in this struggle for a better world, in the effort to give to all people those things that are necessary so that they can fulfill their human destiny, and lead a life that is worthy of the children of God? Hence, we must come nearer to each other, not only through the modern means of communication, through press and radio, through ships and airplanes. We must come together with our hearts, in mutual understanding, in respect and love. We must meet each other, not only as tourists, but as pilgrims who have set out to find God, not in temples of stone, but in the human heart. Men and nations must meet each other as brothers and sisters, as children of God. In such mutual understanding, in such friendship, in this holy fellowship, we must begin to work together in order to build the common future of the world. . . . May [the Lord] transform us into the one family of His children!

The Pope's speech was evidently inspired by the enlarged Declaration, with its confession of unity and all-embracing kinship of human beings as well as the dignity of the non-biblical religions. The Church has always believed and taught that humankind is one. But it is one thing to grasp a truth with the mind, and quite another to experience it in life. The technological inventions of the last decades, from the airplane to radio and television, with their consequences, such as the fight against hunger and disease, illiteracy and unproductive methods of labor, all these have made the one world a personal experience of many through caring for the needs of others.

The speed of the means of transportation and communication has transformed our vast earth into a "global village" (Marshall McLuhan) with many inhabitants. In the view of the Council, the geographical neighborhood alone does not suffice; its dwellers must also become neighbors in mind and spirit. Just as the Church-in-Council has rethought her bond to the people from which she sprang, so must she re-evaluate her ties with the peoples among whom she lives. Thus, she could examine her relations to the world in which she is placed and which she is meant to serve. As every human being is both an individual and a member of a community, the Church is meant to care not for isolated individuals, but for individuals as members of religious bodies and, thus, for these bodies themselves.

In her longing for unity and love among people and nations, the Church "gives primary consideration in this document to what human beings have in common and to what promotes fellowship among them,"[105] as the final text of the Declaration expresses it, speaking of the one origin and goal of humankind. The human situation is metaphysically the same everywhere. Everywhere people ask the same existential questions, but not everywhere do they receive the same answers. Wherever human beings breath, they search for the meaning and the end of life, for what is good and what is sin, for what is the way to true happiness, and what is the Primeval and Ineffable Mystery of our existence from which derives our being and for which it longs. Different cultures give different answers to these basic questions. The Council is not at all discouraged by this variety, but sees the finger of God in these religions. Though God is not present in them in the splendor that illumines the biblical revelation, He is nevertheless present in them. Otherwise, the Council would not have been able to express its reverence for those who believe, worship, and live according to the light of the religion in which they were born.

It was a great moment when the ecumenical gathering of the Bishops said for the first time, and a year later solemnly proclaimed, that the Church despises nothing that is genuine and good in the different spiritual traditions of peoples. "The Catholic Church rejects nothing which is true and holy in these religions"—this is the keynote of the first section, which treats of the various religions of humankind. Timid souls were afraid that the Council Fathers had come close to indifferentism when pronouncing this thesis. The truth is exactly the opposite. The Bishops did not at all think that it made no difference what people considered to be true and what they worshiped. They only confessed what is perfectly, if not exclusively, Catholic: namely, that whoever proclaims a religious truth has received his or her thought and word from the Holy Spirit. Wherever goodness is taught and lived, God is well pleased. Whoever conquers selfishness can only do so because victory had already been achieved on Golgotha. Wherever there is grace, there is the Church.

Exponents of relativism assert that all traditions are true and, at the same time, none; that every tradition is true only for its believers. The respect for the values present in the various world religions, such as the Council Fathers affirmed, was so far removed from such a mentality that they could claim the authority of Christ Himself for their view. As soon as they had affirmed that the Church rejects nothing she finds to be true and holy in other religions, they continued: "Indeed, she proclaims and must ever proclaim Christ, 'the Way, the Truth, and the Life' (Jn 14:16), in whom God has reconciled all things to Himself" (see 2 Cor 5:18-19). He is obviously the Way, the Truth and the Life of those who follow Him, but He is also, though in a hidden way, the power of those who do not yet know Him. Thus, the openness of the Council has no other source than Christ's work of reconciliation.

When the Apostle expressed his joy that God had reconciled the world in Christ, he wrote that "God gave us the ministry of reconciliation" (2 Cor 5:18). Thus, because the Bishops were Ministers of reconciliation, they acknowledged the groping of primitive religions for the Power hidden in all things and events, and their search for the Supreme Being. As servants of this reconciliation, they valued the deep longing of Hindus and Buddhists for the Ultimate and their desire to be free from the wants of the human situation or of the fleetingness of life. They also expressed this respect for Muslims, who "adore one God, living and enduring, merciful and all-powerful, Maker of heaven and earth, who speaks to men," and acknowledged the submission of pious Muslims to the will of God which resembles the obedience of Abraham. Bound to reconciliation, the Bishops implored both Christians and non-Christians to forget the past with its dissensions and hostilities and to "strive sincerely for mutual understanding," asking to make common cause in fostering justice, peace and freedom among all.

The Fourth Draft. A new phase was reached when the Declaration was extended to the whole sphere of humanity's thirst for the Absolute and its awe of the Primordial Mystery of the world.[106] With this the fourth draft was born. When the Council recognized the spiritual experience that is the foundation of the non-Christian religions in many lands, it did not mean to deny the tremendous differences between the way of Israel and the ways of the heathen. The difference consists ultimately in this: The God of Abraham, Isaac and Jacob, the God of revelation, seeks human beings, His creatures, while the gods of the pagan world are sought by creatures. Hence, it is strange that such a keen observer as Johann Christoph Hampe should write:

> It is not only Catholic style, but also the special style of the Council, not to note distinctions and separations or, if so, very irenically. The Declaration does not mention that the gods of the Hindus, and the attempts at redemption of other religions, or the Buddhist pessimism about the world with its demand to shake off any conception of God, are incompatible with the Christian faith, just as it says nothing of Israel's historical protest against the Messiah Jesus of Nazareth.[107]

To allege that it is "Catholic style" not to formulate distinctions or, at best, very irenically is a new catchword in the criticism of the Church. The Secretariat for Unity had anticipated Hampe's complaint that the Council had erred by omission. The last version of each draft was accompanied by an Account (*expensio modorum*) of how the relevant commission explained its dealing with the objections and proposals of the Fathers. In this Account of the new paragraph added to the Declaration the Secretariat said expressly:

> The aim of the Declaration is not to present in an exhaustive manner the world religions with their faults and weaknesses, but rather to point to the bonds between peoples and their religions that serve as a basis for dialogue and cooperation. Hence, it takes more notice of that which unites [Christians and non-Christians] with one another.[108]

The Declaration does not in the least indulge in a blind optimism that would bypass problems; it is rather the sign of a great hope. Its depth cannot be discovered at first sight. It has rightly been said that the Council is the end of the Counter-Reformation. It may be equally true to say that the Declaration marks the end of the Reformation. More exactly: the main concern of the Reformation is no longer our concern. Today, a devout Christian is no longer worried by Luther's question: How do I get a gracious God? The question that troubles believers of our time is rather: How does God work the salvation of all creatures?

This throws new light on the reason for linking the Declaration on the Jews with the Church's attitude on the religions of humankind. The whole Declaration makes it clear that all singularity exists for the sake of universality, all separation for the sake of communality. Israel's election, too, is directed toward the all-embracing kingdom of grace. Thus, the Declaration on the Jews has taken on a dimension far surpassing its original importance. It proved its value by becoming the nucleus around which old-new insights and expressions could gather.

Abbé Laurentin, whom I have quoted before, seems to be one

of the few men to have grasped the depth of this new attitude. He said of the new text that it has drawbacks as well as advantages:

> The drawbacks: [It seems that] the Jews are no longer included in the ecumenical concern. If this were really so, the Decree on Ecumenism would have been mutilated. Whether we like it or not, the separation of the Church from the people of Israel was the consequence of the Christ event, hence it took place on the Christian plane. The disadvantage [of not making the Declaration on the Jews part of the Decree on Ecumenism] is, however, mitigated by the fact that the Declaration—or, more precisely, the responsibility for the dialogue with the Jews—is still in the hands of the Secretariat for Christian Unity.
> The advantages: The difficulties the Church encountered concerning the text on the Jews had a positive result. They made it necessary to be open to entirely new horizons. ... What must be emphasized is the importance [the concern with all religions, i.e. with hundreds of millions of humans throughout the world has] for the problem of the Jews: "Their misstep means riches for the Gentiles," as St. Paul says (Rom 11:12). The principle seems to have found an unexpected application when the Decree on the Jews was enlarged to become the Declaration on all non-Christian religions.[109]

Before continuing, it seems advisable to reproduce the Council Fathers' proposals for emending the text. [1] The overwhelming majority of those who spoke stressed that it was necessary to issue a declaration on the Jews, but insisted that the Council return to the spirit and content of the text that had been submitted at the Second Session. [2] Five Fathers demanded that the loving spirit of the former draft, which they thought was absent from the text placed before the Third Session, be restored. [3] Twenty-one Fathers demanded a special rejection of the accusation of deicide. [4] Ten required a strong condemnation of the persecution of Jews in the past as well as in the present. [5] Four enlarged on the bad consequences of prejudiced teaching, which might easily lead to hatred or scorn. [6] Six Fathers wanted an emphasis on the fact that the sins of all humanity had caused the death of the Savior. [7] Two asked that the Declaration include a confession of guilt on the part of Christians because of the persecutions of Jews. [8] Three speakers pleaded to introduce the image of the good olive tree and its branches in order to make graphic the relation of the Christian to ancient Israel. [9] Four wanted the words about Christ, the Peace between Israel and the nations (Eph 2:15), to be included. [10] Twelve speakers wanted the eschatological hope of the Church expressed in such a way that even the semblance of any proselytizing among the Jews would be avoided. [11] Three considered it necessary to emphasize more strongly the common heritage of Christians and Jews. [12] Six Fathers regarded it as very important that the Declaration take due notice of the religious values of contemporary Judaism.

By contrast with these many positive proposals, there were but a few critical *modi*. The extreme suggestion that the Declaration be abandoned altogether has already been mentioned. Three Fathers wanted the negative tendencies among Jews to be pointed out. Some sought a clarification that Rom 9:4 referred only to the Israel of the past, not to contemporary Jewry; one demanded more prudence when speaking of the common heritage, still another warned against the dangers of dialogue. One Bishop thought the warning to teachers and preachers not to abuse Christian instruction too sharp.[110] In a similar context, Fesquet quoted a remark of Bishop Lamont of Southern Rhodesia, a member of the Secretariat for Unity: "It would be offensive to insinuate that Antisemitism is rampant among Catholics, too."[111] I am afraid the Bishop, a very kind man, judged the world by his own heart. With great pride he wore a ring that had been given him by a Jewish friend in what is now Zimbabwe.

If we compare the negative with the positive voices, the former appear thin and timid. The "conservative" opposition to the Declaration on the Jews sprang from the same source as the "conservative" opposition to other drafts: the fear of admitting that previous leaders and members of the Church had made mistakes. Another source of opposition was the opinion

230 THE NEW ENCOUNTER

that the task of a Catholic as well as of a Council was, first of all, to defend everything that has come down to us from the past, all that is *called* Catholic, rather than bear witness to the good tidings of Jesus and serve the gospel so that it be a leaven in the world.

After the Great Debate, the Subcommittee for Jewish problems was temporarily enlarged so that the wishes expressed on the Council floor might be more easily sifted and incorporated into the new text. At first, Barnabas Ahern, C.P. (U.S.A), Pierre Bênoit, O.P. (Ecole Biblique, Jerusalem), Bruno Hassard, O.P. (Neve Shalom, Israel) and the seminary rector Nicolaus Persich, C.M. (St. Louis) were co-opted as advisers, later also, Thomas Stransky, C.S.P. (from the staff of the Secretariat for Unity) and Msgr. Ramselaar (Holland). At the last meetings of the enlarged Subcommittee, the English Bishop Holland presided, as the text was transformed bit by bit.

It was generally considered one of the great advantages of the new version that it emphasized the love which had caused Pope John to order the Secretariat for Unity to produce such a document. According to the opinion of most commentators, the clear rejection of hatred of Jews was another advantage. Most emendations have been mentioned in connection with the Great Debate of September 28 and 29, 1964. Hence, a brief summary will suffice.

Especially new is the statement that the Declaration on the Jews is an essential part of the Church's self-understanding, the principal task of Vatican II. The Church knows herself to be called by God because Abraham, Isaac, and Jacob had been called. Her mission is the fruit not only of the mission of Christ, but also of that of Moses and the Prophets. The Church's being implanted in the Israel of the Patriarchs and Prophets is now expressed in a different way. The Church, "a new creation in Christ, the people of the New Covenant," is no longer said simply to continue the people of divine mercy and revelation. Rather are the pagans seen as branches of a wild olive tree grafted onto Israel, the well-cultivated olive tree, so that the whole Church draws its nourishment from the root of the tree. Earlier in the document, the faithful had been reminded of the Jewish lineage of Jesus, Mary, and the Apostles; now, they are also told that the first messengers of the good tidings of Jesus who were sent into the world sprang from the Jewish people.

The new version repeats the Pauline teaching that the non-acceptance of Jesus by a large part of Israel did not invalidate the special call of the Jewish people. Thus, it differs from the Third Draft; the same truth had already been stated in the Second, though in other words. The people continues to be loved and called by God; it necessarily occupies a special place in the eschatological hope of the Church. But the new version emphasizes this hope and its universality more strongly. It avoids even the slightest hint that the confession of a future unity is a hidden call to proselytize the Jews.

The Council seemed at an impasse on how to do justice to Jewish objections as well as the Church's hope. When I proffered the present wording: "The Church awaits that day, known to God alone, on which all peoples will address the Lord in a single voice and serve Him with one accord," the suggestion was enthusiastically accepted by the Fathers and Jewish officials present in Rome.

Need I stress that the Jewish and Christian vision of the age-to-come differ? The Council had no intention of ignoring the difference, yet, it wished to bridge this gap. Traditional Judaism expects a time when all the nations of the world will join the people of Israel and accept the Torah as the law of life. The Christian hope, however, is that when the end of ages comes, the righteous of the world will turn to Christ. In repeating the prophetic vision of all peoples addressing the Lord "in a single voice and 'serving Him shoulder to shoulder, [that is, with one accord]" (Zeph 3:9; see Is 66:23; Ps 65:4; Rom 11:11-12), and implying another that graces every Jewish service: "The Lord shall be King over all the earth. On that day, shall the Lord be one and His name one" (Zech 14:9), the new version points to a day-to-come, when concord and harmony will reign, when "all will be well, and [we] shall see that all manner of things will be well" (Dame Julian of Norwich).[112]

A common study of Scripture is counselled as a way to further mutual knowledge and respect. After present and past persecutions have been denounced, the blood-baths initiated by Christians, and the gas chambers invented by anti-

Christians, the Conciliar document exhorts all concerned never to give religious instruction or preach the Word of God in such a way "that hatred or scorn of the Jews could develop in the hearts of the faithful." The document warns further never to represent the Jewish people as a nation rejected or condemned by God or as guilty of deicide. The Fourth Draft culminates in the compelling message:

> What happened in [Christ's] Passion cannot be attributed without distinction to all Jews then alive, nor can it be attributed to the Jews of today. . . . Christ underwent His passion and death for the sins of all people out of His infinite love. This the Church has always held and holds now. Sent to preach, the Church is, therefore, bound to proclaim the Cross of Christ as the sign of God's all-embracing love and as the foundation from which every grace flows.

After the Subcommittee and the four working committees had finished their respective texts, the five sections were combined into the Declaration on the Relationship of the Church to Non-Christian Religions. The Statement on the Jews remained the heart of the whole document, though the other parts were not reduced to secondary importance. In his summation, *the relatio* of November 20, Cardinal Bea applied the parable of the mustard seed to the growth of the Declaration: the seed, that is, the brief statement on the right attitude of Christians to the Jewish people, had become a tree in which many birds built their nests; in a certain sense, all non-Christian religions had found a place in it.[113] After innumerable individual votes on a paragraph, a sentence, or even an expression, the document was accepted by all Bishops belonging to the Secretariat. The last voting took place on October 30.

Critics unfamiliar with the many problems of the Declaration and the difficulties of having to work in common have asked why the drawing up of the document took so much time, and why long discussions within the Secretariat should have been necessary. Some have even doubted the sincerity of the

Declaration. They argued that something that had caused so many difficulties could scarcely have been genuine. Spontaneity is certainly a wonderful gift; yet, it can never be the working method of a team, let alone the style of a Council.

A brief passage from the discussion of the draft on Religious Freedom might illustrate how lively and lengthy teamwork can be. At a certain stage of the shaping of the text, one of the sentences dealing with the dignity of Man was: *Homo* qui *persona est, in eadem instantia est ens sociale*, "A human being *who* [by his or her nature] is a person, is at the same time a social being." After the sentence had been read aloud, one of the members asked to speak: "No," he said, "not so! In my view, the idea that underlies this sentence would better be expressed like this: *Homo* quia *persona est, in eadem instantia est ens sociale*, "*Inasmuch* as a human being is a person, he or she is also a social being." Here the alteration is so minimal—a single letter has been added—that it could easily be overlooked. But however small the change, it holds many philosophical consequences. Another speaker even wanted the text to read: *Homo,* qua *persona, est ens sociale*, "As a person, a human being is also a social being." After a discussion rich in thought of more than half an hour, the original version was accepted, because it could not be the task of the Council to solve philosophical problems.

Not every problem was so intricate, not every discussion so concerned with subtleties of expression. But the complexities of teamwork—which, in matters of global significance, has more advantages than disadvantages—were not the only element that delayed the final shaping of the text. The resistance of Arab governments, which I mentioned before and will have to deal with again, produced repeated delays of the final decision.

It was the indecision of the Council's authorities on how to meet Arab interference that caused three weeks to go by before the revision of the text, which had been criticized in the Great Debate and decided on October 30, was handed to the Fathers. Only very few people knew where the draft, which the Secretariat transmitted to the President of the Coordinating Commission, remained for three weeks. But, as happened so often in the history of the Declaration, here too, stout-heartedness conquered exaggerated caution, though surely hesitation was not overcome by natural daring but by grace.

The Declaration was distributed to the Fathers on Wednesday, November 18, 1964. At the same time, the Secretary General announced that the voting on it would take place on Friday, November 20. Hence, the time allowed for studying the document was short. There was reason to fear that the Declaration on the Jews would meet with the same fate as that on Religious Freedom, that is to say, that the minority hostile to it would demand a delay of the voting because the time was so short. But such a delay would have meant a transfer to the Fourth Session, since the solemn final meeting of the Third Session was to take place on November 21. Thus on Friday morning, there was a rumor that the Declaration on the Church's Relation to Non-Christian Religions had again been removed from the schedule. The rumor was false; the draft was to be voted on.

Before the voting, Cardinal Bea did his utmost to convince the Fathers that the Secretariat for Unity had done its best to comply with the wishes of the Council, whose organ it was. At the beginning of his *relatio* he declared: "Our Secretariat has taken pains to consider all suggestions honestly and sincerely in order to produce a document that would be, as far as possible, worthy of the discussion which led to it, and worthy of the Council."[114] A little further on in his speech, he returned to this subject and said that the Secretariat had done everything to comply, as far as possible, with the wishes of all. He quoted the words of the Apostle to the Gentiles: "Remain at peace with all men as far as it depends on you" (Rom 12:18), and added: "which evidently is not always possible."

> It was impossible to draw up a Declaration in which no statement could be misinterpreted and which would fully satisfy everyone. Besides, it must be borne in mind that it is more important for such a solemn Declaration by the Council to exist than to satisfy everyone, even if that were possible.[115]

Cardinal Bea further insisted on stressing the paramount importance of the Declaration:

> What matters here is acknowledging the salvific will of God and His gracious acts, of condemning without exception hatred and injustice, and exhorting the avoidance of [these sins] in the future. The Church and thus also the Council must therefore fulfill their task and may not be silent.

He added emphatically:

> Unless I am mistaken, no Council in the history of the Church has ever set forth with such earnestness how to interpret the existence of [non-Christian religions] .... We are dealing with more than a billion human beings who have never heard of Christ, never recognized Him.[116]

In this connection, the Cardinal made two points: one, that this immense multitude may achieve salvation if they follow the light of their conscience; two, that it is the duty of the Church to begin a dialogue with those who do not believe in Christ. It would have been a token of good will, had the Pope been able to present this Declaration to India as a gift to his hosts. But as this was, unfortunately, no longer possible, Cardinal Bea continued, it was all the more important that the Council do as much as it could, because this Declaration reveals to non-Christian nations the true face of the Church.[117]

Thus the voting took place, as announced, on November 20, 1964. The situation in the Council hall was not favorable. The atmosphere in St. Peter's had been tense ever since Cardinal Tisserant, the chairman of the four Presidents of the Council, had announced the day before that the voting on the draft, On Religious Freedom, had to be delayed because there was not enough time to examine it. When the Pope did not comply with the most urgent request to make possible, by no means final, voting during the Third Session, because he did not want to reject the decision of the Council's Presidents and the judgment of the Conciliar Court that had confirmed it, there was profound discouragement. This may have been one of the reasons for the rather small vote. Moreover, voting took place toward midday, that is, at a time when the vigor and interest of the Fathers were always at a low ebb. 2,219 Fathers had voted on the Decree on Ecumenism, rather early in the Session, while only 1,996 took part in the voting On the Relationship of the Church to Non-Christian Religions. This was a difference of 223 votes, which was remarkable, even if not overwhelming. It should also be remembered that the opponents of the Declaration were, almost without exception, violently opposed to it, hence did not stay away from the voting, whereas not all those in favor of the Declaration were passionately attached to it. But we will say at once that on the day of the solemn voting on October 28, 1965, that is, a year later, 2,313 Fathers cast their votes.

Voting took place in three stages: the first vote was concerned with sections 1-3 (Preamble, the oneness of humanity; the natural and the higher religions, especially Hinduism and Buddhism; Islam), the second with sections four and five (the Jews: the rejection of any discrimination), the third with the Declaration as a whole. The first three articles received 1,838 affirmative and 136 negative votes; thirteen were invalid. On the last two articles, 1,770 Fathers voted Yes, 185 No; again fourteen votes were invalid. In the vote on the whole, the proportion was 1,651 Yes, 99 No, 242 Yes with reservation, and four invalid votes.

The reaction to the result was not long in coming. An American daily had the headline "History is Written" for one of its articles.[118] The Catholic press in Switzerland welcomed the Declaration as a "new beginning of the Church's encounter with the Jews."[119] A leader of the Hamburg daily, Die Welt, said that the Council had given back to the Jews their theological dignity.[120] Xavier Rynne saw in the provisional acceptance of the Declaration a justification of the long activity of Cardinal Bea and his collaborators.[121] The frequently critical Swedish journalist Gunnel Vallquist wrote simply that the voting was "the happy event of the day, the text was wholly positive." She only hoped that it would not be tampered with between the Sessions: it was certain that the Arab States would be working for this end.[122]

The "Holy War" Against the Declaration. The fears of Gunnel Vallquist were only too justified. Though the Declaration on the Jews had been given a new framework, and though the new Declaration, On the Relationship of the Church to Non-Christian Religions, was to be appended to the Constitution on the Church,[123] the Arab reaction was, to put it mildly, most unfriendly. The attempt to include the Declaration on the Jews in the Constitution on the Church or to append it to the latter had been made, not least, in order to reconcile the Arabs. A Catholic weekly in the United States wrote that since for the Arabs, still living in the theocratic age, religion and politics were almost the same, the Council Fathers had tried to place the Declaration in a context which would emphasize its theological meaning.[124] But all this was of no use. On November 18, two days before the voting, the Syrian radio in Damascus stated semi-officially:

> The new text says nothing new about the Jews. It is the same old Decree that has been given a facelift no one could be deceived by. For twenty centuries, the Church has held onto the view that the Jews are deicides, responsible for the death of Christ. Why does she change her opinion just now, when the Arabs are involved in a bitter struggle with their Jewish aggressors, aggressors who have invaded Palestine and expelled a million Arabs from their homes, whom they now allow to perish in refugee camps? Why did the Church not have the courage to display the same favorable attitude when millions of Jews were persecuted by the Nazis? Can the Church find no more favorable time to rehabilitate the Jews than when they are persecuting the Arabs? If the Council wants to absolve the Jews from the murder of Christ, this is her own affair. But the Arab world is horrified that she has chosen just this moment for her purpose. The coordination of time proves that political factors are at work behind the façade of religion. . . .[125]

238 THE NEW ENCOUNTER

That the Jews are deicides was never the official, i.e. defined doctrine of the Church. Again, Churchmen in many lands protested vehemently against the crimes of the *Kristallnacht*.

While the Syrian authorities responsible for this radio commentary were content with bitter complaints, the Jordanian Prime Minister Bahjat Talhouni threatened "punitive measures." During a session of the Jordanian parliament on November 25, both Christian and Muslim members condemned the Declaration. The Prime Minister then said he did not want to be involved in the Declaration's religious aspects, but from a political point of view he could only deeply regret it. His government would "blacklist those Cardinals, Archbishops and Bishops of the Vatican Council who sign the Declaration."[126]

It seems that the entire Middle East was drawn into the whirlpool of these hostilities, governments and people, Muslims and Christians, Orthodox and Catholics, laymen, priests, and Bishops. Shortly after the end of the Council session, two bombs were placed in the Christian quarters of Aleppo for which the "Muslim Brotherhood" seems to have been responsible. The leaders of the Catholic community of Damascus sent a telegram to the Pope: Despite its religious character, they said, the decision of the Council will have inevitable political consequences which will harm the Arabs, whether Catholics or Muslims. "The greatly excited Christian young people are about to organize demonstrations; we, therefore, ask your Holiness to preserve us from this calamity."[127]

One of the saddest accompaniments of the Arab fight against the Declaration was the attempt of some Orthodox Christians to exploit the difficult situation of the Church in the Middle East to their own advantage. On November 25, the Orthodox Bishopric of Latakia organized a demonstration against the Council's work of reconciliation. In the service following the demonstration, a Greek Orthodox Bishop, one of his priests, and the Protestant pastor of the town spoke.[128] On the same day, the Jacobite Patriarch of Antioch and the Orient, Ignace Jakub III, whose many claims, to be an orthodox Christian, the legitimate successor of St. Peter, and the head of the whole Oriental Church, are untenable, delivered this contemptuous protest:

> In these days, when Christendom complains bitterly about the so-called Ecumenical Council that declares the Jews to be innocent of the blood of Christ—a declaration which is nothing but the fruit of the [surreptitious] "night work" of the chief and the members of the Council—in these days, when Rome has sinned by its Declaration against holy Scripture, the apostolic tradition, the truth of history, and the teaching of the Fathers and Doctors, We consider it our bounden duty to proclaim before the whole world the true centuries-old belief concerning this important question. We do this as the legitimate successor of St. Peter and head of the first Apostolic See of Christendom, indeed, as the head of the whole Oriental Church.

The Patriarch then indulged in an exegesis of the New Testament totally untouched by biblical scholarship. Thus, he asserted that it was certainly not the lower classes who had shouted: "His blood be on us and our children," but rather "the high priests, the Pharisees, the scribes, the teachers of the Law, the elders, the heads of the people, the Sanhedrin and the whole people, the inhabitants of Galilee and Judaea and those scattered over the other countries." After all, at every Passover, just as at Pentecost, Jews from every nation under heaven were in Jerusalem. Certainly, "Jews" from all countries, Galileans and Judeans, too, went on pilgrimage to Jerusalem at these sacred times, but not *the* Jews, *the* Galileans, *the* Judeans, nor could all those mentioned by the Patriarch have assembled before the palace of the governor. For so sizable a group to gather there would have been a physical impossibility. And how can the assertion that the lower classes were not implicated in the death of Jesus be reconciled with the statement that the whole nation was guilty?

To charge all Jews then alive with the death of Christ did not satisfy Ignace Jakub III. According to his view, which he believed to be the unshakable faith of the whole Church,

Israel's "crime is laid at the door of all its descendants, just as Adam's sin is transmitted to his descendants." One could fill a book with the exegesis of this speaker and its refutation. Here I can only reproduce the conclusion of his radio talk:

> From the day of Jesus' Crucifixion until our own, [the Jews] have sought to declare their people innocent of the blood of Christ. Indeed, they will try to destroy Christianity through Christians. Their latest effort in this direction is their influence at the Second Vatican Council, which has provided them with a document asserting their innocence. ... We and the whole episcopate of Our synod emphatically disapprove of this Roman heresy. It contradicts the clear truth of the Bible and the teaching of the Christian Church throughout the centuries. The belief of the Church, according to which the responsibility for the Crucifixion of Christ remains with the Jewish people until the end of the world, will remain deeply embedded in the spirit of Christianity, whatever changes may occur in the ideas, views and customs of people.[129]

Not only is the notion that the Jewish people bear responsibility for Christ's Crucifixion not the true belief of the Church, but what is worse, the assumption that the Christian faith stands or falls with that tenet is a case of religious pathology.

On Sunday, October 22, a message was read in most of the churches of Damascus, warning the faithful against believing all the rumors, explanations, and commentaries that would reach them. It affirmed that the Ecumenical Council had not yet come to a decision and that, in any case, it was not a question of absolving the Jews from being guilty of the death of Christ, as some people were trying to persuade the public. The only point was to make it clear to Christians that they should show good will to all men regardless of race and religion, including the Jews.[130] An Anglican prelate, Bishop Najib Atallah Cuba'in, said that the Declaration of the Vatican Council was due only to Jewish machinations. These, he alleged, followed faithfully the Protocols of the Elders of Zion, which he—like the Czarist Secret Police and Adolf Hitler—believed to be a genuine historical document.[131] One cannot point out often enough that in the Protocols of the Elders of Zion the Jews are accused of imperialistic plots that are not theirs, but those of their enemies.

There were, however, other Arabs who did not succumb to this hysteria. On December 6, *L'Orient* (Beirut) published an article by Hassan Saab, "Christianity and Islam vis-à-vis Zionism." These are the most important passages on the Council:

> The Arabs ought to be happy about such an awakening of the Christian conscience . . . . It is a pity that the fear of Zionist exploitation of the Declaration prevents them from closely examining its contents. Probing her own faith, the Church experiences a great change: for the first time, she sees the reflection of truth in other religions. Islam is presented as a sister religion. The Christian is exhorted to end all disparagement, not only of the Jews, but of all non-Christians. This new attitude of the Church would deserve to be imitated rather than criticized.

That, in the Declaration, the Council sees the reflection of truth in other religions for the first time is not exact. The Church Fathers had had similar perceptions. What is new is that a Council made them its own. Somewhat triumphalistically, the Muslim author continued:

> Here [the Church] approaches the idea of the Koran of the unity of God's family, as well as the other idea of the Koran that the People of the Book is one, the people that consists of Jews, Christians and Muslims, of all who worship Allah, the Father of Abraham, who is the father of all who believe in the one God. Christianity and Islam must be reconciled in this Declaration and congratulate themselves on its spirit . . . .

The same edition of *L'Orient* printed parts of an article by Mohammed Naccache, which had appeared in an Arab weekly. Its original heading was "Does the Declaration that the Jews Are Not Guilty of the Blood of Christ Diminish Our Rights?" *L'Orient* entitled it: "The Revision of the Attitude of the Catholic Church Toward the Jews Corresponds to the Arab Standpoint." Neither author is free from the clichés of Arab propaganda, hence it is to be appreciated all the more that they should have written so clearly and objectively concerning the Declaration. Mohammed Naccache writes:

> I ask myself in what way the Jews' innocence of the blood of Christ could affect us. We have never accused the Jews of having crucified Jesus. The Declaration is a manifestation of the tolerance of the Catholic Church. [The term "tolerance" is not part of Vatican II's vocabulary, J.M.O.] And this tolerance is not only practiced toward the Jews but extends to all religions . . . . The decision of the Council with regard to the Jews abolishes all disparagement of one religious group by another. It ends, at least in principle, the wars pretending to be crusades. Now humans will be able to live as brothers and sisters. It will be left to God to ask them to justify their faith on the day of the last judgment.

Unfortunately, these two authors were voices in the wilderness. The Declaration continued to be heaped with reproaches, even slander. Before its provisional acceptance in October, 1964, a Syrian newspaper called the draft "ridiculous, inspired by the Zionists." At the same time, the state-controlled Syrian radio declared that when the Jews dipped their hands into the innocent blood of Christ, they actually wanted to murder the principles and teachings of Christ.[132] After the acceptance of the Declaration, the language of the Syrian press became even more dastardly and insidious. The Council was called "a second Judas who betrayed Christ for Jewish money." The statement that "the Church is selling Christ once more, not for thirty pieces of silver, but for American dollars," became a constant refrain.[133]

In Jordan, the *Jerusalem Times* spearheaded the attacks on the Council: "Who Crucified Christ? The Vatican in the Year 1964." A number of Christian members of the Jordanian parliament declared they would ask the government to take over the control of all Catholic schools. They even urged Jordanian Catholics to break with the Vatican. An Orthodox member of parliament invited them expressly to join the Orthodox Church.[134] The 88-year old Greek Orthodox Patriarch of Alexandria and Africa, Christophoros, threatened that the decision of the Council would place new obstacles in the way of the present efforts to achieve unity.[135] The Coptic Pope Kyrillos VI was convinced that the action of the Council was due to a conspiracy. He protested together with all the Archbishops and Bishops of his Church against an imperialistic plan of exploiting the Second Vatican Council.[136] On November 25, a manifesto of the so-called "Constituent Council of the Islamic World" was read on Radio Cairo, in which the Catholic Church was reminded that its hostile policy would produce enmity between the Islamic and the Christian worlds. The interests of the Vatican in the Islamic states would also be endangered, as it had institutions and communities there.[137]

All this shows that the Arab attitude was not only governed by misunderstanding and opposition; its leaders, the political as well as the religious ones, were so passionately attached to their cause that they carried on a "holy war" against the Council. True, it was conducted *mostly* with words; nevertheless, it was a war with all its attendant perfidy. The story of this whole war shows that to turn the salvific meaning of the Passion, its ultimate blessing, into a murder story is not only wrong, it stands Christianity on its head.

Surrender? In the realm of nature, a thunderstorm is usually followed by a calm and purified atmosphere. But nothing like that happened here. On the contrary, the torrent of public propaganda was replaced by the drizzle of secret diplomacy. What the fury of the Arab press and radio had been unable to accomplish, endless representations, complaints, criticisms, discussions, and proposals were able to achieve. Abbé Laurentin describes the activities of Arabs in the period between the Third and Fourth Sessions unsparingly:

> The famous Declaration . . . was causing agitation in Arab countries; as a result, Catholics in these countries were threatened with persecution, serious persecution. The Arab States, which had more or less officially agreed to recognize the exclusive religious nature of the texts already voted upon, found themselves outflanked by their own troops. Diplomatic offensives multiplied with the support, advice, and help of the Bishops and Patriarchs of those countries who furnished biblical objections and other religious motives to counter the Declaration. Let us not forget that two of the Bishops from these countries were members of the Secretariat for Promoting Christian Unity, where opinions were thus divided.[138]

Laurentin goes on to say that the Israelis unwittingly assisted Arab propaganda, for part of the Israeli press had given a political, that is to say, a Zionist, interpretation to the rejection of the charge of deicide by the Conciliar document. This ran counter to the repeatedly expressed intentions of the Secretariat for Unity, and thus called into question the statement that the Jewish people was not guilty of deicide. Laurentin gives no source for his assumption that Israel's effort had been counter-productive, that is to say, that it had achieved the opposite of what had been intended. True, there had been rumors in Rome that the Israeli radio had misused the Declaration to further Israel's political ends, and a number of people were only too ready to take this at face value. I think all these rumors originated in Cairo or another Arab city. At least, I have never had any evidence that the accusation was based on fact. There had been isolated voices, mostly those of self-appointed Jewish spokesmen who declared that the Church should top off the Declaration with the diplomatic recognition of Israel. However imprudent, indeed, irresponsible these private statements, they were in no way semi-official, let alone official statements that the Conciliar Declaration guaranteed, as it were, the dignity and rights of the State of Israel.

Laurentin is right, however, when he says in the course of his description: Some interventions seem to have given the impression that, by renouncing the deicide charge, the Church was dissociating herself from belief in the divinity of Christ. Arab diplomats had a fine opportunity to exploit notions of this kind. From some clumsy interventions they deduced theological arguments that served their purposes. What a scandal in the eyes of the Orthodox if "deicide" were dropped from the Church's vocabulary. This would convert the Catholic church to Nestorianism, according to which only an acquired unity of the divine and the human subsisted in Christ, rather than a union of the two natures in the one Person of the Eternal Word. The whole argument developed around the slogan introduced by Cardinal Ruffini, which Maximos IV had tried to take up to calm Arab opinion: "To speak of deicide is absurd, since one cannot kill God."[139] Whatever the merit of that argument, the Secretariat, already divided on this question, found itself compelled to modify the text far beyond what the Fathers' vote required and allowed.[140]

But the situation was not as simple as that. What had forced the Secretariat as a Commission of the Council to reconsider the problem of deicide was, in fact, certain *modi*, "amendments" suggested by the Fathers. One of these—signed by thirty Fathers, most of whom had not been prominent in the discussions—demanded that the warning not to call the Jewish people "rejected, condemned, guilty of deicide" be changed so that it would read: "Never should all the Jews *individually* be represented as rejected and guilty of *formal* deicide." They maintained that the Jewish people corporately had been guilty of material deicide because of the actions of its leaders by citing 1 Thess 2:15.

Undoubtedly, the argument went, some of its leaders had been guilty of deicide, since Jesus Himself had said: "If I had not done among them the works which no one else did, they would not have sinned, but now they have seen and hated both me and my Father" (Jn 15:24). The proponents misread the utterance. First, the words attributed to Jesus in John 15:25 speak of the few who persecuted Him, not the entire people. Second, biblical speech is impassioned, often hyperbolic, and every sentence in it is not meant to be a dogmatic statement.

Thus the problem was posed. The experts who had to deal with the *modi* did not find it difficult to make a decision. Their conviction emerges from the words with which their Account of Modifications, the *Expensio modorum*, begins:

> *Textus a Concilio approbatus quoad substantiam mutari non potest. Praeterea argumenta quibus culpam deicidii et reprobationem populi Iudaici probare conantur, valida non sunt.* "A text approved by the Council cannot be substantially changed. Moreover, the arguments by which [some] attempt to prove the guilt of deicide and the reprobation of the Jewish people are not valid."

As to the arguments produced by the *modi*, the *Expensio modorum* says that in 1 Thessalonians 2:15 Paul did not speak of the Jewish people as a whole, but of the authorities in Jerusalem and Judea who persecuted Jesus and those who believed in Him, and who are the descendants of the murderers of Prophets (see Mt 23:20-32; Ac 7: 51f). The words of Christ in Jn 15:24 refer to the sin of those who sought to kill Him. John frequently calls these men *Iudaioi*, "Jews" ("Judeans" might be a better translation). That the expression "the Jews" does not refer to the whole people emerges from the fact that the same Evangelist records that "many of the people believed in Him" (Jn 7:31) and also that "many of the Jews . . . believed in Him" (Jn 11:45). Other Evangelists report that the opponents of Jesus did not dare lay hands on Him because they feared the people (Mk 14:2), that when the high priests and scribes are said to have made plans to lay hold of Jesus, they were terrified saying: "Not during the feast, lest there be a tumult among the people" (Mt 26:5).

Instead of clarifying the relationship between leaders and

people, the *Expensio* continued with the equally important
statement that Scripture never characterized as formal deicide
the sin of those who engineered the death of Jesus and of those
who actually caused it; neither in the Fourth Gospel nor elsewhere. Not only that; according to Scripture, the enemies of
Jesus, however great their guilt, did not know that they had
killed "the Holy One of Israel" (see Ac 3:17; 13:27), even though
the Gospels often speak of their blindness and hardness of
heart. In the parable of the householder who planted a vine-
yard, which the more than thirty Fathers had also quoted in
support of their proposal, the Lord's threat was addressed to
the leaders, not to the people; His original hearers, at least,
understood it this way, for the Gospel continues: "When the
chief priests and the Pharisees heard His parables, they per-
ceived that He was speaking about *them*" (Mt 21:45).[141]

This attitude of experts was thus clear and unwavering. The
attitude of some Bishops, however, was less firm. They found it
difficult to give up ancient prejudices which so easily disguise
themselves as the sacred tradition of the Church. They would
not accept that the reading of the Vulgate: *Auctorem vitae
interfecistis*, "You have killed the author of life" (Ac 3:15), was
wrong. According to the original text and the context, it should
be translated: "You have killed the Leader to life," that is, Him
who rose first and prepared the way for others, leading them
into life. Still others wanted to avoid possible controversies or
were very much in sympathy with the Arab Bishops.

When, during the plenary session of the Secretariat at Ariccia in March, 1965, those, who wanted to abolish the expression
"guilty of deicide" seemed to be in the ascendancy, Cardinal
Shehan intervened. Filled with prophetic zeal, he said that he
had not asked to be assigned to the Secretariat when he became
a Cardinal, nor was he one of its members when the Declaration on the Jews was first drafted. He had, therefore, no part in
its formulation, but now he was a member, and therefore
responsible for its text. Hence, he felt he must say that the
rejection of the charge of deicide ought not to be dropped.
"Deicide" had become a key word, a symbol of everything the
Jews had ever been accused of. It is a word too easily misunder-

stood. He was also firmly convinced that, by excising these words, the document would be emasculated and its effect would be seriously weakened. He exclaimed: "With my whole heart, I beg that the text be retained as it stands and as it has been approved by the overwhelming majority of the Bishops of the Council." This summary cannot reproduce the vigor and ardor of his speech; under its influence, the attempt to change the text was rejected but, alas, not forever.

The accounts reaching Rome from the Middle East became ever more frightening. It was said that the final acceptance of the Declaration on the Jews would lead to serious attacks on the Christian minorities. The inevitable result would be the closing of Catholic schools in Arab lands and the burning of churches, in fact, the destruction of Christian life. The Council's friendly gesture toward Islam had evidently not impressed the Arabs. It seemed that only the complete omission of the Declaration could satisfy their stubbornness. In order to investigate the rumors and ascertain the facts, Paul VI sent Bishop (now Cardinal) Willebrands and Father Duprey, P.A., to the Near East. The result of this journey, with its visit to all the leading Christian personalities in question, was not encouraging. Both confirmed that the fears existed and were probably justified. In any case, they did not dare contradict the Arab Bishops who were worried about the future of the Church in their countries. Some people might be tempted to speak of "pusillanimity," but no one who has not been in a similar situation has a right to do so.

The impressions Bishop Willebrands and Father Duprey brought home from their journey were given to the last plenary session of the Secretariat, which took place in May, 1965, some months before the Fourth Session. Their largely pessimistic outlook was shared by not a few members and consultors of the Secretariat. In those days, the opinion was often heard that it was morally impossible to pass a Declaration which might result in tumult, killings, and misery, in other words, the immediate fruit of which would be the physical and mental oppression of Christians in the Middle East. Thank God, Jews were not exposed to direct danger, but the Christians in Arab countries were, some Consultors thought. One could not heal the wounds of one side and inflict them on another. Here, it was a question of a piece of paper—after all, a document was nothing else—but there, of living men and women. I cannot help calling the juxtaposition of human beings to paper wrong, however enticing it may sound. A document such as the Declaration on the Jews is not merely a few printed pages. It is part of a psychological and spiritual restitution, the embodiment of the will to reconciliation, of a refound brother-and sisterhood, a living testimony to God's faithfulness.

The mood I just sketched produced varied plans. Some were of the opinion that it might be better not to publish the Declaration at all. The Fathers should be told instead that because of the tensions in the Near East, it was in danger of being misinterpreted. Hence, some members preferred to leave the Declaration in the hands of the Secretariat for Non-Christians or of the Secretariat for the Unity of Christians as a basis for their work. Its content might prudently be published at the appropriate time. these and other proposals were roundly rejected, as well as a new version of the Declaration which refrained from making any specific statements or even allusions with regard to "disturbing" problems. The "new version" was an unsigned draft of one page which contained hardly more than a high-flown paraphrase of the command attributed to the aged Apostle John: "Children, love one another!" On his venerable lips these words must have been a striking testimony; on the lips of Council Fathers from whom the world was expecting concrete statements, they would have been regarded as an "escape into piety," that is, false piety, one that rejects any clear-cut commitment. The anonymous proposal met the worst fate that could befall any suggestion: it was laughed to scorn.

Nevertheless, there remained the possibility that the Declaration would be quietly tabled. In this situation, a number of Bishops and Consultors asked to speak. One of the most stirring interventions was that of the usually silent Bishop of Würzburg, Josef Stangl. On May 12, he said:

> The question of the acceptance or rejection of our decree is

a decisive hour for the Council. Will the Church take the
road of incorruptible truth and justice or that of tactics, of
diplomacy, and of least resistance?

The Bishop confessed that he came from the country of Hochhuth, the author of *The Deputy*. He was besieged by publica-
tions that carried diatribes on Pius XII, the German Bishops,
and the Church in the Third Reich. He went on that the typical
explanation of past attitudes no longer reached the hearts of
people. Today's Christians no longer take seriously considerations of prospective dangers and pastoral prudence. "The question is always: Has the Church been walking in the way of the
children of this world who calculate and follow earthly considerations? These questions are asked by the faithful, especially
by young Christians, and even priests." Growing more intense,
the Bishop continued:

> If we speak in the name of God, in the name of Jesus Christ,
> as His representatives, our speech must be Yes—No, that
> is, truth not tactics, for "anything more than this comes
> from evil" (Mt 5:37).

What was at stake was the credibility of the Church. The
whole world knew that the Declaration had already been
accepted by the Fathers, the whole world was waiting for its
promulgation. The Council was enjoying an extraordinary
reception and the greatest esteem because of its openness, its
honesty, and because it was no "respecter of persons." If our
Declaration were not to be promulgated, everybody would be
asking: Why not? The reply "diplomatic considerations or
whatever" would appear as a sign of weakness; it would be a
defeat of the Church before the whole world. Bishop Stangl
continued:

> It is not only a question of the credibility of the Church but
> also of her claim to moral leadership. The Council wants
> the Church to be perceived as *Lumen Gentium*, "Light of

the Nations." The Council ought, according to the wish of John XXIII, to be a new Pentecost. We must be absolutely honest and put our cards on the table.... Numerous people who doubt, others who seek the truth, still others who err, numerous Christians of the various denominations need our witness of fearless truthfulness and justice which will restore to the Church the claim to moral leadership that she has lost in the opinion of many. It may be that it is precisely the Arabs, Israel, the entire Near East who need the experience of the Church as grace. Do not the words of St. Paul apply to us, too: "In the presence of God and of Christ Jesus who is to judge the living and the dead, I charge you: preach the word, whether convenient or inconvenient" (2 Tim 4:1-2) and "Put on the armor of God, if you are to resist on the evil day . . . having girded your loins with truth!" (Eph 6:13-14)? In this decisive hour of the Council neither diplomacy nor tactics, not even some great move of pastoral prudence will set us free, but only out-and-out justice and truth (see Jn 8:32).

The speech of the Bishop of Würzburg had a sobering effect, in the deepest sense of the word. It laid bare the difficult situation of the Bishops and the gravity of their decision. No longer could they flirt with easy solutions, no longer try to get rid of the obstinate problem by dropping the Declaration altogether. Yet, the struggle about individual phrases went on. Time and again, members tried to drop the condemnation of the deicide charge, but all efforts came to naught, until one day a two-thirds majority favored eliminating the relevant words. The majority had become convinced that a rigid clinging to the text would endanger all ecumenical efforts in the Near East and thus destroy all hope of a reunion of the Eastern and Western Churches or, at least, of closing some of the wounds of centuries—the great dream of Paul VI. If, after the vote, somebody had told the Bishops: "Now you have capitulated to the Arabs after all! Moreover, you have done violence to your own conscience," one of those who had voted for removing the words "guilty of deicide" would certainly have answered: "Not at all! We have made a *verbal* compromise for the sake of a higher good; we have removed a few words, without doing violence to the meaning, for the sake of the well-being of our Christian brethren in the Middle East but, above all, for the sake of the Church's unity."

This, at least, is the way things were seen in the Account of Modifications by the Secretariat. According to the conviction of the majority of the Secretariat's members, those words could be removed because they did not belong to the substance of the text. The idea is contained in the preceding sentences in which a collective guilt of the Jews is expressly denied and the view that they are rejected or cursed by God is clearly dismissed. The following reasons are given for the omission of the phrase "guilty of deicide":

> Whatever the context in which the word *deicidium* occurs, it has an ugly, a hateful sound (*odiose sonat*). Hence terms like *deicida* (Godslayer, Christkiller) and others must be removed altogether from the Christian vocabulary. Besides, the term *deicidium* might lead to wrong theological interpretations. These have already occurred and caused difficulties in pastoral work as well as in the ecumenical dialogue with some Churches.[142]

Some commentators consider the first reason unsatisfactory. Whether a commentator deems it satisfactory or not, he ought to support the elimination of words like "Godkiller" from Christian vocabulary. He ought to see to it that the ban be carried out everywhere, so that all might realize the tragic effects of this epithet. Only thus can the Declaration on the Jews lead to the purification of religious language which preaching and teaching so badly need.

Alarm About the Declaration. The struggle for a just Declaration on the Jews within the Secretariat was accompanied by public requests that the Council emphasize its profession of God's constant love for Israel. There were repeated rumors in the world press that the Declaration was going to be suppressed, or at least considerably weakened. Sometimes, such a rumor was only a journalistic stratagem for acquiring information. Looking back, however, it may be said that the false reports, too, had contributed to keeping the discussion alive. Both well-founded and unfounded reports brought about reactions that were not without influence on the Council Fathers.

On June 20, 1964, the Jesuit periodical *America* published an editorial that mentioned the widespread disquiet the news of a weakened Declaration on the Jews had caused, and therefore asked for a sincere and unmistakable Declaration. Many letters by readers welcomed this editorial. James C. Tower thought that the opposition of the Oriental Christians to a Declaration on the Jews was, in the last analysis, only a provincial reaction. They saw the matter from a point of view that allowed only a distorted picture drawn by local Israeli-Arab tensions. The demand that the universal Church take over their limited point of view was obstruction rather than cooperation with the Council. What they sought to prevent was a proper gesture of Christian contrition for the massive and cruel persecutions the Jews has suffered at the hands of nominal Christians.[143] The Paulist editor of *The Catholic World* in New York, John B. Sheerin, thought that the editorial had cast much light on a most pressing question. The Declaration on the Jews such as it had been presented to the Second Session showed not only prophetic foresight, but also contrition for the injustice Jews had suffered for two millennia.[144]

The author of this commentary emphasized the view of the editorial "that the great question was that of deicide." The killing of Jesus was undoubtedly deicide, for it was the murder of God Incarnate. But does this make formal deicides of the actors in the drama of the Passion—the Jerusalem judges and the Roman hangmen, the Jewish crowd before the palace of the governor and the soldiers (probably Syrian) who mocked, crowned, and crucified Jesus? The answer is obviously, "No." None of the people concerned knew whom they crucified. This, after all, was the testimony of the Victim Himself: "Father, forgive them, for they know now what they do" (Lk 23:34).

Jesus' plea notwithstanding, some people insist on calling deicides not only the actors in the drama of salvation, but the whole Jewish people. Since we are all sinners, and thus spiritually guilty of the Crucifixion, we have become brothers and sisters in guilt just as we are children of mercy. Why, then, should a Christian, a sinner who has been forgiven, want to burden the Jews with his bitterness, even his hatred? Why should he or she want to accuse anyone, instead of rejoicing that his or her own, indeed, the world's sin "deserved so great a Redeemer?"[145]

I would be much more readily convinced that the motives of the persistent defenders of the deicide accusation are pure, were they equally anxious to give the Jewish people credit for being, as it were, the womb of Christ. The conclusion seems inevitable to me: If the whole Jewish people bears the guilt of the few who tried and condemned Jesus, they must in the same breath be named "Mother of Jesus." But, I have never heard anyone who calls the Jews deicides say that they brought forth God-made-Man and ought, therefore, be called "Israel, the Godbearer." Could it be that the source of the charge is not faith or love of Christ, but love of self, or an even more sinister force?[146]

The examples of a public discussion of the Declaration, and its then uncertain fate I have just given, stem from earlier times when the first news of the draft launched by the Coordinating Commission reached the public. They might easily be multiplied by others of the same time, or of later days. All these comments belong to the history of the text, because they are visible proof of the fact that at the Council, the whole Church was engaged, even though only the Bishops were the spokesmen of her convictions and emotions.

However often the expression "deicide" may have been employed by Christian writers and preachers, it does not form part of the authentic tradition of the Church. This was demonstrated, for example, by Cardinal Journet as early as 1945 in his book, *Les Destinées d'Israël*, with the following quotation from Augustine:

> The Lord rose again and many [Jews] believed in Him. Without understanding [what they had done], they crucified Him. Yet, later they believed in Him, and this very great sin was forgiven the *homicides*. I do not speak of *deicides*, for had they realized it, they would not have

crucified the Lord of glory. The killing of an innocent man was forgiven them: through grace, they drank the blood which they had shed in folly.[147]

The months between spring and autumn 1965, that is, the time before the Fourth Session of the Council, were particularly depressing. One piece of bad news followed another. In March of the same year, an obscure Italian Bishop was made famous by the world press far beyond the borders of his own tiny diocese and, indeed, of his country. In an Italian clergy review, Bishop Luigi Carli opposed the Declaration which had been approved during the first reading by an overwhelming majority of the Council Fathers. According to him, the Jews were collectively guilty of the Crucifixion of Christ, and this guilt endured because the Judaism of today was "the free, willed continuation" of the Judaism of the time of Jesus and its "No" to Him. Thus, it must indeed be called "rejected, cursed, and deicidal."[148] As if this frontal attack on the Declaration were not sad enough, it occasioned all kinds of rumors, such as that the Pope had established a commission of four, to which Bishop Carli was said to belong, in order to examine the Declaration. Such a commission would have meant the cassation of the document.

The rumor seemed to be confirmed by a sermon given by Pope Paul. On Passion Sunday, 1965, he conducted the principal service at the Church of Santa Maria della Guadalupe in Monte Mario, a Roman suburb. Explaining the Gospel (Jn 8:46-59), he said, according to the *Osservatore Romano*, that the Gospel of the day was "a serious and sad page, giving an account of the conflict between Jesus and the Jewish people. This nation, chosen to receive the Messiah whom it expected for thousands of years... did not recognize Him when He came; it even fought, slandered, insulted, and finally killed Him." Turning his attention to the present, Pope Paul stated that this drama continued to be repeated even to this day, through the works of all those who offended and denied Christ.[149] The main points the Pope made in connecting the mystery of the Crucifixion with the modern world are these:

> This drama ... is being repeated in our own times: a large part of the human race is proud of acting in contradiction to God; there are people who think themselves superior to others simply because they assail Christianity and its message of peace and brotherliness . . . .
>
> Christ did not curse His crucifiers, but prayed the Father to forgive them, for they did not know what they were doing. And in our own time, too, opposition to God is more than anything else a sign of ignorance, of a lack of knowledge of Christ and His teaching. For this reason, it is necessary to be honestly and correctly informed as to what Christ's message consists of. It is necessary for our own sake, for the sake of our souls, that we remove ignorance . . . .
>
> It is necessary that we believe in Him, we put our trust in Him, we accept Him totally, and that in the midst of all our cares, He remain the center of our lives. We must not be afraid of Christ, but must give Him our faith and our love.[150]

These words show that the tenor of the sermon had been misunderstood. Yet, this does not change the fact that the way the Pope expressed himself was unfortunate, though it does prove that any anti-Jewish intention was far from his mind.

For a time, it seemed as if real communication had broken down. Paul VI had spoken in pre-conciliar language. This was regrettable, because it was hardly compatible with the spirit and letter of the Declaration on the Jews to say that the Jewish people, that is, all the Jews had fought, insulted, and killed Jesus. It seems as if the content of the Declaration had not yet reached the Pope's subconscious, so that, in this probably spontaneous sermon, he still used the "old" language without being aware of it. Most journalists did not realize what the Pope was driving at, and suppressed his application to the present. But the reference to the everpresent and almost ubiquitous resistance to God was the chief point of the homily. No wonder the sermon caused consternation. Most readers of the homily thought to discover a regressive movement in it. Some saw in the gaffe—which happens to the best of speakers, especially in a state of fatigue—a well calculated plan: Paul VI wanted to examine the reaction to his words in order to see how the elimination of the Declaration would be received. These people did not realize that such a calculation was quite foreign to the character of Paul VI, who was, moreover, far removed from any contempt for or hatred of Jews.[151] What had happened was the breakdown of healthy communication.

Two leading Italian Jews, Chief Rabbi Dr. Elio Toaff and the President of the Union of Israelite Congregations, Sergio Piperno, sent a telegram of protest to the Secretary of State, Cardinal Cicognani, in which they expressed their "pained astonishment" that the Pope had renewed the ancient accusation of the guilt of all the Jews in the death of Christ, after the Declaration of the Council seemed to have put an end to it.[152] In the United States, some Rabbis objected to the sermon of the Pope. Several Catholic and Protestant periodicals were no less vociferous in their protests against the "lapse" and "bigotry" of the Pope. But none of those who protested had taken the trouble of reading the whole sermon. Had they done so, they would still have been unhappy about the Pope's injudicious reference to a conflict between the Jewish people and Christ, but they would have seen that he meant no harm.

In such an atmosphere, disquieting rumors were almost inevitable. On April 25, the *New York Times* reported that the Declaration on the Jews had been exposed to renewed attacks, this time not by Arabs, but from "traditionalist" elements in the Church. It now seemed more than probable that far-reaching verbal changes would have to be made. Thank God, this prognosis was wrong, though it is true that the Declaration had been under fire from some (not from "the") "conservatives." It is one of the ironies of life that even a very subtle antagonism often leads to an attitude similar to that which it attacks. Thus it seems that certain opponents of the Declaration on the Jews resembled Annas and Caiaphas, those lovers of the status quo. Afraid of renewal, they wanted to cling to the old state of things.

Nevertheless, the alarming news continued to mushroom. On June 20, the London *Observer* declared, without substantiation, that the Declaration had been removed from the agenda of the last Session of the Vatican Council. Also on June 20, the correspondent of the *New York Times* alleged to have learned from a highly placed source that the final fate of the Declaration was once more to be thoroughly examined. Similarly, the *Frankfurter Allgemeine Zeitung* reported on June 21 that the Pope had sent an instruction to the Coordinating Commission in which he had demanded the removal of the Declaration from Conciliar discussion. These most disturbing rumors, made the Coordinating Council of the German Societies for Christian-Jewish Cooperation appeal to their Bishops. They urged that the Bishops do all they could to have the Declaration, essentially unchanged, promulgated before the conclusion of the Fourth Session.[153] Exactly a month before, German Catholics had addressed a magnificent petition to the Pope. I call it magnificent because the request is expressed clearly and without circumlocution; the language is humble without being obsequious, urgent without being arrogant:

> The undersigned have read with deep interest and joy the Council's Declaration of November 20, 1964, on Non-Christian Religions, including Section 4 on the Jews, which they regard as the basis for a new beginning in Christian-Jewish relations.
>
> The importance of this Declaration cannot be overrated. All Christians who have desired it welcome the fact that old unjustified reproaches against the Jews can be upheld no longer (e.g. the corporate guilt in the Crucifixion of Christ). Thus the ground is cut from under Christian Anti-semitism. After the painful events of the past, this must be a profound satisfaction for all Christians who are aware of that past. For innumerable friends of reconciliation between Christians and Jews, this achievement is one of the finest fruits of the Council. At the same time, we hope that the new bonds to the ancient People of God will also open new ways toward the unity of Christians; after all, the Old Covenant, evidence of God's saving grace, is the common heritage of all Christians and a bridge toward the unity of the entire people of God. Therefore, the undersigned hail the fact that the Council has thus spoken and look forward to the coming promulgation as a task incumbent on our time that will have meaning for ages to come.[154]

Antisemitism on the Periphery of the Council. A quite different phenomenon in the history of the Declaration was the slanderous pamphlets distributed on the periphery of the Council. Even during the First Session of the Council, the Fathers received a book of several hundred pages entitled *Complotto contra la Chiesa*, "Conspiracy against the Church." Maurice Pinay was given as the name of the author. Despite the French-sounding pseudonym and the fact that the first edition appeared in Italian, the book is of Hispanic origin, as is evident from its bibliography. References are normally to Spanish translations, even if the original had been published in another language. Though the book referred frequently only to one author, for example: "All rights reserved by the author," the preface stated that the book "has been written by a group of idealists who are strict Catholics," and who are firmly convinced "that the Catholic Church passes, at present, through one of the most dangerous periods of its history." The Church is threatened by international Communism, whose secret driving forces are Jewry and Freemasonry, whose hidden strength is Jewry again, which in itself is the "synagogue of Satan."

The first three sections of the book deal with the "Jewish threat" to the Church, while the fourth "exposes" the "fifth column in the clergy." This "fifth column" is the creation of Marranos; even the Gnostic and the Arian heresies were the work of the Jews, Arius having been a Jew. How droll! Scholars know nothing of Arius' birth and early schooling. "Pinay" seems the only one able to state that Arius was a Jew. One chapter treats of the Jews as the most dangerous enemies of the Church, another calls them the betrayers of their most faithful friends and protectors, still another states that they spread the cult of Satan. Thus "Pinay" goes on and on: The barbarian invasion was a Jewish triumph; the Albigensian heresy had been instigated by the Jews. At all times, the Jews had attempted to infiltrate the clergy to accomplish their work of destruction more easily. The same was going to happen at the "coming Council." That the author spoke of the Council as a future event shows that the book had been in preparation for a long time; that the words were not removed from the translation shows in what slipshod a manner the "information" had been gathered.

The author(s) write(s):

> We know from a reliable Jewish source that the statute, which will regulate the relations between Jews and Christians and be presented to the next ecumenical council by agents of Jewry in the higher echelons of the clergy, was planned in dark synagogues and high Masonic circles. Its aim is to oblige Jews and Christians not to attack one another and thus to impede Catholics from defending their nations or their Catholic families from the destructive activity of Jewry, which on its part does not appear to attack the Church and the Catholics directly but will do so according to the classic system of casting the stone while hiding the hand that throws it.[155]

American Bishops thought the book so disgusting, so meaningless, and so boring that they threw it into the wastepaper basket.

While "Pinay" considers conversion (which, according to the nature of the Jews, can only be feigned) the secret weapon of subversive Jewry, "Bernardus," another agitator who concealed his name, regards the conversion of the Jews as the only way by which they can get rid of the curse that lies upon them. In a pamphlet written in Italian, *Gli Ebrei e il Concilio alla luce della Sacra Scrittura e della Tradizione*, distributed during the Second Session, Bernardus defends the view that the Jews are indeed a deicide, damned, and pernicious people. The Church must defend herself against them even today, as she has done in the past. He asserts that measures suppressing the Jews or, rather, restraining the freedom of Christians and Jews to interact, and demanding their social separation are not conditioned by the times. They are eternal norms, whether they are just or unjust. Thus, he considers the decree of 1751 by the Inquisition, "Concerning the Jews," a sacred law.

That decree teems with directives; I shall quote only a few that show what happens when the Church imitates a police state. According to it, Jews may not buy or receive any books whatever, unless they have been presented to the competent censors. During the burial of their dead, Jews may not observe any rites, and on the way to the cemetery they may neither sing nor carry lights, under pain of financial or corporal punishment. Jewish men and women must wear a yellow badge. There may be no dispensation from this; if a clergyman of inferior rank were to grant it, he is to be punished by his superiors, as they see fit. Jews are forbidden to distribute, give, or sell meat of any animal killed by them to Christians; the same applies to milk and milk products. The punishment of a fine of 100 "Kronen" and imprisonment is incurred by Jews and Christians involved in such transactions. No Jew may spend the night away from the ghetto; he must return before 1 a.m. and may not leave it before daybreak. Those who disobey the order are threatened with flogging in public, three strokes with the rope for men and with the whip for women. Jews are forbidden to play, eat, drink, or even converse with Christians. Neither are they allowed to visit places of entertainment, castles, farms, or other places for any reason whatsoever, even if they needed a change of air.[156]

Some prohibitions, e.g. that Jews must not observe any burial rites, are contrary to the traditional stance that allowed Jews to keep their liturgy. One must be benighted to regard such precepts as the law of Christ. Regulations like these are enacted when pettiness and fear take the place of faith.

During the crisis of October 1964, the Bishops received another scurrilous publication in the mail, entitled "The Jewish-Masonic Action at the Council." This purported to have been written by unnamed priests and religious of an unnamed diocese; two of them were said to have been members of the Council. Since the authors enjoyed the protection of anonymity, the avowal of their membership in the Council could not be verified. They wrote that their hearts were heavy when they saw the audacity prevailing at the Council. Some of the Fathers had evidently lost the faith. The writers further maintained that Jewish converts were trying to destroy the divine work.

The authors also wished us to believe that "international Jewry," made proud by its temporal triumphs, was now staging a new attack on the Catholic Church, pretending to honor the Jewish people before the world, an attempt contradicting the traditional teachings of the Church. Jews who had attained a high rank in the hierarchy had fraudulently persuaded John XXIII to create a Secretariat for the Unity of Christians. The Secretariat served them as a platform from which to launch their propaganda "in favor of the Jews, the eternal Anti-christs." This work was in the hands of the following Jews, the authors "revealed:" Cardinal Bea, Monsignori Oesterreicher and Baum, together with Bishop Walter Kempe (all from the country of Luther) and Bishop Méndez Arceo, Mexico.

Two things are intriguing. First, the authors evidently do not know which card to play, that of Judeophobia, or that of Luthero-phobia. Secondly, they are not even good liars. Cardinal Bea is as little Jewish as the authors are Congolese. At the time of the Council, Gregory Baum was an Augustinian, not a Monsignor. I do not come from the land of Luther. The Bishop called "Kempe" is evidently Auxiliary Bishop Kampe. Neither he nor Bishop Méndez Arceo had anything to do with the authorship of the Declaration on the Jews.

If one has no real cause, one must fabricate it. Hence, the authors boldly state that the many Fathers who supported the "theses of the Jews" had done so only because they had been deceived by the aforementioned agents of international Jewry "who have so far been able to conceal their identity." Know-ingly or not, the authors implied that the more than two thou-sand Fathers who in the end voted for the Declaration on the Jews had not obeyed the voice of their conscience, but rather the blandishment of Antichrist. It is not surprising that Fes-quet, the special correspondent of *Le Monde*, wrote that these statements made their authors ridiculous in the eyes of every reasonable person.[157]

Still another pamplet complained about a "Jewish-Masonic conspiracy." We read there:

> In our day, the Roman Curia, the Pope himself, and espe-cially the Fathers assembled at the Second Ecumenical Vatican Council no longer realize what lurks behind the alleged reforms of Cardinals Bea, Suenens, Frings, Döpfner, and their associates when they seek decentralization or the

creation of a parliament around the Pope. If such plans are not checked, the Catholic Church and the Pope will suffer the same fate as did the Christian monarchs, who were first deprived of their authority and then deposed. The Vatican will then be turned into a beautiful museum such as the Louvre, Versailles, or other European castles.[158]

According to the writers of this pamphlet, these castles were taken away from their owners through the machinations of Jews and Freemasons, because the former did not oppose the latter.

This pamphlet also alleged that Cardinal Bea's name was not of German, but of Jewish-Spanish origin. It was said to have derived from the Sephardic Beja or Beha. Actually, it derives from Böheim, "the one coming from Bohemia."[159] The pamphlet claimed that "the principal author of the Decree on the Jews, the supposedly converted Jew, today Monsignor Oesterreicher," said, in a sermon at St. Patrick's Cathedral, New York, "We no longer read the many statements of Jesus Christ against His people which are contained in the Gospel. Monsignor Oesterreicher then dared to censure the Gospel of our Lord Jesus Christ." Not only were the authors of these slanders cowards who did not dare to give their names, they deliberately misquoted me, although they maintained they had quoted verbatim. In 1961, I preached in St. Patrick's Cathedral, New York, during the Octave of Prayer for Christian Unity, taking as my theme the stirrings of the Holy Spirit in the Church of our own days. I said:

> We no longer read the many harsh sayings the Gospels record of Jesus against His kinsmen as if they were words of contempt rather than of care, as if they were sweeping condemnations rather than merciful proddings. We now realize better than ever before that, in spite of their past or present opposition to the gospel, the children of Israel remain dear to the Lord. For He is a God of fidelity (see Rom 11:28-29).

From this passage the authors took about a third, presenting it as the complete thought, and omitting the rest.

A man, called Giorgio Trillini, produced a pamphlet under the name of Fra Giorgio da Terni in order to give his statements ecclesiastical character or feign a special mandate. In reality, he was neither priest nor monk. In it, he wrote:

> All famous Popes, Saints, and Fathers of the Church . . . had warned against the "Jewish plague," which is more contagious than the Black Death or one of the venereal diseases. . . . Jews have been found everywhere, from the first Freemasons' lodge to the Bolshevik Revolution, from Rome to the bestial, savage and bloodthirsty Marx, Engels, Lenin, Trotsky, Stalin, Krushchev and Brezhnev. [Of the above-mentioned seven, five are not Jews! J.M.O.] The six million Jews gassed in the concentration camps never existed except in the lies of those crafty children of Israel. The truth has just begun to appear in the newspapers of Egypt, Syria and Jordan. Go ask the Arabs who the Jews are, and you will learn how much they hate Jesus.[160]

In my view, the affinity between the Nazis, the authors of the Antisemitic pamphlets, and hostile Arabs is here quite obvious.

The connection between the last two is even clearer in a publication of the year 1965 with the lengthy title: "The Declaration in favor of the Jews lays the foundation for a new form of racism which impairs the right to the legitimate defense of other nations." The author calls himself Dr. Edoardo di Zaga. He manages to reproduce a correspondence between the leader of the Palestinian-Arab delegation in New York, Issah Nakleh, and Cardinal Bea. As the Cardinal refuses to comply with the wishes of his correspondent, he is at once compared with Machiavelli. The author goes on:

> The Jewish problem is not only serious—it is *the only problem* of the world today, because all other problems which have brought our present age to the threshold of death are the result of the unnatural fertility of this serious problem. To be free or not to be free, to have a fatherland with all that the word implies, or to be part of the world of Leviathan, the world that is controlled and enslaved by Zionism—*that is the question!*

Here are a few "gems" from the pamphlet: the Council seemed to assert that the blood of Abraham made the Jew into a sacrament, that "as an individual and as a community [the Jew] is *ex opere operato* the end and object of the divine promises and the divine blessing." Cardinal Bea had condemned the Church in order to satisfy Jewry. He condemned all persecutions of the Jews, not only in our own days but in all ages of the Church.

> Thus his condemnation is one *en masse*; it is a condemnation of more than thirty Popes who have raised their voices against the excesses, the intrigues and crimes committed by the Jews, that is by the Mafia, who are without sin, because Abraham's blood flows in their veins.

With this general condemnation of the fictitious "crimes of the Jewish people" [meaning probably: "committed against the Jewish people," J.M.O.] a new, sacred racism was to be introduced, "A Jewry protected by the Church and the Council." Two Messianisms had to be distinguished: [1] the Jewish one, which is political, indeed nothing but a desire for power and the subjugation of the world, and [2] the divine one, that is the redemption and salvation of all through the sacrifice of Christ on Calvary.

The author lives in a primitive world, in which there is only black and white, no grey, no transitions, no concert of colors, in a world, not of humans, but of angels and devils, where all justice is on one side and all wrong on the other. Indeed, it may be asked what kind of God he worships. Certainly not the God of Abraham, Isaac, and Jacob, the God of the living, the God of surprise, of grace, of wonder, whose ways are not the ways of human beings. Peter thought it enough to forgive seven times seven—certainly a good measure—but Christ expects us to forgive seventy times seven, that is again and again, without counting. Dr. di Zaga, on the contrary, thinks that "we," Christians, "may not love a people that is the incarnation of the war against Christ and His Church."

It is complete nonsense to assume, as does our author, that, "today as always," Zionism "seeks to eliminate and destroy

Christ, its rival." That Christ and Zionism should be rivals is odd indeed. To assume such opposition is to take Zionism more seriously than it takes itself. But supposing Dr. di Zaga's view of Zionism were correct, ought we to follow him in his hatred? This sentence, indeed the whole paragraph, tells why I have treated the anti-Jewish campaign *ad nauseam*. This hostility toward Jews threatens the Church much more than it does the Jewish people, because it wishes to drive Christians into the arms of a pagan god. However much hate mongers like Dr. di Zaga may speak of Christ, their god is the god of a dark, irreversible fate. The God of Israel, who shows mercy unto the thousandth generation (Ex 20:6), is alien to them. It is a scandal to such hate mongers that the Lord should be faithful to Israel, that He has not rejected it, even though it does not recognize Christ.

The obstinacy with which the Antisemitic opposition was carried on to the end can only be explained by a profound *ressentiment* against the incomprehensibility of God's grace and the election of Israel. In mid-October, a few days before the final vote, the Fathers received "a last warning," this time signed by about thirty so-called Catholic or Christian organizations. Most were unknown in Rome; a few were certainly fictitious. One of the few identifiable groups, which had supposedly supported the attack in the eleventh hour, was the "Traditionalist Movement of America." The leader of this ultra-conservative group, Father Gommar De Pauw, was in Rome when the last warning appeared, and simply denied that this movement had anything to do with the attack. When he was asked to make sure what was behind the signature of his movement, he decided to telephone its headquarters. On the same afternoon, he announced that the spokesmen of the Traditionalists who had remained in the States asserted that they had neither seen, nor approved, much less signed, that paper. This should suffice to show how unreliable were its authors.

Once more, the Bishops were adjured to realize that their approval of the Declaration on the Jews would make them heretics and the Council a kind of "robber synod," while the Pope would show himself as a false Pope were he to promulgate it. The authors considered themselves empowered to issue such a warning because their only motive was "to save the Catholic Church from such a disgrace." Moreover, they only followed Christ and His Apostles: "[The authors] bear witness that Christ and the Apostles John and Paul were the first Antisemites, and that the New Testament was the first [anti-Jewish] pamphlet of our era." Neither the Pope nor the Bishops were frightened by the voice of this adversary masquerading as God's advocate. In the words of the French historian of the Council, Antoine Wenger, A.A., the arguments of the pamphleteers "were so vile, their allusions so repulsive, their origin so uncertain and even suspect" that the Fathers did not allow themselves to be influenced by them in any way whatever.[161] A few days later, the Declaration was accepted and shortly afterwards promulgated.

The End of the Road. On October 28, 1965, the day of the promulgation, the arduous journey had come to an end. Despite certain defects, the Declaration on the Jews was a triumph over the law of inertia which had carried certain prejudices through the centuries. One defect, the dropping of the express condemnation of the charge of deicide, has already been mentioned. Another was the heading of Article 4 in the whole Declaration. One amendment had proposed saying "On Judaism" instead of "On the Jews," in order to make it clear that Article 4 dealt with the religion and not with the people. The proposal was accepted, but unfortunately not in the form suggested. The heading chosen was "On the Jewish Religion."

A Jewish religion without the Jewish people, however, is a fiction, it exists only in a "History of Religions," that is to say, in books. Those who chose the heading were simply unaware of the fact that the Jewish religion cannot be separated from the Jewish people. The latter is, no doubt, a people *sui generis*, a community of shared experience and destiny which can hardly be called anything but "people," whether or not it lives in its own country and has a State of its own. It is a question of Jewish existence which is the existence not only of individuals but eminently of a community. The change was made principally to break Arab resistance, and the only mitigating factor about it is that all titles were provisional, because they served only to find one's way more easily through the working documents. In the final edition, all headings, including that "On the Jewish Religion," have been eliminated.

The provisional version of 1964, and even earlier ones had the phrase: "The Church of Christ acknowledges with grateful mind (*grato animo*) that the beginnings of her faith and election are to be found in ancient Israel." A proposal signed by only two Fathers suggested eliminating the words "with grateful mind" because they sounded as if gratitude were owed to the Jews of today for the fact that our roots are in the Patriarchs. It cannot be denied, on the one hand, that the present generation of Jews is responsible for the evil done by an earlier one while it is asserted, on the other hand, that the present generation should be credited with the merits of the past. This objection was possible only because philosophers and psychologists had not yet worked out the difference between the solidarity which binds the members of a community to one another, and the concept of collective guilt. Biblical theologians, alas, have not contrasted sufficiently the Scriptural teaching of the unity of the Patriarchs and their descendants—the coalescing of forebears and future generations into one corporate personality—with collectivist thinking.[162]

But apart from this elementary distinction, ought not a Catholic give thanks and honor to the Jews of our time also for those gifts that God had showered on them for no merit of their own? The battle cry: "Honor to God alone!" is not part of the Catholic vision of the universe of grace; rather, do Catholics believe that honor given to God's creatures, as *His* creatures, is honor given to Him. Is it not this attitude that speaks in the Church's constant veneration of the Holy Land that has borne Christ and of the holy places, even though they were not conscious of the great deeds God accomplished in them? If the Church lovingly greets these dumb and lifeless witnesses, should a Christian not do the same for the living witnesses, through whom the revelation of the First Covenant has come to us? It is regrettable that the words of thanks were eliminated from the Declaration, not only because the affectionate tone that distinguished the Declaration from other such documents has thus been diminished, but also because the fullness of faith and the courage flowing from it have been harmed.

In the draft of 1964, the disapproval of the hatred and persecution of Jews was expressed by the verbs *deplorare et condemnare*, "to decry resolutely and to condemn." In the final version, the text was shortened; only *deplorare* remained. The explanation that in the language of Councils "condemn" was applied only to heresies, not to sins or crimes, did not convince anyone. For the Constitution on The Church in the Modern World condemned expressly—God be praised!—the inhumanity of total war.[163] In any case, Antisemitism is not only sinful, but also heretical. It is true, however, that the first drafts did not contain the term "condemn," since Pope John had charged the Council not to issue condemnations but to proclaim the good news of the gospel. Moreover, "the special mission of the Secretariat is one of dialogue, formation, and education, not one of hurling anathemas."[164]

One *modus* had asked that persecutions be rejected in a stronger and more comprehensive manner, so that a particular rejection of Antisemitism would be unnecessary, and could, therefore, be eliminated. The Secretariat rejected the second part of this proposal while accepting the first. The fact that the majority preferred the shortened form may have been due to pity for Arabs. The Arab members of the Secretariat felt neglected and complained constantly that the "Arab cause" was at a disadvantage: the injustices done to the Jews had been duly considered, but the wrong done to the Arabs in Palestine had been passed over in complete silence. The lengthy debates on the alterations had, in the end, some positive results. The rejection of Jew-hatred was given new depth. In the words of Laurentin:

> The fact that the Jews are here mentioned among the other persecuted peoples does not make them less important; on the contrary, they appear as the prototype of the persecuted people, from the Egyptian genocide prior to the Exodus to that of Hitler at the time of the Second World War.[165]

Some obvious alterations in the final version deprive the Declaration on the Jews of some of its vigor, but serve a definite purpose. I have in mind the three additions that precede the relevant sections of the old text: [1] Jerusalem's failure to recognize its extraordinary hour of grace; [2] The fact that the Jewish authorities and those who followed their lead pressed for the death of Christ; [3] The Church as the new people of God. They are, as it were, the answer to the frequent objections that the Secretariat had rewritten the gospel, that it had modified Scripture in favor of the Jews, and quoted only those passages or parts of a given text that flatter Jews but not those that criticize them.

Thus, on the eve of the promulgation, when even the slightest change was out of the question, a Papal Delegate from the Middle East asked that the statement on the role of the Jews as a people always dear to God be modified. For this statement reproduced only the positive half of the Pauline text, omitting the negative one on Jewish hostility to the gospel. He was only pacified on being told the obvious, namely that those responsible for the text of the Declaration had not meant to quote Paul verbatim, wherefore there were no quotation marks; further, that the negative aspect was expressed by the addition that not a few had rejected the propagation of the gospel, and finally, if one had to split hairs, that the Conciliar text was not as pointed and straightforward as that of St. Paul. The Apostle says quite emphatically that the Jews are beloved of God, whereas the Declaration weakens it by adding *adhuc*: that they are *still* beloved. Thus the Conciliar Declaration loses something of the self-evidence and assuredness of the Letter to the Romans. Here was a Bishop—true, an opponent of the Declaration from the beginning—who could not get over his seemingly theological difficulties. What would happen to ordinary Catholics if the anti-Jewish and, at the same time, anti-Catholic agitation continued after the Council? The additions were inserted to prevent those Catholics from being helpless victims of a hostile campaign.

Despite all the modifications, the text is a triumph of truth and justice. This is the sober judgment of all competent critics. Mario von Galli, S.J. could write:

On the whole, I think, it may be said that the new version has not drawn back an inch in all essential statements, but it reflects the violent attacks to which it had been subjected in the meantime. This is a relative weakness, but it would be downright foolish were the changes to spoil our joy in a Declaration that corresponds essentially to the ecumenical turning of this Council.[166]

To quote Abbé Laurentin once more: In a meditation on the meaning of October 15, 1965, the day of the final acceptance of the Declaration by the Council Fathers, he reminded the readers of *Le Figaro* that he had said the year before that this text, which was so compact, clear, and attractive to the people of our time, was perhaps the finest success of Vatican II. He went on to say that he maintained this judgment, despite the alterations:

> I have just read the text again, such as it is, trying to forget what had been before. I do not take back my judgment of the year before: the text is still beautiful. It resembles one of those women who are still admired though they are about to fade; those who had known them before still whisper: "If you only knew how beautiful she once was!" A stiff look has replaced the candid smile with which the Church, in a moment of extraordinary grace, had regarded the people from which she had sprung. . . . Some people are bitter about this. However, at first glance, this stiffness is not noticeable.[167]

In another context, and almost a year later, Abbé Laurentin repeated this judgment, adding that the transition from centuries-old hostility to warm friendship could not be made in a day. In such a situation, it might even be dangerous if words and gestures were too much in advance of the feeling on which they must be based. Perhaps the present modest and cautious text was the most appropriate first step. The Statement on the Jews opens locks that have been jammed for centuries. Not without difficulty or pressure in the opposite direction, a door has been opened. The dialogue and friendship between the Catholic Church and the people of Israel may now develop on a sound foundation.[168]

I have anticipated events in speaking of a triumph of truth

and justice. Before the Declaration could be promulgated, some difficulties still had to be overcome. In order to facilitate the voting and make it as precise as possible, the Secretariat had arranged that several individual points be submitted to a vote. These were:

[1] The preamble.
[2] Nature religions, Hinduism, and Buddhism.
[3] Islam.
[4] The Church's roots in ancient Israel.
     The irrevocable grace of Israel's election.
     The common heritage of Jews and Christians.
     Brotherly conversation and common studies.
[5] The rejection of collective guilt of the Jews.
[6] The alleged curse on and the rejection of Israel.
[7] Unprejudiced sermons and catechetical instruction.
     Incompatibility of contempt for Jews with Christian love.
     The special relationship between Christians and Jews.
     The Cross as the sign of the all-embracing love of God.
[8] Universal brotherhood which must exclude none.
[9] The Declaration as a whole.

The voting took place on October 14 and 15, 1965. On October 11, three days earlier, at the eleventh hour as it were, the Bishops received a letter from the *Coetus Episcoporum Internationalis*, "International Association of Bishops," instructing them how to vote. This international committee was an organization of "ultra-conservatives," men to whom standstill was the sign of authentic Catholic life, indeed, an idol. They were almost a council apart from the Council. The "instructions" purported to have been drawn up at the request of Council Fathers seeking advice, and were dated November 11 [sic], 1965. They were signed by Bishop Carli and Archbishops Lefèbvre and Rigaud. In the light of these "instructions," readers who think of Archbishop Lefèbvre as a man who suffers from nothing but nostalgia for the so-called Tridentine Mass must now realize that he is a man who objected to the Council as a whole. Like his colleagues in that committee, he was, I am sorry to say, anti-vernacular, anti-Protestant, anti-Jewish, anti-everything.

To let negative attitudes get the upper hand threatens one's spiritual life. It may be well to recall appropriate words addressed by Paul VI to the Observers, that is, those of Communions separated from Rome, when he first received them in audience. Professor Skydsgaard, a Lutheran, in his words of greeting, had quoted Augustine's "we seek in order to find, and find in order to seek." The Pope took up this theme, making the stirring comment: *Le vrai Chrétien ne connaît pas l'immobilisme,* "the true Christian knows no standstill."[169]

Questions 1-3, the "instructions" held, should be answered in the negative (*non placet*). As a reason for the negative first *votum,* the leaders of the *Coetus* gave, among others, that for centuries the Apostles and their successors had not followed the suggested principle; on the contrary, they had fearlessly rejected errors and plainly confessed the truth of Christ. The authors of the "instructions" seemed to be unaware of the fact that the time in which we live requires new, indeed, courageous ways. The defenders of the status quo could not understand that the Church no longer ruled, but had realized that her mission was to serve believers and not-yet-believers. Still, the authors dared assert that "the vision of the draft" was that of "a professor in his study," because it considered "only religious concepts or, more correctly, a comparative 'ideology'." They wrote:

> The faith that justifies us, however, is not merely an intellectual system in which . . . one might think out a so-called *terrain d'entente* with others, or a so-called "common denominator" or, at least, a certain *apertura,* "an opening toward others." Through faith, the Catholic does not adhere to certain propositions as if he were a philosopher, but submits to a revealing person, believes in His authority, and gives himself completely to Him.[170]

It is intriguing to see how the leading men of the *Coetus* here make use of a theology of faith which is incongruous with their other ideas.

On Question 4, the spokesmen of the *Coetus* said that they liked the first five paragraphs apart from what is said of God's friendship for the Jewish people and the eschatological hope of the Church. The Pauline text of Rom 11:28 was mutilated and changed, they complained; the words "according to the election" were missing and *carissimi sunt propter patres* had been changed into *adhuc carissimi manent propter patres.* Moreover, the critical part of the Pauline text had been suppressed. This objection has been dealt with above (see p. 270). Instead of speaking of mutilation, it would be more correct to say that the Conciliar document was weaker than the Letter to the Romans. The letter says forthrightly that the Jews *are* beloved of God, whereas the Conciliar text, which had to counter a centuries-old prejudice, said that the Jews *continue* to remain the beloved of God. To do away with the ghastly prejudice that the house of Jacob is a people hated by God was sufficient justification for an alteration that leaves the deepest meaning completely unchanged.

The second objection by the *Coetus* showed the same narrow outlook. According to them, it was "unworthy of the Council" to have changed the suggestion of "the future conversion of Israel" in such a way as to exclude any proselytizing. The authors were evidently incapable of understanding that a pastoral Council devoted to renewal and reconciliation had to avoid giving unnecessary offense to others and, that after centuries of injustice, it was particularly necessary, both inside and outside the Council, to speak of Jews with a deliberate *délicatesse de coeur.* Their objections were directed not so much against the Secretariat for Unity and its text as against Pope John and his "theology of the heart."

The same directives said that Question 5 might be answered with *placet* if the term "the Jews" was to be understood in its ethnic, not in its religious sense. Question 6, received a *non placet. Placet* and *non placet* were the terms for an approving or a disapproving vote. Of the text which concerns Question 7, the signatories said that it would have been acceptable had the Secretariat approved the *modus* that demanded the rejection of an Antisemitism "of race or religion." This limitation agrees partly with the demand of the pamphlet with the long title that

I discussed above, and that had been distributed in the first half of October. According to the pamphlet, it was not permissible to qualify

> as persecutions and anti-Jewish excesses those just measures of legitimate defense of the Church and of many nations taken by Popes, Councils, and political leaders against the conspiracies, attacks, and other crimes of the Jews that had greatly damaged the Church and many peoples.[171]

Question 8, too, did not meet with the approval of the three Bishops who signed the "instructions," because the section on the brotherhood of all people had not distinguished clearly between natural and supernatural brothers, that is, fellow creatures and those reborn and sanctified through Christ in baptism, they maintained. First, it is not the duty of a brief Conciliar document to spell out every distinction. Second, there definitely is a brother-and sisterhood that embraces all human beings regardless of their sacramental status. The last question which concerned the document as a whole was simply to be answered *non placet*. These "instructions" undoubtedly made a few Bishops unsure, but they did not influence the vast majority of them. They did not produce the result the authors had intended, namely, the defeat of the Declaration.

The result of the voting was decisive. The first question received 2185 votes, of which 2071 were positive and 110 negative. The few invalid votes regarding this and the other questions are not included. The figures for the other questions are as follows:

	Votes	*Placet*	Non *Placet*
Question 2:	2183	1953	189
Question 3:	2105	1910	189
Question 4:	2099	1937	153
Question 5:	2072	1875	188
Question 6:	2080	1821	245
Question 7:	2118	1905	199
Question 8:	2118	2064	58

2023 Fathers took part in the final voting on the whole draft; 1763 voted in favor, 250 against it, and 10 votes were invalid. These figures must be briefly analyzed. 250 negative votes seems a comparatively high figure; but it should not be forgotten that this comprises not only the opponents of the section on the Jews, but also those dissatisfied with the text on Islam or Buddhism, or even those missionary bishops who had wanted a special mention of Animism. The 245 negative votes on Question 6, too, are more than those on the other questions of the Declaration on the Jews. This was the question where the affirmative vote meant the approval of eliminating the words "guilty of deicide." In the days before the voting took place, Bishop Leven and Abbé Laurentin had asked for a negative answer to Question 6, the former through a brief circular letter, the other through an important essay. At first, many Fathers were inclined to protest against the change, but finally most were convinced that it was better to leave the matter alone, since the Declaration was now at an advanced stage. A vote of protest could easily have turned out to favor the opponents; excellent canonists that they were, they could have used the fact that a high number of negative votes—over a third— required the restoration of the original text. Had this happened they could have demanded yet another delay. This, in turn, might have made it impossible to pass the Declaration in the Fourth and final Session of the Council. Hence, all those in favor of the Declaration preferred one with minor defects to none at all.

On October 28, the day of the promulgation, another solemn vote was taken. 2221 Bishops voted for, 88 against the Declaration and 3 votes were invalid. Whoever had seen the struggle for the Declaration, whoever had witnessed the many crises, its vicissitudes, regarded the triumph of that day as a miracle. As usual, the Pope addressed all those within St. Peter's and many without on the occasion of the solemn promulgation. He saw, in this epoch-making Declaration, the wonder of life. He exclaimed:

> The Church is alive. Well then, here is the proof, here the breath, the voice, the song . . . . The Church lives. The Church thinks. The Church speaks. The Church grows. We

must take account of this astonishing phenomenon. We must realize its messianic significance.

Paul VI hoped that the world, too, especially the Christians separated from Rome, would contemplate the growth of the Church and its new face, more beautiful than ever. The same applied to the followers of other religions, among them especially those "who are related to us in Abraham." He continued with great warmth: ... *maxime Hebraei, quibusdam sic agitur, ut non reprobentur neque iis diffidatur, sed ut erga eos reverentia et amor adhibeatur spesque in iis collocetur*, "... especially the Jews, whom we never ought to view with disfavor, whom we never ought to mistrust, but whom we must meet with reverence, love, and hope." If proof were necessary that the sermon the Pope gave on Passion Sunday, 1964, was not meant to disparage the Jews, his fervent plea to give Jews the honor that is their due and the love we owe them reveals his genuine reverence for the people from whom Jesus sprang. His words crowned the work on the Declaration; they were the perfect "end of the way."

A New Beginning. Beginning and end belong together. No sooner had the mandate of John XXIII been completed when voices were heard asking that the Declaration be implemented. On November 20, 1964, Cardinal Bea pleaded:

> The Declaration must ... lead to effective action. Its principles and spirit should inspire the lives of all Christians, indeed, of all men and women, so that the kind of dialogue Pope Paul discussed in the Encyclical *Ecclesiam Suam* may be begun. It is here, in the fruits which this Declaration should and will have after the Council, that lie its importance and worth.[172]

At the time of the promulgation, on October 28, 1965, the Cardinal gave an explanation to the news agency ANSA in which he said:

> The Declaration on Non-Christian Religions is indeed a

significant and highly promising beginning, but no more
than the beginning of a long and demanding way toward
the not easily attainable goal of a humanity whose members
feel themselves children of the same Father in heaven and
act as such.[173]

The theme of a new beginning was taken up by many different ecumenists. Jacques Madaule, the President of the *Amitié
Judéo-Chrétienne*, spoke along similar lines as the Cardinal:

> In my view, the Declaration must not be seen as an end, but
> as a first attempt, a new beginning. After so many centu-
> ries of bitterness, the Church at last resumes the authentic
> dialogue with the Jews. It is incumbent upon all of us to
> make this dialogue as fruitful as possible. I am convinced
> that it initiates a new era not only of Christian-Jewish
> relations, but also of the relations between Christians and
> all non-Christian religions, among which I count first of
> all Islam.[174]

J.P. Lichtenberg, O.P., goes into greater detail:

> A first stage of the difficult, but necessary dialogue
> between the Church and Israel; a first invitation to Chris-
> tians and Jews to understand each other better in order to
> love each other earnestly, that is the true meaning of the
> present text. Another stage could be reached when the
> Church acknowledges Judaism as a living and effective
> religion . . . . Finally, to reach a third stage, the Church
> would have to recognize the State of Israel.[175]

This third stage proposed here is not in keeping with the
attitude that most champions of the Declaration on the Jews
displayed during the Council. They stated, time and again,
that the Declaration was in no way meant to prepare the
diplomatic recognition of the State of Israel; some even suggested that such a measure was out of the question for a long
time. Nevertheless, this demand turns up again and again
among Catholics; there are many signs that it may become
stronger. The Arab campaign against the Declaration, a campaign replete with tricks, threats, and blandishments had

turned into a boomerang; the conduct of the Arabs during and after the Council had deprived them of the sympathies which they had enjoyed before, and thus freed the hearts of many Christians to turn to the State of Israel and the hopes it holds out for Jews, indeed, the world.

Even if the Holy See finds it impossible to establish diplomatic links with the State of Israel, it must not be forgotten that there are relations between the two, and that the Holy See has morally recognized the State of Israel. Whenever an Israeli Prime Minister visits the Pope—the latest such visit was that by Prime Minister Shimon Peres on February 20, 1985—the Israeli flag is flown at the Vatican. At that last meeting, the Pope invoked "God's blessing on Israel . . . and all peoples everywhere."[176]

To return to the theme of a "new beginning," Lucien Lazare, the Jewish partner in tripartite conversations held at Strasbourg after the end of the Council, presented it in this way:

> Two thousand years of enmity, the Second World War, and twenty years of reflection were needed to achieve this Declaration. Nevertheless, we sincerely welcome the signs of change without reservation. It is something new when the Church remembers that Jesus was a Jew and that the Apostles were Jews, and that she also teaches this. It is new for the Church to acknowledge the vigor of Jewish spirituality and that the rich religious life of Judaism possesses a dignity all its own.[177]

I appreciate Lazare's response, though I do not agree that the Council's teaching on the Jewishness of Jesus was something altogether new. True, the awareness of it may not have been a very lively one with every Church member. The centuries-long celebration of the Feast of the Circumcision on January 1, or the Presentation of the Child Jesus in the Temple on February 2 are celebrations of His descent from a long line of Jewish ancestors and His being part of the people of Israel, to give only these two examples. It is undeniable, however, that in the Council the Church awakened to the spiritual significance of Jesus' Jewish Humanity.

Lazare's brief remarks, however, are of a special quality. His joy in the Declaration has not been clouded by the bitterness of the past; his simple acknowledgment is free of condescension or pride: secure in the change that has taken place, he has refrained from making demands. To do so would not be in keeping with the newly unfolding spirit. Moreover, the positive attitude of Lucien Lazare will contribute more to the dialogue than the oft-repeated carpings of those who say that only future actions will prove the real value of the Conciliar document.

Cleansing of Speech. The truth of the last sentence cannot be denied but *c'est le ton qui fait la musique.* I hope that I myself shall find the right tone in order to sharpen the theological sense, the feeling, indeed, the conscience of all concerned. The demand of the Declaration that the Jews never be made an object of contempt by the faithful is not only a question of elementary justice, but also one of Christian self-understanding. A few examples of pseudo-theological bias from pre-Conciliar missals should illustrate my concern. Even though they are no longer in use, I chose them for two reasons. First, because I know some of the editors sufficiently well to realize that their commentaries were not motivated by vulgar Antisemitism. Second, because now and in the future, liturgical life will be the principal source of religious instruction.

On the Ninth Sunday after Pentecost in the former liturgical order, the Church read a text from Chapter 10 of 1 Corinthians: "Brethren, these things are warnings for us, not to desire evil as they did. . . ." (vv. 6-10). The editor of the "Schott" missal, the most popular German missal that carries more explanations than English missals, thought it necessary to identify the "they." He did not choose, however, an expression like "the people in the desert" or "those freed from the slavery of Egypt," or, following St. Paul, "our fathers in the desert," but simply: "the Jews in the desert." Taken by itself, "the Jews"—the whole for a part—is a legitimate figure of speech, used in literary and every day conversation. Yet, not everything legitimate is therefor helpful.

It is not in the least dangerous to say "the Swedes" instead of the "Swedish football team"; hardly anyone will assume that

the good or bad qualities of these few Swedes are those of all
Swedes. Things are different in the case of the Jews. Centuries
of errors by Greek and Latin writers, by Christian teachers and
believers, above all, the Nazi attempt to do away with all
European Jews, Auschwitz, and other places of mass murder
should alarm the conscience of all Christians, particularly of
speakers and writers, against using "the Jews" when but a few
are meant. Mortification of mind is needed to make us refrain
from easy use of global terms like "the Jews." An attentive
reading of 1 Corinthians ought to have the same effect. For
though St. Paul first says that "God was not pleased" with
most of those Jews who had passed through the sea and were
baptized in it, he later says again and again "some of them."
Some became idolaters, some committed fornication, some
tempted the Lord, and some grumbled (10:7-10). The punishments inflicted on them were examples: "Therefore, let anyone
who thinks that he stands take heed lest he fall" (10:12).

If a Christian worshiper hears time and again "the Jews," he
or she will become deaf to the delicate distinctions of the passage, indeed, be cheated of the humility the First Letter to the
Corinthians ought to instill. I think much too little attention is
paid to Pauline usage. The Apostle counts among the spiritual
ancestors of Christians not only the servants and friends of
God—Abraham who entrusted himself entirely to God's guid-
ing hand, Isaac who submitted to the will of the Lord, and
Jacob who wrestled for His blessing—but also "the stiff-necked
Jews," the men and women who resisted God's grace in the
wilderness.

Similarly, on the Tenth Sunday after Pentecost, the Church
used to read the parable of Pharisee and Publican (Lk 18:9f),
an incomparable opportunity to emphasize some fundamental truths of the Christian life. Unfortunately, this opportunity
is often passed by, because the historical circumstances of the
parable are stressed too much and, moreover, misrepresented.
A characteristic example is the, in many ways excellent, *Missel
de l'Assemblée Chrétienne*, edited by Belgian Benedictine
monks. In it, a publican is defined as "a Jew who through his
profession as a tax collector was in constant touch with pagans
and therefore unable to fulfill the many prescriptions of [ritual]

purification and the inexorable forms of sanctification demanded by the Pharisees."[178]

The commentator failed to mention that these tax collectors not only were in touch with some pagans, but that they were also servants of the Roman authorities. Protected by them, the publicans exploited their own people for the sake of idolatrous Rome and to their own advantage. Can one call unprejudiced a definition which overlooks that the publicans must have appeared to their own people as swindlers, extortionists, and traitors? One would have thought that editors, whose country was twice occupied and itself a colonial power, would have better understood the tension between the majority of the Jews and the tax collectors. While trampling down their own, the publicans kowtowed to their foreign masters. They were not criticized for entertaining friendly but harmless relations with the Romans; the publican knew very well what he meant when he prayed: "God, be merciful to me, a *sinner!*" (Lk 18:13).

Another footnote describes the Pharisees as "members of an integralist sect which had added minute prescriptions to the Law in order to preserve the Jewish people from contact with the pagan world; their prideful care for religious purity was accompanied by total contempt for other spiritual families and other people." The Pharisees were a movement, not a sect which, strictly speaking, means a community cut off from the main body of a religion. It is true that they regulated life in great detail; still, we do them wrong if we regard them as punctilious legalists who believed that religious life consists in nothing but the external, meticulous keeping of rules.

The description of the Pharisees as a *secte intégriste* is certainly in keeping with the idea, current among Christians, that they were a static element, as would seem to be suggested by the conflict between them and Christ; but it does not correspond to the actual role played by the Pharisees in Jewish history. I take it that the expression *secte intégriste*—what a contradiction!—has been borrowed from modern Catholic usage, according to which integralists are people who are convinced that Catholics, to safeguard the integrity of their faith, must shut themselves off from the movements of history, oppose all innovations, and persist in the old ways.

It is true that the Pharisees were in favor of a certain measure of isolation for the Jewish people, but they were certainly no advocates of immobility. While the Sadducees, the real conservatives at the time of Christ, admitted only Scripture as the source of Jewish life, the Pharisees believed in the resurrection of the dead, even though there is no clear evidence of this truth in the Hebrew Scriptures. Pharisaism was most certainly not the total opposite of Christianity, as can be seen from Paul, who, without any fear of compromising his faith, was able to declare before the Sanhedrin: "I am a Pharisee, a son of Pharisees; I am on trial with respect to the hope and the resurrection of the dead" (Ac 23:6).

The Sadducees, holding rigidly to the old ways, refused to respond to new needs caused by the destruction of the Temple in 70 A.D., and thus died out. The Pharisees, however, did their utmost to.ensure the survival of Judaism into the new era of exile. To this end, they were prepared to reinterpret the precepts of the Torah in order to bring them into line with the reality of Jewish life, with its needs and its possibilities. After the destruction of the Temple, and with it, of the priestly cult, they taught that fasting, charitable acts, and prayer—the "worship of the heart"—made up for the cult required by the Torah. They were not integralists in the anti-modernist sense of the word; it would be much nearer the truth if we acknowledged their genius for combining the old and the new, fidelity to tradition and openness to the call of the hour.

The idea that the Pharisees were concerned only with their own salvation contradicts even the Gospels; according to Matthew (23:15), they "traversed sea and land to make a single proselyte." They clung to the oracle of Isaiah that out of Zion will go forth the Law, and the word of the Lord from Jerusalem: that in the latter days all the nations will flow to the mountain of the Lord (2:2-5). I know of no Pharisee teacher who rejected the prophecy of the same biblical author that there would come a day "when the idols of Egypt will tremble at His [the Lord's] presence" (19:1). On that day, the Lord will make Himself known to the Egyptians and they will know Him. He will smite and heal them, they will even turn to the Lord (19:21-22). The Lord will say:

> Blessed be Egypt, my people,
> and Assyria, the work of my hands,
> and Israel, my heritage.
>
> (19:25)

A Christian concerned with the truth should not disregard this gospel-before-the-Gospel; this confession of love for the whole earth, for Israel as well as for her hereditary enemies is a cause for joy.

The American *Bible Missal*, published in 1962, an offspring of the Belgian *Missel Biblique* and the *Missel de l'Assemblée Chrétienne*, used to have the same interpretation with but minor alterations. What worries me is not so much the errors I have mentioned, as the fact that the editors responsible did not realize that the parable does not speak of *the* Pharisees and *the* publicans but of *a* Pharisee and *a* publican. The parable is not a description of Pharisees nor of the role of tax collectors; it is not a historical or socio-political excursus, but a call of repentance to all Jews and Christians, individuals and communities.

How is it that when compiling the notes in question, these authors did not think of those canonists to whom a paragraph of canon law seemed more important than the Gospels, or of those moral theologians who pretended to know the heart of God, unhesitatingly declaring that reading thirty pages of a book on the Index was a venial sin, but thirty-one a mortal one that separates the sinner from God for all eternity? How is it that they did not remember the many Catholics who never forgot to confess that they had eaten meat on a Friday, but were not conscious of any sin against justice or charity? How is it that they were apparently not worried by the fact that the care for the purity of the faith led to the perversion and carica-ture of the gospel which was called the *holy* Inquisition? Ser-mons on this parable about a Pharisee and a publican ought to speak of our sins. By concentrating exclusively on a treatment of the historical setting of the parable, an inexact one to boot, the commentators bar their readers from a true understanding of the spirit of Jesus—indeed, they foster, though certainly without realizing it—in their listeners or readers the unhealthy attitude: "I thank you, God, that we Christians are not like those conceited Pharisees."

The Meeting of Two Spiritualities. The mistaken exegesis of the parable runs parallel to the misunderstanding of Judaism at the time of Jesus and after. Many Christians used to assume that Judaism after Christ is without life or grace. Here, too, a new attitude is needed. Whoever meditates on the prayers of the synagogue cannot possibly imagine that God has abandoned His people. One of the most moving is this:

> Lord of all worlds,
> We approach You with our petitions,
> Not because of our own justice,
> But for the sake of Your great mercy.
>
> What are we,
> What is our life,
> What our love,
> What our justice,
> What our salvation,
> What our strength,
> What our power?
>
> What shall we say before You,
> Lord our God, and God of our Fathers,
> Are not all heroes as nothing before You,
> The famous, as if they did not exist,
> The wise, as if without wisdom,
> The knowers, as if without knowledge?
> For their many deeds are as nothing,
> And the days of their life are as a breath before You....
>
> And yet we are Your people, children of Your Covenant.
> Children of Abraham, Your friend,
>   to whom You have sworn on Mount Moriah,
> Descendants of Isaac, his only son,
>   who was bound on the altar,
> The congregation of Jacob, Your son, Your firstborn—
> In Your love, with which You have loved him,
> In Your joy, in which You have rejoiced in him,
> You called his name Israel and Jeshurun.

Therefore we are bound
To laud, praise, and glorify,
To bless and sanctify,
Yes, to give praise and thanks to Your name.

Blessed are we, how good is our portion,
How lovely our lot, how beautiful our inheritance!
Blessed are we, that we may speak with love early and late.
In the evening and in the morning:

Hear, Israel, the Lord our God,
The Lord is the Only One.

(Daily Morning Service)[179]

Can the close relationship between Judaism and Christianity be proved more clearly than by this prayer, with its surrender to the Lord, with the consciousness of each member's unworthiness and, at the same time, the people's God-given mission? The new insight the Declaration introduced demands a mental change. Indeed, the Declaration was never meant to be a document favoring ease or comfort. On the contrary, it is, in the words of Herbert Vorgrimler, a revolutionary document in the good sense, a document intended to change a centuries-old mentality in the service of reconciliation. As once the sins of Israel were sent out into the desert, so now, through the Declaration, "the sins of the Christian world are expelled into the desert, whether they have been committed horizontally, among the peoples, or vertically, throughout the centuries of history. Not in vain is the figure drawn by these two lines a Cross."[180]

NOTES*

¹ For details on the involvement of the *B'nai B'rith*, see *Hommage Solennel* à *Jules Isaac* (Salle des Centraux, October 10, 1963).

² For Jules Isaac's visit to John XXIII, see J. Toulat, *Juifs mes frères* (1962), pp. 152-154. Isaac's appeal is reproduced in *Du Redressement Nécessaire de l'Enseignement Chrétien Concernant Israël, Mémoire présentée par Jules Isaac* (1960).

³ *Acta Apostolice Sedis (AAS)* 51 (1959), p. 595; *Freiburger Rundbrief (FR)* 12, 7f. (The abbreviations given in this and other notes—set in parentheses—will be used later for identification of sources.)

⁴ Pope John is here narrowing the breadth of Judaism. He is not alone in this, for Christians have often looked on Judaism as a religion which ceased to develop once the Bible had been completed. Post-biblical Judaism, however, is determined not merely by the Hebrew Scriptures; it takes its distinctive character from *halakha*, the legal tradition formed by the Rabbis. Nonetheless, the reduction of Jewish existence by the Pope does not rob his injunction of its force.

⁵ *Osservatore Romano, (Oss Rom)* October 19, 1960.

⁶ *Ad Petri Cathedram*, 4. The encyclical is dated June 29, 1959, and was first published in *Oss Rom* on July 3, 1959.

⁷ The full text can be found in *Dialogue* (Montreal, 1966), 3, 7.

⁸ Ira Hirschman, *Caution to the Winds* (1962), p. 185.

⁹ Chaim Barlas in *Davar*, Jerusalem; reprinted in *Jewish Newsletter*, December 29, 1958.

¹⁰ *Documents conciliaires*, 2, 204.

¹¹ Laurentin, *Bilan du Concile* (Paris: Seuil, 1966), p. 129.

¹² *Acta et Documenta Concilio Oecumenico Vaticano II Apparando* (Typis Polyglottis Vaticanis, 1961), Series 1, 4, 132-134.

¹³ *La Documentation Catholique (DC)* 39, 1480.

¹⁴ *AAS* 42, 126.

¹⁵ The final sentence of this prayer, following the second reading that prepares for the blessing of baptismal water, is doubtless an echo of the theology of Rom 9 to 11, while the *transeat* of the Latin text is probably an allusion to the *transitus*, the *Pasch*, the "Passover" of Christ.

¹⁶ In his Commentary, *Der Galaterbrief* (Freiburg: Herder, 1974), pp. 416-417, Franz Mussner lists several interpretations but opts for the one that has the Apostle ask God's mercy upon all Israel.

* A tight pre-publication schedule made it impossible to adjust all bibliographical references to the style prevailing in this book.

¹⁷ "Umfrage zum Konzil," special issue.of *Wort und Wahrheit*, ed. Mauer, Schulmeister, Schmidthüs, & Böhm (Frieburg i. Br.: Herder, 1961).

¹⁸   Belief that but a single love is at work in the Church must not be taken to mean that this love is reduced to one level. It is not that God loves all men and women with equal affection, but that He takes to Himself every human being with infinite love.

¹⁹   Charles (Cardinal) Journet, *Destinées d'Israël* (1944), p. 112. See also "The Mysterious Destinies of Israel," *The Bridge*, 2, 35-90.

²⁰   We must not forget the fact that the cry, "His blood be on us and on our children!" (Mt. 27:25) was not, in itself, a curse. It was, rather, an assertion of innocence and is reminiscent of the words employed to warn witnesses in capital trials before they made their statements. Footnotes and commentaries often refer to 2 Sam 1:16 and 3:29, but make no mention of the *Mishna*, which is much more important. *bSanh.*, 4, 5, states specifically that it was customary to instill fear into witnesses as a means of encouraging them to keep to the truth.

A reminder was given that capital trials were quite different from property disputes. In the latter, it was possible for a person to make up for any false statement by paying an appropriate sum of money. But not so with capital crimes, where the blood of a man unjustly executed and that of his descendants would be upon the perjurer until the end of the world. If this warning is kept in mind, it can be seen why the crowd outside the governor's residence unhesitatingly declared their readiness to bear responsibility for Christ's execution at the hands of Pilate. They felt themselves, quite simply, to be without guilt.

This is almost certain if we assume that the crowd was made up to some extent of members of the resistance movement. These "Zealots," as they are called, had long believed that Jesus was "their man." Even though Christ dissociated Himself from their attempt to crown Him king (Jn 6:15), even though He taught that the kingdom of God was incompatible with violence (Mt 11:12; Jn 18:36), even though He passionately rejected Messiahship as understood by the Zealots (Mt 6:8-10; Mk 8:33), and called those who had raised such a claim before Him "thieves and robbers" (Jn 10:8), and even though He accepted Jerusalem's homage upon a gentle donkey and not on a battle-charger, the men of the resistance lived in the illusion that He was simply waiting for the opportune time to assume leadership. The very moment, however, the Zealots realized they had been mistaken and Christ would not make common cause with them, but would go the way of the Suffering Servant (Is 52:13-53:12), they "dumped" Him in a rage. Obsessed as they were with their militarist ideology and their disillusionment, they thought themselves fully justified in abandoning Christ to "the Romans" and the shameful death of crucifixion.

For the question of Christ and the Zealots, see O. Cullman, *Christ and Time*, (1950), and *The State in the New Testament* (1963), and the popular work of J. Pickl, *The Messias*, transl. A. Greene O.S.B.(St. Louis: B. Herder, 1946). For the liberation movement in general, its religious attitude and political orientation, see M. Hengel, *Die Zeloten* (1961).

²¹   A modern translator, Jörg Zink, *Das Neue Testament* (1965), p. 358, has translated Rom 11:25 with an excellent feeling for the text: "Part of Israel is *closed (verschlossen)* to Christ." The same translator renders Rom 11:7 as: "A part determined by God is [in harmony with Him], the rest are as though *fettered (gefesselt)*."

²²   The pastoral letter was printed by *DC* (Paris, 1960), 42, 299f.

²³   The expression "Israel according to the flesh" has no pejorative meaning. It does not stigmatize the Jews for any supposed carnality, sensuality, or worldliness. It refers simply to the Israel that has come forth by natural generation, the offspring of the loins of Abraham. It is never a moral designation; it is first biological, and since the Israel according to the flesh is the one with whom God concluded the Covenant, it acquires a theological quality.

²⁴   K. Staab, *Pauluskommentare aus der griechischen Kirche* (1933), p. 156.

²⁵   *PL*, 79, 108.

²⁶   Staab, *ibid.*, p. 526.

²⁷   *PG*, 14, 1190-1191.

²⁸   For a comprehensive treatment of Patristic understanding of Paul's theology on Israel, see Karl Hermann Schelkle, *Paulus Lehrer der Väter* (Düsseldorf, Patmos, 1956).

²⁹   See H. Kosmala, *Hebräer—Essener—Christen* (1959), p. 345.

³⁰   See N. A. Dahl, "The Johannine Church and History," in *Current Issues in New Testament Interpretation*, ed. W. Klassen and G. F. Snyder (1962), pp. 134f.

³¹   In Lincoln Cathedral is the burial place of an eight year old boy named Hugh, who, according to legend, is supposed to have been "murdered by the Jews" in 1255 for ritual purposes. In 1955—seven hundred years later!—a text reviling the Jews was removed from the walls of the Cathedral. The following inscription was put up in its place in reparation:

Trumped-up stories of "ritual murders" of Christian boys by Jewish communities were common throughout Europe during the Middle Ages, and even much later. These fictions cost many innocent Jews their lives. Lincoln had its own legend, and the alleged victim was buried in the Cathedral. A shrine was erected above and the boy was referred to as "little St. Hugh". . . . Such stories do not redound to the credit of Christendom and so we pray: "Remember not Lord our offences, nor the offences of our forefathers."

Asked about the reasons for the alteration the Dean of the Cathedral replied that untruth had no place on the walls of a cathedral (cf. *FR* 12, 66).

³² For the complete text, see Edward A. Synan, *The Popes and the Jews in The Middle Ages* (New York: Macmillan, 1965); for this and other ecclesiastical documents condemning the slander of ritual murder, see Cecil Roth, *The Ritual Murder Libel and the Jew* (London: Woburn, 1934).

³³ In his *The Catholic and His Church* (1960), de Lubac gives a pointed treatment of this subject.

³⁴ *Catholic Bulletin*, (St. Paul, Minn.: Catholic Bulletin Publishing, 1965), p. 115.

³⁵ Audience of October 13, 1962; *Council Daybook (CD)*, ed. F. Anderson, 1, 34, and 36.

³⁶ J. Hershcopf, "The Church and the Jews," *American Jewish Yearbook*, 1965, pp. 111-112.

³⁷ *Relatio*, November 18, 1963; cf. A. Bea, *The Church and the Jewish People* (1966), p. 159.

³⁸ *Neue Zürcher Zeitung*, Dec. 12, 1962; reprinted in *Herder Korrespondenz (HK)* 17, 92.

³⁹ H. Fesquet, *Le Journal du Concile*, ed. R. Morel (1966), p. 142.

⁴⁰ The exact text of this and other documents of the New Delhi Assembly are to be found in W.A. Visser 't Hooft, ed., *New Delhi Report, Third Assembly of the World Council of Churches* (1961).

⁴¹ According to an unpublished memorandum to which the Cardinal himself referred at the end of his *relatio* of November, 1963; cf. Bea, *ibid.*

⁴² Audience of October 13, 1962; *CD*, 1, 33-34.

⁴³ *New York Times (NYT)*, July 1, 1963: *The Advocate* (Newark, N.J.) July 4, 1963, interview with me about Fr. Weigel's statements.

⁴⁴ *FR* (July, 1965), p. 5; cf. also W. P. Eckert and E. L. Ehrlich, *Judenhass—Schuld der Christen?!* (Essen: Driewer, 1964), pp. 428f.

⁴⁵ The Latin text of the second version can be found in Eckert and Ehrlich, *ibid.*

⁴⁶ Unless stated otherwise, the official daily resumés of the various press offices were used for these and all the other interventions.

⁴⁷ A. Wenger, *Vatican II, Chronique de la Deuxième Session* (1964), p. 175.

⁴⁸ *Ibid.*

⁴⁹ Cf. *CD*, 1, 271.

⁵⁰ Press office, *Handreichungen in deutscher Sprache*, 28, 2-3 (Nov. 20, 1963).

⁵¹ *CD*, 1, 272.

⁵² R. Laurentin, *Bilan de la Deuxième Session* (1964), p. 150.

⁵³ By an "ecumenical theologian" in this context, I mean one who specializes in ecumenism, as distinct from those who serve the reconciliation of the Church and Israel. With regard to the latter, see (among others): K. Thieme, "Der ökumenische Aspekt der christlich-jüdischen Begegnung," *FR* (October, 1955) 8,9; P. Démann, "Israel et l'Unité de l'Eglise," *Cahiers Sioniens* (March, 1958), 7, 1; C. F. Pauwels, O.P., "Ist das Mysterium Israels eine ökumenische Frage?", *FR* (December 1959), 12, Nos. 45-48.

⁵⁴ B. Lambert, *Ecumenism, Theology and History* (1967), pp. 446-448.

⁵⁵ Fesquet, *ibid*, p. 351.

⁵⁶ *CD* 1, 316.

⁵⁷ Bea, *ibid*, p. 156.

⁵⁸ *Ibid.*

⁵⁹ *Ibid.*, p. 159.

⁶⁰ Bea, *ibid.*, p. 157.

⁶¹ *Ibid.*, p. 157.

⁶² *AAS* 52, 960.

⁶³ Address at Rome airport: M. Maccarrone, *Il Pellegrinaggio di Paolo VI in Terra Santa* (1964), p. 25.

⁶⁴ Maccarrone, *ibid.* p. 104.

⁶⁵ *Ibid.*, pp. 72f.

⁶⁶ *Ibid.*, p. 41.

⁶⁷ *Ibid.*, p. 72.

⁶⁸ *Ibid.*, p. 90.

⁶⁹ X. Rynne, *The Second Session* (1964), p. 313.

⁷⁰ *Frankfurter Allgemeine Zeitung* (*FA*), January 4, 1964.

⁷¹ *New York Herald Tribune*, January 6, 1964; quoted in *HK* 18, 306.

⁷² *New York Herald Tribune*, January 5, 1964.

⁷³ See *ibid.*, January 7, 1964.

⁷⁴ Quoted in Eckert and Ehrlich, *ibid.*, pp. 418f.

⁷⁵ *Ibid.*, pp. 430-432; cf. *FR* (December, 1959), 12, 7.

76   *Ibid.*

77   Bea, *ibid.*, p. 160.

78   *Ibid.*

79   *Ibid.*, p. 161.

80   In his *Jesus of Nazareth*, Joseph Klausner calls this lament a "street ballad." The "clubs" refer to the violent methods used by the slaves of that house in gathering the tithes. The "whisperings" refer to the secret sessions where new suppressive measures against the people were devised. The "pen" is the instrument with which the exploiters' decrees were signed. The last lines, which may possibly have been added later, present a sorry picture of the financial machinations of the high-priestly clique. In view of that lament, one seriously wonders whether the leaders of the Sanhedrin, those malevolent caricatures of "*high* priests," can really be looked on as the representatives of the people.

81   Bea, *ibid.*, p. 161.

82   *Ibid.*, p. 162.

83   *Ibid.*

84   The exact words of Rabbi Heschel are quoted in *Time*, September 11, 1964.

85   *CD* 2, 64.

86   *Ibid.*, p. 82.

87   *FR* (1965), 16-17, 13.

88   Gunnel Vallquist, *Das Zweite Vatikanische Konzil* (1966), p. 292.

89   The contributions to the Great Debate are reproduced here in the form of a mosaic. Their chronological order can be found in the *Council Daybook* (See note 35).

90   W. Becker, "Die Erklärung über das Verhältnis der Kirche zu den nichtchristlichen Religionen," *Catholica* (1966), 20,120.

91   See page 138, above.

92   For a refutation of the Cardinal's statement that Gentiles are considered "wild animals," see my "History of the Declaration" in *Commentary on the Documents of Vatican II*, pp. 80-82, n. 105. For a full treatment of the nature and role of Gentiles as presented in Jewish literature, see the *Jewish Encyclopedia*, 5,615-626.

93   See G.S. Higgins, "Christian-Jewish Relations," *The Yardstick*, N.C. Features (January 25, 1965), p. 3. This essay contains several quotations from the Patriarch's communiqué and Higgins' own reply.

94   See René, Laurentin, *ibid.*, p. 82.

95   Fesquet, *ibid.*, p. 578.

96   According to the regulations, only the Moderators or the Pope himself could transfer the competence for a Conciliar document from one commission to another; *Orientierung*, October 31, 1964, quoted in X. Rynne, *The Third Session* (1964), p. 64.

[97]   Vallquist, *ibid.*, p. 319.

[98]   Rynne, *ibid.*

[99]   See Fesquet, *ibid.*, October 17, 1964; Rynne, *ibid.*, pp. 65-66.

[100]   Laurentin, *Troisième Session* (1965), p. 140.

[101]   *FA*, October 14, 1964.

[102]   A.-M. Henry, ed., *Vatican II*, Unam Sanctam 52-53 (1966), p. 62.

[103]   See *CD*, Session 2, p. 150.

[104]   Henry, *ibid.*, p. 62.

[105]   *Nostra Aetate*, 1.

[106]   See E. Schillebeeckx, *Vatican II: The Real Achievement* (1966), p. 58.

[107]   Eckert and Ehrlich, *ibid.*, p. 424.

[108]   *Schema Declarationis de Ecclesiae Habitudine ad Religiones Non-Christianas* (1965), Expensio modorum ad 1,2, p. 13.

[109]   R. Laurentin and J. Neuner, *The Declaration on the Relation of the Church to Non-Christian Religions*, Vatican II Documents (1966), p. 35. The text quoted is from a different translation.

[110]   Bruno Hussard O.P. *Le Religioni non cristiane nel Vaticano II*, pp. 38f.

[111]   See Fesquet, *ibid.*, p. 506.

[112]   See my Commentary on the Declaration in *American Participation in the Second Vatican Council*, A. Yzermans, ed. (New York: Sheed and Ward, 1967), p. 609.

[113]   Bea, *ibid.*, p. 166.

[114]   *Ibid.*

[115]   *Ibid.*, pp. 167-168.

[116]   *Ibid.*, p. 168.

[117]   See *ibid.*, pp. 168-169.

[118]   *New York Journal American*, November 21, 1964.

[119]   This headline forms the title of an exhaustive article by Dr. Willehad Eckert, O.P., in the *Basler Volksblatt*, November 7, 1964.

[120]   *Die Welt*, November 21, 1964.

[121]   See Rynne, *ibid.*, p. 266.

[122]   Vallquist, *ibid.*, p. 416.

[123]   When the Declaration was provisionally accepted on November 20, 1964, it was still considered as an appendix to the Constitution on the Church (Bea, *ibid.*, p. 167).

[124]   *America*, October 31, 1964, p. 305.

[125]   According to *HK*, March, 1965, p. 80.

[126]   *NYT*, November 26, 1964.

[127]   *HK*, March, 1965, p. 80; likewise *The Catholic Messenger* (Davenport), December 24, 1964, on the basis of reports of the N.C.W.C. News Service.

[128]   *HK*, March 1965, p. 80.

[129]   From a French translation of the radio talk distributed in Rome; cf. *HK*, March 1965, p. 81.

[130]   *Ibid.*, p. 80.

[131]   *Catholic Star Herald* (Camden, N.J.), December 18, 1964.

[132]   *The Providence Visitor*, October 9, 1964, on the basis of reports of the N.C.W.C. News Service.

[133]   *HK*, March 1965, p. 80.

[134]   *The Advocate*, December 3, 1964.

[135]   *The Providence Visitor*, December 11, 1964, on the basis of the Religious News Service.

[136]   *FA*, November 24, 1964.

[137]   *The Jewish World*, December 1964, p. 19.

[138]   Laurentin and Neuner, *ibid.*, p. 37.

[139]   Cardinal Ruffini's exact words were: . . . (*Iudaeos*) *vocare deicidas non possumus, eo magis quod nomen 'Deicida' insulsitatem quamdam exprimit, nemo enim Deum occidere unquam valeret.*

[140]   Laurentin and Neuner, *ibid.*, pp. 37f.

[141]   For the whole argument, see M.-M. Cottier O.P., *Vatican II. Les Relations de l'Eglise avec les Religions non-chrétiennes* (1966), pp. 73f.

[142]   See *ibid.*, p. 75.

[143]   *America*, July 4, 1964.

[144]   *Ibid.*

[145]   *Exsultet*, liturgy of the Easter Vigil.

[146]   *America, ibid.*

[147]   Journet, *ibid.*, p. 153; *Ennarat. in Ps.*, 61,5, *PL*, 36,791.

[148]   Bishop Carli's paper appeared under the title "E possibile disintere serenamente della questione giudaica?" in *Palestra del Clero* (May 1, 1965) 9,465-476.

[149]   See *FA*, April 9, 1965; *New York Times*, April 11, 1965.

[150]   For the thrust of the whole sermon, see *The Catholic Bulletin* (Minneapolis), April 16, 1965.

[151]   See Paul VI's words in the Promulgation of the Declaration, below, pp. 276-277.

[152]   The discussion that followed the Pope's sermon is summarized by Hershcopf, *ibid.*

[153]   The entire text of the letter has been reprinted in *FR*, (July 1965), 16-17,4.

[154]   *Ibid.*, pp. 3-4. The memorandum was signed by 52 noted Catholics of Germany.

[155]   *Verschwörung gegen die Kirche* (Austrian edition, 1963), pp. 730f.

[156]   The Inquisition Edict is reproduced in detail by Laurentin and Neuner, *ibid.* pp. 24-28.

[157]   Fesquet, *ibid.*, p. 504-505; cf. *FA*, October 15, 1964.

[158]   Here and at other points in this section I am omitting exact page

references, etc., since the pamphlets discussed are not obtainable through the legitimate book trade. Moreover, most of them appeared without any publisher's name.

[159] Buchmüller, *Augustin Kardinal Bea* (Augsburg: Winifred Werk, 1971), p. 32.

[160] See Hershcopf, *ibid.*, p. 55.

[161] Quoted from J.-P. Lichtenberg O.P., *L'Eglise et les religions non-chrétiennes* (1967), p. 18.

[162] The term "corporate personality" was coined and the phenomenon first discussed by H.W. Robinson, *Corporate Personality in Ancient Israel*, Facet Books (Philadelphia: Fortress, 1964). Among other books treating the subject are: J. de Fraine, *Adam et son Lignage* (Bruges: Desclée, 1959); R.P. Shedd, *Man in Community: A Study of St. Paul's Application of Old Testament and Early Jewish Conceptions of Human Solidarity* (London: Epworth, 1958).

[163] *Gaudium et spes*, art. 77,2; 72,2; 80, 3-4.

[164] See Cottier, *ibid.*, pp. 72f.

[165] Laurentin, *Bilan du Concile*, p. 303.

[166] *Die Furche* (1965), p. 12.

[167] *Le Figaro*, October 16/17, 1965.

[168] See Laurentin and Neuner, *ibid.*, p. 54.

[169] See L. Kardinal Jäger, *Das Konzilsdekret über den Ökumenismus* (1965), p. 139.

[170] The "instructions" had no publisher or page numbers to which I could refer.

[171] The reference to a *certain* similarity in the wording of the two circulars—the Antisemitic and the Conservative—is not to suggest that the *Coetus*, in particular Bishop Carli, and the "anti-Jewish International" at work outside the *aula* had been making common cause. This has often been insinuated. But I think it too facile to identify the opposition of the Conservatives with the crude hostility of the pamphleteers.

[172] See Bea, *ibid.*, p. 168.

[173] Quoted from Fesquet, *ibid.*, p. 1020.

[174] *Ibid.*, pp. 988f.

[175] *Esprit*, June 1966, p. 1178.

[176] *Christian Life in Israel*, publ. Israeli Interfaith Association, Spring, 1985.

[177] *Esprit, ibid.*

[178] *Missel de l'Assemblée Chrétienne* (1964), p. 831.

[179] The translation is patterned after that by Else Schubert-Christaller in *Der Gottesdienst der Synagoge* (1927), pp. 9f.

[180] From an unpublished letter.

RETURNING BY ANOTHER ROUTE

The story of the Magi has it that, after seeing the Child Jesus, they went home by another route (see Mt 2:12). Preachers have often given the phrase a moral turn, implying that the Magi went back with minds and hearts changed. "Returning by Another Route" may thus well serve as a title for papers that discuss a new vision and sentiment engendered by the Council. What wonder that the Church of Christ can be rejuvenated and yet remain what she was ordained to be.

Humanity's Many Paths To God

OCTOBER 28, 1965, is a proud day in the history of the Second Vatican Council. On that day, Pope Paul voiced his happiness at the renewed face of the Church, and his hope that many would now see her unveiled beauty. Some were startled. Why did the Pope express this hope on the very day that the Council offered the world a Declaration which did not speak so much of the Church as of those outside it?

Could it be that no one is fully "outside?" At once exclusive, the Church is all-inclusive. She sees herself as a "little flock" (Lk 12:32), and yet she is far wider than her visible boundaries suggest. A decade and a half before the Council, Cardinal Journet spoke of the millions who, in an incipient and hidden way, are tied to her, who despite their errors have not

299

refused the grace of living faith which God offers them in the intimacy of their hearts, God who wills that all be saved and brought to the knowledge of truth. She herself does not know them by name, yet she senses their number-less presence about her, and ofttimes, in the silence of her prayer, she hears ascending in the night the confused sounds of their march.[1]

On October 28, the Council confirmed these words. In part, it even went beyond them.

The Church and Humanity

THE DECLARATION has several parts: one on various religions, another on Islam, a third on the Jewish people. The preamble to the first part points out that in modern times the earth has shrunk, that technological advances have turned distant peoples into neighbors. This changed geography is a spiritual challenge to the Christian. Never before has it been so clear that humankind is one, that its members depend on one another, that they are joined for good or evil. They either prosper or perish together. In its first and last statements—the "Message to Humanity," issued at the beginning of the First Session, and the pastoral Constitution on The Church in the Modern World, passed at the end of the Fourth—the Council insisted that Christians make the earthly concerns of all people their business. "All Men are brothers, irrespective of the race or nation to which they belong," the Bishops proclaimed.[2] Christians must then see to it that humankind endure: that no one go hungry; that all peoples attain freedom; that human beings everywhere live in a state consonant with human dignity. But this is not all. "Man cannot live on bread alone; he lives on every word God utters" (Mt 4:4).

But how did the word of God come to those who were outside the realm of God's dealings with Israel, who were, or still are, outside the orbit of the gospel? How did God speak, how does He speak to them? The Declaration gives no direct answer to these questions. It states first that, though culture, custom, outlook, thought, and language differ, the human condition is very much the same everywhere. The basic problems, the fears and hopes, the weakness and strength native to people, vary little from continent to continent. Thus the Declaration affirms:

> Human beings expect from the various religions answers to the unsolved riddles of the human condition, riddles that agitate the hearts of people today as much as they did in olden times: What is a human being? What is the meaning, what is the purpose of our lives? What is the moral good, what is sin? Which is the road to happiness? What is death, what is judgment, and what is retribution after death? What, finally, is that ultimate, ineffable mystery which, encompassing our existence, is its source as well as its destiny?

Following this, the Declaration devotes a few lines to the more primitive religions and several paragraphs to some of the world's great religions, to Hinduism, Buddhism, and Islam. The brief allusions to their teachings make no pretense at being definitive. Rather than offering comprehensive descriptions, they invite Catholics to become acquainted with the religious experiences of people everywhere.

True, there is something dubious about human attempts to reach God. The god we find may be one of our own making. If we call on him, we may not be heard, for the gods are deaf. In all that can be known about the world and humans, they are initiators and judges; in all that can be known about God, the latter are neither. The true God cannot be found by our search. It is we who are found by the God who seeks. In contrast to the pagan deities, the God of Scripture goes after His creature. "Adam, where are you?" (Gn 3:9), He asked at the beginning. At the fullness of time, however, He came in the flesh, like a shepherd climbing after a stranded sheep, like a woman bending down for a fallen coin, like a father on the lookout for a runaway son (Mt 18:12; Lk 15:8,20).

On the one hand, it matters little what people think or expect of God; what matters is what He plans for, and demands of them. On the other hand, religious strivings do matter: Though they are often infected by selfishness, by our drive to insure or assert ourselves, grace is still at work in these strivings. Thus,

St. Paul told the Athenians that he had made his way through their city and had looked at their shrines. While doing so, he had noticed "an altar bearing the inscription: 'To an unknown God'." In Greek, the words "to an unknown God" can also mean "to God, the unknown." Thus the Apostle was able to continue: "What you worship but do not know—this I proclaim to you" (Ac 17:23).

Justin the Martyr (ca. 100-165) could say that Christ "is the Logos, the Word, of whom all humanity partakes." Hence, he held, men like Socrates or Heraclitus—men who lived according to the *logos*, that is, the dictates of reason—were really Christians even though they were considered godless.[3] Again, when touching on the virtuous life the Stoics strove for, he gladly acknowledged that they had reached a certain degree of truth and goodness, "because of the seed of the *logos* sown into every human heart."[4] Christians, he thought, were privileged to live, not only by a grain or two of the Word, but by "the whole Word, which is Christ."[5] It may be well to repeat Justin's important distinction: There are "the little words of God," strewn all over the earth. And there is the one great Word. Its sound was heard in Israel at various times and in various ways; when the time was ripe (Eph 1:10), however, the Word was enfleshed. It appeared not obliquely, not partially, but fully, personally, in Jesus. Once uttered, His message never rests: it was, is, and will be "shouted from the housetops" (Mt 10:27) till it encircles the globe. Far from splitting humanity, Justin's distinction shows its ultimate oneness before God. As the axiom *distinguer pour unir* implies, all distinctions are for the sake of a higher unity.

The hidden work of God among humans, so different from His public revelation in Israel and the Church,[6] made the Second Vatican Council avow:

> The Catholic scorns nothing that is true and holy in these religions [that is, Hinduism, Buddhism, and others]. She regards with sincere reverence those ways of action and of life, those precepts and teachings which, though differing in many aspects from the ones she holds and sets forth, nonetheless carry a ray of that Truth that enlightens

all human beings. Ceaselessly indeed, she proclaims Christ, "the Way, the Truth, and the Life" (Jn 14:6), in whom humans may find the fullness of religious life, in whom God has reconciled all things to Himself (see 2 Cor 5:18-19).

The Omnipresence of Grace

SOME MAY ARGUE: "The Apostolic Age spoke of 'the unknown God' and 'seeds of the Logos,' the Council of rays 'of that Truth which enlightens human beings.' How is it possible that the Christians of past centuries considered those who did not know Christ as separated from Him altogether?"

Medieval Man had a distinct sense of objective reality. The majesty of truth was plainly evident to him; he knew that its summons was unconditional and that humanity was made for it. Our age, however, has unveiled human subjectivity: Even in the finding of truth, one is dependent on a thousand inner and outer forces. Though on the way to eternity, he or she is a pilgrim held by the here and now. Thus we can no longer say, as Medieval Man—blinded by a great light—often did, that all who do not share our faith stubbornly resist God; that if only they willed, they could accept His whole revelation. To assume as much would be presumptuous on our part. Humbly, we have come to recognize the limitations of every human being.

It is the particular grace of our age that we can stand in awe before the mystery of the infinite God who respects the finitude of His creature. It is the particular grace of our age that none of the differences and divisions among people can shatter our belief in the victory of God's saving plan. That it will ultimately prevail is the strength of Jews and Christians. We are privileged to realize that His salvific will breaks through human dissensions, even now. Two pitfalls threaten us: an "objectivist" or a "subjectivist" approach. The two terms are obviously meant in a pejorative sense, of people who give exclusive attention to one of the two aspects of the human search for truth. Both attitudes wreak havoc on the life of society and that of the individual. One leads to persecution, the other to chaos; one tends to make the individual pitiless, the

304 THE NEW ENCOUNTER

other spineless. We are fortunate to set objectivity and subjectivity, not as opposites that must needs be hostile, but as polarities that wait for us to unite them.

For millennia, far-off lands were impenetrable. Even a century or two ago, their cultures were still riddles, their faiths seemed superstition or deviltry, and their men and women hell-bound. When the scattered impressions and preconceived notions of the Christian West gave way to findings of scholars, we were first treated to fanciful theories, consciously or unconsciously designed to end forever the uniqueness of Christianity. But far from gainsaying Christ's claim, the discovery of once unknown patterns of life makes us understand His sovereignty better. We are able to see in many native religions rays of the everlasting Sun, even to relate their insights and expectations to the message and hope of the gospel. During his visit to India in December, 1964, Pope Paul VI did exactly this.

No doubt, the longing for salvation, the craving for rebirth, the groping for the absolute have at times pushed human beings on the road to wickedness. They have, strange though it is, led them to the performance of corrupting, even diabolical rites. Thus, the thunder of Prophets stormed against the orgies of the Canaanites. Yet, as there are aberrations of humanity's religious search, so are there genuine and positive thrusts. A "savage" who shed his own blood to appease the anger of his gods made such a thrust. Dark clouds on the horizon and rumblings from the sky reminded him of his relish as earlier in the day he watched the death struggle of two animals. Fearing that his punishment was at hand, he cut his flesh in order to offer his lifeblood in expiation for his sin.[7] His notions about God and the weather may be primitive—his religious instinct, however, has depth. So much so that I would call him representative of religious people outside the Jewish and Christian orbits.

In going after the Fountain of all being, these people often stumble; yet even when they stumble, the arm of the living God may hold them. Whenever they find a partial truth, their finding is a gift of the Spirit. Whenever they strive for goodness, God's pleasure is with them. In trying to understand the secret of love and of suffering, they are not without Christ. Nor are they without grace, and where grace is found, there the Church has cast anchor. If I were asked to sum up in a few brief words that part of the Declaration which we have examined, I would say that it hymns the omnipresence of grace in the world.

Hearts Longing for God

IT MAY BE well to illustrate, indeed, to document that omnipresence with examples of non-Christian piety. A scholarly presentation would have to investigate in each instance the exact meaning of the word "God" as well as the entire religious setting in which it is used, and this is, of course, impossible in a brief article.[8] Most of the quotations that follow are taken from the work of one of the great missiologists of modern times, the late Thomas Ohm O. S. B., on the love of God in the non-Christian religions.[9] I shall let the utterances of men and women, from primitive as well as from civilized backgrounds, speak for themselves.

Ohm has a pygmy chieftain say:

We are not born like beasts.
When we come into the world the Creator looks upon us
and we upon Him, with our face turned toward Him.

Several days after the birth of a child, a feast is held at which the pygmies of the equatorial forests chant:

To you, the Creator, to you the mighty One,
I offer this new shoot, new fruit of an ancient tree.
You are the Master, we are your children.

Among the pagan Galla, tribal folk from eastern Africa, this evening prayer is offered:

O God! You have let me spend this day in peace,
let me pass the night in peace as well.
You, the Lord who has no Lord over him!

There is no strength except in you.
You alone are without debt.
In your hand, I pass the day,
In your hand, I pass the night.
You are my mother, you are my father.

In the third century, B. C., the Stoic leader Cleanthes composed
this hymn, possibly the most beautiful in Greek:

Most glorious of immortals, Zeus all powerful,
Author of Nature, named by many names, all hail.
Thy law rules all; and the voice of the world may cry to thee,
For from thee we are born, and alone of living things
That move on earth are we created in thy image.
So will I praise thee, ever singing of thy might
By whom the whole wide firmament of heaven is swayed
And guided in its wheeling journey round this earth.[10]

Much earlier, around 900 B. C., a saintly woman poet of the
Tamils of South India sang:

Thine is all my love, from the day that let me breathe and be,
From the day that saw the first word spring from my mouth.

To take a great leap in time, the deepest phase in the development of India's religion is *bhakti*, loving surrender to, worship of, and communion with God. A relatively late and ripe
fruit are the utterances of an unlettered weaver. Kabir (1440-
1518), full of longing for and joy in God. Here is an instance:

When I am parted from my Beloved
My heart is full of misery.
I have no comfort by day, no sleep at night.
To whom shall I tell my sorrows?
Who has felt one single ray of the great Love
Is saved, is with God.[11]

Another Bhakti singer is Tukárám (1608-1649):

Thee, thee alone, O God
My soul desires:
No gaudy Heaven I seek,
No bottomless plunge into the Absolute:
Life in this world of death is good, is all I need,
For I have thee:
All shall know it, Lord:
I am thy servant, thee I love, thee I adore.[12]

Sūfīsm, a mystical sect of Islam, is based on the doctrine that God, the entirely Other, is utterly near and inward. A Sūfī of the ninth century is said to have prayed:

O my God, in public I call You as lords are called,
but in private as loved ones are called.
Publicly I say, "O my God,"
but privately, "O my Beloved."[13]

The Persian Sūfī Bābā Tahir confessed:

O God, my heart is breaking,
    I weary of its smart.
It sigheth without ceasing:
    If merciful thou art,
Take thou away my heart.[14]

Many more examples of a rare spirituality among non-Christians could be given but it might be best to conclude this list with a simple story of a simple people. It belongs to the lore of a tribe living on a remote plateau in Vietnam, a tribe till recently unreceptive to the Gospel; it is reported by a missionary who went to them, barely a decade ago.

> Once the ocean swelled and inundated the earth: the flood covered and destroyed everything. The angels had to flee; to find refuge they sought shelter in the mountains, in the trees. . . . God alone need never flee for He dwells neither here nor there.[15]

Many and One

THESE RELIGIOUS testimonies of various lands and times are not a purely human achievement. Such heights could not have been reached unaided. Though His ways are hidden, God is indeed at work outside the biblical revelation, for He wills the salvation of all and their march toward truth (see 1 Tm 2:4). To be sure, in non-Christian religions truth is often mingled with error, moral purity with deformity. Yet, who dares say that God disdains all their tenets, rites, and acts; He may well use some or many for the spiritual good of those who live by them. Since they are not grown on the chosen soil that He cultivated for many centuries till the coming of Christ, it may seem to many that, no matter what their beauty, they are of no lasting value.

The Church had made her own Peter's ecstatic profession that we—indeed, the whole world—are saved in the name of Jesus, and no other (Ac 4:12). At the same time, she maintains against the so-called fundamentalists that men and women can please God without express belief in Christ, that they are loved and may respond to God's love, even though they do not know or accept the Good News, even though they are not visible members of the Church. If the universe of grace really reaches to the four corners of the world, why do Christian missionaries preach the gospel of Christ in far away lands? Why are we anxious to have the Christian witness heard all over the globe? No less a lover of world and humanity than Teilhard de Chardin has said that, should Christianity disappear, "the presence of a loving God would disappear from the psychological equipment of the world—darkness and coldness beyond any we could even begin to imagine [would reign.]"[16] What Christ's Life, Death, and Resurrection discloses is this: God is not an absent God; His wooing is not like the flirtation so frequent in Greek mythology, not like the "game" of the Hindus, not like the pursuit of the Hound of heaven, not even like the courtship in the Song of Songs—though all these are in varying degrees images of God's search. The events of Jesus' ministry tell the Christian that God is engaged in a life-and-death struggle for each individual.

To say it again. God's grace is at work in many places and in many persons, though they may be unaware. To embrace Christ, then, is to believe in God's universal love.

NOTES

[1] Charles Journet, *L'Eglise du Verbe incarné* (Paris: Desclée, 1951), 2,1114. See *The Bridge* (New York: Herder, 1955), 1,312.

[2] "Message to Humanity," *The New York Times*, October 21, 1962.

[3] *Apol.* 1,46; *PG* 6:397.

[4] *Ibid.*, 2,8; *PG* 6:457.

[5] *Ibid.*

[6] In his penetrating book, *Christianity and Other Religions*, R. C. Zaehner describes this difference. The Church, he says, has inherited Israel's experience of God, an experience quite unlike that of any other tribe, people, or race. "The Jews are a peculiar people," he continues, "simply because they are the chosen people. Others 'grope their way towards' God; and God delights to play this game of hide and seek with them (and for the Hindus God's dealings with men are constantly likened to a 'game'). But the Jews He chose from all the nations of the earth to be His own people: they alone were granted the terrible privilege of hearkening to the voice of the living God as an awesome objective reality who issues commandments and prohibitions." (New York: Hawthorn, 1964), p. 134.

[7] Taken from the notes on a lecture by a missionary living among members of a "primitive" tribe.

[8] For the higher religions, Zaehner's book previously referred to provides the necessary information.

[9] *Die Liebe zu Gott in den Nichtchristlichen Religionen* (Munich: Wewel, 1950).

[10] *The Oxford Book of Greek Verse in Translation*, ed. T. F. Higham and C. M. Bowra (London: Oxford University Press, 1944), pp. 533-534.

[11] *Songs of Kabir*, transl. Rabindranath Tagore (New York: Macmillan, 1915), p. 98.

[12] John S. Hoyland, *An Indian Peasant Mystic* (London: Allenson, 1932), p. 59.

[13] Reynold A. Nicholson, *The Mystics of Islam* (London: Bell, 1914), p. 8.

14 Arthur J. Arberry, *Poems of a Persian Sūfī* (Cambridge: Heffer, 1937), p. 17.

15 Jacques Dournes, *Gott liebt die Heiden* (Freiburg: Herder, 1965), p. 69; the original edition *Dieu aime les païens* (Paris: Montague-Aubier, 1963) was not available to me.

16 *Letters from a Traveller* (New York: Harper's, 1962), p. 302, n.

The Rediscovery Of Judaism

YOU MAY ALL HAVE experienced my predicament; I have to speak on something that I have treated before, even more than once. *Timeo virum unius libri* says an old Latin proverb; freely translated: "Beware of the man who has only one topic." The danger of becoming stale and boring is too obvious to belabor. In looking, then, for a fresh approach, it occurred to me that I might begin with a one-sentence summary of the Statement on the Jews.

A Rabbinic Model

The Torah in a Nutshell. No sooner had this possibility flashed through my mind than I realized, happily, that in doing so I

311

would follow in the path of the Rabbis who were fond of summing up the teaching of Scripture in concise terms. George Foot Moore has called it "the Law in a nutshell."[1] Anyone with even a slight knowledge of Judaism knows of an unnamed pagan's request to be taught "the whole Torah while standing on one foot," *kol ha-torah kulah al-regel ahat.* Equally well, does he know Hillel's answer: "What you yourself do not like, do not do to your fellow man. This is the whole Torah. The rest is commentary" (*bShab.* 31a).

Christian writers have used bottles of ink to show that this negative phrasing of the Golden Rule is inferior to the positive wording Jesus gives it (Mt 7:12; Lk 6:31), while Jewish apologists have gone to great lengths to show that the two phrasings are exactly the same in content. Maybe so, maybe not. The different wording has nothing to do with the basic views of the two teachers, Jesus and Hillel; its reason is the different people they spoke to. While Jesus addressed Himself to Jews who had lived under the discipline of the Law and had been trained to walk in the sight of God, Hillel spoke to a pagan to whom *imitatio Dei* was something alien—his gods were hardly models of holiness. To my mind, the negative form shows Hillel's sensitivity, his awareness of speaking to a man nurtured by a far from perfect, probably utilitarian morality, a man still to be brought under the wings of the living God. The negative cast is characteristic neither of Judaism nor of Hillel himself. In fact, Hillel used to say: "Be of the disciples of Aaron, love peace and pursue it. Be one who loves his fellows and brings them near the Torah" (*Ab.* 1, 12).

Almost as familiar as Hillel's answer is the dispute between Rabbi Akiba and Ben Azzai (early second century, A. D.). For R. Akiba, "Love your neighbor as yourself" (Lv 19:18) was the all-embracing rule of the Torah, whereas for Ben Azzai, "This is the book of the descendants of Adam. When God created Adam, He made him in His likeness" (Gn 5:1) was the Torah's foundation and crown.[2]

Not quite so well known is a charming homily by Rabbi Simlai (late third century, A. D.). He delighted in searching for the basic principles of the Torah. First he found eleven in

Psalm 15, later six which he saw expressed in Isaiah 33:15. With Micah, he reduced the manifold rules to three:

> You have been told, O Man, what is good
> and what the Lord requires of you;
> Only to do what is right, to love kindness,
> and to walk humbly with your God.
>
> (6:8)

With the second Isaiah, R. Simlai narrowed them to two: "Maintain justice and do right" (56:1). Finally, he saw the unity of the Torah in the words of the Lord, spoken through Amos: "Seek me and live" (5:4).[3] How warm an image, how different from the conception so many Christians have of Judaism!

In the context of these rabbinic insights, the conversation between Jesus and a Pharisaic scholar appears in a noncombative light. It must have been an earnest student of God's words who asked Jesus: "Master, which is the Torah's greatest commandment?" Jesus' answer was a happy one indeed: "'Love the Lord your God with all your heart, with all your soul, with all your mind.' This is the great, the first commandment. A second is like it: 'Love your neighbor as yourself.' On these two commandments, on these *mitzvot*, depend all the Law and the Prophets, *kol ha-torah ve-gam ha-nevim*" (Mt 22:36-40).

For many exegetes, to whom biblical, that is passionate, thought and speech remain a riddle, Jesus' relationship with the Pharisees is bound to appear as one of complete estrangement and uninterrupted bitter dispute. Thus they take the legitimate desire of the *talmid hakham* to test Jesus' teaching as an attack or an attempt to trap Him. Consequently, they understand Jesus' answer as a counterattack, the "unmasking of Pharisaic legalism." One goes so far as to write: "Instead of a commandment that a juridical mind could grasp, Jesus offers a purely moral one; the expert in the Law—a jurist—did not know what to make of it."[4] In my opinion, there is no warrant for this in the Matthean text. Older translations, like King James or Douay, say of the young scholar that he "tempted"

Jesus, whereas most modern versions use the verb "test." The Greek word *peirazein* means exactly this: "to put to the test." By itself, it tells nothing of whether the "tester" is led by a search for truth or by antagonism against the one to whom the test question is put. If the word itself is ambiguous, the situation on which Matthew based his story must have been entirely free of hostility, rancor, or even dispute.[5] For it was a perfectly natural one. Jesus was asked a question with which any teacher in Israel might have been confronted, and He answered like a true teacher in Israel. However singular the juxtaposition, indeed interdependence, of the love of God and the love of neighbor may have been,[6] it was not of an explosive nature. In no way did it transgress the frontiers of Judaism. The conversation implied no criticism of the many minutiae of the Law,[7] only the emphatic truth that, without love, all deeds, great or small, are nothing.[8]

Without Flattery or Contempt

The Conciliar Statement in a Nutshell. I may have tried your patience; I promised to give the sum and substance of the Statement in a brief sentence, but then seemed to have lost myself in recalling rabbinic ways to defend my method. In discussing the method, however, I have already touched on the content. What the Rabbis did for the Torah, I would like to do for the Conciliar Statement on the Jews. To put it within the compass of one sentence, section four of *Nostra Aetate*, the Council's Declaration on the Church's Relationship to Non-Christian Religions, bespeaks the discovery, or re-discovery, of Judaism and the Jews in their intrinsic worth, as well as in their import for the Church.[9]

This summary may be the last thing you expected. If it surprises you, I am happy. A person who can be startled, thrown off his or her preconceived ideas, can also be convinced. But if you reject the view I propose outright, without probing my arguments, I stand little chance of being heard by you. My words will simply go past you. I can also conceive of one who is neither amazed nor rebuffed by my interpretation, but brushes it aside as purely subjective comments. My comments are indeed subjective in that I stand fully behind them. They are not subjective in the sense that they spring from my imagination, without a corresponding reality. I do not think I need apologize for offering a summary, in other words, for my conviction that the Conciliar Statement requires a commentary. What is Christian teaching if not a commentary upon Scripture, and what is the rabbinic tradition if not commentaries upon commentaries? It is no proof of want of meaning or of ambiguity but of richness when a sentence or series of sentences need interpretation. I would consider it deceptive were I to read my own predilections into the text. Yet, I consider it my duty to let the text speak in all its power, to let it give voice to meanings that are not on the surface.

For there are those who will reject my summary by saying that the Conciliar Statement does not recognize the Jewish people as a spiritual reality, that, in fact, it denies that reality by calling the Church "the new people of God." Some Christian scholars think that "the new people of God" is not a felicitous phrase. Even so, the phrase is part of a compound sentence. If one reads the first clause: "Certainly, the Church is the new people of God," by itself, independently of the second, one undoubtedly gets the impression that here the old theologoumenon is repeated which sees Israel as having been replaced or superseded by the Church, or, to put it differently, which views Israel as a servant dismissed, a son disowned, or a wife divorced.[10] But as soon as one continues to the second, the main clause: "nevertheless, the Jews are not to be presented as rejected or accursed by God, as if this followed from Holy Scripture," it becomes clear that Israel is not driven from the presence of the Holy One, blessed be He.

For all their differences, the Church and Judaism need not be antagonists, rather does the Covenant bind them to a common task, to a partnership before God. In the words of the Swiss scholar Clemens Thoma, the Conciliar Statement

> confirms the biblical profession that God's calling and gracious gifts are irrevocable (see Rom 11:29), that the Jewish people is, therefore, still God's special possession

(see Ex 19:5), and that the particular distinction of Christians, as God's people, is to be joint heirs, joint members,
joint partners with the Jews. (See Jn 10:16; Eph 2:11; 3:6;
1 Pt 2:7-10).[11]

Men of Vision. Some may counter that in the text of the Conciliar Statement the recognition of Judaism is so skimpy as to
be practically absent or worthless. I would like to analyze and
answer this second objection historically. Undoubtedly, the
vast majority of Christians down the ages did not ignore the
Jews, but they reduced them to mythical figures: devils incarnate, assassins of Christ, embodiments of malice and
obstinacy. Against them stood a small minority of Christians
who, now and then, tried to do justice to the Jewish reality.
Edward H. Flannery accuses Christian historians of having
torn from their books and their memories the hard fact of the
persecution of Jews by Christians.[12] It is of great importance to
tell the story of Jewish tears and blood. Still, the opposite is no
less important. Some time ago, Edmond Fleg, the great French
literary interpreter of Jewish thought, rejected the view that
life was "a tale told by an idiot, full of sound and fury, signify-
ing nothing" (*Macbeth*, V, v, 27); in the Jewish tradition, he
held, another vision prevailed, that of meaningful history, He
had been asked to prepare a history of Jewish suffering, to
which he replied that he would rather write a history dominated by the friends of the Jews than one by their enemies.[13]
    In the framework of this paper, I can refer only to a few
representative figures whose attitude toward the Jews was in
no way negative. One is the twelfth century thinker Peter
Abelard. Among his minor works is *A Dialogue Among a Philosopher, a Jew, and a Christian.* The *Dialogue*'s philosopher is
a pagan for whom reason and nature are the sole foundation of
morality. He finds the vision of the Jew and that of the Christian stultifying because both have recourse to revelation. In the
course of the exchange, the Jewish partner delves into the
suffering of his people. This is but part of his tale of woe:

> Despised are we and hated by all. Anyone who wrongs us
> considers it supreme justice, indeed a service lofty and

pleasing to God.... Even when allowed to exist, we are not permitted to own fields, vineyards, not even a patch of land—and there is no one to defend us against open or concealed attacks. Thus filthy lucre is all that is left to us. To keep our miserable life going we must charge exorbitant interest, which in turn makes us hated by those who think that we oppress them.... Truly, the state we are in speaks louder than a tongue ever could (*PL* 178:1618).

This plaint of the Jew is really that of Abelard. I am convinced of this because now and then Abelard makes his Jewish companion use terms that only a Christian would use. The latter thus calls the seal of God's covenant with Israel *circumcisionis nostrae sacramentum*, the "sacrament of our circumcision" (*ibid.*). Prior to this, the Jewish colloquist calls the Christian *frater iste qui Christianum profitetur*, "that brother who confesses to be a Christian" (*PL* 178:1615). If one remembers that the Jewish speaker, however realistically drawn, is Abelard's disguise, one is bound to conclude that it is he, the Christian, who calls Jews his brothers and sisters.

Startling, too, is Johannes Reuchlin's *Gutachten*, his *Expertise on Whether One Ought to Seize, Do Away With, and Burn All Books of the Jews*. His opinion, addressed to Emperor Maximilian in October, 1510, sought to answer the question of whether the Talmud should be destroyed because, among other things, it was written "against the Christians" and "insulted Jesus, Mary, and the Apostles . . . as well as the Christian order."[14] Interestingly, he based his judgment on those excerpts that had been used to misrepresent rabbinic teaching. For, despite all possible efforts, he had not been able to get hold of the entire Talmud.[15] Here is one of his significant points:

Suppose the Jews had deliberately written their books against us—something I do not really hold and which, in any case, would require convincing demonstration—they could plead that they did so, not to harm anyone but to defend themselves. On Good Friday of every year, we publicly abuse them by calling them *perfidos Judaeos*, that is "treacherous Jews," or without mincing words, "men in whom there is neither faith nor trust." To this they could well counter among themselves: "They slander us. We have never betrayed our faith."[16]

When Reuchlin took up the defense of rabbinic literature, he stood alone. Yet what is so remarkable about his brief is not only his courage and scholarly honesty, but also his sympathetic understanding. I would go even further; the last sentence I quoted betrays an extraordinary stance: Rather than sit in judgment over the "obstinate Jews," Reuchlin is convinced that they have no other motive than to be faithful to their calling.

As a third witness, let me single out Abbé Henri Grégoire of the late eighteenth century, one of the champions of full rights of citizenship for Jews. His paper on the physical, moral, and political regeneration of the Jews—a paper that carried off the prize of the Metz Royal Academy of Arts and Sciences—ends with this plea:

> You nations, for eighteen hundred years you have trampled on the remnants of Israel. The severity of divine vengeance has fallen on them[17]—but has God appointed you His instruments? The fury of your fathers chose its victims from among this tormented flock. What kind of treatment have you saved for those frightened lambs that escaped the slaughter and fled into your arms? Is it enough to let them stay alive, all the while robbing them of the things that make life bearable? Will you bequeath your hatred to your children? Do not judge this people except in the light of their future. . . .
>
> A new age is about to begin. . . . The Jews are members of that universal family that is bound to establish brotherhood among all peoples. Over them, as over you, revelation spreads its majestic veil. Children of the same father, rid yourselves of every pretext for antipathy towards your brethren. Some day, they will be united with you in the same fold. Give them homes where they may rest their heads in peace and dry their tears. Then the Jew will return tenderness to the Christian and embrace in me his fellow citizen and his friend.[18]

I cannot discuss the style so characteristic of the Enlightenment, but one comment may be necessary. Though Grégoire
seems to cling to the traditional Christian hope that some day
Jews and Christians will be one in Christ—in his words, "united... in the same fold"—he is no proselytizer. He is every bit as
emphatic in stressing the common humanity of Jews and Gentiles, and the common roof spread over men and women of
biblical faith as well. For him, Jews and Christians live under
the same firmament, the spiritual firmament of the revealing
God. He does not refer to the Church and the ancient Israel, but
to the people of his time: the Christians who are free and the
Jews who are prisoners of the Ghetto.

A final witness. In the summer of 1935, the Catholics of
Czechoslovakia held a national convention to which the Chief
Rabbinate of Prague bid the delegates welcome. The Bishops of
the land acknowledged the greeting with the following letter:

Prague, June 30, 1935

Gentlemen:

You were kind enough to welcome the National
Assembly of Catholics with a biblical wish of peace
which recurs again and again in the books of the Old
and New Testaments. From the depths of our souls,
we thank you for this message and, with all our
hearts, we return the greeting.

Fiat pax in virtute tua, "May there be peace in your
strength" (Ps 122:7 Vulg). The words of the Psalm
you have quoted form part of the daily prayers of the
Catholic Church. We are certainly of one mind with
you, Gentlemen: Mankind is divided today into only
two camps, the camp of those who proclaim faith in
God and the camp of His foes. We also trust that the
common values of faith and morality be, without

320 THE NEW ENCOUNTER

exception, a rampart to those who build their lives on the sacred truths of divine revelation. The sublime commandment of the love of God and of neighbor, already contained in the Old Testament, is the common base of all that is sacred to Jews and Catholics.

The message of peace that goes out from this National Assembly of Catholics is addressed to the entire world and to all Men without distinction. For every human soul is of infinite value before God. You have greeted this Congress with the words of the singer of the Lord. Permit us to respond with the high priestly blessing, with these lofty words: *Yeverehoho Adonay veyishmereho*, words we apply to all humankind without exception:

May the Lord bless you and keep you
May He let His face shine upon you,
And give you peace—
Ve-yosem leho shalom (Nu 6:24-26).

The letter was signed by Leopold Precan, Archbishop of Olmütz, and Charles Kaspar, Archbishop of Prague. Need I emphasize that this moving exchange of mutual well-wishing took place thirty years before the Council? It is a document of the post-Conciliar spirit in pre-Conciliar times.

The People of Pain. To return to Edmond Fleg's perspective, I cited him, not to gloss over the long history of Christian wrongdoing and Jewish suffering—it is, after all, injustice and pain that made the men of conscience I quoted speak out—but to show that the Conciliar Statement, however great a break-through, was not entirely without forerunners. Justice is indivisible. A man like myself, who considers it his duty to clamor that justice be given to Jews and Judaism, must take particular care not to tolerate clichés and over-generalizations about the role of Christians. Please, do not misunderstand me. I dislike the Elizabeth Ardens of Christian Church history who use their cosmetic art to make everything look beautiful. But I equally dislike the modern flagellants who delight in phrases like this: "We Christians worship the Cross, but the Jews carry it." There is truth in this avowal. Still, I cannot join in the global confession of some well-meaning Christians: "We are all guilty of the Holocaust." This high-sounding phrase is just as dangerous as apathy, for if all are guilty, meaning equally guilty, then for all practical purposes none is guilty.

What troubles me about most attempts to castigate the moral involvement of all those not directly participating in the murder is their vagueness. A scholarly analysis would have to take into account notions like "Man is nothing but a highly developed animal" or "Right or wrong are but conventions." It was Hitler's demonic logic that put these and other ideas characteristic of the "modern mind" into practice, concluding that people could, indeed ought to be, bred as well as slaughtered like cattle and that anything *der Führer* willed was justice. Again, those who blame the Nazi atrocities only on pseudo-theological notions like deicide—notions I abhor—seem to forget how fragile the influence of religion is on the lives of human beings. In many instances, what appears as a religious prejudice is really a political or psychological impulse—the will to power, self-righteousness—religiously disguised.

In my opinion, the agony of the Jews must not dominate—I repeat, dominate—the theological thinking of Christians on the reality of the Jewish people. Not that I wish to say with Rabbi Johanan (second century, A. D.):

Every distress
    in which Israel and the nations of the world share
    is a real distress.

Every distress
    confined to Israel
    is no real distress.

(*Dt. R.* 2:22)

I confess that the superhuman magnanimity of R. Johanan's dictum has me both awed and dumbfounded. No doubt a homiletic hyperbole, it seems to offer little comfort to the sufferers, little to their spiritual kin. Neither does its interpretation by the learned translator of *Deuteronomy Rabbah*[19] shed light on the abysmal character of Auschwitz, Dachau, Bergen, Belsen, Treblinka, and all the other substations of hell. Still, R. Johanan's opinion stands like a marker indicating the heights to which rabbinic thought, often maligned, has been able to rise. Do I stand this saying on its head when I read into it a summons to Christians to see in the victims of Goebbels' extermination policy[20] not only Jewish witnesses but also witnesses that belong to humankind? If I am right, not Jews alone but Christians, too, must speak of the Nazi victims as "our martyrs."

This summons notwithstanding, I do not wish to dwell on the torment of the Jews. It must not be the foundation of our dialogue. True, we must make Jewish pain lovingly our own, but such is the paradox of the Jewish-Christian co-existence conditioned by centuries of wrong thinking and wrong doing that we can speak of it too much and too often. I beg you not to confuse this statement with the complaint of many Gentiles that Jews are obsessed with the Nazi slaughter. Of course they are, and they have every right to be. My statement that we can speak of the Holocaust too much and too often is not born of that protective mechanism by which we seek to insulate our hearts against pain, its sight and its sound. I am motivated by exactly the opposite desire.

The People of Life. Some hold that the Statement hardly bespeaks a new vision of Judaism since it does not even mention the Holocaust—this is but another version of the objection that the attention paid to Judaism in the document is skimpy. I am sure the Fathers of the Council thought they were expressing their horror, disgust, and indignation at the tortures inflicted on Jews by the Nazis when they said that the Church "decries hatred, persecutions, displays of Antisemitism, staged against Jews at whatever time in history and by whomsoever." Many may think that these words are not strong enough, not explicit enough. I will not contest this criticism. Yet, are there words in Latin or English, or any other language, forceful and graphic enough to deal with the abysmal event of the slaughter of Jews by the Nazis, when hell went on a rampage the world has never seen before?

When you remember that the medieval Christian was nurtured on the hardly Christian legend of the Wandering Jew; when you remember that the emphasis among the best Christian writers has often been, as in the case of Léon Bloy, on "the people of tears"; when you remember that even Jews, Marc Chagall for instance, like to portray the sufferings of their people in the image of the crucified Jesus—please, do not take this as criticism, I love Chagall's several Crucifixions—you may understand my misgivings about any attempt to base the new Christian vision of Judaism on the anguish of the Jewish people. Christians, good Christians, may find it easy to look upon Israel as the people of pain, whereas they may never think of it as the people of life.

Christians may become so fond of the image of the Jews as a people crucified that they forget Israel's primary witness. It is of the greatest moment that Christians learn that Israel's primary witness is simply *to be*, to live, to live in the presence of the living God. There is no other people whose members commemorate the death of one of their loved ones by a prayer that is, in the deepest sense of the word, an assertion of existence, the *Kaddish*:

> Mighty be His great Name, and holy,
>   in the world fashioned by His pleasure.
> May He establish His reign
>   while life and days are granted you.[21]
> May He do so swiftly—soon,
>   and let us say: Amen.

The *Kaddish* can be understood only if one realizes, as the Jewish tradition evidently does, that to live is not only to eat and breathe, but to worship. The eminence of the *Kaddish* in Jewish life springs from an impetus embedded in the Jewish soul not to break the chain of those called to sing God's praise. Thus, in every generation, the son, for instance, taking the

place of his departed father continues the line of those who
hallow God's name.

Again, I doubt that there has ever been another people who,
in celebrating a marriage, whether in a palace or in the ghetto,
prayed:

> Praised are You, Lord our God, King of the universe.
>   You created joy and gladness, groom and bride,
>   mirth and song, pleasure and delight,
>   love and harmony, peace and companionship.
> Soon, Lord our God, may there be heard
>   in the cities of Judah and in the streets of Jerusalem
>   the jubilant voice of marrying couples
>   from under the nuptial canopy,
>   and the song of young people, feasting and singing.
> Praised are You, O Lord!
>   You cause the groom to rejoice with his bride.

Comment would destroy the beauty of these lines.

Israel is truly the people of anguish, and yet the people of
merriment. It has died a thousand deaths, and yet it is alive.
Am Yisrael ḥai, "The people of Israel lives." The survival of the
Jewish people through the centuries is not only a physical or
biological fact, it is a theological reality. This reality a Jew
experiences in his or her innermost being. It ought to be, as
much as is humanly possible, the experience of Gentile Christians, too. Jewish survival must therefore be, I hardly need
stress, a political concern, but it must also become a theological
category, an affirmation of faith, the Christian faith. Christian theological textbooks dare not ignore this sign of God's
faithfulness.

A Divine Élan. May I beg you to remember that, when I questioned making the anguish of the Jewish people in the past and
in our day the one lever of our dialogue, I did so because I am
speaking to men and women who do not have to be convinced
that the Holocaust was an outburst of hellish forces. Any sensitive person is struck dumb by its malice. Hence any sane indi-

vidual is loath to offer rational explanations and glib consola-
tions. This is not to say that God, who gives meaning to human
events, has ceded His throne to meaninglessness. The various
attempts proclaiming that in Auschwitz God, too, was
destroyed—a proposition absurdly different from the theology
of the Suffering Servant, and no less from the Midrash that has
the Holy Spirit weep over the agonies of the Chosen People
(*Lam. r.* 1, 45-46) or the one that has the Shekhinah go into exile
with exiled Israel (*Lam. r.* 1, 33)—hand to Hilter that victory
which history denied him.

According to Rabbi Meir, when the noose tightens around a
criminal's neck, the Shekhinah laments: My head hurts, my
arm is heavy. "If God," Rabbi Meir continues, "is so grieved
over the blood of the wicked . . . how much more over the blood
of the righteous!" (*bSanh.* 46a). True sensitivity sees not only
the volcano of evil that erupted in Auschwitz, Treblinka, and
Bergen-Belsen, but also the ultimate failure of the greatest
poisoner of history; for all his successes, he did not triumph.
Horrible though it was, the "Final Solution" was anything but
final. Six million Jews died, but the Jewish people lives. What
this sentence really means is exemplified by the State of Israel.
Here, an ancient people that for almost two thousand years
was severed from the soil, that as a whole had not been
involved in statecraft, that in the days of Hitler had been
defaced in every possible way, was rejuvenated.

Prior to the founding of the State of Israel, it was an uncon-
tested axiom among Gentiles, even among many Jews, that
Jews were incapable of building up and sustaining a state
because of their over-developed individualism, their lack of
discipline, the desire of each one to go his or her own way. But
Jewish individualism notwithstanding, Israel was founded
and has survived innumerable odds. As you all know, when
Israelis are asked how it is that, each time war with the Arab
states erupts, they are victorious even though they are a handful compared with the multitudes of Arab soldiers, they
answer: "We have a secret weapon, called *aleph bet*." These
first two letters of the Hebrew alphabet stand for *Ain b'rerah*,
"No alternative," or "No way out." In this instance, it means
"No way out but to fight, and fight to the last." Surrounded by

hostile armies on three sides and with the Mediterranean threatening from the fourth, they have no choice but to defend themselves unless they wish to drown in the sea.

Ain b'rerah, however, has a still deeper meaning: Israel's survival is due to a force greater than the common instinct for self-preservation or even an extraordinary tenacity for life. When the age-old desire for regaining sovereignty came close to fulfillment, all sorts of projects were talked about: Jews were to find a new home in Uganda, Madagascar, or Argentina. It would have been much easier to follow one of these plans than to return to the eroded land of their fathers. When they did return, they could have chosen an international language like English or French as the official tongue of the country. This would have been the sensible thing to do but the pioneers were "foolish enough" to reawaken the language of their ancestors, which few people understood, and to refashion it for modern use.

Why was Israel resettled against all sober calculations, and how has it been able to survive against all odds? I see only one explanation: With all respect for the idealism, the self-sacrifice, the industry, and the valor of the forerunners, the planners, the founders, the keepers, and the plain citizens of Israel, one has to profess: *Ain b'rerah*. Ultimately, Jews had, and have no choice. They are driven by an élan that is a divine gift, for they are wedded to God; they are a covenanted people. To be His people means that they cannot get away from Him, even if they wanted to. After the Emancipation, European Jews tried to be fully assimilated into the nation in whose midst they lived, but it did not work. Even when they throw off the yoke of service to the God of Abraham, Isaac, and Jacob, they cannot escape Him. "Israel alive" is a wonder that should inspire Christians, first to awed silence and then into praise.[22]

It has often been said that the Conciliar Statement on the Jews is an answer to Auschwitz. It is a fearsome truth that the unspeakable horror of Auschwitz was needed to awaken Christian conscience and consciousness. Yet, to say that the Statement is a belated response to the Holocaust would be, at best, a half truth. The Statement is, above all, a witness to Jewish existence, to the reality of Judaism; it confirms the Jewish self-awareness that expresses itself in *Am Yisrael hai*, "The people of Israel lives." Ezekiel's vision of the valley of dry bones—of bones, bereft of life and strength, being fleshed out, coming alive again by the power of the Spirit—spoke of an event uniquely located in time and space, that is, Israel's regeneration and reunion after the Babylonian Exile (Ez 37:1-14). Though the prophetic vision is thus linked to a definite date, it is not dated. Like many other biblical utterances, it has lasting meaning; it describes the perennial wonder that is Israel. Should not Christians, whose lives are marked by the power of Christ risen, be the first to look in amazement on the repeated revitalization, indeed resurrection, of God's people?

A Hand Extended. I am still dealing with the objection that the Statement's recognition of the Jewish people is skimpy or, as some critics put it, that it speaks well of biblical Israel but ignores the Judaism of later days. I have always been amazed at this hasty reaction. True, the Council did not expressly say that Judaism is a living faith and a grace-filled way of life. But, let me ask, do friends ever preface their profession of friendship by stating the philosophical conviction that the one loved is real, and not a figment of the imagination? This is very much the way it was with the Conciliar Statement.

Some of you may raise your eyebrows or burst out laughing at my comparison when you recall the difficulties and polemics at the time of the Council. It is true, the document did not have easy sailing, but does the fact that it met with hostility on the part of a few Council Fathers and of a frenzied, Antisemitic lobby outside the Council not to testify to, among other motives, their fear of its inherent power? I do not deny the lacunae of the Conciliar Statement nor its weakness in certain parts; still, for all its imperfections, it was a work of love. Its architects and champions were driven by affection for the Jewish people, and they did—at least for some wonderful moments—inspire an imposing majority of the Council.

The Conciliar Statement expresses the wish that Christians and Jews learn to know one another; that they grow in respect; that they study the Scriptures, seedbed of their lives, together, and that they engage in loving dialogue. No one can converse with a corpse, no one talk with a relic of the past. Even though it is not spelled out in the text that Judaism is a living force, it is implicit in these recommendations of the Council. It is not to the Israel of old that the Church extends her brotherly—or if you prefer her sisterly—hand, but to the Jews here and now. The common patrimony the Statement speaks of could obviously not refer to the treasures Christians share with Israel of patriarchal or prophetic days because Patriarchs, Prophets, Singers, indeed, all the Teachers of ancient Israel are the ones who "established" this patrimony or handed it down.

All this is stated, not just implicitly but explicitly, by another passage of the Conciliar document. I mean the one that refers to the Church's living memory of the fact "that the Apostles, the Church's foundation stones and pillars (see Ap 21:14; Gal 2:9), sprang from the Jewish people, as did most of the early disciples who proclaimed Christ's gospel to the world." I am sure you noticed that the past tense "sprang" for this grateful recollection is preceded by an emphatic statement in the present tense: "Theirs *is* the sonship and the glory and the covenants and the law and the worship and the promises; theirs *are* the Patriarchs and from them *is* the Christ according to the flesh (Rom 9:4-5)." The unexpected use of the present tense by the Apostle as well as the Council is a singular witness to that dignity of the Jewish people which nothing "in heaven, on earth, or in the depths"—to use another Pauline phrase (Phil 2:10)—can kill.

Paul's enumeration of the divine gifts granted to Israel has been a stumbling block to exegetes. Christians have often assumed that Jews not believing in Jesus as the Christ are banished from the sight of God and deprived of His love. How, then, can the Apostle put the bestowal of these graces in the present tense? One exegete asks himself: "Why does Paul set forth all these advantages of Israel?" only to answer: "to make the mystery of the rejection of Israel truly great and inconceivable."[23] Yet chapters 9-11 of the Epistle to the Romans were written to proclaim, not Israel's rejection but God's righteousness and fidelity. The Apostle himself poses the problem of whether God has rejected His people and replies with a resounding *Mē genoito*, "Never!" (11:1)

Another exegete is so bewildered by Paul's attributing Israel's "prerogatives" to those Jews who do not share his belief in Jesus that he has the Apostle speak here, not of the Israel of history but of "God's Israel," that is, the nation after God's own heart, the "ideal" people fulfilling His plan.[24] One need not be a scholar to realize that Paul was concerned with the empirical, not an ideal people, not with an ultimate concept of Israel dwelling in a transcendental realm but with those Jews the Christians of Rome knew.

The most drastic solution to the difficulty the present tense poses to exegetes has been offered by the English translator of the contemporary Jerusalem Bible, rendered in French by Catholic scholars. Contrary to the Greek original and the French translation, the English edition has Paul of Tarsus say: "They (my kin, the Israelites) *were* adopted as sons, they *were* given the glory and the covenants; the law and the ritual *were* drawn up for them, and the promises *were* made to them." Here the translator is guilty of violating one of the most primitive rules of scholarship, never to twist a text to conform to one's preconceived ideas. If a biblical passage does not fit one's theology, surely one must revise one's theology, not the text. I am sorry to add that the translator of the Epistle to the Romans in the new American Catholic version, the most recent of translations, outstanding in many respects, has chosen to be as arbitrary as the one responsible for the Jerusalem Bible in English.

The Sustaining Root

The Old Testament, Source of Life. This excursion into New Testament interpretation reveals, I think, a fact often overlooked: Paul's vision of his kinsfolk is one of the most important parts of the whole Statement on the Jews. In fact, it is a key, if not the key, to the proper understanding of the Statement. This is not the place to analyze Paul's vision, word by word. What the key sentence tells is simply this: Israel—that is, the Israel of all times—is a unique people. But it is not merely a people, or merely a faith community, it is a covenanted people. Forever, Israel is like a son to God. Forever, God stands by this son of His and the promises given him. The son was chosen to hallow God's name. When Moses and Aaron first appeared before Pharaoh, they conveyed this message of the Lord, the God of Israel: "Let my people go that they may worship me in the wilderness" (Ex 5:1). The Hebrew words *yaḥogu li*, which I have rendered perhaps too simply as "worship me," are often translated as "celebrate a festival for me," or "keep my pilgrim feast." Martin Buber reads the divine command as *Entlass mein Volk, dass sie mir rundreihen in der Wüste!*[25] which might be rendered: "Set my people free, that, dancing round and round, they may honor me in the desert!"

Slave laborers that they were, the Israelites were called to serve God in joy. Not that they were to imitate the wildness of pagan orgies. On the contrary, they were and are to serve God in disciplined joy; therefore the Torah was given them. If we keep in mind the tradition that all Jewish generations stood at Sinai—or as the Haggadah puts it: "Every [Jew] in every generation is bound to look upon himself as one who has personally gone forth from Egypt. . . . It is not only our fathers that the Holy One redeemed, but ourselves, too, did He redeem with them"—then it is clear that the people of Israel is meant to be a special and lasting witness to the Holy One, blessed be He. It is to remind us that the world is to be ruled, not by human instinct but by righteousness. To put this into a contemporary context, as the Cain-like instinct of Hitler clearly felt, Israel is for all times a symbol of conscience, a sign that makes some burst into praise and others withdraw into rancor.[26] These few remarks are not meant to exhaust the meaning of Paul's saying. All I intend to show is that what he says in Romans 9:4-5 makes concrete and more explicit his other saying, also quoted in our Statement: "God has not withdrawn His gifts and calling" (Rom 11:29).

I hardly need to stress that a thoughtful writer will be on guard lest he or she violate the sequence of tenses. Never will he or she shift from the past to the present or vice-versa, unless there is a reason. I have discussed one deliberate shift in tenses by the framers of the Statement on the Jews. A second one reads:

> The Church, therefore, cannot forget that she *received* the revelation of the Old Testament through the people with whom God, in that enduring love words cannot express, deigned to conclude the Covenant of old. Nor can she forget that she *draws* sustenance from the root of that well-cultivated olive tree onto which the wild shoots of the Gentiles have been grafted (Rom 11:17-24).

A whole book would be necessary to do justice to the first, and for that matter to the second part of this passage. In fact, a few years ago I wrote a book on the roots of Christian teaching in the *Tanakh*.[27] To treat those roots, however, runs the risk of being misunderstood by many, as if such a treatment implied a deliberate shoving aside of the rabbinic parallels of Christian teachings. I had and have no such intention but, as a Christian, I cannot say loudly enough that the only Scripture the Apostles knew was the Old Testament. Since it filled and guided their lives and that of the early Church, "old" could not possibly mean antiquated; rather does it imply that, in the Ancient Scriptures, the revealing God makes His first giant steps into the midst of human beings.

"Giant"—denoting only magnitude—is an inadequate adjective for the unique saving deeds by which God intervened in Israel's history, the age-old love with which He loves His people, and the unfailing care He maintains of them (see Jer 31:3). Still, God's singular covenant with Israel does not gainsay His salvific will toward all human beings, the "omnipresence of grace." That the statement on the Jews is placed in the wider context of non-Christian religions may point to a deeper meaning than the expediency that led to its present location: Israel is God's very own, a treasured possession, *segulah mikol ha-amim* (Ex 19:5), but God's love embraces all: "The earth is mine" (*ibid*). The universality of His love is the teaching of the gospel, but it is far from foreign to Judaism. The Talmud records, for instance, Abba Arika's exposition of Malachi's oracle that God is honored by sacrifice and His name great among the nations (1:11). When he said that certain nations "know Israel and their Father who is in heaven. . . . and others do not," his pupil Shimi pointed out that the prophetic saying spoke not of some nations but of the world from the rising of the sun to its setting. Abba Arika brushed the objection aside: "You, Shimi!" which I take to mean: "How can you, of all my pupils, not understand!" He simply continued: "They (the nations) call Him the God of Gods" (*Men.* 110a). Even more impressive is a verse from Ibn Gabirol's "The Royal Crown" which devout Jews recite during the night of *Yom Kippur*:

> You are God! All creatures are in Your service.
> Not diminished is Your glory
> by those who pay homage to a being of their fancy.
> For they all strive to draw near You.[28]

I must return to the Hebrew Scriptures as a living source of vibrant Christian faith. Recently, an outstanding American Catholic exegete, speaking on "The Relevance of the Old Testament for Preaching in the 1970's," was quoted as "admitting only a modest claim for Old Testament relevancy at any time. The problem is obvious—the Christian religion is not the religion of the Old Testament."[29] Quite true, but neither is it that of the New Testament only. To follow Jesus means to embrace both Testaments.[30] In the words of the German Protestant scholar Claus Westermann,

> The Old Testament was the Bible of early Christianity; the writings of the New became Scripture, that is, part of the Bible, by being added to the Old. Since the Ancient Scriptures proclaimed the deeds and words of the God from whom Jesus knew He was sent and whom He addressed as His Father, they could not be cut loose from the words and deeds of Jesus Himself.[31]

Time was when it was customary to say that the Old Testament was the manifestation of the God of anger, and the New Testament that of the God of grace. Yet, one and the same God, the God of judgment and of mercy, of wrath and of love, speaks in both Testaments. Time was when Christians used to set the Gospel against the Law, but again the whole of Scripture is Law and Gospel, Gospel and Law. Time was when Christians were wont to say that the Ancient Scriptures concern themselves only with the blessings of earthly goods, while the apostolic writings speak of spiritual blessings alone. This and all similar dichotomies are artificial, man-made, and thus wrong; they must go; they must disappear from the pulpit as well as the classroom. These dichotomies must go because they are in keeping neither with modern scholarship nor the thrust of the Conciliar Statement.[32]

In everything the Gospels proclaim, the Torah and the Prophets are presupposed. They are the foundation of its teaching and, even when not explicitly referred to, they are present. None can grasp the gospel of redemption without fully understanding the gospel of creation, and without hearing Israel's God thunder against sin as well as offer hope. Again, a Christian may be tempted to reduce the incredible message of resurrection to rational proofs of immortality, if he or she has not made Israel's vision of human nature really his or her own. Nor will a Christian accept as neighbor a man or woman whose speech, garb, and custom stamp as enemy (see Lk 10:29-37), unless he or she accepts the proclamation of the Hebrew Scriptures that every human being is God's image. Hence, in all human relations, in all social concerns, the Christian cannot dispense with the teachings of the Hebrew Scriptures.

The Rabbis, Guides to Understanding. However important the Hebrew Scriptures are in the life of Christians, they must not ignore the teachings of the ancient Rabbis. After all, Matthew has the Pharisaic scribes "sit in the chair of Moses" (23:1). It is of no small moment that the Evangelist attributed this saying to Jesus and placed it at the beginning of a pericope that reflects the struggle between the early Church and the Pharisaic leaders after the destruction of the Temple or, more concretely, the hurt of Jewish Christians whose desire to stay within the body of Judaism had been rejected.

Two examples will make clear, I hope, what I mean by the

indispensable role of the Rabbis in understanding the New Testament. The first instance is that of the woman suffering from a flow of blood (see Mk 5:25-34; Mt 9:20-22; Lk 8:43-48). If one listens, without the Rabbis' help, to the story of her cure by a power going out from Jesus as she touched the fringes of His cloak, one might easily interpret the work of healing as plain magic.[33] But, the fringe the woman wished to hold in her hand, be it only for a second, was doubtlessly the one that every Jew wore at the four corners of his garment, to which "a cord of blue" was attached (Nu 15:38). The fringe, *tsitsit*, was meant to be a call to observe all the commandments of the Lord; a reminder not to follow the heart's instinct, or a lustful urge, but to be holy to God (15:39-40). For the woman who hoped to be made well by Jesus, holding the *tsitsit* of His robe was thus a way of manifesting visibly her desire to be near to God and to do His will.

This interpretation is confirmed when one considers the meaning of the blue cord. Rabbi Meir (second century, A. D.) explains: "Blue is the color of the sea, the sea mirrors heaven, and heaven is like the throne of glory" (*bMen.* 43b). On the strength of this quotation, William G. Braude concludes that

> for the woman, the act of touching was an act of adoration. The sick people believed, which is what the authors of the Gospels mean to tell us, that Jesus was the Messiah, the living rule, so to speak, through whom one might come to know Him who sits on the throne of Glory.[34]

The second instance relates to the resurrection of Jesus. If a Christian exegete is at home with the thought and speech patterns of the ancient Rabbis, he will not be embarrassed by, nor go through mental acrobatics to explain, the credal profession that Jesus rose from the dead on the third day. As the clock moves, the span from Good Friday afternoon till Easter morning is not even two days. Karl Lehmann, formerly Professor of Dogmatic Theology at the University of Mainz, now Bishop of that city, has drawn our attention to the fact that in rabbinic literature "on the third day" is not an attempt to date an event or measure its duration, but a statement pertaining to the history of salvation.[35]

Midrash Rabbah interprets the phrase "on the third day..."
(Gn 22:4) this way: "It is written 'After two days, He will revive
us, on the third day, He will raise us up that we may live in His
presence' (Hos 6:2)." This Midrash goes on to give the example
of Joseph who "on the third day said to [his brothers]: 'This do,
and live' (Gn 42:18)"; of the spies who were told to hide three
days (Jos 2:16); of the prophet Jonah who was in the belly of a
great fish for three days (2:1); of Esther who, on the third day,
put on her royal garments in which she appeared before the
king to plead for her kinsfolk (5:1), and other examples. The
English translator of the given Midrash adds: "The point of all
these quotations is that relief from distress or the climax of
events occurred on the third day."[36] Even more enlightening
are these words: "The Holy One, blessed be He, never leaves the
righteous in distress more than three days" (*Gen. R.* 91, 7).[37]
"On the third day" thus designates the revelation of God's
glory, His saving power—an understanding presupposed by
the New Testament writers but never spelled out. It is made
explicit only in midrashic literature.

Modern Jewish Interpreters. I am still discussing the Conciliar
reminder that the Church is nourished by the sap rising from
the root of the well-cultivated olive tree. In probing the hidden
depths of the New Testament, the Christian requires the tute-
lage of the Hebrew Scriptures as well as that of the ancient
Rabbis. I will go even further and say that he or she needs to
listen to those Jewish teachers of today who themselves are
eager to understand the Gospels. To perceive the full measure
of Jesus, the Christian must see Him as His contemporaries
were able to see Him. To view Him thus, he or she may do well to
seek the help of a gifted, open-minded, and interested Jewish
scholar. Though there are several, I shall quote only two.

Each year, German Protestants gather for what is called the
German Evangelical Church Day. One of its most significant
workshops is that on "Jews and Christians." At the 1969 Convention, held in Stuttgart (July 16-20), Rabbi Robert Raphael
Geis addressed that workshop on "Jews and Christians Facing
the Sermon on the Mount." He said that, for Jesus, Sinai no
longer sufficed, since the time of salvation had begun. To

Rabbi Geis, the Sermon on the Mount is a majestic anticipation of the kingdom-to-come, while the Beatitudes resound with a mighty "Onward! Onward!"[38]

Rabbi Geis further speaks of the Jewish people's long road of suffering and of Jewish responsibility today. Jews must not be part of the arrogance of silence, as millions of human beings here and there endure "a Jewish fate." He seeks to unsettle them by referring to some rabbinic sages of the fourth century A. D. who knew that messianic days were not to be days of ease:

> Ulla and Rabba declared: Would that the Messiah appeared soon but that we were no longer around to see him. Only R. Josef said: Would that he came soon and that I be considered worthy to sit near the dung of his donkey (bSanh. 98b). So grave are the things to come! So grave the overturning of the old order! So grave the revolution that breaks with all we are accustomed to but lets the pure features of human Man radiate, that Man for whom we long and whom, at the same time, we fear![39]

Turning to Christians, R. Geis stresses that he in no way considers the realm of the beyond in Christianity as insignificant and marginal; still, he reminds them of the words of James: "My brothers, what use is it for a man to say that he has faith when he does nothing to show it?" (2:14). He professes to have witnessed in his Christian friends that justification by grace allows no lazy life of compromise but clamors for the works of faith.[40]

To get the full flavor of R. Geis' insight, more than a few phrases are necessary. Here, then, is a larger excerpt:

> In proclaiming the nearness of the time of salvation, Jesus is no visionary, no fanatic, who overlooks, indeed mercilessly disdains, human weakness. Still, the way Jesus disavows the existing human order has a revolutionary element without parallel. The Sermon intends the transformation of this earth: "How blest are you poor, the Kingship of God is yours. How blest are you who now go hungry, your hunger shall be satisfied. But woe to you rich, gone is your solace" (Lk 6:20-21, 24). In these utterances of

Jesus, there throbs an eschatological impatience. One almost hears the mighty "Onward! Onward!"....

Together with many Jews, most Christian "functionaries" want to have none of Jesus the revolutionary, as Karl Barth calls Him. Still, this changes nothing, diminishes nothing. The Man of mercy, the Bringer of righteousness and peace has appeared. Might and the power play of the world are about to vanish. Yes, so unsettling can the demand be that Man live with his eyes on the coming of God's Kingdom, that one begins to lead life within the Kingdom in a world that is not yet ready for it. The Sermon on the Mount is one great anticipation.

In saying this, one must not forget, even for the wink of an eye: Jesus is a Jew, he speaks the language of His people. *Malkhut shamayim*, literally translated "the kingdom of heaven," means but one thing, God's kingship on earth. The reason for saying heaven is simply the reserve of a Jew that makes him shun pronouncing God's name and makes him substitute "heaven" for it. As a Jew, Jesus means by redemption a public act on the stage of history; only on the strength of his public act does the redemption of the individual soul emerge. He who asks in the Sermon: "Is life not more than food, the body not more than clothing?" (Mt 6:25) cannot be pushed off into the hereafter and thus have His mighty bidding dulled.

It is *this* bidding in the proclamation of Jesus, and only this bidding, that matters; it does not merely "interest" us, it grips us. A Man appears with the intent of propelling what the Prophets announced to the very point where salvation begins, in order to burn into all of us, Christians or Jews, an image of humanity that should never let us be content with the human being—as he or she is. Christians and Jews may shake their heads in bewilderment. I cannot keep a Christian from doing so. A Jew, however, should reflect on how Leo Baeck, a master at weighing his words, said something hard to ignore: "Judaism may not pass [Jesus' gospel] by; Judaism may not misjudge nor dispense with it."[41] In like manner, Buber speaks of Jesus' great place in the history of Israel's faith.[42] (Baeck and Buber) are joined by another Jew who up to now has had, as far as I can see, the deepest perception of [Jesus].

David Flusser, who teaches New Testament at the

338 THE NEW ENCOUNTER

Hebrew University, has made these incisive comments: "Jesus is the only Jew of antiquity known to us who proclaimed not only that humanity was at the threshold of end-time but also that the new age of salvation had already begun."[43] Our anxious times must not serve as an excuse for us Jews to draw back behind these clear markings. All the less should we do it because the Christian world sees things anew and, unless we are deluded, hears again Jesus' saving message on the kingdom of God on earth in its concreteness and directness. The singular interest in the religious "I," fostered for so long, pales before the kingdom of God. . . .[44]

I have quoted Rabbi Geis extensively in order to show that the Church still draws sustenance from the root of the well-cultivated olive tree, though in a rather unexpected manner. With Karl Barth, the great theologian of the 20th century, I would like to say:

The Bible . . . is a Jewish book; it cannot be read, understood, or interpreted unless we enter into the speech, the thought, and the history of the Jews in complete openness, unless we are ready to become Jews with the Jews. Thus we are asked to take a stand toward the continued existence of the Jews as a proof that God is and works through history whether we affirm it or intend to howl against it with the wolves.[45]

The wolves here are, of course, the Jew-baiters, the vulgar as well as the sophisticated ones. Since Barth wrote these words in 1938, he no doubt thought in particular of the Nazi cacophony and all those Christians who, afraid of being discovered as not part of the pack, joined in the howling.

Another contemporary Jewish voice is that of Professor Gerald Blidstein who ends his yet unpublished paper on "Judaism in the Gospels" with these uncompromising words: "For the Christian [Jesus] is more than a Pharisaic sage; for the Jew He is less."[46] Still, he makes these startling observations:

The student of Judaism is fascinated by the gospels—
indeed, by the phenomenon of Christianity as a whole—
because it represents, at least in part, the development of
certain elements of his own faith that in his own faith are
preserved in a radically different proportion and so create
a different experience. I do not mean the clearly recogniza-
ble similarities, the many values and structures which,
despite their differences, Judaism and Christianity share
as against, say, Buddhism or Taoism, the transcendence of
God and His personality, the reality of good and evil, and
so on. I speak rather of differences that are often, in all
actuality, the working out of a new balance, a new proportion, between elements that are quite traditional. Christianity is often, then, a re-proportioning of Jewish elements, the striking of a different balance. The student of
Judaism is fascinated by the potential of the doctrines and
institutions of his own faith, and moves to explore the
"atomic structure" of these elements, if I may call it that,
and to understand afresh the meaning of the proportion
and balance in which Judaism holds them.[47]

In the course of his paper, Professor Blidstein deals extensively with Jesus' attitude toward the Sabbath. He discusses,
in particular, the controversy with some Pharisees occasioned
by the hungry disciples who had plucked and eaten some ears
of corn on the Sabbath (see Mt 12:1-8; Mk 2:23-28; Lk 6:1-5).
Without wishing to identify myself with all his remarks on the
incident and on rabbinic parallels, I find his suggestion on
Matthew 12:6—though different from the interpretation common to Christian exegetes—quite penetrating:

If I may be allowed, parenthetically, a bit of textual second-
guessing: May I suggest that the "something greater than
the Temple" is not Jesus, but rather, as the sentences
immediately following suggest, the doing of mercy? For
the passage as a whole reads, "I tell you there is something
greater than the Sabbath here. If you had known what that
text means, 'I require mercy and not sacrifices,' you would
not have condemned the innocent. . . ." The "something,"
then, is the feeding of the hungry; since one sacrifices on

the Sabbath, certainly one ought to be able to do all deeds of goodness.[48]

I wish time permitted me to treat the work of Professor David Flusser and that of Professor Asher Finkel, and to do so extensively. Still, in limiting myself to the words of Rabbi Geis and Professor Blidstein, I have indicated the deep potential for a certain theological exchange, or cross-fertilization, if you wish. I trust I have succeeded in showing that, despite the separation of the two faiths, Christians would do well not to live independently of the people of Israel. They must not behave as if Judaism did not exist or had nothing to offer them. Some may counter that I have gone beyond the literal meaning of the Conciliar Statement that the Church "draws sustenance from the root of the well-cultivated olive tree," that is, the Israel according to the flesh. The objection is justified, if the emphasis is on "the root," but if the oneness of the "olive tree" is stressed, then I have applied the words of our document in what I think is a legitimate way.

Cast in Jewish Idiom. I have given two examples of how Christians need the help of their Jewish brothers to understand themselves better. But this fact pales before another to which, in my opinion, readers of the Conciliar document have not given sufficient attention or weight. Twice the Council clothes its message in traditional Jewish terms.

[1] In saying, with the Apostle, that "God holds [the Jews] most dear, for the sake of the Fathers" (Rom 11:28), the Council did not speak condescendingly, as some critics assume. "For the sake of the Fathers," is a happy echo of that precious rabbinic doctrine of "the merit of the Fathers," *zehut avot.* According to rabbinic tradition, the Patriarchs were created before the world was made (*Gen. r.* 1, 4). Elsewhere, they are considered the rocks and the hills, in other words, the very foundation of the world. Abraham, in particular, is called the "rock" on which the Holy One, blessed be He, built the earth (*Yalkut to Pent.*, §766). Again, it is because of the merits of Israel's great forebears, that is, because of God's mighty Covenant with them, that the people was delivered from the Egyp-

tian bondage and safely passed through the waters blocking their way to the promised land (*Ex. r.* 1, 36). It is on account of their virtues that Moses was allowed to ascend Mount Sinai and receive God's revelation in the Torah. When the people abandoned their Deliverer by dancing around the Golden calf, Moses' pleading with God was in vain till he said: "Remember Abraham, Isaac, and Israel, Your servants" (Ex 32:13). As soon as he recalled them, God heard him at once.[49]

To plead with God that He be merciful because of His love for Abraham, His friend, Isaac, His servant, and Jacob, His saint, is part of Jewish literature even prior to the Rabbis. When, in the revolt of Judas Maccabeus, his army had to face Nicanor, a commander determined not only to defeat the Jews but to send them into slavery, many fled in terror. Those who remained prayed to the Lord to save them, "not for their own merits, but by virtue of the covenants God had made with their ancestors, and because of His holy and majestic name they bore" (2 Mc 8:15). Again, the apocryphal *Testament of Levi* predicts that the Temple will be razed and Jerusalem's inhabitants dispersed throughout all nations as captives. Yet, destruction and exile are not God's final word. He will be gracious again. The author of the *Testament of Levi* thought it necessary to remind his readers that "were it not for the sake of Abraham, Isaac, and Jacob, our Fathers, not one of our issue would be left on the earth" (*Testaments of the Twelve Patriarchs*, Levi 15). Asher, too, foretells the desolation that will come over the land and the scattering of Israel unto the four corners of the earth. He, too, concludes his dire prophecy with words of hope: "In His fidelity, the Lord will gather you together again through His tender mercy, for the sake of Abraham, Isaac, and Jacob" (*Ibid.*, Ash. 7).

Among many Christians, the word merit does not have a pleasant ring. The mischievous sale of indulgences during the Middle Ages may, in part, excuse the bias. Another source may be the mistaken notion that Christianity is superior to Judaism in that the Christian is bidden to love God, without seeking any reward, whereas the Jew is told to pile merit upon merit, reward upon reward. This is sheer myopia, not to say ignorance. On the one hand, Jesus taught His disciples to suffer insults and

342 THE NEW ENCOUNTER

persecution gladly, and theirs would be "a rich reward in heaven" (Mt 5:12). He also said:

> Do not store up for yourselves treasure on earth
>> where it grows rusty and moth-eaten,
>> and thieves break in to steal it.
>
> Store up treasure in heaven
>> where there is no moth and no rust to spoil it,
>> no thieves to break in and steal.
>
> (Mt 6:19-20)

On the other hand, there are numerous rabbinic sayings that praise love of God as the one governing rule of life: "Whatever you do, do not do it except for love" (*Sifre* on Dt 11:13). Indeed, it is the hope of the Rabbis that those who obey out of lesser motives will come to obey out of the highest. Safra, a Babylonian Rabbi of the fourth century, prayed:

> May it be Your good pleasure, O Lord our God, to make peace among your family above and your family below,[50] also among the disciples who occupy themselves with Your Torah whether for its own sake or not; and may all those who do not occupy themselves with it for its own sake come to do so (*bBer.* 16b-17a).

I do not claim that the Conciliar Statement on the Jews is a perfect document, but honesty demands that I complete this admission by another statement: Many criticisms by Christians, and even by Jews, betray little knowledge of Judaism, or little application of that knowledge. To my mind, it bespeaks the openness of the Council, its courtesy and nobility, that it should acknowledge what the Jewish people means to God in terms borrowed from the storehouse of Jewish thought.

[2] There is another instance of the same phenomenon, even more remarkable than the first. Jews and Christians are brothers and sisters in hope; both long for, and walk toward, God's universal rule. Though they both believe in an age-to-

come when God will be all in all, they differ in the interpretation of their common hope. Who would have thought that, in
professing her own expectations, the Church in Council would
use, not the New but the Old Testament? Who would have
dreamt that, basing herself on one of Zephaniah's utterances,
she would say: "The Church awaits that day, known to God
alone, on which all peoples will address the Lord in a single
voice and 'serve Him with one accord' (Zeph 3:9; see Is 66:23; Ps
66:4; Rom 11:11-32)" (*Nostra Aetate*, 4)? Can there be any doubt
that, by clothing her own eschatological hope in traditionally
Jewish language, the Church honors the people of Israel?

Another, somewhat later, oracle proclaiming the same hope
for the universal acknowledgment of the one living God is that
of the Prophet Zechariah:

> And the Lord shall be King over all the earth:
> On that day shall the Lord be one, and His name one.
>
> (14:9)

Obviously, it could not have entered the mind of the Prophet to
deny, ahead of its revelation, the triune life of the Lord God,
rather does he emphasize the uniqueness of the God of Israel,
peerless and sovereign. His saying is, in the words of the late
Chief Rabbi of the British Empire, Joseph H. Hertz,

> one of the fundamental verses of the Jewish conception of
> the Kingdom of Heaven. It proclaims the Providential care
> of God for all mankind, and the future recognition of the
> true God by all mankind. It closes all synagogue services.[51]

The spirit of this prayer is akin to that of the prayer Jesus
taught His disciples, sharing with it the ardent desire for the
complete unfolding of God's kingship: "Thy kingdom come!"

Plainly, the Jewish and Christian concepts of the age-to-
come differ, and no council would wish to gloss over the difference. But it ought not to go unnoticed that the Council wished
to bridge the gap in an unusual way. Though no dogma, a

344 THE NEW ENCOUNTER

traditional Jewish view speaks of a time when the nations of the earth will submit to the Law of God, as written in the Torah; the Christian tradition, however, looks toward an end point in history when all will turn toward the Way that is Christ. As the Council quotes one prophetic utterance and implies another with which the Jewish liturgy resounds, it points to an age when words, far from losing their meaning, will reveal their full wealth; when they will no longer separate, but unite; when the reality-to-come will far surpass our present stammer.[52]

Problems of the Day

The State of Israel. I am obviously unable to deal with every problem raised by the Conciliar Statement, but there are two I must touch on. The Council said nothing about the one reality that is paramount to Jewish existence today: the State of Israel. I can be brief on this since I have spoken of the challenge the State poses to Christians on more than one occasion.[53] To me, the State of Israel is the visible expression of the God-willed permanence of the Jewish people. As is Judaism, so is the State of Israel, a banner of God's fidelity. Jewish history began with the promise of the Land. More precisely, the promise of the Land antedated the existence of the people. Scripture has God bid Abram: "Go forth . . . to the land that I will show you" (Gn 12:1). The Christian must not ignore that the foundations of the State are thus deep, not limited to an act of the world community and a decision of the settlers of the Land, however essential they were to the birth of the Jewish State.

One of the difficulties the State of Israel presents to most people is that it does not fit into the usual categories and preconceived ideas. To give only one example: Here is a state whose neighbors have been at war with it for years; terrorist bands threaten the lives of its people again and again. Yet when one of the neighboring states felt itself menaced by the same terrorists and became engaged in an armed conflict that took many lives and destroyed many homes, the people of Israel did not rejoice in the misfortune of its enemies. Instead, Israel was the first country to send help to Jordan, help to the wounded, help to the hungry.

There are few instances that show the depth of Israel's mentality as much as the particulars of this effort. The Jordanian authorities accepted Israel's aid only under certain conditions. The whole relief program had to be carried out under the patronage of the International Red Cross instead of Israel's *Magen David Adom*. The sixteen vehicles loaded with medical supplies and the ten trucks carrying over two hundred tons of food were not allowed to show Israeli license plates. So disinterested was Israeli assistance that the men in charge were ready to "cover up" their act of mercy as long as those in need were helped. I venture to say that many Israelis who think of themselves as non-religious are religious despite themselves. Here is a state human in a way that none of its accusers is.

In Jesus' great parable, a passing Samaritan takes pity on a Jew who had been the victim of highwaymen and left him in the care of an innkeeper. The Israelis took some two hundred people wounded in the Jordanian civil war into their own hospitals and those located in the occupied territory. If Jesus praised the good Samaritan, what would He say of the good Israelis? Of course, this is a rhetorical question. I have no doubt what He would say of them if He walked again the roads of His land. My concern is: When will Christians come to say the right word about *Eretz Yisrael*? When will they recognize that it is more than several thousand square miles but that it is a spiritual reality. Fruit of divine promise, it has itself become a promise. To me, at least, the unselfish acts I have just noted are prophetic signs.

Proselytism. A major obstacle to constructive dialogue between Christians and Jews is the suspicion of some Jews that the Statement is but a screen for missionary efforts and the dialogue but a new device to win converts. A few Jews, by no means unfriendly, may even say that the Church cannot help it: She is missionary by her very nature.

I will be as candid as the problem demands. Let me begin by saying: The Statement is an honest document. It means what it says, never something else. It is not a cryptic invitation to Jews to enter the Church; it cannot be, for it is not even addressed to Jews but to Catholics. Yet, it is quite correct to say

346 THE NEW ENCOUNTER

that it is the mark of the Church to be missionary. In other words, she would have to disobey her vocation as the "city on the hill" (Mt 5:14), were she to forget that she is sent into the world to serve men and women and offer them the healing power of Christ. The Church must bear witness to Him. Even without preaching, she bears this testimony by her very presence, and so does the individual Christian. This witness wells forth from the very heart of the Christian existence, and no Christian can change it without unmaking himself or herself.

Close to, but different from this inner mission, is organized missionary activity, or "the missions." I hardly need tell an audience as knowledgeable as this one that missionary activity is part of the Church's Jewish heritage. I wish there were time to describe the efforts and successes of Jewish missionaries prior to Jesus' time. But I must at least disavow as a fallacy the common stereotype that Christianity is, by its inner dynamic, missionary and outgoing, while Judaism is self-contained and thus non-missionary.

To come to the contemporary scene, there is in the Church today no drive, no organized effort to proselytize Jews, and none is contemplated for tomorrow. Though the Church will always profess Jesus as the Savior of all; though she will never abandon her vision of a humanity united in the living God; though she will continue to welcome wholeheartedly to her ranks Jews who have been led to believe in Jesus as the Christ—they are, after all, essential to her make-up as the Church of Jews and Gentiles—she cannot treat the worshippers of the Holy One, blessed be He, as if they dwelt "in the land of death's dark shadow" (Mt 4:16 NEB; Is 9:2). These words of Isaiah referred to the hungry and despondent survivors of the Assyrian invasions of 733-732 B.C.; they may not be applied to the religious nature of Judaism, nor may the servants of the living God be approached as if they were servants of idols or some anonymous power.

It may not be sufficient to rule out a Christian approach to Jews that resembles the mission to animists or humans worshiping figures of their own making. This would, after all, be a purely negative stance. Elsewhere, I have raised the question, as have others before me, of whether Judaism and Christianity are not two ways of righteousness that have complementary functions. Among other things, I wrote:

> I have no doubt that, at the end of ages, the chasm will be closed, even though I do not know exactly by what wonder of grace unity will come. Is it necessary, indeed, possible that in the present eon—for the Christian the "age of the in-between," between the first and the second comings of Christ—we do away with the opposing visions of Christians and Jews? Is their polarity not rather meant to be an agent that makes both communities, and the world with them, run toward that final consummation of which the Prophets dreamed? Do not both communities, each in its own way, serve the will of God, and though seemingly apart, push together toward the ultimate goal: God's perfect reign and humanity's delivery from all and every evil?[54]

Further, various guidelines for Catholic-Jewish relations, foremost among them those of the American Bishops, expressly warn against the abuse that would turn dialogue into an attempt to proselytize the partner. There have been, however, a few voices, like those of John Cardinal Heenan and Fr. Arthur Klyber, that have strongly criticized all anti-conversionist views. Few major theologians have spoken on the subject. Hans Küng is one. He writes:

> Only one course of action is permitted to the Church on this common pilgrimage—not "tolerating," not "missionizing," not "converting," but only "stirring [Israel] to emulation," (see Rom 11:11-14). The Church can make Israel jealous of the "salvation" she has received, so as to spur Israel to imitation. How? The Church, in her whole existence, must bear witness to the messianic fulfillment. In her whole existence, she must vie with Israel in addressing herself to a world that has turned its back on God, and in demonstrating to it, with authority and love, the word that has been fulfilled, the righteousness that has been revealed, the mercy that has been accepted, the reign of God which has already begun.[55]

No doubt, the New Testament is intransigent, at first glance even overwhelmingly so. But it is also conciliatory, indeed, open; it acknowledges deep commitment in "others" and the divine light in their hearts. Jesus declared point-blank:

> He who is not for me is against me;
>   he who does not help me gather, scatters.
>
> (Mt 12:30)

Yet, with no less force, He also said: "He who is not against us is for us" (Mk 9:40). Again, when one whom the Gospels call a "teacher of the Law" agreed that the Lord God was the one and only Lord and that He had to be loved with all one's heart, strength, and being, and that one's neighbor ought to be loved as one's self, Jesus hailed him: "You are not far from the kingdom of God" (Mk 12:34).

Would I could forever lay to rest the suspicion that the Conciliar Statement on the Jews is meant to conceal missionary aggression, the "soul-snatching" of the Church. But after centuries of estrangement, it takes time for confidence in one another to strike root. Let me say only one more word on this point: No matter how firmly we reject any "conversionist tactics," we must, at the same time, love the concept of, and call to, conversion. In the pre-ecumenical age, Christians sought to convert others. Today, Catholics realize much more their own need to be converted.

"Conversion" stands at the threshold of Judaism as well as of Christianity; both ways of righteousness are unthinkable without it. In saying this, I am not thinking of conversion as a change from one religious group or spiritual family to another. I take conversion, in its deepest sense, as a reorientation of one's total existence in the sight of God. The ancient Rabbis taught that repentance was among the seven things created before the creation of the visible world. In more modern terms, *teshuvah*, "repentance," the turning to God, is woven, as it were, into the fabric of our being. The ability to abandon all that is wrong, to heave overboard everything that hinders our pilgrimage, and to turn to God as the true Captain of our ship—this ability is very much part of every human being. The Talmud has collected many rabbinic praises of a human being's power to turn. Here are a few:

> Great is repentance: it carries healing to the world....
> Great is repentance: it reaches to the throne of glory....
> Great is repentance: it brings about redemption.
>
> (*bYom.* 96a)

Every Christian can make these tributes his own.

What is needed, however, is not our eulogy of *teshuvah* but our actual turning. Let me close, then, with the prayer that each of us, be he Christian or Jew, become a *baal teshuvah*, a penitent, a convert; that we learn to appreciate and respect each other's thought and work; that we learn to think as well as speak of each other's tradition with sensitivity;[56] that we discuss our differences with painstaking honesty; that we, hostile cousins of yesterday, learn to be loving brothers and sisters today and tomorrow.

I would like to clothe this request for kinship in words of the Jewish liturgy and make my own this prayer of *Rosh ha-shanah*:

Eloheynu ve-Elohey Avoteynu
Our God and God of our Fathers,
   in Your glory, rule the entire universe;
   in Your majesty, tower above the whole earth;
   in Your mighty splendor, show yourself to all who dwell on it.
Every creature will then know that you created it, and every
                                    being that you made it.
And every living thing will profess:
   Adonay, Elohey Yisrael, Melekh
   u-malkhuto bakol mashalah.

   The Lord, the God of Israel is King,
   His reign embraces all that is.

NOTES*

*Whenever this essay speaks of "Statement" without qualification, it refers to Section 4 of the Conciliar Declaration on the Relationship of the Church to Non-Christian Religions.

¹ Moore, *Judaism* (Cambridge: Harvard University Press, 1944), 2,84f.
² *Sifra, Kedoshim Perek,* 4,12; *J. Talmud, Ned.* 9,4; *Gen. R.* 24,7.
³ See Moore, *ibid.,* 2,83.
⁴ *An Stelle eines juristisch fassbaren Einzelgebotes nennt er ein rein moralisches Gebot, mit dem ein Gesetzeskundiger als Jurist nichts anfangen konnte.* Paul Gaechter, *Das Matthäus Evangelium* (Innsbruck: Tyrolia, 1963), p. 712.
⁵ The adverse interpretation of the Matthean scene follows the model of John Chrysostom. Without much knowledge of the Gospel's Jewish milieu, he writes in one of his homilies on Matthew: "When the Pharisees heard that Jesus had put the Sadducees to shame, they approached Him again. Although it would have become them better to hold their peace, they decided to enter into an argument with Him. They put forth a man well skilled in the Law, not from any desire to learn from Jesus but to trap Him" (*PG* 58:661). Would it not have been more likely for the Pharisees to rejoice in the way Jesus unmasked the weakness of their opponents' stand? Again, why would it have been necessary to select a particularly learned man to ask a question that was on many minds and lips? Wisdom was required to answer the question, not to utter it.

The ignorance of the Gospel's Jewish milieu manifest in John Chrysostom's comments is, I am sorry to say, almost a hallmark of patristic exegesis, not to speak of that of later ages. In the field of New Testament interpretation, the motto "Back to the Fathers!" is not an altogether happy one. A return to patristic exegesis would not only clash with many of the insights of modern biblical scholarship, it would also block the true understanding of Jesus' relationship to His people and its various groups.

This is as good a place as any to quote a great Jewish master of our times. In replying to Alfred Edersheim—who in his *Life and Times of Jesus the Messiah* (New York: Longman's Green, 1917) perfected the "art" of making the difference between Christ and Judaism "one of infinite distance" (2,15)—Solomon Schechter observes: "We venture to hold that the glory of such a sublime figure as that of Jesus Christ in no wise requires the process adopted in dealing with a microscopic object, namely, the obscuration of its surroundings." (*Studies in Judaism*, Third Series [Philadelphia: Jewish Publication Society, 1924], p. 165). Indeed, to darken the background of Jesus' life in order to make Him stand out does Him no honor; worse than that, there is always the danger that what starts out as antagonism against Jews will in the end become hostility toward Jesus Himself.

  6   For a similar teaching, see Test. Iss. 5,2. *The Testaments of the Twelve Patriarchs*, ed. R.H. Charles and W.O.E. Oesterley (New York: Macmillan, 1917), p. 63.

  7   Interestingly enough, the view that there are 613 commandments in the Torah, which the detractors of Judaism never tire of repeating, was first expressed by R. Simlai, the same man who so ingeniously sought to arrive at a unifying principle of the Torah.

  8   A common misunderstanding has it that in Jewish spirituality "fear of the Lord," not love of Him, is the supreme virtue. In reality, the Rabbis consider fear, that is reverence or awe, and love of God synonymous or closely associated qualities. See Ephraim E. Urbach, *The Sages* (Jerusalem: The Magnes Press, 1955), 1,402-403; 2,860-861.

  9   Some writers have described the Conciliar Statement as a "rejudaization of Christianity." I consider this designation unfortunate, indeed, misleading. To give only two reasons: First, in apostolic times, "judaizers" were Christians who insisted that, in order to be saved, Gentiles would have to keep the practices ordained by the Mosaic law (see Ac 15:1). When the Council taught Catholics to be fully aware of the Church's origin in Israel—an origin that has put an indelible character on her—when it reminded them of the Hebrew spirit that does, and must, mark her life, it obviously did not demand that she acknowledge all the biblical or halakhic precepts as still binding on her members. But it is exactly this or some other kind of amalgam that the term "rejudaization" suggests. Our search, however, must be for that clarity without which the dialogue between Christians and Jews cannot flourish.

  Second, among the difficult tasks that will face the Church of tomorrow is to take deep root in the various parts of Asia and Africa. Among other things, she will have to relate the biblical idiom to new thought and speech patterns. Rejudaization, at best a vague term, does not prepare her for the delicate work of adapting herself to new surroundings, without the least loss of her being, an essential part of which is her Hebrew heritage. She must learn new ways to serve while remaining faithful to her everlasting Lord. To be keeper and dispenser of things old and new (see Mt 13:52) is one of her privileges.

  10   Years ago, Jacques Maritain, to whom all engaged in the ministry of reconciliation owe much, said in "The Mystery of Israel": "The

mystical body of Israel is an unfaithful and a repudiated Church (and that is why Moses had figuratively given forth the *libellum repudii* [bill of divorce])—repudiated as a Church, not as a people. And ever awaited by the Bridegroom, who has never ceased to love her." (*Ransoming the Time*, transl. H.L. Binsse [New York: Scribner's, 1941], p. 154) Today an alert theologian would be loath to separate the Jewish people as an ethnic entity from the Jewish people as the Lord's witness.

 11 See *Kirche aus Juden und Heiden* (Vienna: Herder, 1970), p. 16.

12 See *The Anguish of the Jews* (New York: Macmillan, 1965), p. ix.

13 See *La Conscience Juive* (Paris: Presses Universitaires de France, 1963), pp. 5,8f. Fleg's complete statement in translation is:

> Were I to do a work of this kind, it would rather be a history of friendship for Jews for had we not had, at all times, friends more powerful and more numerous than our enemies, we would no longer exist. All through our history, we have been continually helped and saved, and this, too, is one of its essential aspects.

Fleg's view of Jewish history is akin to that of Salo W. Baron who speaks of "the lachrymose conception of Jewish history," i.e., a conception of "the destinies of the Jews in the Diaspora as a sheer succession of miseries." Again, "the Middle Ages were neither in themselves the dark ages . . .; nor were they as dark for the Jews, in comparison to the rest of the population, as is widely held." Baron, *A Social and Religious History of the Jews*, First ed. (New York: Columbia, 1937), 2, 31, 86.

14 See *Gutachten über das Jüdische Schrifttum* (Constance: Thorbecke, 1965), p. 28. The English title in the text reproduces the original title of 1510.

15 See *ibid.*

16 See *ibid.*, p. 84. The German for "treacherous Jews" is *glaubbrüchige Juden*.

17 It is not clear what Grégoire means by "divine vengeance has fallen on them." I doubt that he subscribed to the notion that Israel's dispersion and all its other misfortunes were punishment for the Crucifixion. I think it only fair to stress that the idea of the people's punishment is not one devised by Christians. Rabbinic literature often speaks of the destruction of the Temple, its cause and consequences, in the most stringent terms.

The Jewish liturgy resounds with the awareness of Israel's sin, of

God's judgment as well as of His mercy. The most profound expressions are found in the *Selihot*, "Prayers of Penitence," that are to be said prior to *Rosh ha-shanah*. One of these, as used in the Sephardic congregations of the United States, reads:

> More than all other peoples we have transgressed
> Hence deep is our shame more than any other nation.
> Our joy has gone into exile;
> Because of our sins our heart is faint.
> Our longing is shattered,
> The crown of our glory is ravished
> Our sanctuary is laid waste
> Through our transgressions
> Our homeland lies desolate.
> Its beauty is given to strangers;
> Our strength is spent for others.

(*Prayers for the New Year*, ed. David de Sola Pool [New York: Union of Sephardic Congregations, 1948], p. 25.)

That City and Temple were destroyed because of the people's sins is part of both the Jewish and the Christian traditions. The tremendous difference between them is that Christian teachers, at least in the past, were easily misled by the tone of finality given to many biblical sayings into seeing God's judgment as irreversible, while Jewish interpreters did not. The Jewish response to divine punishment is varied and immensely rich. The Jewish worshiper may voice Zion's lament: "The Lord has abandoned me." He can imagine even God Himself sorrowing: "I am become like a sparrow.... When you take away its young a sparrow is left solitary...I burnt my children...and I sit solitary." Yet, he or she feels assured that, even though Jerusalem be in ruin, God's eyes and heart "will be there perpetually" (1 Kgs 9:3). He remembers that God promised long ago: "I return to Jerusalem with compassion" (Zech 1:16) and "I will be a wall of fire round about, and I will be the glory in her midst" (Zech 2:5). Still more encouraging is God's "fellow-feeling." "The Holy One blessed be He ... sees Jerusalem in desolation ... and two great hot tears fall into the depths of the sea," writes a novelist of the last century. An ancient midrash tells that, when the Holy One, blessed be He, saw the destruction of the first Temple, He wept and said: "Woe is me for my house. My children, where are you? ∴ What shall I do with you, seeing that I warned you but you did not repent?" He then has Abraham, Isaac, Jacob, and Moses summoned from their tombs to mourn with Him, "for they know how to weep." (For full references, see *The Holy City, Jews on Jerusalem*, ed. Avraham Holtz, a B'nai B'rith Jewish Heritage Classic [New York: Norton, 1971], pp. 110,84,68,110,108-109,144,81.

[18]   Grégoire, *Esai sur la régénération physique, morale, et politique des Juifs* (Metz, 1789), pp. 193-194.

[19]   A footnote in the English edition says that a distress of Israel alone is not a true distress "because God quickly hears their prayers. The Yalkut, however, reverses the reading, and this is preferable." (*Midrash Rabbah, Deuteronomy*, trans. J. Rabbinowitz [London: Soncino, 1939], 7,50.)

[20]   In speaking of "Goebbels' Final Solution," I am following the historian of the SS who bases himself on Felix Kersten, Himmler's personal physician and confidant. Himmler once confessed to Kersten that Hitler's original order was to remove all Jews from Germany in an orderly fashion, allowing them to take with them all their movable property. But toward the end of 1941, Goebbels convinced the Nazi leadership that "the Jewish question could be solved only by the unsparing annihilation of all Jews. As long as a single Jew remains alive, he will be an enemy of Nazi Germany. Hence, any kind of clemency and humanity toward the Jews would be ill-advised." (See Heinz Höhne, *Der Orden unter dem Totenkopf, Die Geschichte der SS* [Frankfurt: Fischer, 1969] 2, 343.)

Assuming the correctness of the report, it is psychologically interesting that the idea of the "Final Solution" should not have come from any of the gangster types in Hitler's entourage, but from the member who was the most sophisticated but, at the same time, was a cripple and seemed to have in no way resembled the Nordic man. Without any scruples Hitler made Goebbels' suggestion of murdering all Jews within reach his own.

[21]   In the traditional way, these words are spoken by the one who leads the prayer—hence "while life and days are granted *you*."

[22]   On all this, see Helmut Gollwitzer, *Israel und Wir* (Berlin: Lettner, 1958).

[23]   Anders Nygren, *Commentary on Romans* (London: SCM, 1958), p. 356.

[24]   See Lucien Cerfaux, *The Church in the Theology of St. Paul*, transl. G. Webb and A. Walker, 2nd ed. (New York: Herder, 1959), p. 20.

[25]   "Das Buch Namen" in *Die Schrift* (Berlin: Lambert Schneider, n.d.), 2,21.

[26]   I am referring to Hitler's contemptuous statement that conscience is a Jewish invention. (See Hermann Rauschning, *The Voice of Destruction* [New York: Putnam, 1940], pp. 223-224.) Sayings like these make clear that he and his henchmen hated the Jews, not

because of any faults they might have had, but because of the singular position they held in God's scheme. It is this kind of hatred that makes the slaughtered Jews martyrs in the strict sense of the word.

²⁷   *The Israel of God* (Englewood Cliffs, NJ: Prentice-Hall, 1963). The book is out of print.

²⁸   See *The Order of the Form of Prayers for the Day of Atonement According to the Custom of the Spanish and Portuguese Jews*, 2nd ed. (London: E. Justius, A.M. 5570), p. 42. Fidelity to Ibn Gabirol's thought demands that I mention the lines that follow. In them he calls those who seek the king's highway but stray from it, blind men who fall into a pit, or the abyss of perdition. Though they may think they have attained their goal, they have labored in vain. Only those who travel the straight road will arrive at the king's palace. I wonder whether the latter verses do not weaken the lofty view of those quoted in the text.

²⁹   Daniel Durken, O.S.B., on Roland Murphy, O. Carm., in *America*, May 30, 1970, p. 588.

³⁰   Fr. Murphy's stand may actually be close to mine, for in Fr. Durken's words, he continued: "The solution is just as obvious—the God of the Old Testament is the God of Jesus Christ" (*ibid*).

³¹   *Das Alte Testament und Jesus Christus* (Stuttgart: Calwer, 1968), p. 7.

³²   Westermann, too, disavows these false distinctions. He also gainsays the often mentioned antithesis between the first Covenant as the one of promise and the second as the one of fulfillment. Promise and fulfillment are the marks of both Testaments (see *ibid*.,p. 10).

Exegetes, preachers, and catechists face another danger, that of over-allegorizing. As the Rabbis interpret biblical texts allegorically, so may the Christian teacher. In fact, the use of Israel's songs, the Psalms, as the Church's own prayer presupposes her reading of references to Israel or Jerusalem as references to herself. This is as it ought to be. Again, a Christian, on hearing many of the psalms, may hear the voice of Christ. St. Augustine, for instance, called Him *iste cantator*, "that unique Singer" (*Sermon on Ps 122*), "the Man who is all men" (*On Ps 34*). A worshiper who hears the cry of the poor and afflicted as a cry of Jesus, exercises what I would call the creative imagination of love. A lover sees his beloved everywhere. Likewise, a Christian, who is nothing if he or she is not a lover, sees Christ on many a page of the Old Testament but it is not "fancy" that moves, rather love, the love of Jesus and His own.

The use of allegory, the search for a figurative sense, is thus correct, provided two main rules are scrupulously observed. First, the preacher may well apply "Comfort, comfort my people" (Is 40:1) to the followers of Jesus, as long as he does not suppress that "people" refers originally and first of all to the people of Israel. He may take "I will help you, says the Lord" (Is 41:10) as a promise to believers in Christ, again as long as he does not forget that the offer is made primarily to Israel according to the flesh. Second, the figurative interpretation must not be selective, in the sense that all references to phrases like "Israel, the chosen," "Jacob, the favored," "Zion restored," are applied to the Church and phrases like "Israel, the sinner," "a stiff-necked people," "the people and city punished or doomed" are seen as pointing to the Jewish people. Wisdom, which lives on humility, will lead the Christian to see himself or herself marked by the good and the bad, the promise and the threat, the gift and the punishment the Hebrew Scriptures offer.

[33] Examples of such interpretation are legion. The most recent seems to be by Edward J. Mally, S.J. who writes: "Jesus is described as possessing an almost magical healing power that operates automatically upon contact with Him." ("The Gospel According to Mark," *The Jerome Biblical Commentary* [Englewood Cliffs: Prentice-Hall, 1968], 2,33.)

[34] "A Rabbinic Guide to the Gospels," *Scripture* (London, April, 1967), p. 7. See also the narrative in Mk 6:56 and Mt 12:36.

[35] See *Auferweckt am dritten Tag nach der Schrift* (Freiburg: Herder, 1968), pp. 262-290.

[36] *Midrash Rabbah, Genesis*, transl. H. Freedman, (London: Soncino, 1959) 1,491, n.2.

[37] *Ibid.*, 2,842.

[38] See "Juden und Christen vor der Bergpredigt," *Gerechtigkeit in Nahost* (Stuttgart: Kreuz, 1969), p. 10.

[39] See *ibid.*, p. 12.

[40] See *ibid.*, pp. 12, 15.

[41] *Judaism and Christianity*, transl. W. Kaufmann (Philadelphia: Jewish Publication Society, 1964), pp. 101-102.

[42] See *Two Types of Faith*, transl. N.P. Goldhawk (New York: Harper Torchbooks, 1961), p. 13.

[43] *Jesus*, transl. Ronald Walls (New York: Herder, 1969), p. 90.

[44] See "Juden und Christen vor der Bergpredigt," *ibid.*, pp. 10-11.

[45] *Church Dogmatics*, 1,2 (Edinburgh: Clark, 1956), pp. 510-511.

[46] From an unpublished lecture given on September 23, 1969, at the New York Theological Seminary, titled "About Jews and Judaism: an Interreligious Colloquy."

[47] *Ibid.*

[48] The process of learning from contemporary Jewish scholars

requires discernment, as Professor Blidstein's entire attitude toward
the Christian message shows. In another context—a review of Rabbi
Arthur Gilbert's book *The Vatican Council and the Jews*—he writes:
"Christianity does have a superb myth, of proved subjective efficacy,
and the sociological and cultural situation is one, obviously, that puts
the Jew at a disadvantage in both overt and subtle ways." It is not
clear whether myth is used here as in Gnosticism, as something that
happened nowhere, yet could happen anywhere, or in a modern sense
as a poetic interpretation of ultimate reality. Professor Blidstein also
holds that there has been no meaningful shift in the thought of Christian theologians. The reason is that "[this] task has been thus far
beyond their powers because Christian scripture is in part—whether
read from a fundamentalist or 'symbolic' perspective—Antisemitic."

Were these the words of a Gentile scholar with scant knowledge of
Jewish History, one could understand. They are strange, coming as
they do from a Jewish scholar who must know that the history of
Jewish thought is, to no small extent, a history of fierce controversy.
The polemics in the New Testament, too, are the reflection of strife
among brothers. In any case, they were not one-sided. Take, for
instance, the remark of Rabbi Tarfon (ca. 100 A.D.) that the Jewish
Christians are worse than idolaters: The idolaters deny God without
knowing Him; the Christians know Him but deny Him nevertheless
(*Tos. Shab.* 13,4). New Testament polemics are bound to a concrete
situation in history and are, therefore, not of a dogmatic nature. Yet,
Professor Blidstein wants us to believe that the religious causes of
Antisemitism can "be eliminated only by a thorough secularization."
He seems to have misgivings about his own suggestion for he adds "as
disastrous as such a development may be from other points of view."

To be fair to Professor Blidstein, I would like to quote a few more
passages from the same article. First: "Christianity has meant more
than persecution of Jews, and its religious and moral performance
cannot be dismissed, no matter how heinous its role in Jew-killing."
Again, turning to his Orthodox fellows, he admonishes: "We ought
seriously consider the image of the non-Jew in Orthodox pedagogy
and folk-culture. I do not intend to forego an ounce of Jewish pride and
selfhood; I question, though, whether this pride need be bought with
defensiveness and hostility. All the pieties about *benei Noah* [the
Gentiles as Noah's sons and daughters by virtue of God's covenant
with him as the beginning of a new humanity after the flood] and the
possibility of their spiritual and person [*sic*] integrity are not as potent
as the expletive, *goy*." Interesting, too, is this self-examination: 'The
naiveté of Jewish shock at Christian silence [before, during, and after

the Six Day War] shocked me more than the silence itself. Have our *gedolim* said anything about Biafra? Or more to the point, said anything about South Africa?" ("Jews and the Ecumenical Dialogue," *Tradition*, 2,2, Summer 1970, pp. 103-110.)

⁴⁹   Moore, *Judaism*, 1,537.

⁵⁰   The translator of the Soncino edition of the Babylonian Talmud notes that "family above" refers to the guardian angels of the nations, while, from the context, "family below" would seem to mean the nations of the earth. He also mentions that Rashi considered the latter to mean "the assembly of nations." (*The Babylonian Talmud, Berakoth*, transl. M. Simon [London: Soncino, 1948], p. 99, nn.6,7.)

⁵¹   *The Authorized Daily Prayer Book*, rev. ed. (New York: Bloch, 1952), p. 105.

⁵²   See my "Commentary: Declaration on the Relationship of the Church to Non-Christian Religions," *American Participation in the Second Vatican Council*, ed. Vincent A. Yzermans (New York: Sheed and Ward, 1967), p. 609.

⁵³   See "The Theologian and the Land of Israel" and "A Statement of Conscience" in *Brothers in Hope*, Volume 5 of *The Bridge* (New York: Herder, 1970), pp. 231-243 and pp. 291-295. Also, the Institute Papers "Salute to Israel," "Jerusalem the Free," and "The Internationalization of Jerusalem?"

⁵⁴   For the full text, see *Brothers in Hope*, pp. 27-30.

⁵⁵   *The Church*, transl. R. and R. Ockenden (New York: Sheed and Ward, 1967), p. 149. For another interesting view on the problem, see Kurt Hruby, "Reflections on the Dialogue," *Brothers in Hope*, pp. 124-128.

⁵⁶   There is no doubt that the ignorance, misunderstanding, and misrepresentation of things Jewish by Christians have been more harmful than the misinterpretation of things Christian by Jews. This, however, does not dispense Jewish writers and spokesmen from the obligation of presenting Christian views or tenets with that fairness they rightfully demand for their own.

Teachers of Christians

ONE NEEDS NO SPECIAL learning to know that Christianity sprang from Jewish soil. But I wish to go further and say that this soil is still able to provide nourishment, indeed, have a vitalizing effect. There are, however, Christians who think it preposterous that Jews could teach Christians anything at all. One of the frequent objections is that Jews are worldly, overly given to creature comforts, in short, materialistic. An opponent might say:

Just remember the community of Israel in the wilderness, grumbling. They had been led out of Egypt by the Lord's mighty arm, a mere six weeks before. True, for a time they had been without water and without proper food. Yet, after their experience of God's ever-ready help, they had little excuse for a complaint like this one: "If only we had died at the Lord's hand in Egypt, where we sat round the fleshpots and had plenty of bread to eat" (Ex 16:3).

Our opponent is right. The Israelites had little reason for hankering after Egyptian fleshpots, or dreaming of their former life of abundance; they had never known such a life. An ancient papyrus describes the fate of Egypt's lower classes, its craftsmen, workers, and peasants: "For the last eighteen days we have been rotting away with hunger.... We have no clothes, no oil, no fish, no vegetables. . . ."[1] The Hebrews, who were at the very bottom of society, fared even worse. André Néher, the outstanding French interpreter of Judaism, depicts them as "one densely packed mass of humanity," having been deprived of their individuality. They had been subjected to "exhausting forced labor," to "the murder of their children at birth," to searches, abductions, and punishments, to an "officially sanctioned sadism, pitting a man against his brother." This created "a psychosis of mutual distrust and hatred," making them psychological cripples. Their "misery can be described only as a circle in the inferno of a concentration camp."[2]

The Mirror of Our Sins

MORE CONCRETELY, though the Egyptian overlords were big meat eaters, they never shared these delicacies with their slaves. How, then, could the latter, just freed from oppression and continuous anxiety, identify themselves with their tyrants? Their delusions must have been caused by the unexpected deprivations and the change of their daily routine. The monotony of the desert must have simply unnerved them. True, they lacked gratitude and trust, but their sins can hardly be called specifically Jewish. They were typically human.

Unwittingly, our opponent reminds us that, even in its sinfulness, Israel is a paradigmatic people. Its sins are mirrors of our sins. Christians have been quite ready to see in Israel's gifts and glories their own. Rarely, however, have they said of

Israel's wrong-doings, individual or communal: "These are replicas of my, of our own transgressions." We need to make this admission, not for the sake of Jews, but for our own integrity. True, the sins of ancient Israel and of Jews today are ugly, as sin is ugly, but they are and were no uglier than those of other people, of other nations, except perhaps for those lapses into idolatry, which for Israel were betrayals of the special love with which God had singled it out.

What is truly unique is not Israel's sinfulness itself but the fact that its transgressions were recorded for all the world to hear or to read. The historians of the nations of the world like to conceal, to cover up the wrongs of their people, while the sacred writers of Scripture openly confess the misdeeds of prince, priest, and people, even castigate them. A phenomenon difficult to explain in mere human terms, the life of ancient Israel has been for centuries exposed to public shame and contempt. In the face of such candor, a true Christian cannot, like a heathen, despise or ridicule the people God made His own; rather ought he or she see with awe that in the whole of Scripture God's love outshines all darkness. A Christian who pays more attention to human failings than to God's triumph overturns, as much as it is given to a creature, the universe of grace.

The Wholeness of Human Beings

THE STEREOTYPE of Jews as born materialists seems to have been encouraged, among other factors, by an inability to understand the biblical vision of Man, to use Bergson's terms, as "mind in matter," "memory in the flesh." As early as in the twofold story of creation, we are shown humanity in its wholeness. Created in God's image and likeness (Gn 1:27), the first human being is said to have been fashioned out of the clay of the ground (2:7). Made as male and female (1:21), it is the nature of human beings to love and be interdependent, to live in communion with others (2:18-24). But they are also destined to be stewards of creation (1:28); they are called to labor, cultivate, and care for their abode (2:15). They are in need of food (2:8-9) *and* of the word: humans can master language and song

(2:19,23). All these qualities make a human being partner of the world's Maker and Lord.

Even though the first two chapters of Genesis are silent on it, the biblical vision of human totality is a hierarchical, an ordered one. However important, however vital it is for men and women to gather food or buy it as modern economy demands, that they are made in God's likeness is infinitely more significant. It is a great and wonderful thing that they are stewards of the earth, that they are meant to leave their creative and responsible imprint on nature, but it is a far greater thing that they are able to love each other, and those near and far. To clothe oneself well and beautifully is a sign of a civilized person, but it is more important to be dressed in grace than in finery. Thus in the Christian tradition, things of the spirit have primacy over things of the earth. The same is true of the Jewish tradition, even though the word "spiritual" is not part of the regular rabbinic vocabulary, and though the accents are, at times, different.

To keep the hierarchy, the ascending order of values before one's eyes is not always easy. Our finite nature, our short attention span, or limited psychic energy, may be among the causes that make us ignore either our major vocation or one of our lesser tasks. We Christians often act as if our only role in life were to "save our souls," as if we were not also told to pray: "Give us this day our daily bread." Claus Westermann, a German exegete, emphasizes that in Jesus' encounters with others, in His discourses and actions, the elemental human concerns are dominant. As He moves among men and women, He addresses them in their creatureliness; He responds to it. They are either hungry or thirsty, sick or well, members of a community, men or women in quest of life's meaning or in search of fulfillment. Jesus knows Himself to have been sent by His Father to minister to the life of men and women in its limitations, peccability, evil inclination, suffering, and death. All this reveals Jesus and, no less, His disciples, Professor Westermann concludes, as standing firmly within the tradition and history of the Jewish people.[3]

Much to the point as this depiction is, one important aspect is missing. When finding men and women in their creaturely frailty—beings wounded or vulnerable, exposed to threats and dangers—Jesus did indeed aid them in their needs, cure their ailments, or answer their problems. Yet, He also tried to take them beyond these life-restraining conditions. He demanded fiath—not just the acceptance of a given tenet—but that total surrender which lifts us out of our little ego to that infinite Expanse we call God.

Christians ought to set their minds first and foremost on God's reign, the way of His kingship, and His righteousness (Mt 6:33) but at the same time, keep their hearts open to the wonders as well as the miseries of the earth and life on it. In his or her striving for a total human existence, a Christian should attempt to imitate Christ in His fullness. As much as the gospel, the vision of Genesis must thus be part of our consciousness. Whenever Christians are tempted to ignore an essential component of their humanity, Judaism where and when it has remained true to the total image of the human person, serves as a corrective that counters trends to onesidedness and recalls the fullness of existence.

The Continuing Witness of Israel's Prophets

A WIDESPREAD misunderstanding has it that Christianity is all love, mildness, forbearance, and mercy, while Judaism is the opposite. What a squint eyed view! While Psalm 130 ends with these comforting thoughts:

> In the Lord is love unfailing;
>   great is His power to set men free.
> And He will free Israel
>   from all their sins,

the stern warning: "You cannot serve God and Money" (Mt 6:24), is part of Jesus' Sermon on the Mount. Even sterner is His warning to those who ignore the starving, the ill, or the naked, to those who neglect strangers or prisoners: In the suffering of the disinherited of this earth, you disregard me; and your end will be terror (see Mt 25:41-46).

In both these sayings of Jesus lives the spirit of Israel's

Prophets, those intrepid spokesmen of God who summoned all Israel, high and low, to return to the righteousness demanded by the Covenant. Israel's Prophets urged, admonished, prodded, reproved, threatened, announced punishment, even doom. Yet, shattering judgment was not their final word; heralds of hope, they offered comfort, indeed, redemption. For a Christian, these "men of God" must never be mere figures of the past to be eulogized; they must be part of the Church today—alive so that we may be alive, alive in and for God. Take, for instance, Amos' denunciation of his contemporaries:

> Woe
>> to you who live at ease in Zion. . . .
>>> to the overconfident on the hill of Samaria. . . .
>> To you who loll on beds of ivory
>> and sprawl over your couches,
>> To you who feed on lambs from the flock
>> and fatted calves, . . .
>> but are not made ill by the ruin of Joseph.
>>>>> (6:1, 4-6)

It is easy to escape from these and similar invectives by saying: "Zion and Samaria are far away. Joseph is not one of us. We do not sleep on beds of ivory." Yes, it is easy, but it would be wrong. Though we, with most of the world, suffer from an economic recession, from inflation, from unemployment, ours is still a country of affluence, and many of us are "knee-deep in clover." Again, let no one say that these words by the same Amos are outdated:

> Hear this,
>> You who grind down the needy
>> and plunder the poor,
>> you who say, "When will the new moon be over
>> so that we may sell corn,
>> and the Sabbath . . . .
>> so that we may give short measure in the bushel
>> and take overweight in silver,
>> tilting the scales for cheating!
>> Then will we buy the lowly man for silver
>> and the poor for a pair of sandals."
>>>>> (8:4-6)

Let no one say that this outcry is out of date just because today's exploiters are not content with just a little price fixing and small profits; because they do not concern themselves with bushels but thousands of tons; because they deal not merely in grain but in oil and all the vital supplies.

A community that does not count the Prophets of old as living, present-day witnesses is to be pitied. How can anyone be a follower of Christ if he does not heed the Lord God? He says through one of His Prophets:

> Is not this what I require of you . . . :
>> to loose the fetters of injustice, . . .
> to snap every yoke
>> and set free those who have been crushed?
> Share your food with the hungry,
>> shelter the homeless poor.
> Clothe the naked when you meet them,
>> do not turn your back on your own.
> Then shall your light break forth like the dawn
>> and soon your wound will heal.
> Your righteousness shall go before you
>> and the glory of the Lord follow you.
>
> (Is 58:7-8)

I said that any community which does not wish to heed these heralds of righteousness and redemption, of human hope and God's glory, is to be pitied. The community, however, that allows them to proclaim their message will be rewarded in many ways; it will be safe from false ideologies of freedom, from a fraudulent theology of revolution, and from self-appointed prophets.

Story-Telling Communities

THERE ARE OTHER truths, other practices dear to Judaism that could help Christians rediscover customs that have fallen into disuse, or find new modes to articulate their faith and express their love of God and neighbor. A greater awareness of Jewish celebrations in the home, particularly of Shabbat observance, could help Christians acquire a fresh sense of

dedication. New insights could aid us to turn our Sundays into
mighty proclamations of Christ risen, and thus into a continuous wellspring of love. In August, 1975, *Liturgy*, the journal of
the Liturgical Conference, explored this theme.

Rather than repeat a work well done, I should like to give the
remainder of my time to a fundamental phenomenon that, as a
rule, gets little attention. The mission of the Church, analogous
to that of the Jewish people, is to hand down from generation to
generation, from individual to individual, the message of salvation, as each, the Church or Israel, understands it. This
message is obviously verbal, even though it is concerned, not so
much with words as with facts. The late American exegete G.
Ernest Wright said with regard to the ancient Hebrews: "Biblical Man confesses his faith by reciting the formative events of
his history as the redemptive handiwork of God."[4] The same is
true of Jews and Christians today.

On every Passover, for thousands of years, Jews have gone
on to relate the story of their delivery from Egypt as the core of
their belief and the mainstay of their lives. For a Catholic, the
Eucharist is the epitome of all that he or she believes and lives
by. Still, at the moment of Consecration, the summit of the
Mass, the priest does not recite the creed nor does he profess his
and the congregation's faith in transubstantiation and Christ's
real presence, rather does he narrate what happened at Jesus'
parting meal:

> Before He was given up to death—
> a death He freely accepted—
> while they were at supper,
> He took bread and gave You thanks.
> He broke the bread,
> gave it to His disciples, and said,
> *Take this, all of you and eat it*:
> *This is my body which will be given up for you.*

The priest then continues his narration by relating Jesus' taking the cup, and speaking over it those powerful words of
change, of converting the substance and meaning of wine into
the precious drink of salvation.

If the Church wishes to be true to her mission, she has to state and restate, interpret and define her beliefs to safeguard their clarity, defend their authenticity, and argue their true significance. Yet before she can interpret, argue, and define, she must first recount God's saving deeds, the *magnalia Dei*, "the mighty works of God," (Ac 2:11), the *ḥasidey YHVH*, "the manifestations of the Lord God's covenant love" (Ps 89:2). In the words of the German theologian John B. Metz: *Das Christentum [ist] nicht primär eine Argumentations–und Interpretationsgemeinschaft, sondern . . . Erzählgemeinschaft*, "Christianity is a community, not primarily designed to argue or interpret revealed truth; rather has it been chosen to tell a story,"—*not any story*, not a fairy tale or adventure story one tells children to lull them to sleep, or an anecdote orators and preachers use to enliven their presentation—but *the one* story of the Life, Passion, Death, and Resurrection of Jesus Christ. Need I add that the Church must also relate the narrative of Abraham, Isaac, and Jacob, of Joseph, Moses, and Joshua, Samuel, David, and Solomon, of Israel's Prophets, Singers, Sages, and great women? Without them, there would not have been a Jesus of Nazareth; without the telling of their story, His own would be suspended in mid-air.

Professor Metz, to whom we owe the term *Erzählgemeinschaft*, "narrative community," maintains that certain faith motifs cannot be fully unfolded, except through narration. The prophetic proclamation of the God who overturns what is antiquated or obsolete and makes everything new is, in Professor Metz' view, such a motif. Another is the novel and uncontrivable experience of the Rising of Christ Crucified.

> The world raised from nothingness; Man formed out of dust; the new kingdom whose nearness Jesus announced; the new human being; resurrection as the passage through death to life; the end as a new beginning; the life of future glory—all these beliefs shatter [mere] rational deductions and arguments and resist the perfect transposition of their narrative shape.

Professor Metz seeks to support his theory by references to

several poets and philosophers; his major authority, however, seems to be Martin Buber. He quotes from the preface to *Tales of the Hasidim*:

> Storytelling is itself an event. Since it serves to perpetuate holy events, it bears the consecration of a sacred action.... The story is more than a mere reflection: The holy essence it witnesses lives on in it. The miracle that is told, acquires new force. . . . A rabbi, whose grandfather had been a disciple of the Baal Shem, was asked to tell a story. "A story," he said, "must be told so that it becomes a help itself." And he told: "My grandfather was lame. Once he was asked to tell a story about his teacher. He then related how the holy Baal Shem used to jump and dance while praying. My grandfather rose as he spoke and was swept away by his story to such a degree that he himself felt he had to jump and dance in order to demonstrate how the master had done it. From that moment he was cured of his own lameness. This is the way to tell a story."[6]

For Metz, the Catholic theologian, Buber's text intimates an inner nexus between story and sacrament; so closely are they linked to one another that narratives are, as it were, efficient signs. One may call such a sacramental sign *eine Sprachhandlung,* "a speech action." This is neither the time nor the place to examine Prof. Metz' views. Yet, it would be an oversight not to stress that Hasidism, a Jewish movement which sprang up in the 18th century in Eastern Europe, imbued its members with joy in God's presence everywhere, and led them to loving communion with Him.

It would be an oversight, too, not to point out that the story quoted by Prof. Metz is one that illumines, and carries on an ancient tradition. More than once does Scripture enjoin upon a father the duty of instructing his child. In the Book of Deuteronomy it is said:

> When in time-to-come your son asks you: "What is the meaning of these ordinances, statutes, and decrees which the Lord our God gave you?" you shall say to him: "We were Pharaoh's slaves in Egypt, but the Lord brought us out of Egypt with His strong hand. Before our eyes He

wrought signs and wonders, mighty and terrifying, against Egypt, against Pharaoh and all his household. He led us out from there, brought us into the land and gave it to us as He had promised our fathers." (6:20-24)

The instruction does not end here; still, the lines I have just read show sufficiently that the story of Israel's deliverance serves as foundation and reason for the commandments given it.

There are other instances in which a father is directed to instruct his offspring why the people of Israel celebrates the Passover. "On that day, you shall tell your son: 'It is because of what the Lord did for me when I went forth from Egypt' " (Ex 13:8; see Ex 12:28; 13:14). These very words are repeated at the Passover meal; more than that, the entire celebration centers on that command. It is a marvel to contemplate that the ceremonies and symbols, the prayers and songs serve only to make the story of the Exodus more vital and to heighten the experience. Interestingly enough, the ritual as well as the book that guides the participants through the Seder, is called *Haggadah*, "narration" or "telling." When the tale of redemption is related and listened to with fervor, everyone present lives his or her freedom as something present, as a reality. "In each and every generation, it is a Man's duty (this means, of course, it is the duty of every Jew, man and woman; it is not without significance that the *Haggadah* should say *adam* when it means Jew); it is a Man's duty to consider himself as one who went forth from Egypt."

This spirit of "reality" is no less a special mark of the Catholic liturgy. Every Eucharistic celebration re-presents, makes present and operative, the work of redemption. On every major feast, the celebration of a sacred event makes that past event part of existing time. At Christmas, Catholics pray, "*today* a light has dawned on us"; during Holy Week, "*this is the hour* when [Jesus] triumphed over Satan's pride"; on Easter, "*This is the day* when Christ became our paschal sacrifice." Here past, present, and future are bridged, time divided becomes one, as it were. To make the past live in the "now," to turn it into a force for the future is the meaning of liturgical celebration, as it is that of sacred narration.

Jewish experience in telling the story of God's dealings with His people is a fountain from which Christian worshipers must draw strength. If we only could tell the story of Jesus' Passion and Death with such power that every hearer would be roused, stirred, and feel calmed in body and soul, that one would feel grace of redemption in every fiber of his or her being. Would, the stories on Jesus' compassion, how He cared for the ill, removed their pain, and restored well-being, indeed, life to sufferers of His land and time—would they were told with such trust and compassion that they brought, not necessarily instantaneous healing, but ever increasing relief. I wish all liturgical lectors and all catechists fully realized the grandeur of their office.

Our theme this afternoon is "Learning One from the Other." But in showing that Israel and the Church are communities with a unique story to tell, that for both a liturgical celebration is a *zikkaron*, a memorial, a recollection not merely in mind but also in deed, I have gone beyond the stated purpose of this talk. Story telling (in this highest sense of the word) and bridging the divisions of time through the liturgy are characteristics that the Church inherited from Israel, that are, if you permit the biological metaphor, in her genes. It is in this sense that you must understand the intertwined Shield of David and Cross, our designer—a Jew, incidentally—used for our graduate program and the posters announcing this convocation. The symbol does not plead for a fusion of Church and Judaism but for a greater awareness of their kinship, their interdependence, their need of one another.

It is not enough that Christians free themselves of contempt for Jews, or Jews of contempt for non-Jews—the only state compatible with our respective missions, our origin and destiny is profound solidarity and mutual concern.

Hiney mah-tov umah-na'yim
shebet aḥim gam yaḥad

Bliss and joy it is
for brethren to live in unity.

This first verse of Psalm 133 may well be an admonition addressed to the priests and levites of the Temple, those who had just returned from Babylonian Exile and those that had stayed home, that they end their quarrels and live together in concord, in the sight of the One God they all serve. I trust it is proper to extend the plea of the Psalmist to the coexistence of Christians and Jews. May they dwell side by side, care for one another, be mindful of the fact that they dwell in the presence of the living God, God of Abraham, Isaac, and Jacob, and their partners, Sarah, Rebekah, Leah, and Rachel.

NOTES

[1] As quoted by André Néher, *Moses* (New York: Harper Torchbook, 1959), p. 70.

[2] *Ibid.*, pp. 73, 91.

[3] Claus Westermann, *Schöpfung* (Berlin: Kreuz Verlag, 1971), pp. 159-160.

[4] G. Ernest Wright, *God Who Acts, Theology as Recital* (London: SCM Press, 1952), p. 38.

[5] Johann B. Metz, "Kleine Apologie des Erzählens," *Concilium*, 9,5 (May, 1975).

[6] Martin Buber, *Tales of the Hasidim*, A Commentary Classic (New York: Schocken, 1958), pp. V-VI. See the German original, *Die Erzählungen der Chassidim* (Zurich: Manesse, 1949), pp. 5-6. The translation used in this paper is partly my own.

SINGING OF HIS LOVE

"Of the Lord's steadfast love I will sing" is the opening verse of Psalm 89. In it, an inspired singer leads his people in the joy of hailing the saving events in its history. By the grace of God, the Church and, with her, every Christian, may share in the privilege of praising His presence among His own. In Jesus' Passion God's enduring love is manifest. Psalm 89 may be an apt title for meditations on Jesus' dying for all.

Deicide Under The Microscope

WHEN SPEAKING OF the deicide issue, I have in mind something other than the question of whether or not those Jews directly involved in condemning Jesus and in delivering Him to the Roman governor—or, to speak the language of Scripture, "handing Him over to the Gentiles" (Ac 21:11)—can legitimately be called deicides. To my mind, this question answers itself, and the answer is "No." Nor do I wish to inquire if the designation "deicides" can in all seriousness be applied to the totality of Jews, the entire generation at the time of Christ— living in the Holy Land or in the Diaspora—and to all subsequent generations. Such an inquiry, too is superfluous. The matter has been unmistakably settled. The Council has clearly disposed of the fallacious notion of collective guilt.

375

What I intend to investigate is the problem of whether deicide is an indispensable concept of Christian theology or, if not
an essential one, at least one so vital that it bears witness to the
Christian mystery and truly serves its proclamation. I am
concerned with a theological problem whose solution has not
become easier because of certain developments during the
Council.

Defenders of the Charge

ARAB SPOKESMEN turned the question into a political one;
strange though it sounds, they championed the use of the term
"slayers of God" as applied to the Jews. They did so in complete opposition to the Koran. Islam's sacred book denies not
merely the divine sonship of Jesus and His redemptive death,
but seeks to reinforce this denial by maintaining that He did
not die at the hand of Jews; indeed, He did not die at all. The
Fourth Sura (Chapter) of the Koran has Jews boast, and the
"voice of truth" answer:

> "We have put to death the Messiah Jesus, the son of Mary,
> the apostle of Allah." They did not kill him, nor did they
> crucify him, but they thought they did. Those that dis-
> agreed about him were in doubt concerning his death, for
> what they knew about him was sheer conjecture; they were
> not sure they had slain him.[1]

Moreover, Jewish writers have seen in the invective so often
hurled against them the source of all the evils that have
befallen the Jewish people in the course of the Christian era.
Finally, some Christian leaders in the Near East condemned
the attempt of the Council to free Christian thought and speech
of all stereotypes, of all misleading and often contemptuous
phrases, as a contradiction of "the truth of Scripture and the
perennial doctrine of the Church." One even spoke of "this
Roman heresy."[2]

Just a brief historical aside. I mentioned that Jews blame the
deicide charge for all their sufferings. This is an unproven

assumption, indeed, a simplistic interpretation of history. Yet, I would be less than honest did I not add that the charge has more than once disfigured the face of the Church as it brought disaster to the Jews. Let me give two examples. The first is from the Holy Week service of the Greek liturgy. A troparion of Holy Thursday runs like this:

> The Synagogue, that worthless company of knavish, abominable, and God-slaying men, attacked You, O Christ, and dragged away as an evildoer You, the Creator of all, whom we magnify.[3]

Unfortunately, this is not the only instance of an invective or accusation disguised as prayer; it hardly serves as an instrument of devotion.

The second example is from the time of the Crusades. The *pauperes*—as the disinherited hordes of those days who had joined the knightly crusaders were called—went all through the Rhine valley to kill Jews and loot their homes. This is how the *Lumpenproletariat* of those days justified their massacres: "We have set out to march a long way to fight the enemies of God in the East, and behold, before our very eyes are His very worst foes, the Jews. They must be dealt with first." Addressing themselves to the Jews, they are reported to have shouted:

> You are the descendants of those who killed and hanged our God. Moreover [God] Himself said: "The day will yet dawn when my children will come and avenge my blood." We are His children and it is our task to carry out His vengeance upon you, for you showed yourselves obstinate and blasphemous towards Him. . . . [God] has abandoned you; He has turned His radiance upon us and made us His own.[4]

These two samples of a perverted faith may explain why many Bishops and theologians at the Council were convinced that the true reform of the Church demanded that her language be purified and "deicide" completely eliminated from her vocabulary.

No one maintains that the expression "deicide" is of biblical origin. It was unknown to the Apostles, unknown to the young Church.[5] Yet, that the term cannot be found in Scripture is no conclusive proof against its use. The word "trinity" is not mentioned in any of the writings of the New Testament. Yet, the mystery of the triune God is an essential part of the Church's preaching. It could well be that the *idea* of deicide belongs to the sphere of New Testament thought, without the *word's* having been coined in apostolic times.

Pseudo-Evidence

THAT "DEICIDE" must remain part of the Church's *kerygma*, its proclamation of the Gospel and thus of its vocabulary is the viewpoint of a few defenders of the term. Representative of them is Bishop Carli of Segni, Italy, who in a widely reported essay, "The Jewish Question at the Second Vatican Council," wrote:

> It has been said that one cannot speak of deicide, in the proper sense of the word, since the Jews were unaware of the divinity of Christ. To this we reply: Objectively, *in foro externo*, it was a question of real deicide because Jesus was truly God and explicitly declared Himself to be such. It is therefore legitimate to use the word, at least as St. Peter used it ("... *auctorem* vero *vitae* interfecistis." Ac 3:15) and St. Paul "...qui et *Dominum* occiderent Jesum") 1 Thess 2:15; ("...si enim cognovissent, numquam *Dominum gloriae* crucifixissent." 1 Cor 2:8).[6]

These, then, are the *loci classici* that must be investigated so that the exegetical aspect of our problem may be solved.

[A] *Acts 3:15*. The first phrase Bishop Carli advanced takes us back to the early days of the primitive community of Jerusalem. The Bishop quoted according to the Vulgate: "*auctorem ... vitae interfecistis*," which the Douay version rendered: "the author of life you killed." One only has to read further, "whom God has raised from the dead" to realize that "author of life" cannot possibly be Peter's meaning. The translators of the

King James version were keener when they wrote,"Ye killed the Prince of life." The meaning becomes certain if the passage is read in context and in Greek. In Greek, the words of the Apostle Peter are: *ton de archēgon tēs zōēs apekteinate.* According to Bauer's *Wörterbuch zum Neuen Testament, archegos* means [1] *Führer, Herrscher, Fürst,* "leader, ruler, prince"; [2] *Anfänger,* "beginner"; and [3] *Urbeber, Begründer,* "author, founder." To Acts 3:15, Bauer assigns the first meaning.[7] Being an adaptation of Bauer's *Wörterbuch,* the *Lexicon* by Arndt and Gingrich takes the same position.[8]

The context of Peter's utterance makes the translation "leader of life" a certainty. As I have already mentioned, the Apostle continues: "whom God raised from the dead ... of this we are witnesses." Thus he speaks of Jesus as the One risen or the One raised by God. The accent is on the humanity, not the divinity, of Jesus. He is "the first to rise from the dead" (Ac 26:23), "the first-born from the dead" (Col 1:18) or, in the words of the NEB, "the first to return from the dead." Through His resurrection, He has broken the "power of death" (2 Tim 1:10), not only for Himself, but also for His own, indeed, "announcing the dawn [of salvation] to the people [of Israel] and to the nations" (Ac 26:23). The emphasis on the risen Christ ought to convince anyone wishing to know the mind of the young Church that it is incorrect to read Peter's sermon as an accusation of deicide.

The entire speech makes this clearer still. In the name of Jesus, Peter had returned to a man lame from birth the use of his limbs. When the multitude saw the former cripple nimble as a youth, they marvelled. The Apostle, however, countered their wonderment with the assurance that it was not *his* power that performed the miracle, rather that of the living God, the One who acknowledged Jesus as His appointed Messiah:

> The God of Abraham, Isaac, and Jacob, the God of our fathers glorified His servant Jesus whom you committed for trial and repudiated before Pilate when he had decided to release Him. You denied the Holy and Righteous One and asked for the release of a murderer. You killed the leader to life, but God raised Him from the dead (Ac 3:13-15).

Joyously, Peter declared that it was faith in the name of Jesus, indeed, the name itself that gave the man fettered from the womb the wholeness of his humanity, only to continue:

> Now brethren, I know full well that you acted in ignorance as did your rulers. This way, God brought to fulfillment what He had foretold through the mouth of all the Prophets: That His anointed should suffer. Change, then, your way. Turn [to God] that your sins may be blotted out, that the times of refreshment may come (3:17-19).

Peter pleaded with them to repent so that Jesus the Messiah might return and everything be restored in God (3:20-21). Can there be any doubt that the tenor of this sermon is not one of accusation but of wooing? Whatever the listeners or, more precisely, some of them may have done so that Jesus was delivered into the hands of the pagan Pilate and nailed to the Cross, Peter calls them "brethren" (3:17). He did not sanctimoniously abandon them nor did he make the slightest attempt to disassociate himself from them—an attempt that consciously or unconsciously underlies the use of the epithet "deicide."

Besides, it was not the *murder* of Jesus that stirred Peter— his theme is the *victory* of the Cross. Jesus, the Suffering Servant, is the One truly alive and thus the giver of the true, full life. All designs against Him could not destroy His work. On the contrary, His resurrection proclaims the end of all "nonsense"; it offers blessing for the Jews, the heirs of the Prophets and sons and daughters of the Covenant, but also for the world (Ac 3: 25). Jesus' suffering is thus, to speak with the Canon of the Mass, a *beata passio*, a "blessed passion"—a mystery which the term deicide threatens to suppress.

[B] *1 Thessalonians 2:13.* Quite different from the tone of Peter's sermon, soon after the Pentecostal event, is the second passage adduced by Bishop Carli. It is taken from the probably oldest writing of the New Testament and doubtlessly the oldest Pauline epistle in existence. The calm, indeed, peaceful relationship between the primitive Church and the Jewish people that prevailed at the beginning seems to have given way to one of tension and unrest, at least in certain communities. On his second missionary journey, the Apostle and his companion Silas had gone to Philippi in Macedonia. Their stay there came to a bad end: The two were dragged to the marketplace by pagan troublemakers, accused before the magistrates, and thrown in prison. "These men—these Jews—are making trouble in our city" (Ac 16:20), was the charge. The denouncers characterized the way of salvation the two had proclaimed as "customs running counter to Roman law and mentality" (Ac 16:21). After their delivery from prison, Paul and Silas had to leave the city; in the spring of 50 A.D., they arrived in a roundabout way in Thessalonica, the present Salonica.

On three successive Sabbaths, Paul preached in the synagogue there on Jesus, the suffering and risen Messiah. His words were not without success. A few Jews, a great number of God-fearing Greeks, among them many influential women, accepted the Gospel. Beset by envy, members of the local synagogue—we do not know whether they were the leaders or some irritable members of the congregation—instigated a riot to undo the work of the Apostle and to discourage his helpers as well as the young Christian community. The city resounded with these shouts: "The men who have turned the world upside down have now come here . . . they all flout the emperor's laws, asserting that there is another King, Jesus!" (Ac 17:6f). That very night, Paul and Silas had to flee. Their persecutors, however, would not give up; they followed the two till Beroea in order to wreck their apostolic work just begun (see 17:13).

In a letter the Apostle sent within the year to the distressed community, the anger against his foes, long pent up, seems to have burst through. At first, he had been anxious whether the young church of Thessalonica, inadequately instructed, encircled by paganism, and suspected by the Synagogue, would remain steadfast. On hearing of their faithfulness, he was able to tell them of his gratitude that the word of God had proved a power in their lives (see 1 Thess 2:13). He then went on:

> Brothers! You have fared like the churches in Judea, God's people in Christ Jesus. You have suffered at the hands of the Judeans[9] who killed the Lord Jesus and the Prophets, and who drove us out. They are not pleasing to God and they are hostile to all people for they hinder us from speak-

ing to the nations so as to lead them to salvation. Thus they make full in every way the measure of their guilt. God's wrath is upon them and presses toward the end, *ephthasen de ep'autous he orgē eis telos (1 Thess 2:14f).*

The Authentic View of Paul? Two divergent interpretations of this disturbing passage have been advanced. The first says: These are undoubtedly harsh words, but they are not the words of a man who despises the stranger, who castigates everyone whom he cannot comprehend; they are rather the words of a Jew about his own kinsmen. "An authentic Jew like Paul," a contemporary commentator writes, "cannot be but dismayed and shocked by the resistance of his people to God's advances";[10] hence his strong words. Biblical speech is always passionate; in the Pauline letters, the language is even more passionate than in the other books of Scripture.

To give voice to his deep disappointment, Paul seems to have done something unheard of. He appears to have gone so far as to make use of the pagan polemic against the Jews. The Jews had always been an enigma to the Gentiles: a people that adored an invisible God—the Lord of heaven and earth—not a local deity that could be exchanged with, or united to, another local deity; a people that worshiped a God who imposed on them the yoke of a law compelling them to an almost monastic isolation; a people consecrated to a God who is Spirit served— in the eyes of the Latin poet Marcius Annaeus Lucanus (39-65 A.D.)—an uncertain God.

A people that refused to eat and sleep with others could appear to certain pagans only as godless and misanthropic. "Atheists," "men without pity and hated by the gods," "enemies of other men and of all foreign customs"—this is how some writers of antiquity saw the Jews.[11] Some interpreters think that the Apostle merely echoes what the Gentile authors pronounced before him. What he does, then, is to imply that quite a few of his kinsmen seem bent on justifying the ugly reproaches of their pagan foes.

In seeking to understand what seems an angry outburst, one must not forget that, on the one hand, Paul's heart knows that

Jews resist the Gospel and its dissemination because they are convinced that they offer service to God (see Jn 16:2). Though ill-informed, though unenlightened, their zeal is for God and His Law (see Rom 10:2-4). On the other hand, he vividly remembers when he himself "savagely persecuted the church of God and tried to destroy it" (Gal 1:13). His great fear, then, is that the resistance to the good news drives his people toward a catastrophe.

Heinz Schürmann, whose translation I have largely followed, comments:

> As [Paul] wrote his sentence [of the full measure of guilt and the near wrath of God], he happened to work in Corinth as a tentmaker in the house of Aquila and Priscilla, a couple who, a short time ago, had been expelled from Rome by the Emperor Claudius. It could be that Paul saw in this event, quite concretely, the beginning of the end: The banishment of Jews [from the ancient city] by the Roman world ruler may have appeared to him as the beginning of the disaster which, in the year 70 A.D., overtook them when the Roman armies destroyed Jerusalem and the Temple. An actual event like [the expulsion from Rome] must have left its imprint upon the Apostle; it may have conditioned the particular severity of his language and thus explain it.[12]

What makes this translation and interpretation significant is that Schürmann understands 1 Thessalonians 2:16b in the context of St. Paul's time rather than in a timeless manner: that God's retribution and anger have not come upon the Jewish people "for good and for all" (NEB), *endgültig* (ZB), *pour en finir* (JB). According to Schürmann, then, the Apostle does not say that God's wrath will rest upon his kinsmen till the end of ages, rather that, at any moment, God's judgment may burst upon the inhabitants of Judea.

Even if one accepts this first interpretation of these harsh words in the Letter to the Thessalonians, one must not take them dogmatically. After all, they answered but a particular situation, and are thus not to be taken as Paul's last word on the Jews. His final words on them are in Romans 9-11, written in 56-57 A.D. These were meant to teach, and they are words of love. But even the harsh words of the year 50 in no way support the use of the terms "deicide" and "deicides." In the Letter to the Thessalonians, the Lord Jesus, as a victim of persecution, stands, as it were, in the midst of the Prophets and the Apostles. His Passion and Death are set off against this background as the ultimate example of the fate that God's revelation and grace-filled deeds suffer in this world.

I have deliberately chosen the words "in this world." However much the heart of the Apostle cries out when he thinks of the sufferings that so many messengers of God have endured at the hands of some of his kinsmen; however much it cries out when he thinks of the sufferings that are to befall his fellow Jews—still, it would be wrong to forget, at this outcry, the main thought of the passage in question. It is the martyrdom of the young Church everywhere, in the land of the Jews and the lands of the pagans. Everywhere, he sees the Church and the individual Christian persecuted—poor, weak, alone, ostracized.

Interpolation? Having given voice to one school of thought, I must now give a hearing to a second one, one that takes an opposite stance. Its proponents simply doubt the authenticity of 1 Thessalonians 2: 13-16. To give the word to the one exegete, Birger A. Pearson calls these lines a "deuteropauline interpolation." If the second part of verse 16 is considered, as he thinks it must, a reference to the destruction of Jerusalem in 70 A.D., the Apostle cannot possibly be the author since, according to Roman tradition, he was beheaded in 67 A.D.

Another of Pearson's arguments is the doubtlessly valid assumption that the source or pattern for the accusation of the Jews as men who mistreat their Prophets is 2 Chronicles 36: 14-16, a *topos* commonly used by Christians after the fall of Jerusalem. This argument does not prove Pearson's thesis—all major commentators, even those who do not question the Pauline authorship of our passage, acknowledge its literary dependence on the Chronicler's castigation of his people. Yet, he offers other evidence, the strongest of which is the fact that "the hostile reference to the Jews as agents of the Crucifixion (2:15) . . . does not square with what Paul says elsewhere either of the Jews or [other] agents of the crucifixion (Rom 9-11; 1 Cor 2:8)." Summing up, Pearson holds that his arguments in favor of considering 1 Thessalonians 2:13-16 an interpolation "are bolstered by the clear progression of thought from v. 12 to v. 17."[13]

An entirely different position is taken by Otto Michel, a position that conforms neither to the first nor second. In a paper, first read at a consultation of Jewish, Protestant, and Catholic scholars at Arnoldshain, Germany, in 1966, Otto Michel, of the University of Tübingen, fully accepts the genuineness of what he considers Paul's frontal attack on Judaism. Uncompromisingly, he writes: *Es geht dem Apostel um Kampf und Auseinandersetzung, nicht um Reaktion und Stimmung*, "For the Apostle, [his polemic] is not a matter of mood but one of struggle or contest."[14]

To conclude the exegesis of 1 Thessalonians 2:14-16, Bishop Carli, and others with him, see in the passage the condemnation of only the Jews' attitude to the salvific event in Christ. To read Scripture in such a way that the Jews are always singled out negatively is, however, dangerous self-deception. It goes without saying that Scripture speaks continuously of them. After all, the word of God came first to them; only much later did it break into the pagan world. Hence, the New Testament has little to say about the fate of God's word among the Gentiles. Now, there is a routine to relate words like "election" and "grace," almost as often as they appear in the Bible, to Christians, and words like "infidelity" and "rejection" to Jews, and to them alone. This, I contend, is bad exegesis; it may well betray an unconscious desire to escape Christ's claim on the whole person.

During the Council, a Benedictine monk from Germany told me that the singing of the Passion on Good Friday always shook him to the marrow. In his abbey, the role of the *turba*, "the crowd," to which older Passion books gave the name *synagoga*, was not presented by one singer. The whole community became the *turba* because it represented the men of every age and every part of the world. The whole community, indeed, every monk in it cried out *Crucifige*! "To the cross with him!" In this community of monks, the Gospel was truly heard, understood, prayed—and suffered. This practice is now widespread.

[C] *1 Corinthians 2:8*. Of all three passages of Scripture Bishop Carli considered the props of his theory that the Jews are truly deicides, the third nearly proves him right. Here the Apostle speaks of the Crucifixion of "the Lord of glory," *ton kyrion tēs doxēs*. In the Jewish tradition—in the book of Henoch, for instance—"the Lord of glory" is a title of special dignity, reserved for God alone. In applying this title to Jesus—the One degraded on the cross and now glorified, the One who at the fullness of time appeared as servant and at the end will reveal Himself as the royal victor—the Apostle confirms his faith in the oneness of the Son with the Father.

For a man or woman of faith, the divine glory dwelling in the Redeemer is manifest, even on the wood of disgrace and in His seeming impotence. Is it therefore not reasonable to speak of "deicide" and "deicides"? This at least was Bishop Carli's conviction; under the caption "May One Call the Jews Deicides?" he argued that one may do so legitimately, in the light of the passages quoted from Scripture. As ill luck would have it—if I may be Bishop Carli's spokesman, for only a second— the third biblical passage does not speak of the Jews at all, leaders or people.

In his First Letter to the Corinthians, Paul reveals the purpose that brought him there: to think only one reality, to know only one reality, to preach only one reality, Jesus the Christ nailed to the Cross. Therefore he appeared before the Corinthians without persuasive schemes, subtle arguments, or display of fine words, for human wisdom is of no avail before God: it can never grasp God's saving design (1 Cor 2:1-5). The wisdom God had shared with the Corinthians is "hidden wisdom, His secret purpose, framed from the very beginning to bring us to our full glory," the Apostle states (2:7). He continues:

> But none of the rulers of this eon have known it, for had they known it, they would not have crucified the Lord of glory. [So it happened], to speak in the words of Scripture, "things beyond our seeing, things beyond our hearing,

things beyond our imagining—God prepared them for those who love Him" (1 Cor 2:7-9; NEB).

The "rulers of this eon" or "the powers that rule the world" are not—as one may be led to assume if one does not know the Jewish texture of the New Testament—Caiaphas, Annas, and their clique, nor even the Emperor and his Governor. According to a Jewish conception of those days, and hence according to the Apostle, the "rulers of this eon" are cosmic forces, angelic powers or supramundane beings hostile to God who influence the course of this sinful world. In the light of this conception, it was really *they* who brought Christ to the Cross, *they* who caused His Passion and Death, having been devoid of eternal wisdom and not known His saving purpose. Had they known the divine plan, they would not have laid hands on Christ since what outwardly appeared as His defeat, indeed His ruin, was really their defeat, introduced their ruin, and announced the triumph of those who love God in Christ. Thus the Apostle.

The Reversal of the Passion

THERE IS, I think, only one conclusion that can be drawn from an examination of the three passages Bishop Carli and others based themselves on, and it is this: There is no biblical warrant for the deicide accusation. But is there not at least traditional justification for its use? No doubt, the charge was made often—all too often!—still, there is no real tradition. As early as 1954, Charles Cardinal Journet in his *Destinées d'Is-raël* drew attention to an Augustinian text. Referring to those who had clamored for Christ's death, St. Augustine comments:

> The Lord rose and many among [the Jews] believed. They had crucified Him without understanding [what they did]. But later, they believed in Him, and their great error was forgiven them. The blood of the Lord they had shed was forgiven the *homicides*, "manslayers." I do not say the *deicides*, "Godslayers," for had they understood, they would not have crucified the Lord of glory (cf. 1 Cor 2:8). The homicide of an innocent was forgiven them and the blood they spilled in folly, they now drink through grace.

The Augustinian passage is also quoted by René Laurentin in his commentary on the Conciliar Statement on the Church and the Jews.[15]

During the last session of Vatican II, the question was again debated whether or not the deicide charge ought to be explicitly rejected. In the course of this debate, two memoranda were circulated. They were by two well-known French theologians and writers, one favoring the express repudiation of the term as regards the Jews, the other pleading its theological retention. The latter was Père (later Cardinal) Jean Daniélou, S.J. I am quoting a summary of his views which he kindly put at my disposal:

> My memorandum said that the expression deicide was absolutely correct, provided it was properly understood. The word *theoktonos*, God-killer, appeared for the first time with Gregory of Nazianzus (*Carm*. I,I; PG 37:466A; I,2, PG 37:963A). It is of poetic origin and completely parallel to *theotokos*, God-bearer. Just as *theotokos* does not mean that Christ owes His divine nature to Mary but that He, to whom Mary gave His human nature, is God, in the same sense *theoktonos* does not mean that the Jews wanted to kill God, which would be an absurdity (they would then be the precursors of the "death of God" theologians) but that He whom they wanted to kill and whom they considered but a man, was in fact God. The word deicide is, then, simply the statement of a reality—one that is, theologically speaking, incontestable—namely that He who was put to death by the Jews—and by the Romans— was the Son of God. To deny that would mean the denial of the hypostatic union. This said, it is perfectly legitimate to think that the use of the word should be avoided because of its ambiguous character. But nobody has the right to reject it as erroneous.

(I hardly need to stress that I do not favor the use of "the Jews," "the Romans." Synecdoche is a legitimate literary device, but historical experience warns us against its careless use.)

A different view was given by Abbé Laurentin. His paper is so rich that it is extremely difficult to give a brief account of it. I offer instead a summary of his views as contained in the bro-

chure already mentioned. There he compares the word "deicide" to an "explosive," the manifold "consequences of which
cannot be foreseen or controlled."[16] He calls the expression
"deicidal people" "a myth disguised under notional and even
theological appearances." This is its fault as well as the secret
of its power.[17] With one of the drafts of the Statement on the
Jews, he maintains that it is "unjust and erroneous" to call the
Jews "deicidal" and gives the following reasons:

[1] The expression seems to imply that "the Jews" are the
"*sole* deicides," even though "they played only a limited part in
the trial of Christ. It was not the Jewish authorities but the
legitimate Roman authorities who passed the decisive sentence."[18] And he asks: ". . . why have the Romans never been
charged with collective responsibility for deicide?"[19] [2] Another
injustice inherent in the expression is "that it seems to apply to
all Jews. But those who the Gospels say took "part in the death
of Christ were small in number."[20] [3] "Still more profoundly,
the word 'deicide' has two very different meanings, one formal
and the other material." Yet, a material error is not a sin.
Again, those who put Jesus to death—Jews and Romans—
were not formally deicides; in several places, the New Testament attests to their ignorance.[21] [4] "There is one last confusion to expose. . . . [it has been] proposed that to challenge the
expression 'deicidal people' would be to challenge the title
'Mother of God,' *Theotokos*, for the Virgin Mary.[22] Laurentin
rejects this analogy as false.

"Assuredly," he writes, "it would be legitimate to call the
Jewish people theogenic or *theotokos*, since it is certainly the
quality of a people to perpetuate itself by giving birth to descendants." Thus the Jewish people, through Mary, gave birth
to Jesus, Man and God. But "it is not a quality of a people as
people to put God to death." This is all the more true, he adds,
when one keeps in mind the first three points he made. "Maternity creates a substantial and ineradicable relationship
between persons. . . . The fact of having killed someone [does
not] create a substantial belonging of this kind. . . The argument [that the Jews are deicides] is primitive and empty." In
conclusion he states: "To assimilate divine maternity and deicide, to represent in terms of the same model the unrepented

gift God made to Mary" and the disgrace of those who contributed to Jesus' death "is to fail to appreciate God and to wrong His goodwill and His mercy."[23]

Having quoted the insightful statements by Daniélou and Laurentin, I would like to conclude this study by giving what I think is the deepest reason against the use of "deicide" and "deicides." It is not the lack of a scriptural and truly traditional basis but the fact that the two terms pervert the mystery of the Passion. They move the accent from voluntary sacrifice and loving death to murder, from the gracious deed of God to the vicious act of men. More than that, it is not just a shifting of accent; the whole theology of the Cross becomes Man-centered instead of God-centered, sin-oriented rather than grace-oriented. "Deicide" and "deicides" destroy even what they pretend to assert, that He who made Himself the victim of our sins was God in the flesh. If "deicide" is the proper term, then the One Christians preach and live by is not the One who gave Himself freely for our sake but one who was forced to come to our rescue.

To quote the words of an Anglican theologian:

> God died upon the Cross. This to the Synagogue is supreme blasphemy, and in a sense, it is. It is the most fantastic statement that could be uttered by human lips, yet it is the heart of the Gospel. Karl Barth called it the "humanity of God"—God's solidarity with sinners.[24]

The use of the term "deicide" tends to efface this solidarity. It is thus not only an anti-Jewish but also an anti-Christian term.

NOTES

[1]   See *The Koran*, trans. D.J. Dawood (London: Penguin, 1956), p. 370.

[2]   See book, pp. 230-248.

[3]   *Holy Week and Easter Services*, comp. Father George Papadeas (Hempstead: St. Paul's Greek Orthoox Church, n.d.), p. 641.

[4]   Guibert of Nogent, *De Vita Sua*, and Richard of Poitiers, *Chronicon*, as quoted by Norman Cohn, *The Pursuit of the Millennium*

(New York: Harper Torchbooks, 1961), p. 52. Salo W. Baron gives a slightly different wording of the crusaders' battle cry. He writes:

> The unsophisticated marching bands, even more than the regular armies, were readily persuaded by this simple reasoning: "We are marching a great distance to seek our sanctuary and to take vengeance on the Muslims. Lo and behold, there live among us Jews whose forefathers slew [Jesus] and crucified him for no cause. Let us revenge ourselves on them first, and eliminate them from among the nations, so that the name of Israel no longer be remembered, or else let them be like ourselves and believe in the son of [Mary]." Jesus was supposed to have said that "there will be a day when my children will avenge my blood. . . ." In the opinion of many Crusaders, that time had come.

In a footnote to this passage, Baron emphasizes that the main argument against the Jews as Christkillers is "almost verbatim repeated by all three Hebrew chroniclers" of that time as well as substantially confirmed by Christian writers. Still, Baron continues, the chroniclers "did not quote here literally the crusaders' utterances. They merely applied the accepted technique of ancient and medieval historians to make heroes explain their motivations through imaginary speeches." See *A Social and Religious History of the Jews* (New York: Columbia University Press, 1957), 4,120, 290.

⁵ The first Christian author to raise the charge of deicide seems to have been Melito of Sardes, a second century Bishop of that city, the capital of ancient Lydia in Asia Minor. In his homily on the Passion, he calls on all the nations to look at the "unprecedented murder that was committed in Jerusalem, the City of Law":

> He who hung the earth in its place is hanged,
> He who fixed the heavens is fixed on the cross,
> He who made all things fast, is made fast on the tree,
> The Master has been insulted, God has been murdered,
> The King of Israel has been slain by an Israelitish hand!

This translation is by Eric Werner in his study "Melito of Sardes, the first Poet of Deicide," *Hebrew Union College Annual* (Cincinnati: 1966), 37,202, where all pertinent data and references are to be found.

While Eric Werner sees in Melito's homily "a veritable diatribe against the God-killing Jews" (p. 201), Karl Heinrich Rengstorf thinks that "nothing would be more mistaken than to reproach the Bishop of Sardes with a low-class and malicious anti-Judaism. . . . The Jews he has in mind and accuses are not the Jews of his time, much less the Jews of his diocese but the Jews of long ago, the Jews of the first Good Friday, in Jerusalem." See Karl H. Rengstorf and Siegfried von Kortzfleisch, *Kirche und Synagoge: Handbuch zur Geschichte der Christen und Juden* (Stuttgart: Klett Verlag, 1968), 1,73.

Rengstorf holds further that the "thesis of deicide [is] above all a christological statement whose rightness or wrongness does not depend on whether those who sent Jesus to the cross were Jews or non-Jews" (*ibid.*, p. 74). He stresses the fact that the phrase had no harmful consequences for Jews, either in Melito's generation or in those following upon his; yet, he admits that, "taken by itself the phrase could have been unheard-of brisance" (*ibid.*). Would it not be much more to the point to see in "deicide" a term that endangers Jews and Christians? In the case of the latter, not their bodies but their spirits: It may easily turn them into heartless or self-righteous people. It is a triumphalistic expression that has no place in an *ecclesia peregrina*, a church of pilgrims.

[6] "La questione judaica davanti al Concilio Vaticano II," *Palestra del Clero*, 44, (15 February 1965), 4,192-193.

[7] Walter Bauer, *Wörterbuch zum Neuen Testament*(Berlin: Töpelmann, 1963), col. 223.

[8] William F. Arndt and F.W. Wilbur Gingrich, *A Greek-English Lexicon of the New Testament* (Chicago: University of Chicago Press, 1957), p. 112.

[9] *Ioudaioi* can be translated as "Judeans" or "Jews." In this context, where Paul speaks of "the church in Judea," the first meaning seems to be the one that he had in mind. Still, in the discussion of the text I will proceed from the common assumption that the Apostle spoke of "Jews" without restriction.

[10] L.-M. Dewially, O.P., *La jeune église de Thessalonique* (Paris: Cerf, 1963), p. 44.

[11] Tacitus, in particular, spouts this accusation (*Ann.* 15, 44; *Hist.* 5,5). The frequent attacks on the Jews by Greek and Roman writers have been collected by Théodore Reinach in a bilingual edition (Paris: Presses Universitaires, 1895; reprinted by Georg Olms, Hildesheim, 1963). A more recent bilingual edition, Greek/Latin and English is by Menahem Stern, *Greek and Latin Authors on Jews and Judaism*, 2 Vols. (Jerusalem: Academic Press, 1974, 1980).

[12] Heinz Schürmann, *Der Erste Brief an die Thessalonicher* (Düsseldorf: Patmos-Verlag, 1962), p. 56.

[13] Pearson, "1 Thessalonians 2:13-16: A Deutero-Pauline Interpolation," *Harvard Theological Review* (1971), 64, 79-94.

[14] See Otto Michel, "Antijüdische Polemik bei Paulus," in *Antiju-*

daismus im Neuen Testament? eds. Eckert, Levinson, and Stöhr (Munich: Kaiser, 1967), p. 51.

[15] René Laurentin, *The Declaration on the Relation of the Church to Non-Christian Religions* (Glen Rock: Paulist Press, 1966), pp. 73-74.

[16] *Ibid.*, p. 65.

[17] *Ibid.*, p. 66.

[18] *Ibid.*

[19] *Ibid.*, pp.66-67.

[20] *Ibid.*, p. 67.

[21] *Ibid.*, pp. 69-70.

[22] *Ibid.*, p. 71.

[23] *Ibid.*, p. 71-73.

[24] Jacób Jocz, *Christians and Jews, Encounter and Mission* (London: S.P.C.K., 1966), p. 11.

Season of Love

LENT IS NEAR. Soon the daily Eucharist, homilies, sermons, and devotions will call us and the people entrusted to our pastoral care to live ever more lovingly in the sight of God. This is our great chance: intensive prayer, abstinence, fasting, and most of all, love for all of God's children are to carry us to Easter, that radiant day of the Lord's Resurrection, and beyond. The Archdiocesan Commission for Ecumenical and Interreligious Affairs, together with its standing Committee for Catholic-Jewish Concerns, has therefore asked that I turn to you with a special request.

The Lenten and Easter liturgies abound with references to the Jews. This is as it ought to be. Jesus was born a Jew; His earthly life was lived among His kinsmen; the great events of

His sojourn among Men—"the work of our redemption"—were enacted on Jewish soil; indeed, the whole history of our salvation is tied to the Jewish people. Lent, then, and the Easter season, in fact, the whole liturgical year are never-ending opportunities to praise the mystery of election—the strategy of divine love.

Yet, such are the vagaries of our lives, the "exposure" of human existence, that this great opportunity of the spirit can also become a spiritual pitfall. "The Jews," who ought to remind us of God's merciful involvement in human affairs, His predilection, and thus His covenant, can become a screen behind which we hide from the grip of grace. In the past, Christians often uttered and understood "the Jews" as an invective, an evil incantation, a kind of magic formula by which one could project one's own sins on those "others": "the Jews."

Victim of a Murderous Plot of the Jews?

THE OLD CHARGE: "The Jews killed Christ!" not only ignores the historical setting of Jesus' Passion but also negates the existential significance of His Death. Anyone familiar with the forces that shaped the life of the inhabitants of that little Roman province of Judea may be easily misled into assuming that the "high priest," "chief priests," and the "scribes," so frequently mentioned were the legitimate civil and religious authority of the land. In reality, the high priest and his clique were puppets, creatures of the Imperial Court. For almost two centuries, first under Syrian, then under Roman domination, the high-priestly office was given to the highest bidder. Being in power, the high priests and their families wielded considerable influence. Yet, having acquired their dignity through bribery, they were links in the chain of Roman corruption, but hardly the true representatives of the Jewish people.

Though no love was lost between pagans and Jews, particularly the Roman procurator and the High Priest, the latter seemed to have worked with the former whenever he thought it necessary to protect his own position. The death sentence was pronounced by Pilate, and could have been pronounced only by him. Still, the Passion narratives suggest that Caiaphas and Pilate made common cause in ending Christ's ministry. Both appear to have cooperated in Jesus' arrest. To both, He seemed a dangerous man, a disturber of the status quo. All who wielded power thought of Him as a rival, though He had no political ambition. Loved by the people, He could easily have become the leader of a popular uprising, a seditionist. And it was as such that He was crucified; hence the "inscription" on the Cross, the alleged cause of His conviction: "Jesus of Nazareth, King of the Jews."

I have used words like "suggest," "seem," "appear," for the narratives on Our Lord's Passion are proclamations of our redemption, not transcripts of a court reporter. At the various stages of Jesus' trial, there was no one present to take the minutes, no one charged with recording the proceedings. After all, the details pale before the overwhelming message that Jesus died for our sins, that He gave His life so that we might live in God's everlasting presence. If He died for our sins, then our sins—then we, the sinners—brought Him to the Cross. Let me recall for a moment the historical perspective: a politician and his counselors; a high priest and his entourage; "theologians," called scribes; soldiers, and a crowd; Romans, Jews, Syrians, were among the actors in the drama of salvation. (I speak of "Syrians" because it was the Roman custom to take their mercenary troops, particularly the occupation forces, from the native population. The soldiers in Pilate's service who mocked Jesus and crowned Him with thorns were, historians agree, Syrians. Their sneer "hail, king of the Jews" was an attempt to ridicule the messianic hope of the Jews.) This historical vista renders concrete the theological truth that all humanity is responsible for the Death that raised all humanity to new heights, that opened God's heart to each and everyone, Jew and Gentile, the refined and the rough, those who know Him and those who do not yet know Him.

Bearer of Salvation for All Humanity

WHY DO I EMPHASIZE so much that Jesus is the victim of *all* sinners, as He is their Pardoner and Restorer?

First, Vatican II has warned us anew, *not* to put the blame for the Lord's sufferings on the Jews—the Jews of Jesus' time, even less, the Jews of all times. To do so would be a grave injustice; it would also turn the Good News upside down. This is what the Council said:

> Christ underwent His Passion and Death freely and out of infinite love because of the sins of all people so that all may obtain salvation. This the Church has always held and holds now. Sent to preach, the Church is, therefore, bound to proclaim the Cross of Christ as the sign of God's all-embracing love and the fountain from which all grace flows.
>
> (*Nostra Aetate* 4, conclusion)

Second, in our age, the message of the universality of sin and of the infinitely deeper universality of grace has to be preached again and again. The awareness of sin, its wholesome fear, is rare today. Without the admission of sin, however, there is no hope; and without hope, life is shallow. May I beg you, then, to be alert so that the misleading cliché: "The Jews killed Christ" will not slip into one of your homilies, sermons, or devotions. It has the questionable honor of having been around for a long time, and of sneaking into our speech when we least expect it. It is always easy to let generalizations take the place of exact thought and careful preparation.

The Man of Pain Present in All Sufferers

TO PROCLAIM the Lord's Passion in such a way that its telling begets gratitude, love, and joy in God, but never anger, self-righteousness, or hostility is our priestly task. Whenever the Passion story is read or chanted publicly—on Passion (formerly Palm) Sunday and Good Friday—we ought to introduce its recitation by a few prefatory remarks. It may be best to have the priest who presides over the liturgy do so. The following thoughts may prove helpful in making the proclamation of Jesus' loving death a moment to remember, indeed, a call lovingly to embrace all of God's children, particularly Jesus' kin.

In his "Epistle to the Hebrews," a disciple of the Apostle Paul hails Jesus' sacrifice of His body for our sins as having been offered "once for all" (10:10). As a historical event, it cannot be repeated. Its weight is infinite; hence nothing could be added by its repetition. Yet, for our benefit, it can and ought to be re-presented, sacramentally. When the mystery of Christ's Passion is thus proclaimed, we become witnesses of His saving love, His contemporaries, as it were.

Though a repetition on the historical plane is impossible, the Lord's suffering is mysteriously continued—re-enacted, if you wish—in all those who are persecuted for His sake. As Saul, who had been harassing the Church (see Ac 8:3), approached Damascus, a flash of light threw him to the ground and a Voice asked him: "Saul, Saul, why do you persecute me?" When Saul questioned: "Who are you, Sir?" the Voice answered: "I am Jesus, the One you are persecuting" (Ac 9:5). Similarly, when the Reformation tore the Church apart, threatening her very existence, Teresa of Avila (16th cent.) exclaimed: "The world is in flames. Christ is being crucified anew. They want the Church to perish from the earth."

In these sayings, Christ identifies Himself, or is identified, with those who believe in Him and follow Him. Yet, this is not the whole truth; He is also one with the poor, the neglected, the abused, and the persecuted everywhere. The French writer Léon Bloy (1846-1917) called the modern contempt for Jews because of race "the most horrible slap Our Lord suffers in His ever-continuing Passion, the bloodiest and most unforgivable, because He receives it in the face of His Mother." At the thought of Jewish suffering at the hands of the Nazis, the American-French writer Julian Green cried out:

> Jesus' torment goes on in this world, day and night. Having once been nailed to a Roman cross, He has been persecuted with inexorable cruelty in the person of His own people. One cannot strike a Jew without having the same blow fall on Him who is the Man par excellence and, at the same time, the Flower of Israel. It is Jesus who was struck in the concentration camp. It is always He; His suffering is never ended.

Avenging the Blood of Christ?

THERE HAVE BEEN times and countries when worshipers left the Church after the reading of the Passion to throw stones at Jewish houses and call vengeance down on the Jews as "the murderers of Christ." What a travesty! How can a Christian think, even for a moment, that Jesus' redemptive death needs to be avenged or punished? It is our salvation; were we to respond to it by blaming others instead of our sins, we would deprive ourselves of this very salvation.

"Collective guilt," a dark, indeed, deadly notion, does not form part of Jesus' message. It is far from being an article of the Church's creed. But it is a temptation that assails Christians as much as non-Christians, perhaps even more so. To the preacher or teacher the temptation may come in the form of the phrase "the Jews" as it frequently appears in the Gospel according to John. Now, the temptation is that it be always taken collectively, as if it always meant "all the Jews," the whole community of Israel, then, now, and always.

"The Jews"—Who Are They?

STRANGE THOUGH it may seem, the meaning of the designation "the Jews" is neither obvious nor is it always the same; it may vary from pericope to pericope. When Jesus says to the Samaritan woman: "It is from the Jews that salvation comes" (Jn 4:22), "the Jews" are clearly the Jewish people, chosen to be God's witnesses, the vehicles of His favor. Similarly, in the title on the Cross—Pilate's final verdict—"Jesus of Nazareth, King of the Jews," "Jews" means the people, the body of Jews in its entirety.

John 2:13-25 is a remarkable example of a shift in meaning, not from pericope to pericope, but within the same pericope. It begins: "The Passover of the Jews was at hand," often rendered: "The Jewish Passover was near." There can be no doubt that "the Jews" here means the worshiping community of Israel. Later in that passage, we are told that, after Jesus had cleansed the Temple, "the Jews challenged Him" to show them a sign that would prove His authority for His action (Jn 2:18).

When He points to His Resurrection, under the image of "this Temple" destroyed and rebuilt anew, "the Jews" again take Him to task (2:20).

No special scholarship, only common sense is needed to realize that those inquiring into Jesus' credentials are not the whole Jewish people. It would have been physically impossible for the entire people to conduct such an investigation. In both verses, "the Jews" means the officialdom in Jerusalem and its emissaries, in today's jargon, "the establishment." Thus the "Good News New Testament" reads: "the Jewish authorities" while other translations retain "the Jews" (see Jn 18:28, 19:31, 38; 20:19). Many think that "the Jews" is the only rendering that is faithful, true to the original. I dare say, it is not; it does not convey to the uninitiated hearer and reader the meaning the author intended and the early faithful may have grasped.

A Flawless Proclamation

HOW CAN WE do away with readings that tend to turn the Gospel of Christ, our Peace who made Jews and Gentiles one (see Eph 2:14), into an instrument of Gentile contempt for Jews?

Comments by the celebrant, deacon, or preacher of the day, in short, by the one chosen to proclaim the Gospel, ought to suffice to avoid harmful misunderstandings. Whenever called for, the reader ought to preface the reading with words like these: The designation 'the Jews' in this morning's (evening's) pericope does not refer to the totality of the Jewish people—the Jews of yesterday, today, and tomorrow—it does not even point to the Jews of Jesus' time; it is a term that here and in many Gospel passages stands for the officials of Jerusalem, those leaders Jesus seems, according to some exegetes, to have branded as hirelings men who were not true shepherds (see Jn 10:12, 13).

A comment of this kind may accomplish more than comments generally do. It may make most listeners realize that they must not transform the recital of the Gospel into a hide-and-seek game; turn "the Jews" into a screen behind which they find refuge against the promptings of grace, or make scapegoats out of them. A brief comment may make the listeners aware that it is always they who are addressed, castigated, wooed, and urged to turn from their own selves to God.

That in a number of pericopes "the Jews" does not mean what we, at first sight, think, is not a unique phenomenon. There are many instances where a literal translation is misleading, and a more meaningful one must take its place. To give but one example, in the Beatitudes, Jesus hails "those who hunger and thirst after righteousness" (Mt 5:6). The Vulgate translated the Greek *dikaiosynè*, a rendering of the Hebrew *tzedakah*, with *iustitia*. Some vernacular versions followed suit and wrote: "those who hunger and thirst after justice." Yet, this rendering is wide of the mark.

Justice is that virtue which gives everyone his or her due, which accords to all what is rightfully their own. Yet, *tzedakah*, righteousness, is quite different; it bespeaks God's gracious, loving attitude toward those with whom He concluded a covenant and the faithfulness of the covenanters toward His Will and Law, and toward one another. Hence NAB renders: "those who hunger and thirst after holiness." NEB offers his translation: "those who hunger and thirst to do what is right." The Good News NT reads: "those whose greatest desire is to do what God requires." This is not the time or place to decide which of these translations is to be preferred. All I wish to do is to prove, with the help of one example, that my suggestion, far from being revolutionary, makes good sense.

An ever-increasing number of writers today propose that in all those instances where the Gospel pericopes tell of tension, alienation, distrust, or hostility between Jesus and His audience we say "Judeans" rather than "Jews." I cannot give all the reasons for reading *Ioudaioi* as Judeans, but it may be worth pointing out that these twin words correspond somewhat to the twofold meaning of "Yankee." For a Southerner or Westerner a Yankee is a New Englander, for a Mexican "Yankee" is an unflattering way of referring to any U.S. citizen.

It would be an ideal solution could we say "Judeans" in every instance where *Ioudaioi* seems to have a pejorative meaning, but present-day rules forbid us to make such a change. The time will come when most translations will use "Judeans" wherever appropriate. There is a German translation that employs "Judeans" in all instances described. It is by the late Otto Karer, one of the foremost pioneers of the Ecumenical Movement. The editors of one English version are said to be contemplating such a move.

In this letter I have asked that you preface all passages that might be understood as abusive with a comment as to the proper meaning of "the Jews." I have asked you, for I have no authority to enjoin you, nor would I wish to do so. The proclamation of the Gospel without the least animosity against Jews and with the utmost care for the integrity of the Christian message must be a concern that is not imposed on us from without, but springs from the heart.

When the late Cardinal Bea introduced the first draft of the Conciliar Statement on the Church and the Jewish people to the Assembly of Bishops at St. Peter's, he stressed that to bring light to this relationship is to help in the Church's renewal. He emphatically declared that it would contribute to the purpose of the Council, as Pope John XXIII saw it, the rediscovery of the Church's youthful fervor. May I, therefore, ask you to enter ever more into this great ministry of reconciliation?

Delivered Into Our Hands

The Lord God has given me
   a skilled tongue,
To know how to speak to the weary
   words that will rouse them.
Morning after morning
   He opens my ear
That I may hear as disciples do.

The Lord God has opened my ears
   and I have not rebelled,
I have not turned away.
   I offered my back to those who beat me;
My cheeks to those who plucked my beard.
   My face I did not shield
from insult and spitting.

> The Lord God is my help,
>   Therefore I am not disgraced;
> I have set my face like a flint,
>   I know I shall not be shamed.
>
>   (Is 50:6-7)

Servant of the Lord

THIS IS THE third of the four Servant Songs. The others are 42:1-4; 49:1-7; 52:13-53:12. Throughout these poems the identity of the Servant of the Lord, *Ebed YHVH*, fluctuates between the community and a single person; now he seems to be an individual, now the people of Israel. Such wavering is not a sign of hesitation, rather the expression of a seminal biblical phenomenon. The late English exegete H. Wheeler Robinson called it "corporate personality." *Adam* may mean man the person or the community; the first human being or all humankind. Jacob's life anticipates the lives of his offspring. Again, he is given the name Israel (Gn 32:29), and it is by this name that his descendants are known. They, "the sons of Israel" (Ex 1:1), have grown into "the people of Israel."

This, then, is the principle of corporate personality: One stands for all, and all are gathered up in one; all take on the burden, mission, or responsibility of the one. Many Christian beliefs—original sin or the communion of guilt; vicarious suffering; the communion of saints, the fellowship of grace; the fact that all individual men and women are accomplices in humanity's rebellion against God and that they may become fellow pilgrims on the road to Him—cannot be really understood without this Hebrew principle of solidarity, which threads the Old and the New Scriptures as well as post-biblical Judaism.

Who, then, is this Servant, whose suffering is said to bring light and salvation to the world: In the past, Christian exegetes limited themselves to the individual interpretation, seeing in the Servant Songs exclusive prophecies of Jesus; Jewish exegetes have leaned toward a collective understanding, seeing the Servant as a symbol of the whole people of Israel or of its righteous, faithful remnant.

Both were wrong in their "either-or" attitude. In the second Servant Song, for instance, the Lord says:

> You are my Servant, Israel,
>   through whom I show my glory.
>
>   (Is 49:3)

Yet, this same Servant has a mission to Israel (v. 5). This proves, if proof is needed, how much care must be applied to "fixing" the identity of the Servant. At times, it is impossible to determine who he is, clearly and unequivocally. It is the nature of prophecies to be obscure and, to some extent, open-ended. Only those who assume that the role of prophecy is to still our curiosity, rather than to stir us to a change of heart, and thus to a righteous life can be shocked at the thought that prophetic visions are by nature opaque and often admit of more than one interpretation.

The Servant of the third Song is plainly called to teach and comfort the weary. Yet before he can do so, he must himself listen to the word of God, morning after morning. The bewildering reward for his testimony is to be ignored, even mistreated. Still, he remains steadfast; buffeted, he is not broken. He cannot be put to shame because his trust in the Lord remains unshaken. The question still remains: Who is the Servant of this Song? Could it be the prophet himself who wanted to bring the divine message to the Gentiles and was hindered in his effort by his own people? If someone is tempted to say that this must be the correct view, for to hinder such witness, to hold on to one's privileges, to refuse to share the gifts one has received is typical of Jews, he is right, and yet wrong. Jews are apt to be like that, not because they are Jews but because they are human beings. Christians have been guilty of these sins, too often to relate here.

We said that, like other oracles, the vision of the Second Isaiah is open to more than one interpretation. Hence, in using the third Servant Song for the beginning of Holy Week, the Church can apply it to Christ in His Passion. In doing so, she is far from being arbitrary—she follows the dictates of the heart. Every lover sees the image of the beloved everywhere. Moreover,

406 THE NEW ENCOUNTER

to see in the portrait of one flogged, abused, and spit upon, the likeness of Him who bore these and other pains for our sake is certainly not farfetched. Yet, not only the heart, the learned mind, too, is compelled to share this perspective. "... no nation, not even Israel, ever did, or perhaps ever will or can, measure up to the Servant in the Songs. Only Christ has done that." Even though at the start, the Prophet equates the Servant with Israel—a fact Christians must respect—for them the Servant can be "in the last resort . . . none other than Christ" (Christopher R. North, *The Second Isaiah*, p. 20).

A prophet does not gaze at the world, he does not merely contemplate the past or the future, he acts, seeking to shape history. We are granted a share in this prophetic task. We carry part of the burden, of the responsibility for things-to-come. Again, if we keep in mind the insignificance of our ministries when placed next to the awesome mission of the Servant of the Lord, we may read this Song as a tale of our discipleship. Called to bear witness to God's love, manifest in Jesus the Suffering Servant, and to bring comfort to the weary, we, too, will be rebuffed and mistreated. But one with Him, we will not be disgraced. We will remain firm: weakened, we will yet be strong.

Life for Others

THE APOSTLES rightly see themselves above all as "witnesses to the Resurrection" (Ac 1:22, 2:32, *passim*), as men who bear testimony "that [God] raised Christ to life" (1 Cor 15:14). Theirs is a dignity unique and undeserved. The morning of the Resurrection, the women in their company report that they found Christ's tomb empty and that angels reminded them of His prediction to "rise again on the third day" (Lk 24:2-8). Rather high-handedly, the Apostles dismiss their tale as "hysterical nonsense," as "idle gossip" (24:11). But once they are convinced, they do not waver in their belief in the Resurrection as the consummation of God's saving will and work, as the summit of Jesus' life. Moreover, in the risen Lord, heaven and earth also rose; a new life is promised to all creation.

Still, the Gospel narratives and, thus, the liturgical readings on the Resurrection are brief and limited almost to bare essentials, while those on the Passion are quite long and given to much detail. This is as it must be. "Christ risen" transcends earthly experience and ordinary concepts. The Crucified, however, appeals to human imagination, to our sense of drama and the feelings of pity, sorrow, and sympathy. But both, the proclamation of the Resurrection and the retelling of the Passion are indispensable parts of the Church's Mission. Without the former, the Christian faith is a sham (see 1 Cor 15:14,17), without the latter, the message of Jesus risen is reduced to a dream, or turned into something like a pagan myth. In the past, the Passion's immediate appeal to our senses and emotions quite understandably led to a preponderance of meditations, devotions, and sermons centered on the Cross. The task of today's preacher is not to let one mystery eclipse the other.

In preaching on the Passion according to St. Mark (14:1-15:40) or, for that matter, on any of the Passion narratives, the stirring details must not let us forget the substance of the message. It would be an intriguing topic to inquire into the reasons for Judas' betrayal or into the larger phenomenon that a human's worst enemies are likely to be under his or her own roof and that the Church's most bitter foes have usually come from within her own household. Yes, it would be interesting to examine Judas' hidden motives in betraying his Master, as novelists, playwrights, and psychologists have done, but would such an inquiry—apart from the fragility of its conclusions—increase our gratitude and devotion to Christ? Would it make better disciples of us? This is, after all, the purpose of the telling of the Passion story, is it not?

Again, a preacher could review the "court proceedings," step by step. Were there two trials, a "Jewish" and a "Roman" one? Or was the session at the High Priest's house—strangely enough, in Mark's Gospel the High Priest bears no name—no trial at all but a preliminary investigation, something like a "pretrial hearing in the judge's chamber?" Would a verdict by the Sanhedrin have had any effect? Only the Roman governor could send someone to his death on the cross, by the sentence: *Ibis in crucem*, "To the cross you go" or "You will mount the cross." Answers to these and similar questions are, no doubt, illuminating but they could easily give our sermons the wrong slant. We are not meant to be criminal investigators, prosecutors, or judges. In roles like these, we would be completely miscast. We cannot play investigator or judge because, in the re-telling of the Passion, *we* are the ones who are investigated, accused, and judged. What will our sentence be? Conviction or acquittal? Further alienation or reconciliation?

A character sketch of the High Priest or of Pontius Pilate, a thorough analysis of the Jerusalem crowd before the governor's palace or of the Syrian soldiers who mocked Jesus, crowning Him with thorns, would make the men and women in the pews sit up. But would these efforts bring them to their knees, or make them walk in Jesus' footsteps? To ask the question is to answer it. There are hundreds of problems of scholarly importance that remain to be solved. They must be posed and, as far as possible, answered, but not then and there. A Passion sermon is not a dissertation, much less a "whodunit." The actors in the drama of salvation—the High Priest and his clique, Pontius Pilate and his entourage, the mob and the cohort, in other words, clergy, intellectuals, politicians, military men, and the masses—acted in the name of all of us. They are our deputies. In some monastic congregations, it is not an individual singer who chants "Crucify him!" (Mk 15:14); the whole community shouts it. Such existential understanding makes one say: "It's not only Judas who betrayed Him. I did, too" or: "I, together with Peter, denied Him, not once, but again and again." Without that understanding, the Passion story has not really spoken to us.

To preach that the Lord Jesus suffered and died for us is part of the *kerygma*, the proclamation of Jesus Christ, His Good News. However much we need to stress today that "sin" is not a clerical or, for that matter, a Jewish invention, that it is a dreadful reality, it is still more important to cry into the world that forgiveness is not a pious fraud but a true gift of God:

> The Son of Man did not come
> to be served
> but to serve,
> and to give up his life
> as a ransom for many.
>
> (Mk 10:45)

This saying makes clear that hand in hand with the Passion's redemptive significance goes its moral one: Jesus is the Savior. He is also our Exemplar, our Model. It is quite common today to speak of the servant Church and assume that it is the Pope, the Bishops, the priests who ought to be servants of others. True, but the concept of the servant Church is not limited. All are called, and all will prove to be chosen if they obey the summons to live, not for themselves but for others.

"Life for others" implies, among other things, that we take seriously Christ's conquest of sin. It is plain that His death has not made sin disappear from the face of the earth. In this gigantic, terrifying task, we must be His helpers. This is not a common thought among Christians. We are wont to pray: "For my sake, You accepted death on the Cross, may Your love and torment not be lost on me!" Why should we not add: "May Your willing death not be lost on the world!" and act accordingly?

It is part of the Christian paradox—or of the folly of Christianity—to hold that through His death Jesus ushers in God's Kingdom, His reign. His cry: *Eloi, Eloi, lama sabachthani*, "My God, my God, why have You forsaken me?" (Mk 16:34), though an expression of anguish, is not one of utter hopelessness. As the psalm itself shows, the prayer begins with desperation but ends with trust and sure hope (Ps 22:23-32), with the promise of praise and the vision of a world living in the presence of the Lord.

To end on a note of joy: Hard though life on earth is, the Christian who lives in the shadow, nay, the radiance of the Cross, knows his or her existence to be an eschatological one. "Eschatological existence" means that the glorious fullness we expect for the end of ages is already present in our lives, though still hidden from our sight. Thus, the Christian takes life here and now as a forward thrust toward the realization of all that is to be, as an anticipation of "the new heaven and the new earth" (Ap 21:1). Not just an anticipation by the mind but by deed. Such is our responsibility as men and women hallowed by the Passion of the One who is God's Beloved and ours.

It Was I

The Church prefers that the Passion be read in dialogue form to make us realize our *personal* involvement. We—our sins—nailed Jesus to the Cross; they are forgiven because Jesus freely suffered the anguish and pain of death for us.

Hence it is not only important, but necessary that we acknowledge our part in Christ's death. Were we to pretend that we are without guilt, we would not be redeemed. Christ came to save sinners, not those who think themselves righteous.

That the Lord's Passion is of our making, and not the work of *the* Jews or *the* Romans, is the teaching of the Church. A not often used Eucharistic prayer, whose great theme is reconciliation, recalls, before the mighty words of Consecration are pronounced:

410

When we were lost
And could not find the way to You,
You loved us more than ever.
Jesus, Your Son, innocent and without sin,
Gave Himself into our hands and was nailed to a cross.

Even the best of popular devotion upholds this thought, thus giving the Passion narrative its true significance. The German original of the moving hymn, "O Sacred Head Surrounded," contains this stanza:

O Lord, what You endured is all my doing.
I caused [the pain] You bore.
Wretched sinner, deserving but Your wrath,
Your mercy and Your grace I do implore.

Another Passion Chorale asks:

Who was the guilty?
Who brought this upon Thee?
Alas, my treason, Jesus, has undone Thee.
'twas I, Lord Jesus,
I it was denied Thee;
I crucified Thee!

The story of the Passion is not fiction but history. Still, when the Passion is read as part of the liturgy, it is not to satisfy our craving for knowledge, but to raise our whole being to new heights, to greater devotion, to deeper gratitude, and to more fervent love of God and fellow.

We must not point our fingers at the actors in the Passion but rather beat our own breast. It would be outrageous were we to condemn those for whom Christ pleaded on the Cross, praying, "Father, forgive them for they know not what they do."

When you hear mentioned Caiaphas, the high priest, or Pontius Pilate, the procurator, the Pharisees or the Roman soldiers, Peter who denied knowing Jesus, and Judas who betrayed Him, the hostile crowd and His devoted friends—Mary Magdalene, another Mary, Joseph of Arimathea, and Nicodemus— you should say before God: "They are I; they represent me; they mirror my being, my failures and my good will, too." Please remember through the service that what we do here is to glorify God and to humble ourselves.

Just one more remark. Most of the time when the Evangelist says according to our text "the Jews," (Judeans might be a better translation) he does *not* refer to the Jewish people as a whole, but to the religious authorities in Jerusalem of Jesus' days.

Let love reign among us.

Only where love is, there is God!

BEARING GOOD FRUIT

*All through Scripture, trees have stood
for life. The righteous are likened to
trees planted near running water, bearing leaves that never wither (Ps 1).
Jesus compares the true teacher to a
tree bearing good fruit (Mt 7:18). "Bearing Good Fruit" well bespeaks the message of Vatican II on the Church and
the Jews in its yielding a new sensitivity, a new way of speaking to and of
each other, a new mode of doing, indeed,
living the "truth in love" (Eph 4:15).*

The Covenant: Old, New, and One

THERE HAVE BEEN several Israeli efforts to find the proper rendering of Christian terms into modern Hebrew. It is no easy task to find the right word for Incarnation, *parousia*, or even baptismal font. The most recent effort by the United Christian Council in Israel renders "old Covenant" as *ha-berit ha-rishonah*, "the First Covenant." The whole Bible—the Hebrew and the Christian Scriptures—is called *sefer ha-beritot*, "Book of the Covenants." In this country, a number of theologians and journalists have spoken of "Israel's enduring Covenant." Some Christians are left uneasy by the statement that "God's Covenant with Israel endures," even after the Declaration of Vatican II on the Church and the Jews and similar Protestant documents. They think that with Christ's Death and Ressurection, a new Covenant superseded the old. I have often been asked for the reasons behind that new theological vision embodied in the title.

First, Jews have lived through centuries of exile, dispersion, abuse, oppression, persecution, even massacre, and they are still around and about. Hitler had millions of Jews killed; he planned to have them all exterminated like vermin, yet he is gone while the people of Israel lives. Merely human factors like physical stamina or vitality cannot explain this wonder of endurance. It is without a doubt sign and proof of the Lord's fidelity to the Chosen People.

True, the exile is in part God's punishment—thus even the Jewish sages of old teach. But to be punished is not to be rejected. To suffer is not to be unloved. To say the opposite, to equate human suffering with abandonment by God, is to turn the Christian message upside-down. Jews have lived through many torments and outlived many enemies. Is this not clear evidence that they are not, as Christians in the past often held, a *massa damnata*, a condemned body? They are not banished from God's presence. His Covenant with them remains in force; it is a reality of the spirit.

Second, Holy Scripture tells again and again that the Lord concluded His Covenant with Abraham and Abraham's descendants *le 'olam*, forever. Nowhere is it said that the Covenant is tied to a brief span, that it is given on credit. No doubt, the Chosen People must give account of its fidelity to the Covenant, but God's love in no way depends on Israel's righteousness; in no way is it determined by the people's conduct.

Yet, are not some promises couched in a conditional mood so that their fulfillment rests on Israel's obedience, on its keeping of the commandments? Yes and No. What is given on condition are tokens of the Covenant, not the Covenant itself. For example, when the people is untrue to its calling, the land entrusted to it can be taken away, but only temporarily, because the Lord had pledged it to their forefathers. In any event, *hesed*, "God's loving kindness," His covenant love, His mercy, lasts forever.

Third, in his Epistle to the Romans, the Apostle makes clear that the Lord is not so fickle as to revoke what He gave out of the fullness and freedom of His heart. Since He drew Israel to

Himself, not because of its virtue or might, but because of His love—that love which has no other reason or explanation than itself—Israel, once chosen, remains chosen for all time. Vatican II made St. Paul's vision its own, declaring: "Now as before, God holds them most dear, for the sake of the Patriarchs; He has not withdrawn His gifts or calling—such is the witness of the Apostle."

Fourth, if the people whom the reworded Good Friday intercession calls the one "to whom God spoke first" is not dismissed from the realm of grace; if the Christian Church has not superseded Judaism; if, in short, the relationship between the Church and the Jewish people is not a negative one, is it then positive? Vatican II answered that question in the affirmative: "The Church . . . cannot forget that she draws sustenance from the root of that well-cultivated olive tree onto which the wild branches of the Gentiles have been grafted." The well-cultivated olive tree is the people of Israel brought up under the discipline of the Torah, the rebukes and comforting words of Prophets, the prayers of its Singers, and the wisdom of all its Sages.

An ancient prayer that now precedes the blessing of baptismal water at the Easter Vigil describes the bond between the Church and the Jewish people still more powerfully:

> Even in our days, we witness the splendor of the wondrous deeds You wrought in days of old. What Your mighty arm once accomplished for the one people, when You freed them from their Egyptian pursuers, You do now for the salvation of nations, through the water of rebirth. Grant that all men and women become Abraham's sons and daughters and so share in the dignity of Israel.

If Israel had lost or been deprived of its God-given dignity, how could the Church pray that the whole world, *plenitudo totius mundi*, participate in that dignity?

Dare I spell out the reaction of some of my readers? I imagine its being: Though not fully convinced, I am impressed by your explanation, that is, by your arguments from history, the Scriptures, the liturgy, and the Council. I am also intrigued by your theory of one Covenant, if I understand you correctly.

To this, my answer is: Yes, I believe there is ultimately one, all-embracing Covenant, whose sun shines through the ages. There is one universal Covenant since a divine-human covenant is but an articulation of God's majestic love affair with the whole of humanity. The special Covenants, with Noah, for instance, with Abraham, Moses, and the people of Sinai, or David, the various covenant renewals in the history of Israel and, of course, the New Covenant with all humankind in and through Jesus, are manifestations of His lasting embrace of the whole earth and, thus, interrelated. How could it be otherwise, since the goal of the spiritual universe is not divorce, but wedlock, the joining together of all who were apart?

For all its magnitude, this theological view, some may ask, belittles Christ's salvific work, indeed, deprives His Life, Death, and Resurrection as well as His Church of their unique significance, does it not? I do not think so. In the world of the senses, a light-colored object needs a darker background to sharpen its outline. A white flower, for instance, shines more brightly in a meadow that is deep green. The same effect is achieved when a skyline is placed against a nocturnal firmament. Some people or groups whose self-awareness or self-esteem is not very strong need other persons or groups that are alleged to be inferior. They seem to be unable to live without such contrast, without a real or imagined adversary or antigroup.

The Lord Jesus, however, needs no darkened milieu, no evil or empty environment to be seen in His unique grandeur as the Teacher of teachers, the Savior of saviors. I do not have the least difficulty in believing, on the one hand, in Jesus, the Son of God without equal and, on the other, in the universality of God's love, the basic oneness of the Covenant. In fact, belief in the One seems to demand belief in the other. Such is the height, length, and breadth of salvation.

The Challenge of Shalom

THERE IS AN Israeli folksong whose initial words are *Shalom Haverim,* "Peace, my friends." You may have heard it, you may even have joined in singing it. *Shalom Haverim* is a parting song, thus a good way to end the Eucharistic Service. Still, what made the song journey from the youth of Israel to the worshipers of our churches? Was it its haunting melody? Was it the power of briefness? Was it the sound of Hebrew? Or just *shalom,* one of the key words of Scripture? All of these may have attracted us, but mainly the last. The word *shalom* has truly invaded our ranks. Men and women who speak no Hebrew use *shalom* as a greeting. The word heads some people's stationery or appears on bumper stickers; not a few Christians wear pins, medals, or necklaces with *shalom* on them. To top all this, some religious houses have been christened *Shalom.*

The Goal: Shalom

WHAT IS BEHIND this word explosion? Ours is a time of
violence, restlessness, and alienation, yet also, if not chiefly,
an age in search of peace. The summons of Israel's poet: "Seek
after peace and pursue it" (Ps 33:15) resounds even in the souls
of many who otherwise do not listen to the voice of Scripture.
But why is this longing expressed in Hebrew? Why not in
English? "Peace," after all, is a strong word; related to the
Latin *pax*, it bespeaks a pact, an agreement between warring
powers to stop bloodshed. Covenants that bring an end to
human slaughter are worthy of praise.

Yes, let us honor the word "peace." The power of *shalom*,
however, is greater. It opens biblical horizons: Prophets and
Psalmists prayed for it. The Lord Jesus greeted His disciples
with *shalom*; it is His messianic gift. *Shalom* derives from a
root that means "whole," "unblemished," "intact." Hence, it is
more than a cessation of hostilities, more than the silence of
guns and bombs. It is well-being, prosperity, unity within a
human being, among human beings, and above all, between
God and us. It is present where strength abounds, where abundance and security prevail, where things are as they ought. To
render it into contemporary idiom, *shalom* is integrity of existence, integrity of relationships.

I wonder how many of those who sing *Shalom Haverim* send
this greeting in the direction of the men and women who gave it
birth. Is *shalom* not the mark of the true relationship between
Christians and Jews? Is it not also the goal of all Catholic
education? Is it not, in particular, the motto of every enterprise
that fosters kinship between the two communities? Indeed, this
kind of peace is the particular burden, responsibility, and challenge of today's generation. I dare say, as educators, it is your
special responsibility.

The Requirements

Understanding the Holocaust. The Conciliar Statement on the
Jews speaks clearly of the rich patrimony common to Christians and Jews, of the need for mutual knowledge and respect,

of the importance of theological studies and fraternal dialogues. It also implores teachers and preachers to speak of Jews in such a way that their instruction follow, not the letter but the true meaning of the gospel. The guidelines of the American Bishops' Secretariat for Catholic-Jewish Relations are quite explicit on all this, they even list a number of the themes that "merit the attention and study of Catholic educators and scholars."

Before I discuss more fully the challenge we face, I would like to mention a phenomenon that ought to give us pause: Jews have changed. Jews today are different from what they were thirty or forty years ago. A cataclysmic experience has left its mark on them; the Nazi annihilation of six million of their brothers and sisters makes their hearts ache. People counter: "Why can't Jews forget what happened to their kin in Auschwitz and in the other death camps? Why do they have to cling to the calamity that befell them over twenty years ago? Other nations had to suffer, too!" Then they go on enumerating other disasters: At the turn of the century, a million Armenians were massacred by the Turks. In the Potato Famine of 1847 and after, two million Irish people perished. Stalin built his economy and rule on the death of, some say, fifteen million Kulaks. The victims of World War II from many nations, women and children included, numbered fifty millions.

All this is true; indeed, these are painful truths that none of us must forget. Yet, for Jews to know that other peoples suffered as well does not end their own agony. The Holocaust differs from other catastrophes. The extermination plants were organized to the last detail. Prepared on the drawing board, death was delivered on the assembly line. The mass murder of Jews was born, not of a momentary passion, but of a hatred that was like no other, a fiendish, diabolical hatred.

But it is not just this fiendish character of the "death factories" that makes the hearts of Jews still ache. Nor are they agitated only because their relatives and friends were Hitler's victims. Almost every Jew experienced the Holocaust as something that happened to *him* or *her*. Each was abused, degraded, deceived, and choked to death. Under the Nazis, Jews were called "sub-human;" compared to vermin; considered a danger to the body politic, as if they were the most dreaded disease. In the concentration camps, they were herded together, they were taken to what they thought were shower baths, only to discover that the shower heads did not work, and that the room was slowly being filled with fumes of poison gas.

Horrible though the agony of suffocation must have been, the worst pain, present at every step but most of all at the end, was the feeling of being alone, of being forgotten by the world. To most people today, the destruction of European Jewry is a thing of the past, a part of history's dark frame. But to Jews, the Holocaust is an overpowering event, a continuous reality, an everpresent nightmare. Every Jew has had to descend the ladder of horror—if not in his or her waking hours, then in dreams.

If we wish to understand Jews, their needs and concerns, their fears and hopes, their actions and reactions, we must descend that ladder with them. Hence, the Holocaust is a theme for our pulpits. It must be given its legitimate place in our teaching of religion and history. First, a few words on its universal impact.

The man-made hells of Auschwitz and similar places would not have been possible without modern technology. The blessings of the technical advance in our time are obvious. But the boon is, at the same time, a threat to every individual's humanity. Just think of the invasion of our privacy made possible by all sorts of modern inventions. This is just one example, and not the worst. The Nazi Holocaust is a warning to us to guard against the pitfalls of the computer age. Never must we be its slaves.

If men and women of faith look at the Nazi design against the Jews, we know ourselves to be face to face with evil. To quote Emil Fackenheim:

> Where else and at what other time have executioners ever separated those to be murdered from those to be murdered later to the strain of Viennese waltzes? Where else has human skin ever been made into lampshades, and human body fat into soaps—not by isolated perverts but under the direction of ordinary bureaucrats? Auschwitz is

a unique descent into hell. It is an unprecedented celebration of evil. It is evil for evil's sake.[1]

Long before the Holocaust, in 1939, the German Catholic
thinker Theodor Haecker realized that Nazism was a child of
hell. In his Journal, he begins a prayer continuing the thoughts
of Psalm 74: "You have shown us, O God, the very nature of
evil, its arrogance, its triumph in an undreamed-of measure
and to the point of despair."[2]
The Nazis were able to triumph, though Hitler in no way
concealed his murderous design. Hardly anyone would believe
that human beings could be so monstrous. Though trust is a
virtue, credulity is not. There were far too many Christians and
non-Christians who fooled themselves with that hollow adage:
"Things will straighten themselves out." To my mind, Auschwitz, Bergen-Belsen, or Maidenek summon us to watch out for
evils on the social horizon. The Holocaust begs us not to repeat
the ostrich pose of people the world over who blinded themselves to Hitler's scheme.
The celebration of evil that took place in Auschwitz or Treblinka has led some Christians and some Jews to pronounce the
death of God. Yesterday, the "God is Dead" avowal was much
thought, talked, and written about. Today, that assertion is as
dead as the fossils in the deep layers of the earth. It could not
live because it was no answer to the problem of evil. In fact, it
emptied life of meaning.
After the war, Allied soldiers found a lonely inscription,
written on a cellar wall of the then devastated Cologne:

> I believe in the sun,
>   even when it is not shining.
> I believe in love,
>   even when I feel it not.
> I believe in God,
>   even when He is silent.

It is impossible to lift the veil of anonymity and tell with
certitude the writer's identity. Was it a man or a woman? Was it
a Jew who, trying to escape the horror of a concentration camp,

had gone underground, that is, had been hidden by Christian friends in their basement? Or, was it a Christian who had had to endure ten long years of Nazi oppression and then take shelter from Allied bombs? In any case, whoever it was, the writer was gifted with the valor of faith.

The answer to the many faces of evil in the world is not less or no faith, but more faith; not less or no concern, but deeper concern. All evil, in particular the Holocaust, is a summons to exert ourselves to do in God's name what we would like Him to do for us, in some easy, miraculous way. The Holocaust and all the other evils of the world are a summons to make the Christian message that God is Love heard again, not by repeating the words, but rather by our being new women, new men.

Doing Justice to Judaism. I called "God is Love" the Christian message, and so it is. But it is also a tenet of Judaism. I stress this, simply because it is so; it is this kind of truthfulness, of doing justice to Judaism, that God and the times demand of us.

Scripture tells that Moses and the Israelites greeted their rescue from Pharoah's hand with song:

> The Lord is my strength and my courage,
> He has been my savior.
>
> (Ex 15:2)

Miriam, too, with tambourine in hand, led the women in dance and chanted:

> Sing to the Lord, for He is gloriously triumphant;
> horse and chariot He has cast into the sea.
>
> (Ex 15:21)

Thus the Bible. The talmudic narrative is different. There, the angels appear, shouting God's praise: "Holy, holy, holy is the Lord of Hosts." But the Lord rebukes them: "My creatures are drowning in the sea, and you would sing?" (*bMeg.* 10b).

Jewish tradition considers all national catastrophes God's judgments—yet the same chastising God mourns at having permitted the punishment. In one instance, the plaint of Jeremiah the Prophet (13:37),

> And mine eye shall drop tears and tears
>   and run down with tears
>   because the Lord's flock is carried away captive,

becomes God's own lamentation (*bHag.* 5b).[3]

Again, Scripture says that the Lord laughs at the wicked who rebel against Him or who plot against the just (Ps 2:4; 36:13). In a few instances, the Talmud stresses that God laughs with the righteous. When they laugh together, righteousness has triumphed, grace has won a victory, and messianic times are at hand (see *bShab.* 30b; *Ab.Z.* 3b).

For a Christian, the messianic times began with the coming of Christ, His luminous life, His loving death, and His glorious resurrection. They proclaim the splendor-to-come, the new heavens and the new earth. Jews, however, desire more than seeds of hope; they long for the final harvest when trees will bend under the heavy beauty of their fruit, and they long for its appearance now.

As long as the ultimate fulfillment has not come, as long as sin is rampant, as long as the evil impulse tends to turn human creatures from their Creator, humanity needs to plead with God for strength and forgiveness. To show you something of the deep wellsprings of Judaism, let me quote a prayer from the eve of Yom Kippur, in which a Jew, living by God's Covenant, states the human condition in His sight:

> As clay in the hand of the potter
>   who widens or narrows it at will,
> so are we in Your hand, gracious Keeper,
>   heed Your Covenant, not our evil turn....
>
> As silver in the hand of the smith
>   who makes it pure or impure at will,
> so are we in Your hand, healing God;
>   heed Your Covenant, not our evil turn....

Convinced of God's mercy, the devout Jew calls on Him with the whole community, in utmost trust:

> Our God, and God of our Fathers,
>   forgive us, pardon us, cleanse us.
> We are Your people, and You, our God;
>   we are Your children, and You, our Father....
> We are Your faithful, and You, our Beloved;
>   we are Your chosen, and You, our Friend.

Though the Jewish worshipers feel themselves beggars, they know at the same time that they are only asking for what God is eager to give:

> Our God, You defer Your anger,
>   You treat with forbearance the wicked and the good,
>   and this is Your fame.

> Our God, act not for our sake, but for Your own.
>   Look at us who are poor and low.

> Bring healing to us, lost as a leaf adrift;
>   have mercy on Man who is mere dust and ashes,
>   cast away our sins and have pity on Your creation.

Can there be any doubt that prayers like these are heard? That Jewish worshipers who speak this way do not speak into a void, but address the living God? The *Siddur*, the daily Jewish prayerbook, calls Him *Ba'al ha-selihot veha-rahamim*, "Lord of forgiveness and of mercies," that is, Judge and Pardoner; Giver of breath and of grace; Lover of all His creatures and, in particular, of His special possession, Israel. I cannot imagine anyone who, knowing Jewish prayer, would dare deny its quickening power.

My reason for stressing Judaism's vitality and vigor is first this: there can be no dialogue between Christians and Jews, no true meeting, unless we recognize Judaism at its depth. Second, we cannot be happy in our own faith-convictions if we are misers, if we begrudge, as it were, others the love of God, if we deny free reign to His grace.

One instance of what grace accomplishes in a Jewish heart may suffice. The prejudice of Christians has often been that the God of the Old Testament is but an Avenger, that the love of enemy is entirely unknown to Judaism, and so on. Let me, therefore, read the prayer of a nameless Nazi victim. To me, the prayer is truly a monument to "the unknown Jew":

> Peace be to men of ill will, and may there be an end to all vengeance and to all talk of penalty and punishment....The deeds of horror mock all yardsticks. They pass the limits of human understanding, and the martyrs are many indeed.... For these reasons, do not weigh their sufferings, O God, with the scale of justice; do not ascribe these sufferings to the executioners, do not demand of them a dire accounting.... Rather credit the sufferings to the hangmen, the informers, the spies, and all evil men, and reckon unto them all the courage and strength of the victims, their resignation, their high-mindedness and dignity; also their quiet efforts, their hope which did not admit defeat, their brave smile that dried their tears, all their love and sacrifice, all their ardent love,...their harrowed, tormented hearts, hearts that nonetheless remained strong and confident, even in the face of death, in death itself and in the hour of extreme weakness.... May all this, O my God, count in Your eyes as ransom so that the guilty might be forgiven and the just rise—may all that is good count, and not what is evil. And in the memory of our enemies, may we no longer be their victims, no longer their nightmares or the ghosts that frighten them, but an aid against their fury.... Only this is demanded of them, that they abandon their rage. And may we, when all this is over, live again as Men among Men, and may peace come to this poor earth for all Men of good will, and peace for all the rest, too.[4]

Please do not misunderstand me. I do not wish to imply that most victims prayed thus; that the unknown worshiper was typical of Jews—how could this superhuman attitude ever be typical? It is certainly not typical of Christians! What I wish to say most emphatically is that if only one Jew spoke like this before God, Hitler's plan for an amoral society was defeated. That Jews survived Hitler's "final solution," that they survived centuries of persecution, was not a chance event, not so much a happy constellation of historical factors as an act of Divine Providence, and evidence of divine fidelity. God cares for the people He chose at Sinai; He will not abandon them; they are for all times His covenanted people. Not because of their merits, but for the sake of the Patriarchs, that is, for the sake of God's loving pledge, they remain a people treasured, dear, and beloved (Rom 11:28).

The words of the song that goes under Moses' name are still valid:

> For the Lord's portion is His people
>   Jacob his own allotment.
> He found him in a desert region,
>   in an empty howling waste.
> He engirded him, watched over him,
>   guarded him as the pupil of His eye.
> Like an eagle who rouses his nestlings,
>   gliding down to his young,
> so did He spread His wings and take him,
>   bear him along on His pinions.
>   (Dt 32:9-11)

No less true is the prophet's warning:

> Whoever touches you
>   touches the apple of my eye.
>   (Zech 2:12)

I do not hail Judaism as the banner of God's fidelity in order to please Jews. I do it, rather, in order to please God. If God is the ever-faithful One, if "He has not withdrawn His calling" (Rom 11:29), faith demands that a Christian acknowledge this wonder of grace. No doubt, in recognizing God's abiding love for His people, we contribute to the reconciliation of Christians and Jews. Less obvious is the fact that the affirmation of the Jewish people as lastingly covenanted strengthens Jewish-Christian cooperation on many planes. Paradoxically, it also serves the Church: it widens her horizon, enriches her spiritual life, fortifies her role as pilgrim.

The Way: A New Sensitivity

THE POSITIVE VISION of Jews and Judaism I am advocating sharpens our sensitivity to God's dealings—a quality that ought to animate the Church at all times and all places. "Sensitivity," then, becomes the word that best sums up our new, post-Conciliar attitude toward our Jewish brothers and sisters. Let me clarify its meaning by giving a few examples from various disciplines. I am beginning with the one that ought to be an area of major concern on all levels of education, English Literature.

English Literature. As you well know, one of Shakespeare's great plays, "The Merchant of Venice," is a stumbling block for many. There are Christians as well as Jews who would like to see it removed from the curriculum, or consider its performances by the drama club of any school taboo. I am not one of them. As a matter of fact, I think it a perfect means for transmitting the sensitivity that should be a feature of our post-Conciliar outreach. It is not a play hostile to *Jews*, rather does it castigate Christians *and* Jews, that is to say, the sinfulness of humans.

Not a single character in the play is a person of moral integrity. Antonio, for instance appears to be a man of noble heart, kind and unselfish; in reality, he is no less a seeker after profit than Shylock. The difference is that Shylock's business is despised, whereas Antonio's is praised. Yet, even the praise discloses its mettle: "Your mind is tossing on the ocean," his friend tells him, "where your argosies with portly sail.., do overpeer the petty traffickers" (I, i, 9, 12). There seems to be so little difference between the big trader and the money lender that, at the end of the play, Portia, disguised as a young lawyer, can ask: "Which is the merchant, and which the Jew?" (IV, i, 174). The arrogance and hypocrisy of the Christians in the play are most obvious at the elopement of Lorenzo with Jessica. Before she is ready to join her suitor, she returns to the house for more money to take with her. When Gratiano hears her resolve to add theft to the betrayal of her father, he says: "Now, by my hood, a Gentile, and no Jew" (II, vi, 51). These Christians, whose faith is no more than skin-deep, welcome Jessica's "conversion," but she does not turn to Christ. Christ is not even mentioned. She wishes only to escape the boredom of her home and the contempt in which her father is held.

The climax of hypocrisy is the little drama in the court of justice. What some will take to be Portia's noble attempt at saving Bassanio is, to her, little more than a prank. (The affair with the ring confirms her as a practical joker.) She plays her role well. For a moment, she even surpasses herself and grows ecstatic. Her rapturous praise of mercy reaches evangelical heights; yet, her whole line of defense is meant to trick Shylock. He leaves the court ill. He is given this choice: either he becomes a Christian (IV, i, 387), or presently he must die! Need I add that this is an utter travesty of the Christian Way? Though Shylock lives, his spirit is broken, his will crushed. Without faith, he is forced to become a Christian—and all this by the champion of mercy. As I see it, "The Merchant of Venice" is far from being an anti-Jewish play; it is, rather, an unmasking of all sham Christians. It could be a textbook for Christian-Jewish relations; it condenses a millenium into the life of one generation. If taught or played with discretion, it would convey to students or spectators the sins of Christendom and implant in them the desire to make amends, to turn the Conciliar Statement on the Jews into a living reality.

I am not one of those who believe that the Holocaust was the inescapable consequence of two thousand years of Christian teachings. The originators of the Holocaust were repulsed rather than moved by anything Christian. Yet, the attitude of Christians of the kind Shakespeare portrays may somehow have made possible, and for some, have camouflaged the netherworld attack on the Jews by the Nazis. Antonio calls Shylock a misbeliever, a mongrel; he is always ready to spit on him (I, iii, 112, 131). For Gratiano, he is a damned inexorable dog (IV, i, 120), and Lancelot sees in him the devil incarnate (II, ii, 228). As if this were not enough, all his Christian neighbors—at the head of them, Antonio—treat him, not as a person but a label. To them, his name is not "Shylock," but "the Jew." He is even less than that; he is just a thing, a tool that one uses for one's convenience, and then hurls into a corner. There are almost limitless possibilities for a sensitive teacher or creative producer to use the play for purging the old leaven of Jew-baiting and planting in the heart of the reader or viewer the new leaven of respect and kinship. I do not have to spell out what benefit the growth of this leaven would have for the entire Church, indeed, for society as a whole.

Social Studies. To move to another discipline, Social Studies. Never before has there been a generation that has had as much knowledge about its Jewish neighbors as does ours. In former times, the information often came from Antisemites and was wrong. Though modern scholarship has made impressive contributions to a deeper understanding of Judaism, the average Gentile of today takes his image of Jews from novels and musicals by Jewish authors, from "Fiddler on the Roof and Fiedler on the Raft," to quote a modern literary critic.[5] They, too, I am sorry to say, mislead. In its mildest form, the distortion is simply that Jews are quaint, that they are individuals brought up on bagels; at its worst, they are all obsessed with their mothers, they are all like Portnoy.

Social Studies can correct this faulty vision. I am not thinking here of an anatomy of prejudice every sensitive social science teacher will offer to his or her students. Rather am I thinking of some tangible, sober facts. To name only a few: the number of Jewish immigrants; the reasons for their coming; their various backgrounds—to understand them one must know the special history and heritage they brought with them. Other factors that should be discussed are the occupations and professions of Jewish newcomers; their distribution over the United States; the impact of the American way of life on them and, as a result, the keen difference between the first and the second, and between the second and the third generation of

American Jews. Additional aspects on which teachers will
have to dwell if they wish their students to understand their
Jewish neighbors are the economic structure into which the
immigrants entered; the jobs wide open, and those firmly
closed to them; their social stratification; to most non-Jews, it
will come as a bolt out of the blue, upsetting their neat categories, when they are told how many low-income Jews there are.
The students will have to be made aware of the organization of
Jewish life, the welfare, educational, and cultural agencies, the
representative bodies and the religious divisions. To single out
only the last, it is impossible to understand Jews without
understanding the religious plurality among them, its causes
and consequences. Nor can one understand modern Jewry
without grasping the exposure of Jews to contemporary ideologies and the consequent polarities in Jewish identification.

All these points sound abstract, but behind them are some
acute problems. One of the best background books, Marshall
Sklare's *The Jews: Social Patterns of an American Group*, [6]
treats many of these problems. The inside flaps of the jacket
single out three:

> Is it possible that alcoholism is increasing among Jews
> as the result of more frequent contact with non-Jews?
> Why is psychoanalysis so much more attractive to Jews
> than non-Jews, and how does the mental health of Jews
> compare with other groups?
> Are Jewish delinquents different from others? And what
> are the differences between those of the past generation
> and those of our own?

Sensitive and competent teachers of Social Studies will not
disdain what other sciences have to contribute to a clear vision.
Above all things, they will seek to convey to their students an
awareness that the individual Jew is not merely a member of a
group, however special, but also a child, a woman, a man, in
short, a person.

History. History is another quarry from which to win knowledge leading to *shalom* between Christians and Jews. Since
our history books are largely silent on Christian-Jewish rela-

tions, it is most important that in discussing the Crusades and the Inquisition, the teacher deal with their impact on Jews, and analyze the legislation on the co-existence of Christians and Jews by the Fourth Lateran Council (1215 A.D.). This is no easy task since most of the literature accessible to non-specialists is far from satisfactory. To be more specific, not all authors discussing the Council's introduction of badges that identified people as Jews mention that the idea was really of Muslim origin. The Conciliar regulations were more like an ill-fitting garment, whose measurements were not of Gospel size. Again, Jews were not the intended target of the Iberian Inquisition. A royal directive of 1292 admonished Inquisitors, who had deviated from the original intent, "to desist forthwith from the inquisition of heresy against Jews [who had not con-verted to the Catholic faith]."[7]

It is intriguing that at the Fourth Lateran Council, ecclesias-tical authorities took a course Christians have often castigated when taken by the Rabbis. To safeguard the Jewish way of life, the Rabbis sharpened many laws in order to keep traffic between Christians and Jews to a minimum. Christians ought to think twice before "judging" the Rabbis and their protective policy. Still, the discriminatory policy against Jews by the Fourth Lateran Council strikes modern men and women as lacking in justice and respect. No doubt, the Council wanted to safeguard the loyalty of the faithful. That it could find no other way than proscriptions and "stoplights" like the yellow badge, thus creating a sort of spiritual apartheid, should make us humble and determined to fight inequity today. When I say "spiritual apartheid," I do not mean to offer a cheap condem-nation, nor do I wish to take the legislation out of its historical context. To examine a historical fact within its setting is hard work and there is no dispensing with it for the minister of reconciliation.

A promising note could be struck by treating the birth of the State of Israel. I happen to think that it is evidence of God's favor, the sign of His fidelity, indeed, a token of the constancy of His love. In asserting this, I do not base Israel's right to exist merely on the thought that her founding may well be divine compensation for the slaying of most European Jews. Again, I do not rest Israel's claim to a sovereign, secure existence on merely theological grounds. Rather do I base it on an act of the world community. In 1948, the majority of the then members of the United Nations midwifed her birth. Jewish settlers had made swamps, hotbeds of disease, into fertile and healthy stretches of land. For twenty years, they not only worked the land but defended it; what is more, they married, raised children, and died there. Their blood, their sweat, their tears have "baptized" their soil; their dreams and hopes, their laughter and prayers have bedewed it. For centuries, the land was utterly neglected; as soon as Jewish pioneers arrived there, it was lovingly cared for.

In saying this, I do not wish to force my views of the Middle East conflict on you. But I do suggest, and this most strongly, that it is your responsibility to give students the facts so that they can form their own opinions, unhampered by slogans or clichés. One of these clichés calls Israel the creature and outpost of Western imperialism. True, the influence of the Western Powers on the recognition of the newly born state was considerable, but it is important to remember that, in May, 1948, one of the Russian delegates to the U.N., Ambassador Tarascenco, denounced the war of the Arabs against the young state in these words:

> I should like to point out that none of the [Arab] states whose troops have entered Palestine can claim that Palestine forms part of its territory. It is an altogether separate territory without any relationship to the territories of the states which have sent troops into Palestine.[8]

Nor ought one forget that all the Arabic-speaking states of today are creations of the Western Powers.

To begin with Egypt: For years prior to World War I, she had been under the guidance of Great Britain. In 1914, she became a British protectorate. Yet, it was not till 1921 that she was declared an independent sovereign state, and not till October, 1922 that she received a constitution. In World War I, Arabs throughout the Ottoman Empire revolted against the Turks, and so did the Transjordanian tribes. After the war, Trans-jordan was freed from the rule of the sultans and administered by Great Britain. In 1922, when Palestine became a British mandate, the country east of the river Jordan was given to Emir Abdullah who ruled it as a benevolent dictator till 1939. In the same year, a move toward some form of democracy was started: a cabinet was formed and a small legislature elected. In 1920, France received a mandate from the League of Nations over what today is Syria and Lebanon. Lebanon's boundaries were its result. In 1925, she was granted a constitution and declared a republic. The first free elections (under French supervision!) were held in the fall of 1943. The rule of King Feisal, disliked by the French army as well as by his subjects, the Syrians, did not last long. His removal in no way ended the troubles of the land. It was not until 1943 that Syria received its independence from the Free French. A knowledge of these facts is important, I think, in order to evaluate the claims of Israel's neighbors.[9]

Our students ought to know, too, that an impressive American tradition favors a Jewish state in Palestine. Declarations by several of our presidents prove it. As far back as October, 1818, John Adams said in a New York synagogue: "I really wish the Jews again in Judea, an independent Nation." In March, 1919, Woodrow Wilson declared:

> I have before this expressed my personal approval of this declaration of the British Government regarding the aspirations and historic claims of the Jewish people in regard to Palestine.... [The] Allied Nations are agreed that in Palestine shall be laid the foundations of a Jewish Commonwealth.

Calvin Coolidge again took up this theme when he stated in June 1924: "I am...glad to express again my sympathy with the deep and intense longing which finds such fine expression in the Jewish National Homeland in Palestine." In September 1928, Herbert Hoover echoed these sentiments:

> I have watched with genuine admiration the steady and unmistakable progress made in the rehabilitation of Pales-

tine which, desolate for centuries, is now renewing its youth and vitality through the enthusiasm, hard work, and self-sacrifice of the Jewish pioneers who toil there in a spirit of peace and social justice.

Franklin D. Roosevelt said:

It is a source of renowned hope and courage, that by international accord and by the moral support of the peoples of the world, men and women of Jewish faith have a right to resettle the land where their faith was born and from which much of our modern civilization has emanated.

In a letter to the King of Saudi Arabia, Harry S. Truman reiterated the American position:

It is only natural...that this Government should favor...the entry into Palestine of considerable numbers of displaced Jews in Europe, not only that they may find shelter there but also that they may contribute their talents and energies to the upbuilding of the Jewish National home.[10]

Though these presidential statements have no binding force, they must not go unheeded, either by us or by our students. It is obvious, I think, that the implications of my suggestion are wide. If carried out, they could lead our students to mature political judgments, to responsible thought, free of anti-Jewish bias.

Theology. Now to the science or wisdom that should be close to us, whether it is our professional field or not, theology. Theologians, alas, have often "goofed" when discussing the fate of the Jewish people after Christ. Let me prove my contention by pointing to a fairly recent text, that is, from the notes accompanying the Latin-English version of the Breviary published by the Liturgical Press in 1964. They are by the late Canon Pius Parsch, a liturgist of considerable merit. He introduced Friday Matins—Matins being the choral service sung by monks and nuns between midnight and dawn until the liturgical reform of Vatican II—with this comment:

> The Matins psalms present a history of the Jewish peo-
> ple which is at the same time a history of falling away from
> God. It is an unbroken chain of sin, infidelity, ingratitude;
> and its final, logical link is the greatest crime of all: the
> murder of their Messiah.[11]

This, I maintain, is wrong from beginning to end. Though
the Old Testament abounds with the sins of the people of Israel,
it is not the history of their sin. The history of Israel, like the
history of Christendom, or to stay closer to home, my life and
yours, is an up and down of the divine call and the human
failing to respond, of God's gift and our ingratitude. Pius
Parsch went on to say: "In the story of Israel's sins, we must
not fail to recognize our own sins."[12] This is all very well, but
saying this as an afterthought cannot undo the blasphemy—
and I mean "blasphemy"—of the first comment. For to give, as
it were, priority and predominance to the infidelity of men and
women is not only misreading Revelation, but also robbing
God of His glory, depriving Him of His reign, His claim, and
His pardon. Again, to interpret the death of Jesus as but a
logical link in a chain of Jewish infidelities is to turn it into a
local affair and to forget that the Jewish actors in the drama of
salvation were but the vicars of every sinner; it is to treat the
Suffering Servant of God as if He were no more than one of the
many temporal rulers to be assassinated by their rivals.

Dr. Parsch annotated a number of psalms in which he found
the history of Israel's infidelities retold, but it never occurred to
him that when the Psalmists, or, for that matter, the Prophets,
dwell on Israel's failings, they warn and woo the people, and
repent in its name. That the sacred writers so freely confess the
sins of Israel—of people, priests, and princes, of the multitude
as well as the elite—is to Israel's great credit. No other nation
has had historiographers comparable to the writers of the
Hebrew Scriptures.

Again, commenting on Psalm 80 in which the Lord of the
Covenant offers the people of Israel a decisive choice, Dr.
Parsch wrote: "In your hands lie death and life; choose: life, if
you obey—death, if you are faithless like your fathers." He
continued: "Christ's death on the cross shows that the Jews

chose death and final rejection."[13] Who, may I ask, revealed this to him? Who told him that the Jews are forever rejected by God? This is not the doctrine of Vatican II. Nor is it the message of the New Testament. Having said that not all in Israel responded to the Good News, having also repeated Isaiah's accusation against them as "an unruly and recalcitrant people" (Rom 10: 21; Is 65:2), St. Paul continues: "I ask, then, has God rejected His people? Never!" (Rom 11:1). How are we to explain that so many commentators contradict him, and do not know it?

To charge the Jewish people with "the murder of their Messiah" is perverted theology. Moreover, it clearly violates the letter as well as the spirit of Vatican II. Canon Parsch wrote thirty years before the Council—that the Liturgical Press reprinted his words close to the end of the Council shows a certain denseness to the ministry of reconciliation. This is all the more difficult to understand since the men at and around the Liturgical Press are otherwise men of vision and merit. I have only one explanation: An inner inertia makes many Christians continue in the rut of centuries.

Writers on Christian spirituality have often quoted Paul who writes that, when hearing the Torah, a veil "lies over the minds" of Jews (2 Cor 3:15) so that they cannot recognize Jesus as the Christ. It never seems to occur to our spiritual writers that, when thinking of the role of the Jews in the history of salvation, Christians, more often than not, hide behind a steel curtain, a curtain that keeps them from recognizing the hand of God in the life of the Jewish people.

It is the task of our generation to strike down this curtain so that no Christian will ever forget that Jesus suffered in freedom—the new Eucharistic Prayer II expressly reminds us of the "death He freely accepted." To shift one's attention from the meaning to the mode of the Passion, from the great Sufferer to the little executioners, is dangerous. It threatens Jews and maims Christians: It makes Christians insensitive to their Jewish kindred and to the great singularity of Christ's pain. The mystery of that pain is, after all, its ability to absorb every other pain and to hallow it. Any shift from the center to the periphery loses sight of the fact that the Man of Pain draws all those in anguish to Himself. Anyone who blurs this vision revolts against the Christ. Yet, whoever does not tire of orientating himself or herself, again and again, to the Vatican II Statement on the Jews contributes to the rejuvenation of the Church.

Conclusion

ALL THINGS MUST come to an end, and so must this long paper. Despite its length, much has remained unsaid. If you keep in mind the two key words: *shalom*, the goal, and "sensitivity," the way to it, you are the best audience I could wish for.

I hope it is obvious that my plea for sensitivity has nothing to do with the new fad for sensitivity sessions. When I speak of sensitivity, I have in mind the injunction of the Second Isaiah to his fellow prophets: "Speak tenderly to Jerusalem" (40:1). To "speak tenderly" is the translation of the Hebrew idiom to "speak to the heart." The periods of strife, indifference, even hatred have lasted too long; it is time that Christians speak with their hearts: that they speak with heart of the People of the Holocaust and that they speak to its heart. Hence the prophet demands of us:

> *Nahamu, nahamu, ammi,*
> *yomar eloheykhem,*
> *Dabru al-leb yerushalayim.*

> Comfort, give comfort to my people,
> says your God.
> Speak tenderly to Jerusalem.

NOTES

[1]   Emil L. Fackenheim, "Jewish Faith and the Holocaust," *Commentary*, (August 1968), p. 33.

[2]   Theodor Haecker, *Tag-und Nachtbücher* (Munich: Hegner, 1947), pp. 28-29.

3   Louis Ginsberg, *The Legends of the Jews*, transl. Paul Radin (Philadelphia: Jewish Publication Society, 1942) 3, 32.

4   Kurt Kupish, *Das Volk der Geschichte* (Berlin: Lettner, 1960), pp. 207-208.

5   John Gross, "A Balanced View," *Commentary*, (April 1969), p. 84.

6   *The Jews: Social Patterns of an American Group*, ed. Marshall Sklare (Glencoe, IL: The Free Press, 1958).

7   See Salo W. Baron, *A Social and Religious History of the Jews* (New York: Columbia University Press, 1969), 13,14.

8   As quoted by Frank Gervasi in *The Case for Israel* (New York: Viking, 1967), p. 161.

9   See, among other reports, the pertinent entries in *The Encyclopedia Britannica*.

10   Gervasi, *ibid.*, pp. 199-201.

11   *The Hours of the Divine Office in English and Latin* (Collegeville, MN: Liturgical Press, 1964), p. 518.

12   *Ibid.*

13   *Ibid.*, p. 529.

OPENING WINDOWS
ONTO JERUSALEM

When the Jewish people languished in the Babylonian Captivity, King Darius imposed on all the inhabitants of his Empire an idolatrous worship. Defying the King's order, young Daniel went home to kneel in prayer to the God of Israel. While doing so, he had the windows of his chamber open toward the Temple in Jerusalem (Dan 6:11). The open windows well describe the concern a Christian should nurture for the well-being of the Holy City and the State of Israel. A prayer offered at an interfaith seminar on the significance of Jerusalem for Jews as well as Christians, at Temple Emanuel, Livingston, N.J., on May 20, 1981, giving voice to such solicitude, may well conclude this book.

GOD OF ABRAHAM, of Isaac, and of Jacob,
  of Sarah, Rebecca, Leah, and Rachel,
  Lord of the Living, Giver of life!
We turn to You:
  Shelter the life of Israel and its neighbors.
  Grant them and us vision, valor, and skill to pursue peace
  Grant them and us patience and perseverance to achieve it.
Give us, friends of Israel, the wisdom and strength
    to uphold its independence and security,
    to champion its cause, with justice for all
    and malice toward none.

Lord, our God, King of the universe!
  You said: "The earth is mine."
  You declared it at the very moment
    You took the people of Israel as Your treasured possession
    and placed on them the burden of being a holy nation.

Lord our God, You are Sovereign of all the lands, cities, towns,
    and villages of the globe.
Still, You singled out the Land of Israel as Your land, and
    the City of Jerusalem as Your city.
Let Your blessing rest on this holy city.
May it, the capital of Israel, be open to all who love its
    beauty and seek its prosperity,
May it be the city of neighborliness, fellowship, encounter,
    and peace.
May it cease to be the object of strife between Jews and
    Arabs,
May it never be a bone of contention between Jews and
    Christians!
May the city ever be dear to us, ever be part of our concern
    and prayer.
May we all learn to feel and say with Israel's exiles by the
    rivers of Babylon:
"If I forget you, Jerusalem, let my right hand wither."

GENERAL INDEX

Fourth Lateran Council, 433
France, 435
Frankfurter Allgemeine Zeitung, 258, 291
Freemasonry, 30, 212, 260
Frings, Joseph Cardinal, 202-203, 217-218, 262

Gaechter, Paul, 87, 99, 350
Galatians, Epistle to (cf. Index of Scriptural References), 125-126
Galli, Mario von, 270-271
Gamaliel, Patriarch, 62
Geis, Robert Raphael, 335, 340
Genesis, 65, 133, 362
Gentile Christians (cf. Abraham, children by faith), 8, 65, 137, 173-175, 203, 210, 228, 324, 331, 400, 417
Gerety, Archbishop Peter L., 23
Germany, 195, 211, 258, 294, 335, 354
Gnostic heresy, 259
God of Israel (of Abraham, Isaac, and Jacob), 45, 49-51, 76, 136, 181, 186, 226, 265, 281, 312, 326, 343, 349, 371, 379, 382, 386-387, 426
  biblical descriptions of (cf. anthropomorphism)
  Covenant with Abraham and his descendants (cf. Abraham, calling of), 34, 51, 66, 109-110, 140, 196, 369, 416-417
  ever-present (cf. God, Name of), 35, 36-37, 360
  faithfulness of, 9, 41-42, 46, 66, 69, 104, 110, 125, 139-140, 150, 169, 174, 184, 188, 209, 212-213, 231, 249, 263, 266, 315, 324, 328, 330-334, 416, 433
  favors what Man rejects (cf. "folly of the Cross"), 34, 38-40, 45, 62
  guidance of (cf. Holy Spirit), 9, 35, 119, 235, 308

  judgments and mercy of, 48, 49, 65-67, 121-122, 139, 141, 159, 165, 180, 186, 209-210, 254, 332-333, 353, 383, 408, 416, 424-426
  love for all creatures, 37, 93, 177, 221, 268, 284, 308-309, 320, 331, 343, 361, 390, 406, 418, 426-427
  Name of, 35, 76, 193, 250, 323-324, 332, 337
  presence of (cf. God, ever-present), 35, 45
  of Revelation, 50-51, 207, 221-222, 224-226, 241, 273, 301-304, 316, 320, 331, 437
  saving deeds of, 44, 133, 135, 200, 235, 268, 366-370 *passim*, 390, 406, 417-418, 424
Goebbels, Josef, 322, 354
Goldmann, Nahum, 160
Gomorrah, 67
Good Friday Liturgy (cf. Holy Week, Services of)
Good Friday prayer for the Jewish people (cf. "perfidia judaica"), 53, 96-97, 108-110, 148, 417
Good News New Testament, 400, 401
Gori, Patriarch Alberto, 170
Gospels, the Four, 48, 81, 122, 137, 274, 333-343 *passim*, 338-339, 348, 389, 406-407
Gospel of Jesus Christ, 9, 46, 98, 147, 207-209, 230, 263, 270, 300, 304, 307, 308, 328, 350, 363, 378, 381, 383, 385, 400, 402, 408-409, 416, 421, 438
grace (cf. omnipresence of), 9, 19, 48, 49, 66, 108, 119, 121, 138-139, 143, 202, 227, 268, 270, 285, 301, 303, 336, 361, 369, 385, 387, 397, 400-404, 425
Great Britain, 20, 434-435
Greece, civilization of (cf. Western philosophy), 33
Greek texts, 34, 69, 90, 95, 182, 281,

INDEX
OF SCRIPTURAL REFERENCES

INDEX
OF POST-BIBLICAL REFERENCES

Jerusalem Talmud

Shab.	1:4	71	Ned.	9,4	350
Betzah	2:4	71			

Midrashim

Gen.r.	1,4	340	Sifra,		
	18,4	356	Ked. Per. 4,12		350
	24,7	350	Sifre on Dt.11:13		342
	91,7	335	Midr. Pss. 40:1-2		75
Dt.r.	2:22	321-322	99:3		64
Lam.r.	1,33	325	Midr. Prov.25:21		63
	1,45-46	325	Yalkut,		
	3,46	69	to Pent. §766		340
Pes.R.	9	212			

Indices compiled by SaraLee Pindar.